Political Consumerism

Political Consumerism captures the creative ways in which citizens, consumers, and political activists use the market as their arena for politics. This book theorizes, describes, analyzes, compares, and evaluates the phenomenon of political consumerism and how it attempts to use market choice to solve complex globalized problems. It investigates theoretically and empirically how and why consumers practice citizenship and have become important political actors. Dietlind Stolle and Michele Micheletti describe consumers' engagement as an example of individualized responsibility-taking, examining how political consumerism nudges and pressures corporations to change their production practices, and how consumers emerge as a force in global affairs. Unlike other studies, it also evaluates whether and how consumer actions become effective mechanisms of global change. Stolle and Micheletti offer a candid discussion of the limitations of political consumerism as a form of participation and as a problem-solving mechanism.

Dietlind Stolle is a recognized expert on political participation, youth engagement, social capital, and diversity. She currently is the Director of the Quebec Inter-University Centre for the Study of Democratic Citizenship. Stolle is the principal investigator of the *Canadian Youth Survey* and serves as the principal investigator, co-investigator, or collaborator on eight other national and international funded projects, including the 2011 and 2015 *Canadian Election Studies*. She is also the principal investigator of the *Student Issues and Protest Survey* in Quebec. Stolle is a past co-winner of the American Political Science Association's Award for the best paper on European politics. Her scholarly achievements have been recognized in recent invitations to serve as a senior research partner at the Max Planck Institute for the Study of Ethnic and Religious Diversity in Göttingen, Germany and on the advisory board of the Institute for the Study of Democracy in Aarau, Switzerland. At the Wissenschaftszentrum Berlin she has received the prestigious Karl W. Deutsch Professorship.

Michele Micheletti holds the Lars Hierta Chair of Political Science at Stockholm University. She was a member of the SNS Democratic Audit, the scientific boards of the Swedish Consumer Agency and the Swedish Society for Nature Conservation and the Ministry of Finance's Expert Group for Environmental Studies. At present, she is co-coordinator of the European Consortium for Political Research (ECPR) Standing Group on Participation and Mobilization. She has contributed to several parliamentary investigations in Sweden and conducted research for and advised Swedish civic associations and political parties. Her scientific network-building activities have been instrumental in putting political consumerism on the scholarly research agenda. Her publications include The *Swedish Farmers' Movement and Government Agricultural Policy* (1990), *Civil Society and State Relations in Sweden* (1995), *Political Virtue and Shopping: Individuals, Consumerism, and Collective Action* (2003, 2010) and co-edited books on political participation and political consumerism (*Creative Participation: Responsibility-taking in the Political World* (2010) and *Politics, Products, and Markets: Exploring Political Consumerism Past and Present* (2004)).

Political Consumerism

Global Responsibility in Action

DIETLIND STOLLE
McGill University

MICHELE MICHELETTI
Stockholm University

CAMBRIDGE
UNIVERSITY PRESS

CAMBRIDGE
UNIVERSITY PRESS

32 Avenue of the Americas, New York NY 10013-2473, USA

Cambridge University Press is part of the University of Cambridge.

It furthers the University's mission by disseminating knowledge in the pursuit of education, learning and research at the highest international levels of excellence.

www.cambridge.org
Information on this title: www.cambridge.org/9781107010093

First published 2013

A catalogue record for this publication is available from the British Library

Library of Congress Cataloguing in Publication data

Stolle, Dietlind, 1967–
Political consumerism : global responsibility in action / Dietlind Stolle, Michele Micheletti.
   p.   cm.
Includes bibliographical references and index.
ISBN 978-1-107-01009-3 (hardback)
1. Politics, Practical.   2. Political participation.   3. Political ethics.   4. Consumption (Economics) – Political aspects.   I. Micheletti, Michele.   II. Title.
JF799.S687   2013
172'.1–dc23   2012044104

ISBN 978-1-107-01009-3 Hardback

Contents

List of Figures

List of Tables

Acknowledgments

This book has been in the making for about ten years. It grew out of the common interests of both authors in the role of collective action and civil society and the recognition that citizens do not only vote at election time to express their political opinions or influence politics. This common scientific curiosity grew into two research projects, "Political Consumption: Politics in a New Era and Arena" and "Sustainable Citizenship: Opportunities and Barriers for Citizen Involvement in Sustainable Development," both funded by the Swedish Research Council (Vetenskapsrådet). Over the years, parts of this book were presented at conferences organized by the European Consortium of Political Research (ECPR), the American Political Science Association, the Swedish Political Science Association, and the Karlstad Seminar on Studying Political Action. We have also presented our research in many different settings, including the 2001 and 2005 International Seminars on Political Consumerism; the workshop on Gender and Social Capital at the University of Manitoba; and various talks in Canada, England, Finland, Germany, the Netherlands, Norway, and Switzerland. We have also been asked to participate in the U.K. research program Cultures of Consumption's workshop "Citizenship and Consumption: Agency, Norms, Mediations, and Spaces" and to give keynote speeches for the Sciences Po Paris conference "Towards Sustainable Consumption"; the Fourth National Brazilian Consumer Studies Meeting "New Directions for Consumer Society"; the Third German Environmental Sociological Summit; the Milano International Conference "Ethical Fashion"; two University of Madison–Wisconsin–organized events on the politics of consumption and the consumption of politics; the European Society for Agricultural and Food Ethics; and the symposium "Shopping for Human Rights" organized at Bergamo University, Italy, by fellow political consumerism researcher Francesca Forno. Our home universities, and particularly the Statistics Speaker series at

McGill University and the Higher Research Seminar series at Stockholm University, have graciously hosted us.

Several people have been very helpful over the last years in this long-term endeavor. We want particularly to thank Åsa Nilsson, research administrator at SOM Institute at the University of Gothenburg, Sweden, for generously offering her time and giving good constructive comments on our surveys. Daniel Berlin from the University of Gothenburg was in charge of the 2009 national survey "Consumption and Societal Issues." Jonas Peretti gave us exclusive access to the 3,600 e-mails he received in the context of the Nike e-mail exchange; the e-mails became original research material for Chapter 6. Barbara Hobson at Stockholm University shared her ideas and feedback on this particular dataset. Matthew Wright, a McGill student at the time, spent uncountable hours coding the entire e-mail exchange. Laura Nishikawa, who was also a student at McGill, was in charge of the thoughtful discourse analysis in the Nike e-mail exchange. Cesi Cruz (McGill) designed the online survey of the participants of the Nike e-mail exchange. The design of the cross-national comparison of the political and economic factors behind political consumerism at the individual level was triggered by a paper authored by Mariona Ferrer-Fons (University of Pompeu Fabra, Barcelona) for an ECPR workshop in 2004.

Jen Brea contributed with outstanding fieldwork on the garment industry in Lesotho. Most of all we would like to thank Jean-François Crépault, who was also a student at McGill University, for his excellent work on collecting the cross-national data presented in Chapter 4, as well as ideas for developing the analyses in Chapters 4 and 7. His research assistance went far beyond the task at hand, which explains why he is included as a co-author in these two chapters.

Seventeen additional research assistants have helped over the years with research on various aspects of political consumerism. We are particularly grateful for the work by current or former McGill students Yale Hertzman, Olga Redko, Maria Surilas, Michael Kideckel, Joël Roy, Mike Robichaud, Kaitlyn Shannon, Rossana Tudo, Joe Heywood, Sheelagh Gough, Marc Trussler, and Arnav Manchanda. In some cases, the contributions of the research assistants are included in special footnotes in this book.

Many colleagues at home and abroad have offered valuable comments on our keynote speeches, work-in-progress conference papers, and chapter drafts as well as on drafts of the survey questions. Among the scholars offering their thoughts and collegial support are Lance W. Bennett, André Blais, Mario Diani, Andreas Follesdal, Aina Gallegho Dobón, Corinne Gendron, Elisabeth Gidengil, Edgar Grande, James L. Guth, Boris Holzer, Marc Hooghe, Kay Lehman Scholzman, Anders Lidström, Andrew S. McFarland, Therese O'Toole, Roberta Sassatelli, Alexandra Segerberg, Dhavan Shah, Kate Soper, Jan Teorell, Mette Kirkegaard (nee Tobiasen), Frank Trentmann, Jan W. van Deth, Ariadne Vromen, and Alan Warde.

I

Reconfiguring Political Responsibility

INTRODUCTION

Citizens in countries all over the world seek ways to solve their economic, social, and political grievances. They appeal to governments on all levels of politics, engage with civic associations, and invent new participative venues to express and aid their political concerns. Political problems and demands are "tugging and pulling" at the capacities and legitimacy of governments, civil society, and corporations.[1] At the same time, the general public in Western societies has been expressing decreasing trust in the representatives of democratic institutions. Civil society organizations, including consumer groups and environmental associations, have consistently been rated as more trustworthy than political, religious, or business groups (Hampel et al. 2001). The combination of declining trust in governmental institutions and rise in demand for solutions to complex problems puts a strain on citizens, politics, parliaments, and governments in industrialized and stable democracies. These developments challenge the conventional framework and mechanisms for dealing with political, social, and economic problems.

This book addresses the ongoing reconfiguration of political responsibility. It asks what kinds of developments and problems are challenging governments' capacity for political problem-solving and how other actors and institutions come to be political agents. Are there models of political responsibility that address these ongoing changes, and are they effective mechanisms for solving political problems? Particularly, what role do citizens play in the reconfiguration of political responsibility? Chapter 1 begins to answer these questions. It discusses the traditional framework of responsibility by outlining and evaluating its assumptions and characterizing the challenges that it faces today.

---

[1] The phrase "tugging and pulling at states" is taken from Princen and Finger (1994), 225.

The chapter argues that the traditional framework of responsibility needs to be revised and expanded into both the public and private spheres and should emphasize the role of responsible choice for political problem-solving.

The emerging framework for political responsibility puts greater pressure on citizens to take daily responsibility in their public and private engagements. But can citizens realistically assume more general and daily responsibility over these matters? Are they equipped to shoulder this kind of responsibility? What structural and individual prerequisites are necessary for citizens to take on more responsibility and, therefore, play a greater role in political problem-solving? This book explores these questions theoretically and empirically by focusing on the role of political consumerism as a problem-solving phenomenon.

Chapter 1 begins the theoretical exploration. With the help of general theoretical findings on the role of citizens in politics, it develops theory on individualized responsibility-taking that can be used to assess the capability of citizens as problem-solving agents. Subsequent chapters in the book study the actual ability of citizens to act as responsibility-taking agents as well as the consequences and effectiveness of such actions. They explore in different ways whether and how political consumerism in the Northern (Western, industrialized, stable democratic) world provides examples of individualized responsibility-taking practices and investigates political consumerism's capability to solve complex political problems. This focus is chosen because political consumerism has been viewed as a phenomenon that both addresses and reveals many of the problems mentioned in scholarly discussions on contemporary changes in politics. Besides the need for new problem-solving mechanisms and platforms due to the large-scale processes of globalization, modernization, and individualization, political consumerism also emphasizes the role that the market, corporations, and family life can and perhaps should play in politics. However, political consumerism is not only about political responsibility-taking for the common good. Our investigations also explore how citizens take responsibility for self-regarding issues and, in so doing, discuss the more central role of personal choice as a mechanism in politics.

LIMITS OF AND CHALLENGES TO THE TRADITIONAL MODEL OF POLITICAL RESPONSIBILITY

The term *political responsibility* is used in the academic discourse to denote answerability for matters of the common and public good (Peters and Pierre 2007, Keohane 2003). Throughout the ages, political scholars and practitioners have explicitly assumed or, at times, just taken for granted that this answerability for the public good is the task and sole responsibility of government. They envision and model government as the collective actor with supreme authority for dealing with problems that threaten the common good. Governments are called on to solve all sorts of problems from the local to the global levels. These problems include issues of land use, water and school quality, police protection, provisions of welfare and social services as well as food, energy, national safety, and so on. Governments are also called on to engage in global problem resolution. The kinds of concerns involved here are pandemics, banking crises, climate change, international drug-smuggling, terrorism, and world poverty.

But even before governments start to work on these issues, they must be convinced that the matters raised are important to public well-being and thus in need of government action. Therefore, mobilizing opinion and support for a problem area as the responsibility of government is a political process in itself (Keck and Sikkink 1998, Fraser 2005, Kingdon 1995, Baumgarten and Jones 1993, Sabatier 1991). Once it is decided that an issue is a responsibility for government, ideally government actors will attempt to solve it through legislative action, public policy, the public administration, and/or the court system. This framework of political responsibility in which public policies are made, implemented, and enforced has been the central way for citizens to demand governmental action and for nation-state governments to assert their authority and answerability for the public well-being or common good of their citizenry. In democratic societies, this framework has structured political ideology, election campaigns, and citizens' engagement in politics. It has also influenced social science and legal theoretical, methodological, and empirical scholarship. The question is, however, whether the premises of the model are in step with political reality.

The traditional framework of political responsibility is built around three assumptions. The first is that government has legal authority for problem-solving – that is, the government must have legal jurisdiction over the source of the problem. The second is the authority and ability of government to identify actors and institutions and prosecute those who have caused the problem. This is sometimes termed "cause responsibility" (cf. Javeline 2003). The third assumption is that government is able to make these actors accountable for their actions and for ending the problems they have been found to have caused. In other words, they have "treatment responsibility" (cf. Javeline 2003, Young 2006, May 1992, Finer 1941, Winthrop 1975, Sabatier 1991, Dearing and Rogers 1996, Pellizzoni 2004).

The political histories of many sovereign states offer ample examples showing that this framework has functioned and functions well as a problem-solving model in many policy fields. Local, regional, and national governments have, for instance, been able to take relatively effective action on citizen welfare, different forms of public safety (e.g., water, public housing, and traffic safety), and the regulation of industry (Weaver and Rockman 1993, Lundqvist 1980, Esping-Andersen 1990). Another field where the traditional model seems to have worked well is related to some aspects of corporate governance. For example, in the wake of the 2001 Enron scandal, when this large energy corporation was found guilty of fraudulent activity, the U.S. Congress swiftly enacted the Sarbanes-Oxley Act in 2002; its goal was to control and prevent corporate fraud through the creation of the Public Company Accounting Oversight Board mandated to regulate and supervise corporate conduct (see Lucci 2003).

The traditional political responsibility model has also functioned well in some areas of public health, as illustrated by the decision of an increasing number of national governments to ban smoking in public places. Studies have, for instance, demonstrated that these bans have been implemented in such a way that they effectively reduce exposure to the harmful effects of secondhand smoke (Naiman, Glazier, and Moineddin 2010, Pickett et al. 2006). The traditional model has even reacted quickly to large and sudden environmental disasters, as most prominently illustrated by the Exxon Valdez oil spill and the recent Deepwater Horizon spill. These two cases are of special interest for this book because they explain when and how government political responsibility mechanisms can be employed, how they can make corporations answerable for problems of the common good, and why there is so much current focus on the role of corporations as a problem-solving actor in domestic and international relations (Bexell 2006, Alger 2010, Fraser 2005, Ebbesson and Okowa 2009, Winter 2006). Moreover, the oil-spill cases illuminate why such political problems can occur in the first place. They also represent new trends in problem-solving now being implemented in many levels of government.

The Exxon Valdez oil spill occurred on March 24, 1989, outside the Alaskan coast, when the tanker *Valdez* hit the Blight Reef and spilled between 11 million and 35 million gallons (42,000 m³) of crude oil that affected 1,300 miles (1,900 kilometers) of the Alaskan coastline. The U.S. Congress acted rapidly and passed the Oil Pollution Act of 1990, which defined the political problem and the responsible actor, stipulated the establishment of a fund for the payment of compensation for identified damages, and formulated regulations to avoid such problems in the future (United States Senate 1990, Birkland 1997, Margulies 2003). Less than one year later, on February 27, 1990, ExxonMobil was indicted on five criminal counts and found guilty of causing the problem through irresponsible conduct (so-called negligence or intentionality by neglect) and mandated by the court to spend more than 1 billion USD to clean up the oil spill. The company was ordered to pay an additional 5 billion USD to victims to settle its civil and criminal charges over a ten-year period (Baura 2006). Although all civil cases against ExxonMobil and many ecosystem and societal problems caused by the oil spill and in its aftermath are, as of 2013, still not resolved, it is generally believed that government assumed good leadership in dealing with the concerns. It enacted the Oil Pollution Act, moved swiftly in prosecuting ExxonMobil, and held the corporation legally responsible for causing the problem and contributing to its resolution (Birkland and Lawrence 2002, Exxon Valdez Oil Spill Trustee Council no date, Gerber, Jensen, and Kubena 2007).

This case shows how the traditional framework can work rapidly and effectively when its basic assumptions are in place. The oil spill occurred in U.S. territorial waters, thus fulfilling the first assumption of legal jurisdictional authority.

Government could identify the wrongdoer (the second assumption) because the tanker accident that caused the spill occurred at a specific time and location. Government passed legislation and used its legal system to find the company guilty of and liable for the damages to nature and society, thus fulfilling the model's third basic assumption of holding actors accountable for their wrongdoings. In these ways, the model held actors answerable for instigating and solving the problem, that is, cause and treatment responsibility (cf. Javeline 2003, Young 2006, Pellizzoni 2004, Solum no date, Jordan, Wurzel, and Zito 2003b).

Interestingly for the discussion that follows, the Oil Pollution Act also acknowledges that an underlying cause of the disaster was complacency on the part of both industry and government in monitoring the operation of the Valdez terminal and vessel traffic. To ensure against similar problems and oil tanker accidents in the future, it proposed two innovations in political responsibility-taking: more active participation by local citizens in the formulation of oil spill contingency planning and the establishment of "a mechanism... which fosters the long-term partnership of industry, government, and local communities in overseeing compliance with environmental concerns in the operation of crude oil terminals" (United States Senate 1990, Section 5002, 274). As developed further later in the chapter, the role of individual citizens and multistakeholder mechanisms continues to be discussed as a necessary element in political responsibility-taking in the 2000s.

Thus, whereas the Exxon Valdez oil spill demonstrates the strengths of the traditional model to react quickly to serious and acute political problems, it also shows that additional efforts and mechanisms are needed to create long-term solutions for large and sudden problems. But what happens when the assumptions for the traditional political responsibility model are not in place? How strong is the model when government does not have full jurisdictional authority, when it is not possible to identify specific actors who have caused the problem, and when government lacks the capability to make these actors responsible and accountable for their actions? A review of contemporary research on political responsibility that takes as its point of departure in complex cross-national problems and the role of the global economy in politics today sheds light on these questions. This review focuses on the scholarship of two political scientists who have offered significant insights and contributions to the reconfiguration of political responsibility for the contemporary world.

First, in his role as the United Nations Special Representative of the Secretary General on Human Rights and Transnational Corporations and Other Business Enterprises, political science professor John G. Ruggie has investigated whether the traditional political responsibility model is applicable in extraterritorial settings outside the legal jurisdiction of national government. Foreshadowing his appointment was the failure of the United Nations in realizing the "Norms on the Responsibilities of Transnational Corporations and Other Business Enterprises with regard to Human Right Attempts," a proposed authoritative guide to corporate social responsibility that scholars argue was "stymied" by politics and "overly ambitious" as an overarching regulation of the activities of transnational corporations and their relationships with host governments (Hillemans 2003, 1066). From his extensive research since his appointment to this post in 2005, Ruggie has concluded that it is difficult to apply in a "territorially fragmented system of public governance" (Ruggie 2009, 2) and for problems that are outside the "areas within their [government's] 'power or effective control'" (UN General Assembly 2007, 5; see also UN General Assembly 2011). In 2011, Ruggie's research team, for example, concluded from current developments in U.S. tort litigation that the courtroom is not an effective venue for holding multinational corporations responsible for allegations of negligence, breaches of the duty of care, and international human rights violations (Meeran 2011), although more recently there are some indications that this may gradually be changing.[2] Ruggie has characterized these weaknesses as a serious contemporary structural problem because the model cannot easily and readily be applied in the jurisdiction of other sovereign states and in international territory. Even though his evaluation focuses primarily on human rights violations associated with free trade and in cross-national cases, his conclusions apply to other large and difficult problem areas and to different territorially fragmented governments. Other scholars focus their attention on investigating how and why the model is hard to employ to solve environmental, economic, safety, and health problems that are cross-jurisdictional in origin and conclude that this difficulty explains why more effort has been put into developing and ratifying international law (Ebbesson and Okowa 2009, Winter 2006, Fraser 2005).

But difficulties in solving political problems with the traditional model can even be found in a single nation-state territorial jurisdiction if political authority is dispersed and problems "spill over" into multiple legal jurisdictions, as shown in the case of federalism in the United States and the multi-layered government of the European Union. These forms of fragmented governmental authority lead to difficulties in determining the common level of governmental answerability and in harmonizing problem-solving efforts to ensure, for instance, equal treatment of all citizens, common environmental protection, and similarities in laws so that legality in one legal jurisdiction does not translate into illegality in another one. Such problems have been found in the United States in the field of gun control, air pollution, treatment of illegal immigrants, and social welfare (Mayors against illegal guns 2010, Revesz 1997, Potoski and Woods 2002, Fix and Tumlin 1997). For instance, differences in social welfare policies among U.S. states have been found to create "marked disparities" in the treatment of similarly situated American citizens (Kinney 1990, 857).

---

[2] Two examples are the California Transparency in Supply Chain Act of 2010 that became law in 2012 and the new forerunning mediation and complains institution "Danish Responsibility" created by the Danish Minister for Business and Growth in 2012 to implement the new recommendations from the UN and OECD on global development of responsible business behavior.

Harmonizing policy across member states also affects the functioning of the European Union, which has, as a result, experienced several instances of time-consuming and even unsuccessful policy delays. An illustrative case of relevance for the coming chapters in this book concerns the failed attempts to harmonize regulatory policy on the cultivation of genetically modified organisms (GMOs) (European Commission DG Health and Consumers no date a).[3] An interesting side effect of this inability to provide a common regulatory framework is that government calls on citizens and consumers to increase their awareness of national differences in food policy (see e.g., European Commission DG Health and Consumers, no date b).

Scholars have also questioned whether the other basic assumptions of the traditional political responsibility model keep up with reality and how the inability to fulfill them can create what they identify as serious weaknesses and structural problems. An important scholar who conducted such investigations is political philosopher Iris Marion Young. Before her death she evaluated the traditional model's second basic assumption: its need to identify specific actors as those who cause a specific problem ("the wrongdoers"). For her philosophical evaluation, she studied the case of labor rights in offshore operations within the globalized garment-making industry, the so-called sweatshop problem that had gained considerable public attention in the 1990s and early 2000s (see also Chapters 5 through 8). She found that, unlike the oil-spill example earlier, when governmental answerability was swift and strong, it is often difficult for government to act and act promptly to identify a specific actor who, as in her case, is not providing satisfactory working conditions or salary and not following the labor standards recommended by the International Labor Organization, an international governmental agency within the United Nations. Her theoretical investigation shows that the globalized garment industry's nature, which involves a vast number of specialized factories manufacturing specific garment parts and doing so simultaneously for several different companies (Andersson 2001; see also e.g., The Walt Disney Company 2008), is one reason it is hard to identify the wrongdoer.

Young concluded that the traditional political responsibility model is structurally rigid because it must assign both cause responsibility and treatment responsibility to specific identified actors. She argued that this rigidity is a serious weakness when problem-solving is reliant on the identification of specific actors because, without their identification, there is a risk that the problem will just continue. Young maintained that such reoccurrences perpetuate individual harms that accumulate into collective harms and develop into what she termed

---

[3] After twelve years of governmental deliberation, fierce environmental protest, and intensive business lobbying, the EU announced in the summer of 2010 that it would not pursue efforts for a common European regulatory framework on GMOs. Instead the European Commission decided to adopt a more flexible approach, which it maintains will ensure the right balance between maintaining the EU system of authorizations based on scientific assessment of health and environmental risks and the need to grant freedom to Member States to address specific national, regional, or local issues raised by the cultivation of GMOs.

"structural injustices" or widespread domination or deprivation of large categories of persons (Young 2006, 114). Similar difficulties in identifying the specific responsible actor or actors and assigning them both cause and treatment responsibility have been found in other large and complicated cross-national problem areas. Prominent examples noted in the literature are deforestation, overfishing, the banking crisis, and climate change (Gibson, McKean, and Ostrom 2000, UN Development Programme, UN Environment Programme, World Bank, World Resources Institute 2000). Such examples have led scholars to conclude that the traditional model cannot solve problems swiftly and effectively when, firstly, identifiable actors cannot be revealed; secondly, when the identity of wrongdoers cannot be established within a reasonable time frame so that problem-solving can commence before it is too late; and finally, when the problems grow incrementally thus making it difficult to hold specific actors answerable as the specific source of the problem (Young 2006, 2010, Ebbesson and Okowa 2009, Winter 2006, Fraser 2005). As part of her solution for this problem, Young discussed the role that corporations and individuals must play in new frameworks of responsibility-taking.

The traditional model's third basic assumption – that government has the capacity to take action to make the identifiable actors accountable for wrongdoing – has also undergone scholarly evaluation. Policy making, policy implementation, and governance researchers identify several different weaknesses in governmental capacity existing on all levels of government and in different parts of the world and argue that they can lessen the effectiveness of the model. An important first weakness is generated when there is a lack of political will among politicians to formulate an effective policy solution. Reasons for this lack of will include conflicting political interests and priorities, as, for instance, shown earlier in the EU example on GMOs. Political disagreement can even prolong the policy-making process so that the problem accumulates and becomes more severe. Political conflicts can also, of course, be solved through compromises, but as scholars have demonstrated, there is a risk that policy compromise results in watered-down measures that are less comprehensive and effective as problem-solving tools.

Such weaknesses are, for example, noted by scholars at the international government level, where ratification processes can take considerable time or when agreements, as in the case of climate change, cannot materialize fully (Carraro 1999, Robertson 2006, Wiegandt 2001). But they have also been found on the domestic level of government when political leaders feel that it is necessary to give priority to certain policy issues over others. A telling example from Ruggie's extensive investigations is when governments decide that offshore oil extraction, foreign investments, exports, and food production are more important for their people's development than stronger protection of their human rights and the country's environment (Ruggie 2009).

A second kind of government capacity problem occurs when legislatures are able to pass strong regulatory policy but policy is not implemented because of other circumstances. In a cross-national perspective, these problems have been found to be greatest in countries with low economic development and where the rule of law is weak and corruption high (UN General Assembly 2008, 6, 11). However, the economic effects of the recent banking crisis are also affecting the ability of government worldwide to deliver on its policy commitments, for instance in the field of education and employment (UK Parliament no date, Johnson, Oliff, and Williams 2011, L.A. County Workforce Investment Board 2011). Even in countries less affected by the banking crisis, such problems have been identified. Two rather recent scandals in Sweden – one concerning the treatment of pigs on farms and the other concerning the presence of toxic chemicals in toys and other household goods – reveal that problems with implementing strong policy can also occur in resourceful, proactive, strong Western industrialized states. In both examples, the public authorities charged with monitoring responsibility maintained that the national government did not give them the necessary resources to conduct their work properly. This lack of resources meant that neither could sufficiently implement proper farm and slaughterhouse inspections to ensure animal welfare or perform the necessary chemical laboratory analyses to ensure that products sold on the Swedish market do not contain illegal toxic substances. In both cases, Swedish government officials and corporate actors involved in the ensuing public debate announced that more conscientious and informed consumer choice and more responsibility on the part of industry are necessary to ensure food and product safety (Sveriges Radio 2009, 2010, Kemikalieinspektionen 2008).

Some problems demonstrate that – even when the assumptions are in place – the model can be weak in solving problems. An illustrative case is the 2010 BP oil spill, estimated as the largest-ever offshore spill (Duvall 2012) and deemed by U.S. President Obama as the "greatest environmental disaster of its kind in our history" (*Financial Times* 2010). The spill, caused by the explosion of the Deepwater Horizon oil rig on April 20, 2010, killed eleven workers and leaked more than 4.1 million barrels of crude oil into the Gulf of Mexico over a three-month period (Calkins 2011). The 1990 Oil Pollution Act was used to identify BP as the responsible actor with "the primary liability for damage caused by the spill" (Bloomberg 2010). In June 2010, Obama pressured BP to create a 20 billion USD fund for cleanup efforts and to compensate affected businesses and individuals (BP 2010). Six months later, the U.S. Department of Justice filed a lawsuit against BP and eight other companies with the charges that they violated federal safety regulations (BBC News 2010). This lawsuit has been disputed by involved corporations but appears now to have been somewhat resolved.[4] However, although BP has taken official responsibility for the spill, further reporting revealed that other corporations were involved in leasing

---

[4] This development is underway during the writing of this manuscript. As of late 2012, BP has agreed to pay 4.5 billion USD in fines and other penalties and to plead guilty to fourteen criminal charges related to the rig explosion (*New York Times* 2012).

equipment and in constructing the rig (Bloomberg 2010). The spill's complexity led President Obama to appoint the National Commission on the BP Deepwater Horizon Oil Spill and Offshore Drilling, which concluded in its final report that the spill was preventable, was caused by BP's and its two key contractors' faulty management practices, and that governmental shortcomings also played a role (National Commission 2011). In particular, the inadequate regulations and oversight resources of a federal agency under the U.S. Department of Interior (the Mineral Management Service) were mentioned.

This case illustrates that the traditional model of political responsibility is applicable to the extent that the U.S. government was able to identify certain responsible actors and is in the process of holding them accountable in various legal and other ways. However, weaknesses in the model are also apparent. For example, responsibility for the spill was even extended to the American people's desire to drive large vehicles and purchase inexpensive fuel. "Our addiction to fossil fuels" is how President Obama included consumers in his Oval Office address on the oil spill recovery (Obama 2010). Thus, while BP and several other companies and even government agencies have been identified as the primary perpetrator of the spill, the lines of "cause responsibility" go beyond the realm of legal sanction and thus to several other actors. Another weakness made evident by the spill is the need to connect cause and treatment responsibility. Because the spill was unprecedented in that it involved a heavier blend of crude oil containing asphalt-like substances, the best cleanup techniques were essentially rendered difficult or even useless (Borenstein 2010). Therefore, charging BP with the spill's cleanup was not necessarily the most effective response for solving the broader complex problem. Moreover, the amount of compensation that should be allotted for the extent of the ongoing damage to ecosystems, employment opportunities, and the local community's way of life, is difficult to calculate and include in treatment responsibility. Prior to the spill, BP's activities were legal, considered largely unproblematic, and not very risky. Finally, the oil spill illustrates an additional and important challenge to the traditional model of political responsibility, namely the increasing proclivity of governments and corporations to outsource work tasks which makes it more difficult to assign and even track responsibility. This oil spill thus illustrates the strengths and weaknesses of the traditional model. Importantly, it demonstrates that laws alone may be inadequate to prevent and resolve complex problems because they may not be able to compel companies to act in the most ethically responsible ways, which may in essence mean volunteering to do more than required by law (see Bernstein and Cashore 2007 cf. Young 2010).

This discussion of the weaknesses illustrates how the traditional model of political responsibility is challenged in the world today. In general terms, its weaknesses can lead to what has been identified as "governance gaps" (UN General Assembly 2008) when there develops an imbalance between the scope and impact of problems and governmental capacity to manage their adverse consequences. Another general conclusion is that the weaknesses seem to be most acute when it is difficult to identify a specific actor as the source of the problem (cause responsibility), when the identified actors have difficulty in assuming treatment responsibility, and when governments find it hard to apply the responsibility mechanism to problems of a prolonged and diffused nature. The model also shows weaknesses when the negative effects of problems are not immediately apparent but rather creep up incrementally and perpetuate a series of other problems for the common good. Some scholars identify these kinds of problems as syndromes that spiral, create, and reinforce each other (Winter 2006, 5ff). Others call them complex webs of political, economic, and social relationships (Schwartz 2009) that are difficult to sort out in policy-making terms, and other scholars go still further with their claim that these problems are the roots of structural injustices (Young 2004, 2006, 2010, Fraser 2005).

In sum, although these problems differ considerably in terms of origin, policy focus, impact, and level of government answerability, they share certain characteristics. Typically, they are found in areas where it is difficult for government to coordinate the needs, interests, and preferences of large groups of actors. What is also striking is that they are extremely complex in nature. Their complexity makes it difficult to clearly assign political responsibility for them. In some cases, more than one government must assume answerability in order for the problem to be solved. In other cases, the solutions require a multitude of actors from different spheres and levels in society. In still others, individuals and groups of citizens are called on to voluntarily develop values, obligations, behaviors, habits, and lifestyles in order to help prevent such problems from happening again.

RECONFIGURING POLITICAL RESPONSIBILITY

Complex problems are encouraging new thinking and policy practice on the taking of political responsibility. The theoretical frameworks and problem-solving proposals now emerging include but go beyond the "command-and-control" regulatory policy of legislation and the legal mechanisms of the traditional political responsibility model. Reconfiguring political responsibility entails encouraging and rewarding both governmental and nongovernmental actors at the institutional and individual levels for their engagements that go beyond the mandates of law. The emerging "beyond compliance" mechanisms and frameworks are believed to be proactive in character and, as such, it is hoped that they have the potential to avoid some of the pitfalls identified in the traditional model. The reconfiguration of political responsibility reflects fundamental changes in how politics is viewed and encourages a multitude of actors to exercise "due diligence" by becoming more aware of, preventing, and addressing problems before they develop into more serious ones (e.g., UN General Assembly 2008, 17, Young 2006). In these new frameworks of responsibility, actors are to act diligently regardless of whether the problems fall within a particular legal jurisdiction or are illegal or not. In these ways, it is expected that the reconfiguration of political responsibility will bring new effectiveness to problem-solving mechanisms by dealing with the intricacies and complications of the internal and external conditions that characterize complex problems (Winter 2006, Ebbesson and Okowa 2009, Ruggie 2009).

The emerging frameworks on a variety of societal levels and policy areas encourage awareness and learning processes as well as responsibility-sharing for problem resolution across different countries, sectors, and actors. This reconfiguration of answerability relies on the direct and active involvement of government, business, civil society, the media, and individual citizens. The new and emerging responsibility-taking institutions include mechanisms to encourage, guide, and prompt voluntary actions. Businesses are, for example, developing policy, mechanisms, and codes for "corporate social responsibility" to deal with the environmental and "structural injustice" problems associated with outsourced and global production processes (Mamic 2004, Kolk and van Tulder 2005; see Chapter 7 for more discussion). Such soft law "beyond compliance" frameworks have and are even being established to deal with the complex problems involved in family household consumption (see Chapter 5). Public-private partnerships – or what some call "participatory governance" (Lovan, Murray, and Shaffer 2004) – are being established on many societal levels to provide welfare services for citizens (Pierre 1998, Bexell and Mörth 2010). Some new efforts seek to promote better procedures for victims to find more effective remedies for corporate-related human-rights abuses and, thereby, give them better opportunity to participate on par with others in societal life (Ruggie 2009, Fraser 2005). Others seek to encourage the participation of citizens in self-governing their rights of social citizenship (e.g. education and health care) (Clarke 2007, Clarke et al. 2007). Domestic and international governmental and nongovernmental organizations (NGOs) as well as transnational corporations believe that more participatory mechanisms and partnerships will improve their legitimacy by involving more stakeholders in complex-problem resolution.

Reconfiguring political responsibility implies a new role for governmental institutions and actors in more "meta-governance" arrangements. These emerging arrangements continue to rely on the capacity of governments to take political responsibility but acknowledge that governments can no longer rely on interventionist policies and that nongovernmental actors from the private sector and civil society now have the capacity to take on responsibility to help solve globalized complex problems (Knill and Lehmkuhl 2002, Midttun 2005). For instance, governments can evoke their commitments to international standards and national laws to encourage and entice other actors to become involved in problem-solving frameworks (cf. Peters 2010, Jordan et al. 2006, Ruggie 2009, Cashore 2002). They may also take on the role of initiating and coordinating various societal actors to take over responsibility. Examples discussed more in the coming chapters concern state action in creating and operating eco- and organic labeling schemes (cf. Boström and Klintman 2011). Other examples involve how states cooperate with private actors to solve problems with ensuring social citizenship. For instance, governments in many countries have coordinated and signed agreements with corporations for the provision of social services (hospital meals, education, elderly care, etc.) and utilities (water, electricity, transportation, etc.) (Clarke et al. 2007, Bexell and Mörth 2010). Reciprocal responsibility frameworks and arrangements have developed between governments in developing countries and multinational corporations, as illustrated by the community water project in Ikot Abasi Idem in the Niger Delta (Idemudia 2010). Even individual national and local politicians get involved in efforts to reconfigure political responsibility by, for instance, participating in voluntary cross-national cooperation endeavors that go beyond their electoral accountability and include their political communities in voluntary "beyond compliance" efforts that supplement the traditional model. Though some of these networks originated earlier, they now focus more attention on problems in the fields of international law, human rights, the environment, sustainable development, and issues concerning chemicals and pesticides in water, waste, and food (De Sadeleer 2009, Alger 2010). Other frameworks for reconfiguring responsibility that directly involve government are the development of fairtrade cities in the legal jurisdictions of municipalities and towns, as well as government as a responsible public purchaser of services and consumer goods (see also Micheletti 2010, epilogue). These are discussed more fully in Chapter 7.

Civil society is, furthermore, directly involved in new problem-solving. Civic groups mobilize members and supporters into political action that engage individual citizens in their role as shoppers. Their calls for action aim at putting pressure on market actors to develop new production policy and practices. By participating in such calls, it is believed that citizens on an individual basis can take more societal responsibility and pressure corporations to do likewise. Governments on all levels tend to view the engagement of civic society as vital in emerging responsibility-taking processes. As stated by a central international governmental agency: "Innovation and change are often the result when individuals come together in the self-motivated activity that a robust civil society fosters" (UN Development Programme et al. 2003, 65). What is noteworthy in most of the emerging responsibility frameworks is the strong emphasis on the role that corporations and consumer choice can play in helping to solve complex problems; the interplay of the two is the focus of this book. This development also signals a de-emphasis on the distinction between the public and private spheres that historically have shaped the working agenda of government and business as well as the division of labor between citizens and consumers (see also Clarke et al. 2007).

CORPORATIONS AS TARGETS FOR POLITICAL RESPONSIBILITY-TAKING

Markets have undergone dramatic changes in character over the past decades. Today, the largest transnational corporations now have a higher gross national product and capital accumulation than many sovereign states (Chandler and Mazlish 2005, Keys and Malnight no date, Risse-Kappen 1995, chapter 1). They have become more complex, powerful, and global in character. Economic globalization and free trade, which are commonly denoted as neoliberalism, have opened up new opportunities for businesses to conduct their operations and to produce their goods in a wide number of countries. *World Investment Report 2009* estimates that there are 82,000 transnational corporations with about 810,000 foreign affiliates across the globe (UNCTAD 2009). Further illustrations of these developments are the complex web of factories and work-force that now makes up a specific industry. For example, by the early 2000s, transnational garment corporations with Northern headquarters employed 24 million workers in about 200 countries; Reebok's annual production involved manufacturing in more than 700 factories and over 500,000 workers, and Nike had in excess of 650,000 workers in more than 1,000 facilities world-wide (Casey 2006, 7).

The freeing up of international trade and the proliferation of markets glob-ally have benefited the world in many ways. Historically, free trade was instru-mental in the democratization process in the Western world, created labor peace, and promoted economic growth through exports of goods to other nations (cf. Trentmann 2008, Micheletti 1995, chapters 2–3). Freedom of com-merce led to wealth-creating networks across nations that built trust and pro-moted both peace and prosperity. A telling example is the treaty establishing the European Economic Community, which had as its objective the creation of a common economic market to promote European unity, harmonious develop-ment, reduction of regional differences and backwardness, and cross-national solidarity by pooling "resources to preserve and strengthen peace and liberty, and calling upon the other peoples of Europe who share their ideal to join in their efforts" (European Union no date; see also Urwin 1995). Similarly, scholars now find that business uses the opportunities that have opened up in contemporary free trade to increase its engagement in international and global commerce (Wacziarg and Welch 2008, Harrison 1993, Winters 2004). Some research shows that the pro-growth policies associated with free trade (i.e., low inflation and openness to international trade) have had a positive effect on the war on world poverty, specifically they have on average promoted higher incomes among the poor as much as they have led to increases in the incomes of other population groups (Dollar and Kraay 2002, 2004). Studies have also found that Export Processing Zones (EPZ) – that is, areas within mostly devel-oping countries where transnational corporations have been encouraged to set up manufacturing operations because governments have lowered their trade barriers and taxes and limited their requirements – have, at least initially, gen-erally proved to be an efficient and productive way of absorbing surplus labor for countries in early stages of industrialization. The presence of EPZs has increased national levels of employment and the host countries' foreign earn-ings and played the role of a preferable alternative to emigration for less skilled workers and, in certain industries, offered women more employment than outside the EPZs (Kusago and Tzannantos 1998, Kinunda-Rutashobya 2003). Despite these developments or perhaps because of them, corporations became a central concern in discussions on new frameworks of political responsibility and an important target of political activism and political consumerism in the 1990s and early 2000s.

There are several ways of understanding why corporations have become targets of political activism and why they are asked to take on more responsibility for their operations. Some critics argue that despite the benefits of free trade, on balance, corporate engagement in the free-trade market system has not done enough to end world poverty, natural-resource exploitation, and the subjugation of people globally. The UN International Labor Organization's World Commission on the Social Dimension of Globalization summarized the problem in this way: "Seen through the eyes of the vast majority of women and men, globalization has not met their simple and legitimate aspirations for decent jobs and a better future for their children" (ILO 2004, x). The UN Development Program, the UN Environmental Programme, World Bank, and World Resources Institute concluded in their report *World Resources 2002–2004* that free trade has created a "responsibility gap" because "Earth has no CEO. No Board of Directors. No management team charged with extracting resources responsibly or maintaining the living factories – the forests, farms, oceans, grasslands, and rivers – that underlie our wealth" (UN Development Programme et al. 2003, 1). Human Rights Watch, a U.S.-based institution with offices around the world that monitor the implementation of human rights, drew the conclusion that "a world integrated on commercial lines does not necessarily lead to human rights improvements. Experience shows that global economic integration is no substitute for a firm parallel commitment to defending human rights" (Human Rights Watch 2001, 2).

These organizations and others have feared that globalization and free trade will facilitate transnational corporations' "outgrowing" the political-responsibility model inherent in nation-state government (International Council on Human Rights Policy 2002, 45; see also Sabel, Fung, and O'Rourke 2000, Ross 1997, Tucker 2002, Nordbrand and Valentin 2005). They claim that corporations apparently have used the opportunities opened up by free trade to avoid taking responsibility for environmental and social justice issues. Their argument is that corporate conduct is at times in direct violation of international and national law and is illegal. However, as clearly illustrated in reporting on the agricultural, mining, and manufacturing sector, the problem is also that laws are not always adequately enforced (Human Rights' Watch 2004, *New York Times* 2007). Corporate conduct has furthermore been found to be problematic in areas of reported abuses in factories, low salary levels, high number of working hours, and insufficient environmental protection in outsourced manufacturing (International Council on Human Rights Policy 2002; see also UN General Assembly 2007).

Thus, corporations became a focus of governmental and nongovernmental criticism because they have not (voluntarily) addressed the findings about how their operations abroad affect the working conditions of those people who are employed on their behalf. Human rights and labor organizations and other activist groups accuse corporations of bad conduct and use statements by corporate leaders about their unawareness of the problem to substantiate how they engage in blame avoidance. For example, an oft-cited response by Nike's general manager in Jakarta was used to mobilize support for anti-sweatshop political consumerism. When confronted with evidence of labor abuses in factories used to manufacture Nike goods, he replied that working conditions were out of Nike's "scope to investigate" (as quoted in Locke 2002, 11; for a general discussion, see Koenig-Archibugi 2004).[5] As discussed in Chapter 6–7, the Nike Corporation and other iconic brands now consider such matters as part of their voluntary responsibility, but this attitude is less prevalent among some small and medium-sized companies and among unknown brands that produce for the Northern and Chinese markets (UN General Assembly 2007).

The negative effects of contemporary free trade, corporate power, and lack of corporate social responsibility are reoccurring topics in protest activities and even as part of the violence associated with the World Trade Organization Ministerial Conferences (for instance, the so-called Battle of Seattle in 1999), the Occupy Wall Street events, and in discussions at more current international summit meetings, including those concerning climate change. The cross-national debate on corporate responsibility is kept alive in transnational activist networks and through political activists with global celebrity status and popular appeal. Perhaps the foremost figure here is Naomi Klein, whose books *No Logo* (2000), published in several editions in English, and later *The Shock Doctrine: The Rise of Disaster Capitalism* (2008) have both been translated into many different languages. Importantly for this book, the critical debates on free trade, corporate globalization, and neoliberalism have been crucial stimuli for the phenomenon of political consumerism. The activist discourse on political consumerism emphasizes not only the responsibility of business but also the role that consumers should play in convincing transnational corporations to take responsibility for the negative effects of free trade.

---

[5] Two examples of this conduct in the 2000s that have been part of media reporting on activist criticisms are the operations of large Swedish mining corporation in Ghana and the clothing manufacturer United Colors of Benetton. The Swedish corporation Sandvik responded to questions of human-rights violations by initially stating that it had not received information about the violations and that it could not exercise control over all its customers (Fair Trade Center 2003, 13). United Colors of Benetton declared in a press release, after accusations brought forth by the animal rights movement for procuring wool from wool producers who engage in a sheep treatment ("mulesing"), that it "has been unjustly and incorrectly involved by PETA (People for the Ethical Treatment of Animals) in a dispute with the Australian Wool Industry, despite the fact that Benetton has no direct relationship with sheep breeding in Australia" (Benetton 2005).

For scholars of political responsibility, policy makers on different governmental levels as well as civic groups and networks active in political consumerism, corporations must also be included in the circle of political responsibility because they are influential actors in globalized commerce. They view corporations as having the capability to make and implement changes that can have positive ramifications on the environment and social justice. Therefore, they are political targets in political activism.

Another reason for the focus on corporations has to do with what scholars call their "buyer-driven" character (Gereffi 2001). This odd term signifies a tendency among brand name corporations to put more resources into maintaining and developing their standing in consumer society than in improving their operations abroad. For the critics of unsolved problems of world poverty, worker treatment, and misuse of common pool resources, this is a problem for three important reasons. First, it demonstrates how corporations invest more in selling than producing commercial goods, a development that they view as jeopardizing the global common good. Once again, the critics have been able to use statements by famous transnational corporations to substantiate their claims and to rally support for their cause. Again, the Nike Corporation has been targeted because its Asia vice president responded to questions about problems in the company's labor practices in outsourced manufacturing in other countries by stating that the company "did not 'know the first thing about manufacturing. We are marketers and designers'" (as quoted in Locke 2002, 11). Thus, the critics argue that the buyer-driven corporations should allocate resources from profiling themselves in consumer society (which also includes numerous philanthropic projects that benefit local Northern communities[6]), to improving their practices abroad.

Second, as discussed in Chapter 6, critical activists view buyer-driven business investment in so-called corporate branding (that is, cultivation of a corporate logotype, image, and culture in order to compete with other similar corporations in the consumer market) (Knight and Greenberg 2002, Smith 1997, Edvardsson and Enquist, 2006, Edvardsson, Enquist, and Hay 2006) as a visible and highly vulnerable target to mobilize consumers and to pressure corporations to implement changes in their way of doing business. Studies show, for instance, that business seems convinced that high investment in corporate branding is necessary for successful corporate development (see Chapter 6). Thus, the activists reason that corporations will concede to changes in order to protect their brand investments.

---

[6] In Northern societies, corporations donate considerable resources to philanthropic causes in local communities. Examples include Nike's sneaker-recycling stations and corporate giving to communities in the United States "where Nike has a significant employee or business presence," IKEA's investment in local community projects in the United States to help children, and the non-profit McDonald's' Ronald McDonald House Charities in operation in several Western and developing countries (Nike 2010, IKEA no date, Ronald McDonald House Charities, no date).

Third, the critics focus on the desires that corporate branding stirs up in consumers, who they also see as important targets for activism (Shaw et al. 2006). For them, consumers must understand how brand advertising attempts to lure them into buying products offering them individuality, a personal style,[7] and exoticism and how these kinds of products contribute to environmental and work-related problems. For instance, these critics argue how the shift from production of standardized, "one-size-fits-all," "off-the-shelf" goods to those catering to a "market for one" that offers consumers a feeling of more personalized or individualized apparel has been found to strain factories, workers, local producers, and the environment.[8] For John Ruggie and other scholars calling for new frameworks for political responsibility-taking, this shift from assembly-line to worker-intensive production in weakly regulated settings jeopardizes both environmental and worker welfare. Today, governments and corporations both recognize that so-called "brand-induced" problems from the shift to flexible production, fast turnaround, surge orders, changed orders, and other rapid production demands frequently have negative effects that need to be remedied through new mechanisms of responsibility-taking (Ruggie 2006, 4).

In sum, corporations are the center of attention in new frameworks of responsibility-taking and a political target for activists because they can play a significant role in preventing detrimental effects on the environment and human rights. Corporations are asked to break what scholars of labor law and industrial relations have termed "race-to-the-bottom" competition, that is businesses that compete with each other by trying to produce goods at increasingly lower cost and consumer price by keeping wages and investments in production down while maintaining the same or even improving their profit margins (Sabel, Fung and, O'Rourke 2000, Kirton and Trebilcock 2004). As stated earlier, free-trade manufacturing has improved the situation of many people in poor countries but for the scholars, government officials, and political

---

[7] Past examples of such marketing include the Nike advertisement about purchasing shoes that you can "build and iD it yourself" that played an important role in the culture jam Nike email exchange studied in Chapter 6, an older advertisement by the very large clothing store H&M with the slogan "Divided spring – real self, real style. The best style is your very own" and Gap's claim that it offers "Clothing and accessories that enhance personal style." These examples have been collected by the authors from street observations in different cities.

[8] A telling example of the problems generated by this shift in manufacturing comes from a quotation from the report by the international humanitarian association Oxfam on the situation of garments workers in Moroccan factories:

"The shops always need to be full of new designs," said one production planning manager, "We pull out all the stops to meet the deadline... Our image is on the line." But the image they hide is of young women working up to 16 hours a day to meet those deadlines, underpaid by 40 per cent for their long overtime working. "There's a girl who's seven months pregnant working ten hours a day," said one garment worker, "and as she has to make a lot of pieces per hour the employer doesn't let her go to the toilet. It's sheer torture for her, but she can't afford to lose her job" (Oxfam International, 2004, 6, italics in the original text are deleted.)

activists involved in reconfiguring political responsibility, it has come at a high cost to the environment and workers. These costs are an important general focus in the problem-solving frameworks within political consumerism.

THE ROLE OF THE CHOICE MECHANISM IN SOLVING POLITICAL PROBLEMS

A common characteristic in the new and emerging responsibility frameworks both within nation-states and globally is their commitment to a looser and more voluntary involvement on the part of a large variety of different actors. Thus, even though societal pressure may be levied on these different actors to become involved in voluntary problem-solving, it is still up to them to decide if they want to participate and also to gauge the degree of their own involvement. Developing problem-solving mechanisms that allow for voluntary degrees of choice and commitment are, therefore, a central focus in current efforts at reconfiguring political responsibility. These efforts ask governments, NGOs, corporations, and individual citizens to partake in both the structuring of such efforts and even to take advantage of them once they are in place. In this way, different actors are asked to put their voluntary choices to work as a tool for problem-solving and governing complex problems.

For example, both corporations and consumers participate in the voluntary "beyond compliance" choice mechanism involved in labeling and corporate social responsibility schemes for more sustainable production and consumption of goods. Governments in different parts of the world also, for instance, employ the choice mechanism to provide public services to citizens in their welfare state reforms. New public management, public-private partnerships, and citizen's charters are examples of policy commitments that include the offering of alternative choice as a means to satisfy more individualized citizen demand and even as a device for service quality control (McCourt 2002, Clarke et al. 2007). The role of the choice mechanism is, therefore, becoming a common feature in welfare policy. In different countries around the world, social citizenship – public education, elderly care, health care, etc. – is increasingly provided through public, private, and hybrid public-private institutions that encourage citizens to make active choices and participate as "entrepreneurial subjects of choice in their quest for self-realization" (Rose 1999, 142). Similarly, because of the growth in the number of media outlets, choice among news providers is now integral to how citizens keep themselves informed in society (Hardin 2009). Choosing among commodities, lifestyles, media, and communities even plays an enhanced role in identity politics. Illustrative contemporary examples of commodity choices for the creation of a more individualized lifestyle and life politics include the "pink money" market for gay identity (BBC News 1998) and the product lines for vegans and vegetarians (Maurer 2002). Thus, although the reasoning for more individual voluntary choice appears to differ from sector to sector, it is generally seen as having the potential to engage and empower citizens by giving them more say in politics, or to improve the general quality of commodities and public services by introducing the element of competition, or to help individuals find new and more comfortable ways of actively engaging in political problem-solving and fulfilling their identity and lifestyle needs (Boström and Klintman 2011, Jordan, Wurzel, and Zito 2003a, Micheletti 2010, Adam Smith Institute no date, Bennett 1998).

Choice has, in sum, become an important feature in a variety of transactions and is employed as an organizing and legitimacy-seeking tool in both the private and public sector. Some current instances of using choice for societal develop-ment have historical roots. In the past, the choice among consumer products was also used as an organizing tool in protest politics in almost all parts of the world (see Friedman 1999, Glickman 2009, Micheletti 2010, Trentmann 2008, Micheletti, Follesdal, and Stolle 2006). Both historically and currently, not all protest shopping promoted(s) the cause of democracy (for a brief discussion, see Micheletti 2010, chapter 2; see also Chapter 8 in this book). Yet, what is significant about the current situation is the magnitude of choices in today's more consumer-oriented society. Some scholars argue that the consumer is replacing the citizen as the central actor in society (Bauman 2007b, Sennett 2006, Guthman 2009), while other observers proclaim that shopping with a conscience can change or better the world (Clark and Unterberger 2007, Jones, Haenfler, and Johnson 2007).

Today, the multitudes of alternative options for shopping for clothes, food, energy provision, schools for children, health care, and so on require indi-vidual citizens to make evaluations and decisions on price, taste, size, brand, quality, and political and lifestyle orientation. Thus, current problem-solving evokes the figure of the "citizen-consumers" as an organizing force in poli-tics. Scholars evaluate the advantages and disadvantages of this fusion of the consumer and citizen differently. The term "citizen-consumers" sparks contra-dictory reactions. For some, it has a negative connotation because it signifies the demise of politics and citizenship by furthering commodity-based and self-oriented identity that can only lead to decline in general social solidarity and to the displacement of politics with capitalism and individual competition (e.g., Bauman 2007a, Klein 2000, 2008, Guthman 2009, Shaw et al. 2006). For others, individual choice has an interesting and creative role to play and can even be likened to the role that competitive voting plays in choosing the future direction of politics (cf. Buchanan 1954, Gabszewicz and van Ypersele 1996, Smith 1990). These divergent opinions lead to different interpretations of the role and the potential of choice in processes of political responsibility-taking. An important research question is, therefore, whether the choice mechanism can be used in an informed and democratic fashion to improve welfare pro-vision (see e.g., Rostgaard 2006, Lundsgaard 2006, Clarke 2006, Vabø 2006, Blomqvist 2004) and, as investigated in this book, to solve political prob-lems concerning public well-being and the common good, such as protecting social diversity, the environment, and workers' rights and, thereby, to make production and consumption more suitable to these values. A related question is about the types of conditions and factors that can facilitate citizens' empowerment through the less expert-determined and more individualized involvement and alternatives evolving from the use of voluntary choice in politics.

THE RECONFIGURATION OF CITIZENSHIP PRACTICE

The current strong emphasis on the enhanced role of individual choice in politics represents provocative and challenging developments for social scientists. Scholars have conventionally distinguished between individuals as citizens, who function in the public sphere with more or less public interests, and individuals as consumers, who function on the basis of self-interests in the private sphere, and have studied them separately in different academic disciplines (primarily political science, economics, and marketing). Analyzing the role of consumer choice as a form of participation in politics, the choice mechanism as a tool in governance, and the fusion of citizens and consumers into political consumers requires new theoretical conceptualizations and methodologies for investigating how people engage with the new frameworks of political responsibility.

Political philosophers were probably first to consider the implications of choice for political responsibility and how it can affect society. As demonstrated in Iris Marion Young's writings discussed earlier in this chapter, philosophers formulate normative claims about how people should make responsible choices associated with complex problems. They have explored the moral obligations that people have with regard to themselves, others, and society and have formulated the normative claim that individuals should engage in the sharing of responsibilities for protecting and promoting justice (e.g. Young 2004, 2006, 2010, May 1992). But what kind of responsibility do they envision individuals taking, and how can this responsibility be specified or even measured empirically? Their general definition of responsibility, as accountability for one's attitudes and actions, is a good starting point for formulating positive theory on choice responsibility for empirical research. Accountability can, in turn, be broken down into two parts: an individual's understanding of the ramifications of her choices in societal affairs and her exercise of reasonable due care or continual watchfulness when making real choices (Young 2010, May 1992, May and Hoffman 1991, Arendt 2006, Walsh 1970).

The question then is which resources and preconditions are necessary for individuals to assume accountability for their choices. To begin to answer this theoretically (and then empirically in later chapters), we introduce the concept of *individualized responsibility-taking* and define it as reasonable individual choice involving considerations about the societal effects of one's actions. Following the philosophical literature, the concept of individualized responsibility-taking has a strong normative element: it asks individuals to engage in reasonable choice-making even when they are not required by law to do so, when it goes against common social conventions, and when it can mean suppressing private interests and changing private lifestyle habits. Theoretically, this operational definition has the potential to generate empirical indicators for Young's claim in her new model of political responsibility (which she calls the "social connection model") because it considers how all categories of people contribute to processes of injustice and harms through their choice actions (Young 2010, 109). It also addresses Young's claim that responsibility is an open-ended idea as to what actions are called for and, therefore, actors themselves must decide how they should discharge their responsibility (Young 2010, 143).

Individualized responsibility-taking is a demanding theoretical idea, is most likely present in different degrees, and is reliant on societal contexts and individual resources. We identify two necessary preconditions for any degree of individualized responsibility-taking. The first one refers to a series of structural prerequisites that enable citizens to make reasonable choices which they believe are best for themselves and society. The second set of prerequisites is personal background characteristics that give individuals the capability and interest to make such reasonable choices in everyday life. Obviously, living up to or even trying to live up to the norm of individualized responsibility-taking does not come easy. As with other citizenship expectations or norms (cf. van Deth, Montero, and Westholm 2007, Dalton 2008, Stolle, Micheletti, and Berlin 2010), its practice can range on a scale from low to high commitment or intensity. It is voluntary, cannot be forced upon people, and must be nurtured through encouragements of various kinds that help people develop their own "ethical compass" (cf. Department for International Development 2008) to inform and guide them about the effects of their personal choices on societal development. Studying available reasonable choice mechanisms and variations in its practice as well as societal and individual prerequisites is the focus of this book. An important purpose of the book is also to address how well real-life individual practices compare with those of the normative ideal of individualized responsibility-taking.

However, before turning to the empirical investigations in the coming chapters, the theoretical operational measures need to be specified more fully. The first necessary structural condition is *information accessibility*. Individuals must be able to find information about the ramifications of their choices on societal development in order to develop what philosophers call a "caring sensitivity," that is, a meta-virtue about the "appropriateness of response to the needs and feelings of others" (May 1992, 60). For some individuals, a caring sensitivity may come easier; they seem to be born with it or, more correctly, are socialized into it.[9] Frequently, however, this meta-virtue needs continuous

---

[9] Research on altruism shows, for example, that the development of a caring orientation in life is fostered by parental dispositions and interactions with children (Clary and Miller 1986) as well as social aspects, such as social network size and social integration (Brañas-Garza and Espinosa 2006). This research is complemented by a growing inquiry into the biological causes of altruistic actions, including studies that suggest an evolutionary basis for caring, as well as more recent

nurturing. Individuals must be taught and reminded through convincing information, encouragements, admonitions, role models, and examples about how their choices affect the common good. News reports and documentaries, testimonials that put a human face on the effects of less reasonable choice on, for instance, worker exploitation, celebrity endorsements for more reasonable choices over others, and even popular culture can provide such sensitizing information (cf. Walsh 1970, 12, May 1992, Micheletti and Stolle 2007; see also Chapter 5 and 6). Social and peer pressure can also function as a sensitizing agent because it brings "softer and subtler pressures to bear, pressures which affect a man not just in his personal capacity but also through his relatives, friends and associates" (Walsh 1970, 13). The general goal of sensitizing information is to make visible the elements about choice that are not always apparent in available information and to cast "moral taint" on less reasonable "bad" choices with the hope that individuals will make more reasonable "better" ones (May 1992, chapter 8, Mellema no date, Appiah 1991, Arendt 2006). In the political consumerist literature, sensitizing information is called the "politics behind products" and has been found to reveal the political, ethical, and environmental impact of what would usually be considered banal choices in everyday life (Micheletti, Follesdal, and Stolle 2006, Hilton 2007). This need for sensitizing information is the theoretical explanation for an investigation of the consciousness-raising campaigns and other efforts discussed in Chapter 5.

The second necessary structural precondition is the presence of opportunities for individuals to make more reasonable choice, which we term *reasonable choice architecture*, an institutional design that offers individuals advice and opportunities to engage in reevaluating their present-day choice preferences and in making new ones (cf. Thaler and Sunstein 2008, John et al. 2011). As discussed in later chapters, this reasonable choice architecture can be provided or fostered by governments, NGOs, corporations, and civic and social networks. For example, governmental units responsible for good nutrition and sustainable development directly refer to the need to develop "choice editing" platforms in their policy recommendations and documents (e.g., SDC and NCC 2006). Such "beyond compliance" regulatory institutions as voluntary labeling schemes for environmentally friendly, organic, and fairtrade products (discussed in Chapters 4 and 5) can be seen as choice architecture that "nudges" and encourages individuals to reevaluate or edit their commodity choices to promote more responsible or sustainable development. In conclusion, the study of individual responsibility-taking requires an evaluation of whether choice architecture (opportunities, institutions, platforms) that encourage and offer citizens alternative forms of choice are available, and how they differ across countries.

inquiry into brain function that attributes at least some of the basis for altruism to neurological activity (Warneken and Tomasello 2009, Krueger, Hicks, and McGue 2001, Smith and Stevens 2002, Hoffman 1978).

From previous research on political participation, we rely on two general findings to develop necessary theoretical conditions for the realization of individualized responsibility-taking at the individual level. First, *individual motivation* is essential (e.g., Verba, Schlozman, and Brady 1995, Leighley 1995). Of course, this individual resource relates closely to the available choice architecture that encourages, nudges, and rallies people to engage in politics. For the concept of individualized responsibility-taking, this means that they must feel motivated to both seek and use sensitizing information to develop values in line with caring insights and to formulate preferences or an ethical compass that facilitates the making of reasonable choices. Second, they must feel that their actions matter. They must, therefore, have a sense of agency or *empowerment* to engage in the choice practices associated with individualized responsibility-taking. Following previous studies, we identify two important elements of empowerment: personal background and a sense of choice efficacy. Personal background includes the socioeconomic resources of income, education, and place of residence but also such aspects as general interest in politics and a set of values and concerns related to reasonable choice. Scholars consider all these factors in explaining why individuals participate in political projects aiming at taking responsibility to improve the common good or their self-interests (Inglehart 1997, Verba 2003, May 1992, 89–92, 106–107, 118–119, 159). Second, individuals must feel or be made to feel that their choices make a difference – that they are efficacious. A sense of internal efficacy is, therefore, considered to be an important individual attribute. It usually has a positive effect on motivating individuals into certain practices by making them believe that their actions matter and, therefore, counteracts proclivities to free-ride and shirk the responsibilities of citizenship (Fraser 2005, Hawkins et al. 1971, Tuck 2008). Attempting to meet the norm of individualized responsibility-taking also, then, depends on the personal background characteristics and beliefs of individuals. From previous research on other forms of participation, it can be expected that people with high socioeconomic resources feel more empowered to engage in various forms of individualized responsibility-taking (Verba, Schlozman, and Brady 1995, Petersson, Westholm, and Blomberg 1989, Micheletti and Stolle 2005, Wolfinger and Rosenstone 1980). Later chapters will investigate how and whether this expectation holds for political consumerism in the cross-national context.

Furthermore, a reasonable choice architecture can be expected to facilitate individualized responsibility-taking. This architecture is, in turn, dependent on other conditions. On a very basic level, the formulation of and access to sensitizing information requires some degree of freedom of information, press, speech, and association in society. Therefore, the theoretical assumption is that individualized responsibility-taking and reasonable choice architecture will more likely be found in countries where civic and political freedoms are well-established and guaranteed. Individuals in these countries, should, without fear of repercussion, be able to seek and access it so that they can judge the impact of their choices on society at large. Within these democratic countries, it is also theoretically expected that there will be a higher level of individualized responsibility-taking where the social rights of citizenship (that is, a welfare state that provides employment, good education, health care, and so on) are well-developed and citizens have generally higher levels of socioeconomic resources. The idea is that these institutional and policy features allow for the development of post-material values (Inglehart 1997; for further discussion, see Chapter 2 in this book), which in turn are linked with values of self-expression and a stronger demand for environmental protection, social justice, and new forms of political action (Inglehart and Welzel 2005). Theoretically then, it is expected that higher degrees of individualized responsibility-taking will be found in Western industrialized stable democratic countries with well-developed welfare states. It is noteworthy that scholars of participation, citizenship, and political responsibility claim that it is mostly citizens in these countries that should take more personal responsibility for their choices and sustainable development (cf. Dobson 2003, Barry 2005, 34, Young 2006, Delanty 2000). Nevertheless, the range of individualized responsibility-taking is expected to vary across and within nations. Therefore, we conduct both a cross-national study based on individuals in Chapter 3 and on country characteristics in Chapter 4, examining how people within these settings and conditions live up to the idea of individualized responsibility-taking in the arena of consumption choices.

This book is about whether, how, and why citizens might increasingly engage in individualized responsibility-taking. The theoretical considerations in this chapter suggest that individualized responsibility-taking might be a rising phenomenon in Western democracies. Whereas governments and conventional political institutions might not be able or willing to adequately address various current global problems, some citizens invent and create new approaches and solutions to global-problem solving and take over responsibility themselves. These actions cover a wide variety of political issues. For example, some citizens perceive that governments might not regulate the flow of immigration sufficiently, and thus might take it upon themselves to patrol the borders of their countries. In Sweden, citizens have come together in groups in order to be in conversation with young people in the city streets at night as they care about the young generations and want to steer them away from substance abuse and crime and promote safety in their neighborhoods, thus taking responsibility alongside public social and police services and municipal governments. In the United States, urban developers have decided to take responsibility into their own hands and stepped in to find a solution to urban sprawling by constructing the green community Prairie Crossing (see Watson 2010). However, the best and most truly individualized example of responsibility-taking is that of political consumerism.

Political consumers might choose to consistently and regularly use labeling schemes or other elements of the political consumerist choice architecture to help them make responsible choices of food and household products. For others, it might take place more sporadically and only for certain shopping practices (e.g., purchasing organic milk, eco-labeled paper, or fairtrade coffee). Still others, as illustrated by vegans and supporters of the simplicity movement discussed in Chapter 5, may decide to make a deeper commitment to the idea of individualized responsibility-taking by letting responsible choice guide and govern their lifestyles. To attempt to practice the idea as much as possible, they commit to a lifestyle politics that changes their lives significantly (Micheletti and Stolle 2010). Other individuals might opt to improve their sense of how choices are related to complex problems by devoting their resources to gaining more information about how their choices affect societal developments. We can even theoretically visualize individuals who decide that they must convince other people to make reasonable choices and, therefore, participate in opinion-formation efforts to get others to do likewise. Examples of this form of discursive effort are culture jamming, sending letters to corporations, and social interchanges about the environmental and social-justice impact of certain consumer products. Chapter 6 examines a well-known case of antibranding and culture jamming.

Finally, although this book studies political consumerism as its focus, individualized responsibility-taking can obviously even involve choices of a different nature but that also include dimensions of importance for citizen welfare, with welfare service choice being the prominent example. Because all these forms of individualized choice are often intimately associated with trends toward neoliberalism and governmental deregulation, the term "individualization" has provoked controversy particularly in the English-speaking world (Lash 2002, Bauman 2002, Beck and Beck-Gernsheim 2002a, 2002b). It is thus important to keep in mind that individualization and therefore also individualized responsibility-taking differ theoretically from individualism. Theoretically individualism can be defined as a self-interested orientation to societal affairs and a retreat from the political sphere or the replacement of governmental responsibility with that of individual actors freely pursuing their economic interests in a private context outside a moral, social, or political framework of responsibility-taking. Individualization and individualized responsibility-taking refer instead to actions practiced in do-it-yourself styles and in different spheres aimed at caring for public well-being and the common good and thus differ in orientation from individualism's endorsement of the primacy of private enjoyments and lack of interference from the outside of one's personal environment (Encyclopaedia Britannica, no date).

CHARACTER AND OUTLINE OF THE BOOK

The aim of this book is broad and ambitious; the subject matter developing, changing, and challenging. There is no standardized format for analyzing the phenomenon of political consumerism and individualized responsibility-taking. Thus multidisciplinary theorizing, multilevel comparative analyses, multi-methods and methodological triangulation, and the creation and application of new approaches are applied. The empirical investigations reported in the coming chapters rely on eight different sources of empirical material: self-generated and available survey data on political participation and political consumerism at the individual level; merged comparative statistical data on Western democracies; interviews with leaders in business and political consumer activism; public and less public documents and materials from transnational corporations, organizations, and networks; media archives; unique material generated from a well-known culture jam (the Nike e-mail exchange); extensive information collected on the political consumerist market, and previous research on specific kinds and instances of political consumerism.

This introductory chapter has evaluated the traditional government-oriented model of political responsibility in light of the complex problems facing the world today. It identifies weaknesses in the model's scope and effectiveness in dealing with complex and more globalized problems as important reasons for the current efforts in constructing more voluntary frameworks for responsibility-taking in all levels of society. Prominent examples of emerging frameworks that reconfigure responsibility are presented. Among their important characteristics are the involvement of a larger number and variety of actors in political problem-solving, their voluntary and process orientation, and the use of individual choice as a tool for taking responsibility in politics. The chapter also discussed briefly the new role for government (see more in Chapters 7 and 8), citizens, and consumers in these responsibility arrangements. To study generally how citizens can use these emerging frameworks, the concept of individualized responsibility-taking is introduced and developed as involving the identification of necessary structural preconditions and personal background characteristics for individuals to be able to take responsibility by making reasonable choices.

Chapters 2 to 7 apply the concept of individualized responsibility-taking in a series of empirical studies. In Chapter 2, the general rise of emerging action repertoires in the Western world and particularly the emergence of political consumerism is investigated. It also introduces the four forms of political consumerism (boycotts, buycotts, discursive political consumerism, and lifestyle politics) as examples of individualized responsibility-taking. The chapter offers a systematic summary of the doubts that have been expressed within the research and political communities about political consumerism as responsible market-based political action and as an effective agent for political change. The two easily measurable forms of political consumerism (boycotts and buycotts) and the individual background characteristics and factors that are related to them are the focus of Chapter 3. Important comparative results are that political consumers do not differ significantly from other citizens active in other forms of creative political participation and also that political consumers consider the material quality of consumer goods as relevant when making shopping choices just as do non-political consumers. However, significantly and increasingly more women than men act as political consumers. Political consumers also have different values compared to other citizens, including the belief that they have a personal responsibility to think politically about their purchasing practices and take personal responsibility by buying products for political, ethical, and environmental reasons. Political consumers also believe more strongly that good citizenship is about values of solidarity to others who are not as well off economically and politically.

Chapter 4 continues in a comparative fashion. Unique measures on political and economic factors are constructed to reveal cross-nationally weak and strong pockets in the practice of political consumerism and the factors related to this pattern. Surprisingly and contrary to some scholarly expectations, economic factors and price premiums are found to be of little relevance. Rather as explained fully in the chapter, political consumerism is clearly most prevalent in postmaterialist long-term (stable) democracies and, within this group of countries, social equality, the legacy of neo-corporatism, social capital, and religion are the most predominant contextual factors.

Chapter 5 shifts the analytical level from individually practiced forms of political consumerism and related individual and country characteristics to eight identified organizational settings of political consumerism. It discusses how and why old and new civic groups engage in the market as an arena for politics and mobilize individuals and groups into their cause. The chapter identifies important developments and problems in the different organizational settings historically to the 2000s, focuses on the central role played by labeling schemes and particularly those for organic food, fairtrade, and eco-labeling, but also discusses briefly third-party certification in the field of forestry and seafood. It finds that some important activist mobilizing, and most prominently in the organizational setting of anti-sweatshop activism, has taken a different trajectory and discusses why it has not developed into a labeling-scheme framework. Three additional organizational fields – socially responsible investing, animal welfare and rights, and more complete consumer lifestyle change – are briefly discussed. The concluding section uncovers some common developments in the organizational settings and especially efforts toward collaboration and harmonization. Three general findings from the chapter are that activism can frequently be explained by a need to fill in governance gaps due to governments' lack of initiative and action on particular problems associated with production and consumption, that there has been a more confrontational activist repertoire in North America and generally a more cooperative one in Europe, and finally that many of the organizational settings have experienced internal conflict over their future path.

Discursive political consumerism is a difficult form to study, yet it forms the main focus of Chapter 6. Most survey research fails to measure any form of discursive political consumerism and thus does not consider it a form of political action. However, it is used as a tool by civic groups and individual activists to target corporations and sensitize consumers and others about the relationship between consumer choice and, among other issues, the treatment of workers abroad. Thus, discursive political consumerism serves as an interesting example of how one of the structural prerequisites for individualized responsibility-taking, namely information accessibility, is at work in real life. The chapter discusses the discursive turn in political action repertoires and why a particular form of discursive political consumerism, namely antibranding and culture jamming, targets well-known corporate brands. It analyses the unique data source generated from the Nike e-mail exchange, a culture jam that has been calculated to have reached around 11.4 million people globally within a few months after its release. The analysis also shows that the culture jam mobilized certain people into responsibility-taking attitudes and action, created a virtual community of like-minded people, and put the "sweatshop" issue on national and international news. The case of Nike shows clearly how and why brand-name transnational corporations can be vulnerable to political consumerist mobilized action.

Chapter 7 takes a critical look at the potentials and limits of global political consumerism. It systematically addresses the doubts about political consumerism's effectiveness to produce social and political change. To study political consumerism's effectiveness it formulates a multi-faceted process model and, in so doing, contributes to the general social-science discourse on the effectiveness of political action. It also includes one evaluative overview of developments and challenges in the fairtrade and organic food industries. The general finding is that political consumerism is effective but limited in important ways. Its market strategies weaken some of its original movement strategies and allow corporations to take the lead in several fields. This development might perhaps be viewed as corporate sensitivity and adaptation to criticism of political consumerism. Others see it as evidence for white- or greenwashing. Regardless of point of view, corporate engagement creates some confusion on the part of consumers about which labels to prefer and trust. Another important result is that political consumerism is not currently equipped to fundamentally change the large existing North-South inequalities or environmental problems, including the complex problem of climate change. Nevertheless, it has put many problems on the agenda of Western democracies, brought governments into the issue area, and has started to change the standard of living of farmers and workers in the developing world.

In the final chapter, we reflect on how the phenomenon of political consumerism challenges social science by calling on scholars to renew their theoretical concepts and methodology in order to keep up with evolving and emerging political developments. The discussion urges scholars to identify the actors, institutions, and structures at the new frontiers of political responsibility-taking and to assess the effectiveness of their actions. Chapter 8 also extrapolates implications beyond the data and cases reported in the book to develop more general theoretical and methodological insights that we hope will inform future debates on the study of citizenship, participation and social movements, governance, and the effectiveness of political action generally. This chapter also weighs the evidence and discusses general limitations of political consumerism as a form of political participation and problem-solving mechanism. Important considerations in this evaluation include the challenges that complexity and scale of production and consumption imply for devising popular and legitimate problem-solving mechanisms within the political consumerism field as well as the need to involve government, public policy, and regulation to coordinate and enhance political consumerism problem-solving processes.

2

Reconfiguring Political Participation

Why would a group of individuals enter a shopping mall in Stockholm and other major cities on a designated day in November, get shopping carts, and file silently through the mall for a considerable period of time without buying anything (Breathing Planet 2009)? Why would groups of people in New York and other large urban areas dive into dumpsters and trash bins to salvage and eat discarded food and devote time to establishing so-called community curb-days (see curbday.com)? By limiting their private consumption, perhaps even by appealing to others to do the same, and creating mechanisms for alternative consumption lifestyles, they seem to be expressing criticism of societal values and practices related to shopping as well as some aspects of market capitalism. Other people have demonstrated their concern about the negative effects of private consumption on the environment and workers in the global economy by participating in antiglobalization demonstrations or Internet campaigns, creating phenomena discussed in Chapter 6 called antibranding or culture jams, or as discussed in several chapters in the book, preferring and deciding to buy commodity goods produced in sweatshop-free or environmentally safe conditions. For others, locally produced goods are important (Bennett 1998, Inglehart and Catterberg 2002, Stolle, Hooghe, and Micheletti 2005).

Citizens express their political views and act in provocative ways as well. Each year several cities host the World Naked Bike Ride, where thousands of participants get naked while cycling. The co-organizer of the Brighton, England ride explains the campaign eloquently: "The economic crisis highlights that we can't rely on the authorities to do the right thing. It's time for people to demand concrete action to reduce carbon emissions and make sustainable lifestyles accessible to all. The World Naked Bike Ride is a welcome reminder that you don't need a big carbon footprint to get around, and you don't need credit to have a good time" (UK Press Office 2009). Lack of government action in other areas triggers citizen efforts as well. The Minuteman Project in California, for example, organizes what they describe as "citizens' Neighborhood Watch on our border," where citizens organized in chapters patrol illegal immigration at the U.S.-Mexican border. Its founder pointed to his frustrated efforts in trying to get a "neglectful U.S. government to simply enforce existing immigration laws" (Minuteman Project 2009) as the main reason for his organization. Consumer choice editing has been used to promote anti-Semitism and racism (Micheletti 2010). These examples and others discussed in this book show how people in the Northern world are rethinking their role in politics. What these examples, as diverse in approach, commitment, and political message as they are, have in common is aware and informed citizens fed up with governmental inaction taking responsibility into their own hands. They use a variety of methods to express their political views, values, and demands and to take action and develop mobilization tools to perhaps even involve other people.

During the past decades, many developments have taken place in the political participation repertoires in advanced industrialized democracies. Growing numbers of citizens are participating in the extra-parliamentary realm, in non-hierarchical and informal movement-inspired networks, in so-called checkbook organizations, and in a variety of lifestyle politics that concern global human rights and global common-pool resources but also local problems. These innovations in the political participation repertoires call into question the widely accepted thesis that citizens are not very interested in participating in Western democratic politics (Pharr and Putnam 2000, Putnam 2002, 2000). A large number of these additional action repertoires include the idea of individualized responsibility-taking.

In this chapter, the rise of these more individualized forms of participation are discussed and embedded squarely into the debates on the responsibility collapse, the transformation of politics, the reconfiguring of political participation, and the rise of individualized responsibility-taking. The point of the chapter is to discuss how these additional action repertoires might reflect a newly emerging understanding of citizenship and the rising responsibility citizens take in globalized politics. It also discusses how this type of citizen engagement can be studied empirically. Then, the ideal of individualized responsibility-taking introduced in Chapter 1 is compared to and distinguished from conventional participation. The third section of the chapter emphasizes political consumerism and its various forms as examples of individualized responsibility-taking and examines how their inclusion into political action repertoires challenges current definitions of political participation. Finally, we present a way to measure political consumerism and an empirical outlook of the rise and spread of political consumerism in Western democracies.

POLITICAL PARTICIPATION IN THE GLOBALIZED WORLD

Since the 1990s, political scientists have called attention to an alleged decline in political participation and citizen involvement (Putnam 2000, Rubenson et al. 2004, Macedo et al. 2005, van Schuur and Voerman 2010). The most systematic account of the alleged erosion of civic and political life in the United States can be found in the work of Harvard political scientist Robert Putnam and more recently in the teamwork by Princeton professor Stephen Macedo (Putnam 2000, 2002, Pharr and Putnam 2000, Putnam, Feldstein, and Cohen 2003, Macedo et al. 2005). According to these authors, Americans have become less active in voluntary associations and increasingly refrain from typical political involvement such as membership in political parties and they attend fewer public meetings on town and school affairs. Especially with regard to the political domain, an impressive array of empirical evidence has been marshaled to substantiate the claims about the decline of political participation and civic engagement. Evidence shows that various conventional forms of political participation have lost much of their appeal. Political parties have traditionally served as a linking mechanism between citizens and the political system, but in a number of countries the party system is confronted with a rapid decline of party identification and membership (Mair and van Biezen 2001, van Schuur and Voerman 2010). Voter turnout as well has followed a downward spiral (Nie, Verba, and Petrocik 1979, Jackman and Miller 1995, Lijphart 1997, Putnam 2002). But also with regard to other political activities, such as writing letters, participating in rallies, and volunteering in campaigns, the numbers fell by half between the mid-1970s and the 1990s (Macedo et al. 2005). There is an assumption that this flight from politics is spreading to other countries (Putnam 2002).

Many scholars and observers interpret this development as a fundamental threat to the survival of healthy communities and democratic political systems. However, not everyone accepts this interpretation or conclusion. Some scholars argue that dissatisfaction and frustration with mainstream politics does not necessarily turn into political apathy and alienation. Rather, they find that citizens have developed a multitude of ways to engage in politics outside the parliamentary sphere that they find more suitable, responsible, meaningful, efficient, and direct for their political interests and needs (Beck, Giddens, and Lash 1997, Bennett 1998, Inglehart and Catterberg 2002, Stolle and Hooghe 2005, Young 2006). According to these scholars, the willingness to participate in politics and societal affairs is still strong but is no longer completely channeled through traditional political membership and action repertoires based in hierarchically structured groups (Eliasoph 1998, Lichterman 1996). Instead, from this angle, citizens want to contribute to societal goods by mingling and conversing with others spontaneously and on their own terms (Wuthnow 1998). These scholars claim that we are witnessing a rise of action repertoires resulting from preferences to do something political without a steady affiliation.

Ironically, alternative political action repertoires are not really new. In some form, they have been present for centuries (Glickman 2009). In survey research, emerging forms of political participation were first noted by Barnes and Kaase (1979), who revealed a whole array of what they called unconventional forms of political participation that accompanied the protest movements of the 1970s. They made a distinction between "conventional" political action (voting, writing one's representative in parliament, etc.) and "unconventional" forms of political action (demonstrations, boycotts, occupation of buildings, etc.) and predicted that unconventional forms were here to stay and on the rise particularly because younger generations and those with postmaterialist value orientations were more engaged in these activities (ibid., Inglehart and Catterberg 2002). Later, Inglehart confirmed these findings and gave evidence that various activities considered unconventional in the 1970s had actually systematically increased and spread through the populations of Western democracies by the mid 1990s (Inglehart 1997). Indeed, by the end of the twentieth century, various action repertoires, particularly protests, the signing of petitions and to a certain extent boycotts – all of which by now have been called "elite-challenging" – have become mainstream tools for citizens to express their political stances and opinions (Stolle and Hooghe 2005, Inglehart and Welzel 2005).

Theoretical work has underlined this turn in political participation and has located the emerging action repertoires more clearly outside the electoral and parliamentary spheres (Koopmans and Rucht 2002). Well-known and widely used concepts representative of this theoretical thinking are subpolitics (Beck 1997), creative politics (McFarland 2010), and everyday-making (Bang and Sorensen 2001, Li and Marsh 2008) As shown in the brief discussion in this chapter, all these theories discuss how citizens attempt to find ways to take responsibility when faced with government inaction and acknowledge the normative claim included in the notion of individualized responsibility-taking discussed in Chapter 1.

Ulrich Beck's theory of risk society focuses on the problems involved with addressing a variety of risks that threaten public well-being and the common good. It includes the concept of subpolitics, which relates the new political action repertoires to processes of globalization and to citizens' perceptions about government's inability to control and take responsibility for the new uncertainties created by public and corporate policy (Beck 1992, Beck and Beck-Gernsheim 2002a, 2002b, Giddens 1996). The responsibility collapse perpetuated by government's incapacity to deal with risks in certain areas of globalization is being filled by *active subpoliticians* – citizens – who take responsibility for the risks on their own (Holzer and Sorensen 2003). For Beck and his followers, this development shows the opposite of a decline in participation. In Beck's words, "What appeared to be a 'loss of consensus', an 'unpolitical retreat to private life', 'a new inwardness' or 'caring for emotional wounds' in the old understanding of politics can, when seen from the other side, represent the struggle for a new dimension of politics" (Beck 1997, 101).

The implication is that everyday acts by citizens, like the ones introducing this chapter and those discussed elsewhere in this book, have the power to potentially restructure society.

The concept of the everyday-maker underscores the political agency implicit in individual actors in many walks of life (Sørensen 1997, Hansen and Neufeld 1999, Ulrich 1999). An *everyday-maker* is a citizen involved with issues in a very local and specific way who may work alone or in ad hoc networks organized outside the formal system of politics and across traditional political ideological boundaries. Like subpolitical action, everyday-makers do not necessarily view their participation as political. Yet, studies clearly show that this kind of citizen involvement has an impact on politics (Li and Marsh 2008).

Similarly, the theory of creative participation focuses on the participation of individuals who are not necessarily connected to politics through conventional political institutions. These "scattered" individuals seek public action toward a common goal, mostly because government and established political institutions do not pursue or want to pursue that goal (McFarland 2010). In order to do this, these individuals, like subpoliticians and everyday-makers, must overcome the dilemma of collective action and find a way to communicate and cooperate in order to reach their common goals. Andrew McFarland, who developed the theory of creative participation, points to the formation of transnational advocacy networks that transcend the established national organization boundaries as well as participation in boycotts and other actions against current policies of major business corporations as examples of creative participation (Keck and Sikkink 1998, Micheletti 2010).

This short review of important concepts in contemporary social science interprets various current forms of citizen actions that take place outside the parliamentary arena as political expressions and forms of political participation. While these accounts accept the decline of some aspects of political participation, they also highlight an accompanying transformation in citizens' action repertoires and maintain that citizens are becoming increasingly active in political arenas previously excluded from the political analysis, e.g. the market, private sphere, and private lifestyle. As argued by theories of risk society and creative participation, citizens take up responsibilities in areas outside the jurisdictions of local and national governments and the mandates of international organizations. They thus fill the responsibility gaps discussed in Chapter 1. Citizens' actions are seen either as a response to government inaction or as a response to governmental or organizational decisions that citizens find to be inadequate. As theories of the everyday-maker and subpolitics explain, citizens act politically in ways that have often been considered outside the political realm. Implicit in these theories is the notion of individualized responsibility-taking.

Some scholars are skeptical (Putnam 2000, Skocpol 2003). Their reactions have sparked a conceptual debate about the locus of responsibility for political problems and the importance of political goals, motivations, and successes of the involvement of citizens in democracy. They have also raised the question about which type of participation matters in politics (van Deth 2010, Johnston 2008). Can "loose connections" (Wuthnow 1998) or the non-institutionalized action repertoires of everyday-making and subpolitics be a stable and effective way of achieving political goals? Before conclusions can be drawn, we need to examine these forms and particularly expressions of individualized responsibility-taking more systematically and empirically.

INDIVIDUAL CITIZENS AND POLITICAL RESPONSIBILITY-TAKING

This section continues the discussion of the expanded political action repertoires by asking what role the notion of individualized responsibility-taking plays in political participation. The analysis focuses on contrasting declining forms of conventional participation with the rising ones associated with participation in globalized politics with regard to: 1) their structure and mobilization methods; 2) substantive issues; 3) style of individual involvement; 4) targets; and finally 5) the increased role of the Internet, an enabling force or "architecture of participation" (cf. Shirky 2008, 17). This analysis will help to transfer the idea of individualized responsibility-taking to empirical research on political participation.

First, the practice of individualized responsibility-taking does not typically take place in traditional (formal, bureaucratic, membership) organizations. Because it acknowledges the political agency implicit in an individual assessment of ability and choice, it relies instead on horizontal, more flexible, and looser structures (Shirky 2008, Wuthnow 1998). Citizens desiring to engage in individualized responsibility-taking opt, therefore, for more horizontal networks that utilize loose contacts and information communication technology that allow more spontaneous expressions and flexible coordination of their actions (Castells 1997, Deibert 2000, Levi and Olson 2000). Citizens may, for example, become activated through sudden Internet alerts, participation alternatives offered on web sites, through friendship networks, or a personal sense of urgency for a cause triggered in a variety of ways. This form of opportunity structure allows individuals to easily enter or exit political involvements and may not bring about regularities in political behavior traditionally found in conventional participation.

Second, participative forms encouraging individualized responsibility-taking focus less on mainstream or routine politics. Instead, lifestyle elements are politicized, and even though many citizens no longer identify their action as "political," they challenge politics by questioning who gets what, where, and how in the world today. In doing so, these action repertoires blur the traditional boundaries between the public and the private sphere so important to established forms of political participation. Spheres traditionally perceived as private arouse political involvement because they concern value, resource, and power allocations that affect the common good. Eliasoph documents how

housewives, rather than entangling themselves in the routine politics of the parliamentary sphere, prefer home-oriented actions including those of consumer
behavior and household waste disposal (Eliasoph 1998). Forms of participation that allow for individualized responsibility-taking often involve globalized
politics and aspects of sustainable development. Examples include recycling
goods, reducing certain consumer choices, replacing the personal car with public transportation, refining choice by following green shopping guides, and
other consumption-related activities. But not only green and environmental
issues build the substance for citizen actions. Individualized responsibility-
taking embraces other global and local issues that national and local governments do not sufficiently reach, including the areas of immigration, racism,
identity politics, organized crime, family values, and textbook policies (Forno
and Gunnarson 2010).

Third, these forms promote individualized responsibility-taking for a reason. Their "individualized" aspects may take several forms, versions, and levels
that are unique across individuals. Unlike conventional forms of engagement
that differ on the individual level of analysis in terms of intensity, time, skills,
and money invested in them (Verba, Schlozman, and Brady 1995), the forms
described here are less influenced by conventional political institutions (parties, unions, etc.) that shape a relatively uniform model of support and engagement among their members. Rather, they promote individualized responsibility-
taking by allowing for more flexibility, choices, and fashions of involvement.
For instance, the individualized practice may involve a citizen's spontaneous
decision to take a day off of work to demonstrate for a cause; formulate and
then forward a politicized e-mail or posting on a political web site; or donate
money to a cause while walking to lunch. As discussed in this chapter and
in Chapter 5, the practice may even include a host of complex and consistent lifestyle choices, including the regular or temporary purchase of certain
products for political, ethical, or environmental reasons (Micheletti and Stolle
2010). The point is that participants have the opportunity to craft their own
ethical compass and choose very much their own fashion of participating in
politics without following an organizational model or script.

The forms of participation that are growing in globalized politics seem to end
the one-size-fits-all style of engagement that characterized most government-
targeting activities. As explained in the theory of creative participation, this
form of engagement does not necessarily lead to group interaction or face-to-
face meetings of the kind we typically encounter in established political organizations. Neither does it require consensus or majority vote to be enacted.
However, more individualized responsibility-taking practices are frequently
triggered by collective and societal concerns (human rights, global social injustice, climate change, wars, immigration, conservative family values, crime) and
followed by aggregate or public consequences (corporate social responsibility,
better environment, lesser private or edited consumption, social control, peace,
etc.). Even the logic of action is collective, when the reliance on numbers and

critical mass (e.g. many participants) for an efficacious result is taken into account. Individualized responsibility-taking increasingly figures in the strategies of established social movements. This leads to a certain paradox: whereas more individualized forms of participation can often be seen as examples of coordinated collective action, most participants simply perform such voluntary acts alone or at their leisure, whether at home before a computer screen or in a supermarket. In order to address some of these insights, Micheletti described these acts as examples of individualized collective action (Micheletti 2010). McFarland explains how "scattered individuals" need to overcome their disconnection and act collectively in order to successfully engage in creative politics (McFarland 2010, 17).

A fourth common characteristic of the forms of participation that allow for individualized responsibility-taking is the diversification of targets. It is noteworthy that most studies of participation and even the most well-cited literature on transnational advocacy networks (Keck and Sikkink 1998) have not emphasized this important point; they focus mainly on government-targeting. For most participation researchers and democratic philosophers, the primary focus of political participation is still government in the nation-state context (Brady 1999, Conover 1995, Verba and Nie 1972, Nelson 1979, Verba, Schlozman, and Brady 1995, Schlozman 2010). In contrast to conventional participative forms, clearly defined as targeting government or government-related bodies within nation-states, the individualized practices of responsibility-taking aim beyond the government at a diversity of targets (both public and private) as long as they influence allocations of common societal resources and values and, therefore, have de facto political power. The point is that responsibility-taking is meant to influence other people, societal values, corporations, and other powerholders.

Finally, in many ways the Internet is *the* infrastructure or architecture for individualized responsibility-taking. It not only helps citizens collect relevant information but also facilitates borderless information communication, problem formulation and solution-seeking, collective identity, political mobilization, political action, and even value change (van de Donk et al. 2004, McCaughey and Ayers 2003, Shirky 2008). The Internet is a communication tool flexible enough for globalized loose network participation and ways of coordinating action outside the framework of traditional institutions and organizations. As such, it enables choice editing, choice architecture, and new kinds of group formation. Through it, activists can target actors who are seen as causing serious global problems but operate outside traditional national politics and formal governmental accountability mechanisms (elections, legislative hearings, regulatory politics). Their political involvement is not stuck in or strapped to particular geographic spaces as has traditionally been the case in labor strikes, voting, and appeals to politicians. It does not need to be funneled through established membership organizations and involve traditional collective action (Micheletti and McFarland 2010). The Internet minimizes the material and organizational costs for mobilization and action coordination and therefore facilitates individualized political action repertoires (Bimber 2003, Chadwick 2006, Vitak et al. 2011).

FROM CITIZEN TO CITIZEN-CONSUMER

One form of participation that relies on individualized responsibility-taking is political consumerism (McFarland 2010). As discussed in Chapter 5, political consumerism is an encompassing phenomenon whose branches emphasize that choice editing and the use of choice architecture is a desirable form of action for concerned citizens wanting to work on the issues of sweatshops, farm animal treatment, overfishing, deforestation, and undesirable working practices in outsourced companies in the developing world. Likewise, it can also be a tool to support nationalism, intolerance, exclusiveness, or other types of hatred. Political consumerism, formally defined as consumers' use of the market as an arena for politics in order to change institutional or market practices found to be ethically, environmentally, or politically objectionable[1] is a specific form of participation that characterizes individualized responsibility-taking. The concept shows how the two traditions of consumption and citizenship, which tended to be "located in opposing spheres of private and public, associated with competing inner and outer-regarding norms and actions, are...today increasingly recognized as porous, indeed overlapping domains" (Trentmann 2007, 76). In short, the practices of citizenship and consumer culture have been increasingly intertwined and thus have broken through traditional academic and societal boundaries. Citizen-consumers might be active through boycotts, so-called buycotts, discursive forms of political consumerism, and lifestyle commitments and communities and more. These citizen activities are part of the phenomenon of political consumerism and are the subject of the remainder of this chapter as well as the book.

Consumer boycotts, a form of choice editing, encourage people to disengage with corporate actors by refusing to buy their products. Their goal is to force change in corporate or governmental policy and behavior by directly rejecting a harmful product or a product produced by a corporation that engages in harmful practice. The rejection of a product is supposed to directly limit the corporation's profit margin, influence the stock's value, and more broadly damage the name, logotype, and reputation of the corporation. Mediated boycotts can also be used as threats to corporations in order to force them to agree to certain demands by citizens and activists. As discussed in Chapter 5, boycotters have engaged in large campaigns, including rejecting products from Nike, Nestlé, Coca-Cola, Shell, and many other multinational corporations.

---

[1] This definition further develops the conceptualization offered in Micheletti, Follesdal, and Stolle (2006), xiv–xv.

Interestingly, "'bad news' that is, information on the negative practices of a firm or negative impacts of a product, is more influential with consumers than positive information," and offers consumers the choice infrastructure to help them avoid certain firms (Elliott and Freeman 2003, cited in O'Rourke 2005, 118). As a result, survey research shows a considerable increase in boycott use (Stolle, Hooghe, and Micheletti 2005; see also this chapter). However, many political consumer activists voice concern about its mobilizing potential and effectiveness. For a variety of reasons, boycotts are viewed as problematic because it is increasingly difficult to decide on whom to boycott and to mobilize consumer support. Privatization of shopping space in shopping malls can mean that boycotting is an illegal activity. Boycotts' actual financial harm to the targeted corporation is hotly debated. Boycotts may also do more harm than good to the cause and potentially threaten the livelihood of workers in targeted firms (see the full debate in Chapter 7), which explains why many global social-justice networks do not support them officially. Even when mobilization is successful, a boycott action can gain support in such a way that it sends an incoherent message to corporate elites. The highly heterogeneous Disney boycott supported by movements on family values, gay rights, and religious values illustrates this point well (Micheletti 2010). Another problem is that activists may have difficulty in demobilizing supporters once the boycott has been called off (Friedman 1999). Finally, cross-corporate ownership makes it difficult to target specific corporations, though it is still possible to focus on specific products as is now done in the ongoing Nestlé boycott that focuses on Nescafé (see e.g., IFBAN 2004b).

Buycotts, or the use of labeling schemes and shopping guides, is an even more widespread form of individualized responsibility-taking, and began to mushroom in the 1990s along with rising environmental and global social justice awareness. Buycotters prefer certain products over others for political, ethical, or environmental reasons. They call for product labeling that seeks to guarantee that goods are produced under certain conditions, such as least damaging to the environment, without child labor, in a certain local or national context, and with a fair wage to producers. Labeling schemes are the necessary link here between the product and its consumers; they require a good working relationship among corporate actors, non-governmental organizations, the academic community, and even government (Cashore, Auld, and Newson 2004a, 2004b, 2004c, Micheletti 2010). The problems with this form of political activism and the choice architecture that it creates are that (1) it may be difficult to convince corporations and other actors to cooperate to adopt selected labeling schemes; (2) many products – in particular clothing and shoes – are not covered by labeling schemes; (3) buycotts lack the mobilizing bite of more protest-oriented forms of political consumerism; and (4) many labeled products require a price premium and are more costly than non-labeled ones (Hamm, Gronefeld, and Halpin 2002; see also Chapter 4). Other problems concerning the clash between an ideological commitment to alternative forms of consumption and the mainstreaming of labeled goods in supermarkets globally are discussed in Chapters 5, 7, and 8.

These problems do not characterize discursive political consumerism, a form of individualized responsibility-taking that is little researched. Discursive political consumerism engages citizens who worry about the "politics of products" by seeking and relaying information on corporate policy and practices. It is defined as the expression of opinions about corporate policy and practice in communicative efforts directed at business, the public at large, family and friends, and various political institutions. Examples of discursive political consumerism are culture jamming and adbusting, public dialogue about corporate policy and practice, and debates and negotiations with business on the need to develop business ethics, codes of conduct, and independent code-monitoring systems. Discursive political consumers discuss the politics of the products with their friends or acquaintances, forward culture jams, wear logos or messages critical of corporate practices, or act in other ways, such as the whirl-mart actions, that provoke thought about the politics of consumption. Discursive political consumerism plays an important role in the anti-globalization and anti-sweatshop movements. It confronts corporations without using boycotts that can jeopardize garment workers, and it offers citizens a marketplace venue for their political involvement even when labeling schemes are not in place. The Internet has encouraged the growth of discursive political consumerism, whose focus has increasingly been directed at multinational corporations and the negative effects of economic globalization (Bullert 2000, Carty 2002, Illia 2002, Rosenkrands 2004, Blood 2000, Bennett 2004a, 2004b, 2004c; see Chapter 6).

In particular, the Internet has enhanced political consumerist culture jamming, which is a more expressive, less instrumental form of political engagement. Culture jamming changes the meaning of corporate advertising through artistic techniques that alter corporate logos visually and by assigning marketing slogans new meaning. Culture jammers aim to show what they see as the hidden politics of consumer goods by targeting particular corporations and products (for instance, a Nike sneaker; see Chapter 6). Without considerable costs, colorful, playful, and poignant visual displays of politicized logos can be flashed across computer screens, downloaded for printouts, and forwarded to others. The messages are often creative and funny. They aim at consciousness-raising and innovative political mobilization. Culture jamming also encourages individuals to use corporate platforms (automated customer service functions, chat sites, e-mail systems, logotypes) as arenas for political action.

Another form of political consumerism is lifestyle commitments, a form of lifestyle politics, as exemplified by vegetarianism, veganism, freeganism, and voluntary simplicity. Lifestyle politics is formally defined as the choice to use an individual's private life sphere to take responsibility for the allocation of common values and resources, in other words, for politics (Micheletti and Stolle 2010, cf. Easton 1965). It is present when there is conscious and consistent choice of values, attitudes, and actions in both the public and private spheres. People engaging in lifestyle politics are goal-oriented and view their personal life as a political statement, project, and form of action. In its fullest form, lifestyle politics requires a state of private and public harmony on the part of the individual, who must consciously and deliberately reject reckless freedom of choice, wantonness, and enticements (no matter how tempting) that would result in a straying from the path of commitment to chosen principles as expressed in values and attitudes. Lifestyle politics, therefore, goes well beyond the other three forms of political consumerism, and really requires the practice of all of them and a political commitment to certain principles within and across societal roles. Ideally, practitioners of lifestyle politics do all they can to change their routines and habits that elicit attitudes, actions, and consequences contrary to these principles. If they do not, they feel what moral philosophers refer to as "pangs of guilt" for betraying their principles. Vegetarians engage in various forms of political consumerism, as they reject meat products (boycott), most likely buy products that are labeled vegetarian or vegan (buycott), might discuss food choices as well as related issues of animal rights and welfare with others (discursive political consumerism), and often change their entire lifestyle to suit their convictions (lifestyle politics).

Boycotts, buycotts, discursive political consumerism, and lifestyle commitments all involve individualized responsibility-taking. All five characteristics of participation forms that facilitate individualized responsibility-taking identified earlier apply particularly to political consumerism. First, there is no formal membership required for political consumerism; its practice might be spontaneous and irregular. Mobilization for political consumer campaigns can be very sudden, often inspired by events or information known from the corporate world (see Chapter 5). Second, political consumerism is practiced by citizens in everyday settings, during grocery shopping, clothes shopping, or any other visits to the shopping mall or marketplace, or during daily food or other consumption decisions; it also is practiced when citizens make larger purchases like cars or when renovating homes. Choices are made depending on the carbon, ecological, or sweaty footprint left by products. Moreover, discursive political consumerism can be practiced in one's everyday conversations with friends, classmates, colleagues, or within social media networks. This way, the various acts of political consumerism bend the boundaries of public and private. Third, political consumerism is practiced in an individualized fashion, where each individual can develop an ethical compass and decide how to take personalized responsibility, for example, which types of political consumerism to engage in and how often and how regularly. In addition, although we will show in Chapter 6 how some forms of discursive political consumerism can mobilize collective identities; generally the activities of political consumerism are mostly practiced in an individualized fashion in front of the computer, in the supermarket, or in one's daily lifestyle decisions. There are some exceptions, of course, to its individualized orientation, such as the organization of and participation in events such as Buy Nothing Day, weekly or monthly meetings of freegan-ists, vegetarian online groups, or some events such as carrotmobs (see more in Chapter 8) or whirl-marts. Political consumerism is practiced individually even though only large numbers of political consumers are likely to exert influ-ence on and change corporate behavior. Fourth, political consumer actions have multiple targets, first and foremost large multinational corporations, and beyond that international organizations, governments, and other powerhold-ers. When rejecting a product, the target is most likely a specific corporation or brand name. Buying specifically labeled or expressively "clean" products might support environmentally safe, child- and sweatshop-labor-free and concerned corporations that have implemented some form of corporate responsibility, and at the same time hurt companies that have not. Similarly, discursive political consumerism targets large corporations or certain aspects of capitalism. Also, lifestyle politics is meant to send messages to other people, shape societal values at large, and indirectly influence the provision of food and consumer goods. The point is that political consumerism is individualized responsibility-taking that goes beyond the targeting of governments, contrary to conventional polit-ical participation. Finally, all forms of political consumerism use the Internet as a mobilizing tool, whether to provide information about ongoing boycotts, corporate updates, newsletters from consumer organizations, interactive fea-tures such as e-mail groups, posts on social networking sites, deliberation and discourse about values and lifestyles, and so on. Thus, political consumerism is a perfect example of those forms of political participation that epitomize individualized responsibility-taking and fits the five criteria set out earlier in the chapter.

SKEPTICISM ABOUT POLITICAL CONSUMERISM AS POLITICAL PARTICIPATION

Several doubts have been raised about political consumerism and the role that individuals can play in political responsibility-taking. The voices range from disbelief that this phenomenon exists and doubts that these forms are able to fulfill the same functions as government-targeting political action repertoires, to a serious rejection of them as a truly political phenomenon. In this section, some of these doubts are discussed in more detail. The remainder of this chapter as well as others in this book offer responses to these reservations.

One important critique is grounded in the lack of systematic empirical research on extra-parliamentary forms of political participation and the polit-ical responsibility that individuals take on their own. Empirical research is difficult not only because the examples and forms are numerous, diverse, and fragmented but also because they are hard to measure with the quantitative methods commonly used in participation studies. For political consumerism, very few survey measures exist to capture the phenomenon, and discursive political consumerism remains largely unmeasured in survey research even to this day; lifestyle politics has been studied mostly anecdotally. This lack of research attention also means that scholarship has not engaged in a systematic analysis of the necessary conditions for individualized responsibility-taking at the structural and individual level discussed in Chapter 1. Previously, memberships in organizations and groups were clearly defined and easily operationalized. Informal participation, as discussed earlier in this chapter, is not necessarily linked to an organizational unit in a clear way. It is, therefore, not possible to draw obvious conclusions in the debate about the decline of political participation because it is unclear whether forms of participation that give rise to individualized responsibility-taking might in numbers substitute for the declining conventional acts. Nevertheless, at the end of this chapter and in several chapters that follow we will bring together all the available evidence about the possibility of measuring the concept of political consumerism empirically and the claim that the phenomenon has been on the rise over the last decades.

The question is not only about whether citizens engage in individualized responsibility-taking or not but whether it is on the rise, and if so, in which fashion. Another important issue is whether citizens exclusively practice these action repertoires instead of the conventional ones or whether they use both more individualized and conventional forms in tandem. The answer to this question is of some importance in the debate about the link between political action and political democracy. In Chapter 3, we will examine both the exclusive or parallel practice of conventional and emerging forms of participation with a particular focus on political consumerism. Moreover, though, does individualized responsibility-taking embrace the functions provided by voluntary associations and other conventional political tools, or does it fulfill new functions? We have described the character of individualized responsibility-taking as more short-lived, more spontaneous, less organized, and more fluid. Under these conditions, the doubt is whether it provides sufficient links between the citizens and the political system (van Deth 2010). One of the problems is, for example, that within parliamentary democracies, decision-making inevitably will be a long-term process, respecting procedures and consultations. If mobilization campaigns are short-lived events, the fear is that the impact of such campaigns and their resulting political actions will automatically be more limited. The fundamental concern is how the long-term institutionalized decision-making processes can be systematically influenced without an ingrained organizational structure that aggregates citizens' opinion. Chapter 7 offers the first scientific attempt to analyze the effectiveness and the limitations of political consumerism to change political, social, and economic outcomes.

Third, political consumerism is criticized for its lack of full legitimacy gained through inclusiveness. Although democratic theories to varying degrees favor the full and equal participation of all citizens (Pateman 1970), most recently more concern has been expressed about the threat of exclusiveness in various political action repertoires (Skocpol 2003). While we know that active involvement in social and political organizations is spread unequally within society, this inequality nevertheless remains somewhat limited because of the fact that even the privileged classes are confronted with an upper limit of time availability. Such an upper limit does not exist for the availability of financial resources or knowledge and in certain ways education (Verba, Schlozman, and Brady 1995). A major shift from voluntary participation toward financial or knowledge-based participation, therefore, would lead to a drastic sharpening of political inequalities, giving even more political leverage to the financially and educationally privileged, the former of which is already the case with regard to campaign contributions in the United States (ibid., Dworkin 2000). This trend might also apply to political consumerism. In order to be able to choose between a variety of products, one needs education and knowledge about various products and often – such is the assumption – the luxury of financial resources. In other words, the problem is that this activity might be a privilege available only to those who have higher education, knowledge, information, and financial resources. Theorizing on individualized responsibility-taking also suggests that those who take responsibility should be the ones with higher levels of resources. On the other hand, the everyday character of political consumerism marks it as an activity that has the potential to draw in various groups of the population, such as young people as well as women in general and housewives in particular. This is after all an empirical question, and indications of the socio-demographic biases of political consumerism are presented in the following chapter. Socioeconomic inequalities might also play less of a role in other forms of political consumerism, such as boycotting, discursive types, and lifestyle politics. More reflections about inequality can be found in Chapters 6, 7, and 8.

Critics of political consumerism point to the hierarchy and exclusion of citizens as well as the lack of an accountability mechanism of civil society organizations. Such organizations arouse and nourish individualized responsibility-taking but are not democratically elected and, therefore, lack open democratic procedures. Criticisms, for example, were made about the non-transparent structures of the organization Fairtrade Labelling Organizations International (FLO), which helps to regulate and support the certification of fairtrade products; see more information later in this chapter. These products are often the choice of buycotters in the Northern world. Fairtrade producers speak of a lack of transparency and an arbitrariness in the monitoring process, with FLO monitors sometimes showing a lack of understanding of local issues or refusing to disclose evaluation results (Lyon 2007, Martinez 2002, Pérezgrovas and Cervantes Trejo 2002, Boersma 2002). This criticism is considered in detail in Chapter 7.

Finally, to several critics the political meaning of the acts of buying, rejecting, or discussing the vices and virtues of consumer products is not clear. We already discussed how subpolitics, creative participation, and everyday-making as well as the ideal of individualized responsibility-taking blur the lines between public

and private in that its practice reaches into societal roles other than that of the
voter and the private spheres of one's personal life by addressing public issues
of sustainability, environment, labor conditions or minimum wage, and others.
The criticism is that private or market concerns are self-interested in character
and therefore cannot be political in orientation (Soper and Trentmann 2008,
Bauman 2008). The fact that self-interested concerns dominate these political
acts implies that they do not sufficiently stand for values of the common good
and collective concerns as is at least in part assumed of those that characterize forms of participation associated with the parliamentary realm of politics
(Johnston 2008). The ultimate question then is whether any such engagements
can be interpreted as political participation or true forms of citizenship? Can
citizenship practices be exercised in arenas other than the parliamentary one,
and, if so, how do we know that the actions refer to citizen virtues and not
simply private interest? How does the study of citizenship and consumption
challenge the boundaries between these as traditionally perceived public and
private domains (Trentmann 2007, Soper 2007)? The scholarly challenge is,
then, to develop measures that distinguish between the people who do not go
to McDonald's because they do not eat hamburgers from those who boycott
the golden arches because they are seen as a symbol of economic globalization
or because of the way they procure eggs and meat. And what about people
in this group who go to McDonald's only once a year (Stolle and Hooghe
2004)? Similarly, there are, for example, people who commit to vegetarianism for pure health reasons whereas others do not eat meat because they are
concerned about farm-animal welfare and thus their motivations and goals
reach far beyond their own personal interests to include the criticism of the
lack of sufficient public policy for the protection of farm animals (Micheletti
and Stolle 2010). In addition, customers of Whole Foods Market, for example, might more unequivocally practice their role as consumers and fulfill their
self-interests in shopping there, as opposed to citizenship practice (Johnston
2008). The criticism is that these activities or at least some of them are not
sufficiently political, public, and democratic, thus the link between citizens and
the political system is not guaranteed through these forms of participation. As
a result, this potential ambiguity also raises concerns regarding the measurements of political consumerism, and how one can best distinguish between
political acts of shopping and conventional ones. These concerns and issues
are addressed in part in the remainder of this chapter as well in Chapters 3
and 6.

RISE OF MARKET-BASED POLITICAL ACTION

Although political consumerism relies heavily on individualized responsibility-
taking, a phenomenon that we argue has recently been on the rise, it is not
a new addition to politics. Boycotts and buycotts played a role in the union,
environmental, student, peace, and women's movements of the 1960s and

1970s. Moreover, they were also used in the abolition movement and during the U.S. struggle for independence and by Southerners to rebuke "the licentious spirit of the North" in the U.S. Civil War (Glickman 2009, 94) and in the colonial struggles for independence in India and elsewhere (Trentmann 2004, Micheletti and Stolle 2008, Micheletti 2007, Cohen 2003). Particularly, boycotts have been a central form of political expression for groups marginalized in conventional politics (Micheletti 2010). In the early part of the 1900s, the White Label Campaign, an anti-sweatshop labeling scheme, appealed to American women to buy cotton underwear for themselves and their children that was certified "sweatshop free" (Sklar 1998). Women in Europe and North America in these years also engaged in "food strikes" and "food boycotts" to express their anger over milk and meat prices and, in so doing, created emerging forms of women's solidarity (Glickman 2009, Orleck 1993, Young 1994). Boycotts were even used in the anti-Semitic crusade of the 1930s, and by the international workers' movement as a tool against Germany's persecution of Jews (Encyclopædia Judaica Jerusalem 1971). In the 1960s, the United Farm Workers successfully employed consumer boycotts throughout Northern democracies to put pressure on Californian farmers and landowners (Jenkins and Perrow 1977). African-Americans have also used the market as an arena for racial politics. They repeatedly incited boycotts to further the civil rights movement, with the Montgomery Bus Boycott as the best-known case (Friedman 1999, Goldberg 1999, King 1999). In the 1970s and 1980s, boycotts were used as a tool in the worldwide campaign against apartheid in South Africa and Nestlé's marketing of infant formula in third-world countries (Seidman 2003). Part of the anti-globalization movement deliberately uses consumer behavior as a political tool (Bové and Dufour 2001).

The ideal of individualized responsibility-taking claims that globalization processes and the weaknesses in the conventional government-oriented model of political responsibility morally mandate citizens to increasingly take politics into their own hands by, for example, utilizing the tools of political consumerism as a form of political participation. This is a normative claim, yet this chapter attempts to transfer the normative theoretical debate into feasible research questions for empirical research. Thus according to the theoretical expectations, we should see a transformation of political action repertoires and a steady rise of various forms of participation that encourage individualized responsibility-taking over the last decades. Yet measuring actions of political consumerism is difficult. Forms of political consumerism such as buycotting and discursive action in particular are difficult to quantify, especially when attempting to distinguish political acts from non-political ones. As discussed earlier, there is a debate about whether purchases solely based on health considerations should be considered political consumerism (van Deth 2010, Micheletti and Stolle 2010). Similarly, online discussion about shopping choices based on health concerns might also not qualify as a form of political participation. If not, then motivations for shopping decisions and other activities arise as important determinants of whether an act is political or not. This, of course, complicates the measurements of political consumerism and possibly affects the definition of and even criteria for political participation. Nevertheless, one of the purposes of this book is to examine various potential measurements of political consumerism for empirical research and to explore how the concept affects the conventional understanding of political participation.

Political consumerism is also not immune to other kinds of measurement problems that are more universal in participation research. The problem is that people overestimate their participation for social desirability reasons, or do not remember correctly when and how often they participate in various political acts. This is a common phenomenon in voter-turnout research, for example (see Holbrook and Krosnick 2010), but also affects other forms of participation (van Aelst and Walgrave 2001). This phenomenon also applies to political consumerism, where the rift between attitudes (in terms of "I should do this") and behavior (in terms of "I actually have done this") is particularly apparent. Thus although many individuals profess to be concerned with ethical issues and willing to shift their consumption accordingly, sales data indicate a slightly different story, namely that consumers do not always follow up on their stated concerns. This has been dubbed the "30:3 syndrome" – "the phenomenon in which a third of consumers profess to care about companies' policies and records on social responsibility, but ethical products rarely achieve more than a 3 percent market share" (Cowe and Williams 2000, 1). We look at this attitude-behavior gap in more detail later in this chapter and present deeper analyses taking this into account in Chapters 3 and 4.

The question for now is: Which empirical materials can be assembled in order to give evidence for the proposition that political consumerism has been on the rise over the last decades? A recent poll conducted by Globescan, an international opinion-research consultancy, demonstrated that a majority of consumers (59 percent) in twenty-four countries surveyed felt empowered to make a difference through their shopping choices (Globescan 2011). But do consumers actually act as citizens? Although there is hardly any survey material on consumer boycotts and buycotts, scholars have shown that the participation in boycotts in particular has been on the rise (Andersen and Tobiasen 2004, Norris 2002, Petersson, Westholm, and Blomberg 1998). Scholars also claim that the number of boycotts organized worldwide is increasing (Friedman 1999, Glickman 2005). Overall, a recent poll found that more than a third of consumers worldwide boycott at least one brand (Global Market Institute Poll 2005). Similarly, well-known political-participation scholar Kay Schlozman writes that "the 2002 *National Civic Engagement Survey* found political consumerism – boycotting and buycotting – to be more common in the United States than any political activity save registering and voting. This result emerged as well in each of the twelve countries included in the *Citizenship, Involvement, and Democracy* (CID) surveys, conducted between 1999 and 2002" (Schlozman 2010, 181).

The various waves of the *World Values Survey* (WVS) are a prime data source for detecting trends in political participation behavior – including political consumerism – during the last two decades. Unfortunately, there is only one relevant question in the *World Values Surveys* on participating in consumer boycotts that can be used longitudinally. We can extend the time series by comparing WVS data with the results from the 1974 *Political Action Survey* (Barnes and Kaase 1979), thus eight countries are available for a longtime series of boycott data.

These survey data for the period between the mid-1970s and 2010 clearly indicate that a growing number of citizens turn to the market to express their political and moral concerns in boycotts (see Table 2.1). In all eight countries there is a rise in boycott action – from 4.7 percent in 1974 to an average of 15.2 percent in 2000 and about 13 percent in 2005/10.[2] In these eight Western countries boycotting was more than three times as likely in 2000 compared to 1974. In all sixteen longterm stable postwar democracies we see a substantial rise in boycotting over the last waves of the *World Value Survey*. In newer democracies, there is more variation. For example, in the Czech Republic there is a slight decline in boycotting activity, and in several other newer democracies, including Spain and Portugal, we find stagnation.

For additional analyses between the years 2002 and 2010, the *European Social Survey* is being used as well, where the question format was changed to ask whether the respondent had boycotted during the last twelve months. Even so, in ten out of seventeen countries for which comparisons between the fifth wave of the WVS and the first wave of the ESS exist, there is a further increase in boycott action in 2002 compared to the percentages in the *World Values Survey* in 2005/10.

The analysis of the later period in the ESS data from 2002–2010 shows stagnation and decline in boycott action, however. Table 2.1 indicates a rise in boycott action in only Finland, Germany, Greece, Hungary, Spain, and Sweden, and the rise was modest. In four countries for which comparative data was available, boycotting was somewhat in decline between 2002 and 2010 but in all other countries there was no real trend confirming some sort of stagnation. Although this is a short timeframe from which to draw any final conclusions, and some of the minor declines happened in high-boycott countries (e.g., Switzerland), this result does nevertheless confirm the insight from Chapter 5 that movement actors navigate citizens away from the complicated consequences of boycott action toward the use of buycotts, discursive, and other forms of political consumerism.

---

[2] There are a few exceptions. In West Germany, boycotting declined slightly from 1997 to 2000 and again from 2000 to 2005/10. In the Netherlands, Sweden, and the UK, we see a drop in boycotting in the last wave, from 1999/2000 to 2005/10, possibly reflecting the declining importance of boycotts as a consumer strategy. However, overall consumer-action trends over the last four decades are generally rising.

TABLE 2.1. *Longitudinal Data on Boycotting, 1974–2010*

Country	'74 Pol Action	'81 WVS	'90 WVS	'95/7 WVS	'99/00 WVS	'05/10 WVS	Trend in WVS	2002 ESS	2004 ESS	2006 ESS	2008 ESS	2010 ESS	Trend in ESS
Australia	–	4.8	–	21.5	–	15.4***	Rise#	–	–	–	–	–	–
Austria	2.1	–	5.2	–	9.8	–	Rise	21.5	19.6	19.5	–	–	No trend
Belgium	–	3.1	10.3	–	10.4***	10.1***	Rise	12.8	9.9	10.5	11.1 ns	9.2***	Decline
Canada	–	15.5	22.3	–	20.5	23.5	Rise	–	–	–	–	–	–
Czech Rep.	–	–	9.6	–	9.2	5.2	Decline	10.8	6.9	–	7.7**	10.2 ns	No trend
Denmark	–	8.0	10.6	–	24.9***	17.9***	Rise#	22.9	28.3	25.0	21.5 ns	21.9 ns	No trend
Finland	1.1	–	13.5	12.2	14.5	23.7	Rise	26.8	29.3	28.3	30.3*	33.1***	Rise
France	–	10.4	12.5	–	13.2*	15.8***	Rise	26.6	30.0	26.1	27.7 ns	28.9 ns	No trend
Germany+	4.3	6.4	10.0	18.1	11.3***	12.8#	Rise#	27.8	23.1	24.6	33.7***	32.4**	Rise#
Greece	–	–	–	–	4.7	–	–	8.5	5.1	–	15.2***	–	Rise
Hungary	–	–	2.2	–	2.8	–	No trend	4.8	5.2	4.5	6.4*	6.1 ns	Rise
Ireland	–	6.8	7.4	–	8.3**	10.6**	Rise	13.6	10.9	12.3	15.6 ns	–	No trend
Italy	0.8	5.7	9.4	–	10.3***	19.7***	Rise	7.6	7.1	–	–	–	No trend
Netherlands	5.2	6.1	12.0	–	21.4***	12.0***	Rise#	10.4	8.3	9.3	9.6 ns	10.1 ns	No trend
Norway	–	6.8	–	18.1	–	17.4***	Rise#	20.3	23.5	25.3	22.5 ns	19.5 ns	No trend#
Poland	–	–	6.4	5.5	4.2	3.5	Decline	3.6	5	4.0	4.8 ns	5.2 ns	No trend
Portugal	–	–	4.6	–	4.6	6.3	No trend	3.4	2.1	2.3	3.1 ns	2.2 ns	No trend
Slovakia	–	–	4.5	–	4.3	2.5	No trend	–	11.5	10.0	6.7	–	Decline
Slovenia	–	–	8.0	5.6	8.2	7.3	No trend	5.1	2.2	5.0	5.1 ns	5.7 ns	No trend
Spain	–	8.9	4.8	5.1	5.6**	7.6 ns	No trend	8.0	14.0	10.1	–	11.5***	Rise

Sweden	–	8.3	16.5	33.1	33.0***	23.7***	Rise#	32.5	34.8	30.6	37.2**	35.6 ns	Rise#
Switzerland	4.4	–	–	12.2	–	13.9	Rise	31.4	24.9	28.5	–	27.4***	Decline
UK	5.3	6.7	14.7	–	16.7***	13.4***	Rise#	26.1	20.6	23.7	–	19.6***	Decline
USA	–	–	–	19.0	25.7	19.7	Rise#	18.2	–	–	–	–	–

Entries are percentages of respondents indicating that they have participated in boycotting.

+ For all data points only figures from (former) West Germany were included.

– Question wording: In the *Political Action Survey* as well as in the WVS, no timeframe was included; in the ESS the question was asked regarding activities in the previous twelve months. In the 1974 *Political Action Survey*, the exact question was: "Are you willing to join boycotts?" with a first answer category: "I have done this." All the other answering possibilities ventured into the possibility that the respondent might consider taking part in this kind of action in the future. In the *World Values Surveys*, the question was asked in the following way: "Now I'd like you to look at this card. I'm going to read out some different forms of political action that people can take, and I'd like you to tell me, for each one, whether you have actually done any of these things, whether you might do it or would never, under any circumstances, do it." The answer options here included: "Have done," "Might do," and "Would never do." For this analysis, we have used only the "Have done" option, since it is most comparable to the option in 1974. In the ESS/CID survey, the question was asked in the following way: "There are different ways of trying to improve things in [country] or help prevent things from going wrong. During the last 12 months, have you done any of the following?" The answer options were just "Yes" or "No," where a "Yes" answer counted as having done the activity.

– Data gathering: The *Political Action Survey* was downloaded via ICPSR; the WVS was analyzed using both the five-wave cumulative dataset available at ICPSR and the online analysis tool available at http://www.worldvaluesurvey.org. The only exception to this is Finland's data for 1981, which is unavailable from the WVS dataset and its online analysis tool. Data for this country and wave was retrieved from the University of Michigan's Online Numeric and Spatial Data Services' World Values Section analysis tool. This instrument can be found at http://nds.umdl.umich.edu/cgi/s/sda/hsda?harcWEVS±wevs. The ESS/CID surveys were downloaded from their respective web sites.

– Coding: With regards to all surveys, respondents citing "I don't know" to any question were treated as missing cases.

– Weights: WVS and ESS statistics are aggregated weighted percentages.

– Indication of significance: *p < .05, **p < .01, *** p < .001 (ns – not significant). The significance tests were done for the comparison between wave 1 and the latest two waves of the same data sets. For example, for Belgium, the value of 10.1 percent in 2005/10 is compared to the value of 3.1 percent in the first wave in 1980. The two values are significantly different at the p<.001 level, so Belgium shows a rising trend in boycotts in the WVS data.

Trend was slightly reversed for last data point(s) in the WVS or ESS series.

Source: Political Action Survey 1974, *World Values Surveys* 1981/1990/1995–1997/1999–2000/2005–2010, and the *European Social Survey* 2002, 2004, 2006, 2008, and 2010. For the United States: CID survey in 2006 is matched with the ESS 2002.

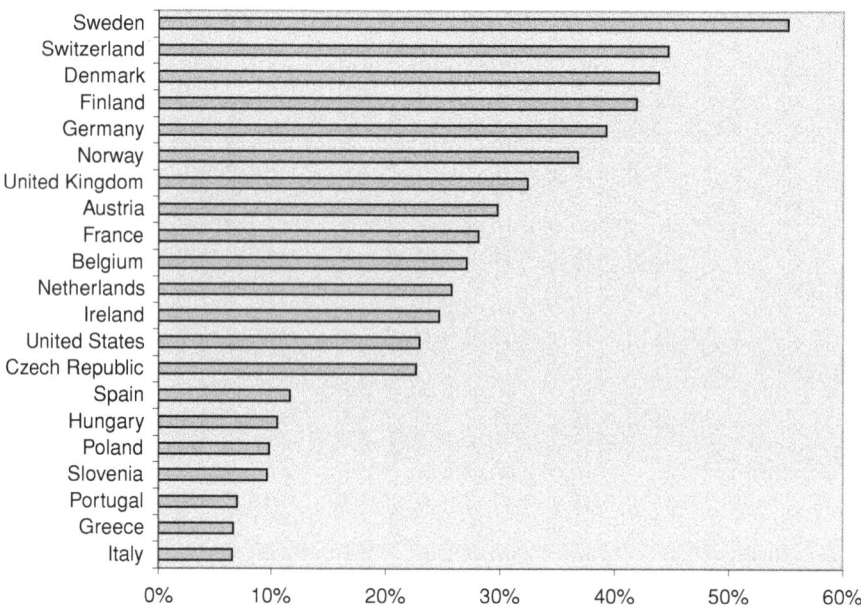

FIGURE 2.1. Buycotting. *Source:* European Social Survey 2002 (Jowell et al. 2003).

There is no longitudinal comparative data available when it comes to the purposeful purchase of products (buycotting). However, first assessments suggest that many more adults actually buycott than boycott. Overall, when asked whether they had deliberatively purchased products for ethical, environmental, or political reasons, about 24 percent of all respondents included in the *European Social Survey* in 2002 said they had done so in the previous twelve months. People living in Northern European countries top the list as most often engaged as buycotters. In Sweden, this form of political consumerism has become somewhat mainstream: as about 55 percent of respondents stated that they had bought certain products for political, ethical, or environmental reasons. However, in many Southern and Eastern European countries, such forms of engagement have not taken off to the same extent (see Figure 2.1), although also here about 7 percent to 12 percent of the respondents indicated that they have engaged in this activity.

    In short, the little survey data available highlight that citizens feel drawn toward acts of political consumerism. This implies that citizens express a heightened awareness of the political meaning of their purchasing choices and claim that they engage in ethical, political, or environmentally-based shopping choices. We have argued that this development of action repertoires is an outgrowth of the rising individualized responsibility that citizens are taking to influence powerful political and economic actors, as structural changes in capitalism and accompanying movements call for a new type of consumer and citizen. Some of these assumptions will be tested in the following chapter.

To what extent can this development be seen as an attitudinal change or as a real change in actions? A step beyond survey data needs to be taken to include an analysis of actual changes in purchasing choices over time. Does the purchase of labeled products increase over time? What kind of information do citizens have about labeling schemes? What actual demand and supply do we see in products that are made under sweatshop-free or exploitation-free working conditions?

Some forms of buycotting provide an opportunity to observe actual, as opposed to reported, macro-level political consumerist behavior. This approach requires creative methodology because sales data for the type of goods and services associated with buycotting are difficult to come by – for most such products, no official statistics are kept. Fairtrade[3] goods are an exception, and organic foods are a partial exception. The Fairtrade labeling scheme is a centralized process, with Fairtrade Labelling Organizations International (FLO) at the helm; the organization keeps comprehensive data for sales (by weight) of fairtrade-certified goods. Less detailed data are also available for organic foods.

Reports indicate that fairtrade products are internationally known. In a study by Globescan in twenty-four countries, six out of ten consumers have seen the Fairtrade certification label (Globescan 2011). Of those who knew the label, about two-thirds associated it with "helping farmers and workers in poor countries escape poverty" (ibid).

A brief review here reveals that the sales of fairtrade food products, especially coffee, bananas, sugar, cocoa, tea, and honey were nearly eight times higher in 2005 than in 1997 (Fairtrade Federation 2005). Between 2009 and 2010 alone, sales of products carrying the Fairtrade label increased by 28 percent globally and more than tripled in countries such as the Czech Republic and South Africa (Globescan 2011). The case of coffee, which when measured by sales is the most popular fairtrade item, illustrates this point. The politics of coffee – its price, harvesting, and, trade – are an important fairtrade focus, and coffee emerged as an emblematic commodity for fairtrade activism because of its popularity among Western consumers, its cultivation by small farmers in developing countries, its role in generating foreign exchanges (Rice 2001), and its ability to illustrate the complex hidden politics of consumer goods in simple fashion (see also Chapter 7). As shown in Figure 2.2, fairtrade coffee sales were at 11,000 metric tons in 1996 and remained relatively stable until 2002, experiencing only moderate growth. Since then, they have increased at annual rates between 22 percent and 52 percent from 2002 to 2007 before leveling

---

[3] The term "fairtrade" (as one word) is used to identify Fairtrade International-certified goods from other products that are marketed as reflecting general "fair trade" (two words) concerns. This is how the terms are used in this book (see Chapters 5 and 7).

Rise in Global Fairtrade Coffee Sales

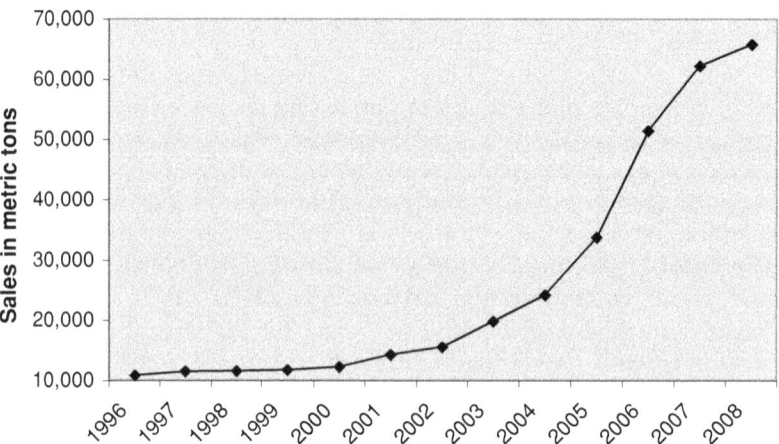

FIGURE 2.2. Rise in Fairtrade Coffee Sales. Data represent total volume of fairtrade coffee sold each year in selected countries (Austria, Belgium, Canada, Denmark, Finland, France, Germany, Ireland, Italy, Japan, the Netherlands, Norway, Sweden, Switzerland, the United Kingdom, and the United States). *Source:* Fairtrade Labelling Organization International 2005, 2009.

off again in 2008. A recent report states that by 2010 the combined sales of fairtrade roast, ground, and instant coffee amounted to 88,000 tons worldwide (Fairtrade Foundation 2012). Some countries have seen a stagnation of the sale of fairtrade coffee though. We consider this development more closely in Chapters 4 and 7.

The sale of organically grown labeled products is also on the rise, and consumers spend increasingly more money on such products. In 1997, global sales of organic food totaled 11 billion USD; they more than tripled to reach 39 billion USD by 2006 (Willer and Yussefi 2006). In 2009, sales were five times higher than in 1997 (see Figure 2.3). The number of organic producers globally increased to 1.8 million from 2008 to 2009, an increase of 31 percent (FIBL, Willer, and Kilcher 2011, 26).

Finally, there is also evidence that socially and ethically responsible investments have been increasing in Western European democracies; the money invested into socially responsible investing (SRI) funds in 2006 was more than three times as much compared to seven years prior (Avanzi SRI Research 2006), and there is some evidence that it is still growing (see Chapter 5). There were about 900 SRI funds in Europe in 2011; and the total assets managed by SRI grew by 41 percent in 2010 and by 12 percent in 2011 (Vigeo 2011).

Yet, whereas actual behavioral change is visible and citizens appear to be more open to choosing responsibly produced items rather than conventional

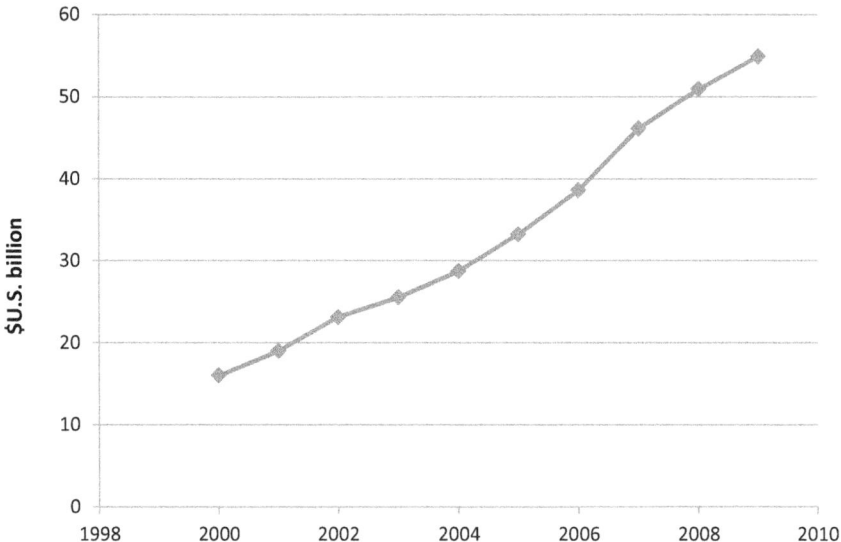

FIGURE 2.3. Rise in Global Organic Food Sales. Data represent estimated total sales of organic food sold worldwide. Numbers have been converted from Euros to U.S. dollars. *Sources:* Willer and Yussefi 2003, 2008, Willer and Kilcher 2009, 2010, 2011.

ones, the actual market share of such products remains fairly low. As mentioned before, ethical products rarely achieve more than a 3 percent market share. For example, although 27 percent of Canadian consumers were aware of the Fairtrade label in 2005, and 16 percent claimed to buy fairtrade coffee, the latter had hardly penetrated the overall coffee market; it held just 0.34 percent in that year (Fair Trade Federation 2005). Even "sixty six percent of consumers in the US and UK agreed that everyone needs to take responsibility for their personal contribution to global warming" (Forstater et al. 2007). However, although quite a number of people are concerned, very few are inclined to take direct action or engage in more difficult behavioral change (ibid).

Variations on the 30:3 syndrome appear to affect consumers in all markets. This gap may reflect the fact that for many political consumers, buycotting certain products may not be a constant or even a regular behavior. A consumer might for example select fairtrade coffee when available at a café but purchase cheaper conventional coffee for home consumption. Individual consumers might also choose the labeled product when sold on its own (e.g., organic eggs), but once eggs are used to make another product (e.g., a cake), the information gets easily lost, and consumers may opt for a conventional bakery good instead, where no organic eggs have been used. Still, in the surveys analyzed previously, such consumers would appear to be buycotters because they buy organic eggs when they decide to purchase them while grocery shopping.

Three other reasons have been suggested to explain this attitude-behavior gap.[4] The first is the higher cost of labeled/certified goods. One shared characteristic of political consumerist goods is that they generally carry a price premium relative to conventional goods. At the individual level, income plays a role for political consumerism; national levels of price premiums may influence levels of buycotting. The next reason is insufficient consumer information about certification, labels, or the products themselves. A consumer's desire to purchase sustainable or socially responsible goods is not enough – it must be accompanied by awareness of and information regarding the consumer's options, as well as trust that the good meets the criteria claimed by the label (Sønderskov and Daugbjerg 2011). In the absence of sufficient information, which is an important structural prerequisite for individualized responsibility-taking (see Chapter 1), a potential political consumer may simply choose to purchase a more familiar conventional product. Finally, consumers may have the perception – whether accurate or not – of inferior quality of an "ethical" product relative to its "non-ethical" counterpart. For instance, organic produce may not be as visually appealing as conventional produce, gourmet coffee buyers may suspect that fairtrade coffee is not up to the quality standards of conventional brands (Dimitri and Greene 2002, Giovannucci 2003) or consumers might believe that eco-labels on clothing signal a lack of fashion style. When this is so, consumers may not be willing to choose ethics over cost/quality considerations, at least not at all times. All of these factors may contribute to this apparent disconnect between attitudes and behavior, which has led some observers to state that political consumerism is "more celebrated than practiced" (Tallontire, Rentsendorj, and Blowfield 2001, 8). However, a less pessimistic interpretation is that if these factors are mitigated – particularly if premiums decline, if information becomes more readily available to consumers, and/or if a choice architecture is in place – political consumerism may become a more regularly practiced behavior. The upshot of the 30:3 syndrome is that the ethical marketplace has immense room for growth (Cowe and Williams 2000).

Citizens also engage in communicative involvements to change the fairtrade discourse and their conceptions of consumer society. Surveys and other systematic data collections have, however, not really begun to tap involvement in discursive political consumerism, and so this book presents a unique case study in Chapter 6.

In terms of lifestyle politics, some changes can be observed over time as well. We look here closely at the example of vegetarianism, which is often motivated by health and/or animal welfare concerns (see more in Chapter 5). Research in the United States suggests that at least among vegetarians there is a perception that vegetarianism is increasingly accepted as socially "mainstream" (Jabs et al., cited in Smart 2004). Vegetarian food items are also more readily

---

[4] These are adapted from Tallontire, Rentsendorj, and Blowfield (2001).

available than before in the Northern world, and vegetarian meals are offered as attractive alternatives in many restaurants. Overall, then, vegetarianism has become tolerated as part of everyday society and to a degree a well-accepted lifestyle. Whereas only a while ago very few people declared to live a vegetarian lifestyle, recent surveys in the United States have noted that 12 percent of females and 9 percent of males aged 18–34 never eat meat (Vegetarian Journal 2009). Among youth in 2010 it was found that 7 percent of eight- to eighteen-year-olds abstain from meat, and 1 percent identify as vegan[5] (Stahler 2010). Taking a longer-term perspective, research in the United Kingdom finds that the number of vegetarians has increased substantially during the last half-century (Phillips 2005). In particular, the number of people rejecting any kind of fish or eggs has risen starkly (Vegetarian Journal 2005).

Most importantly, there seems to be a growing category of specialized vegetarians who reject certain animal products but not others. Even the number of occasional (non-rigid) vegetarians is increasing. Respondents to a 2011 poll claimed that they ate vegetarian for "many, but less than half" of their meals (Stahler 2011). Overall then, these data indicate a growing spread of vegetarianism in stable democracies. The trend also seems to transcend partisanship – 15 percent each of Democrats and Republicans abstain from meat at more than half of their meals (ibid).

It seems, therefore, there is an overall rising interest in a vegetarian lifestyle and diet, a development also reflected in the increase of U.S.-based vegetarian food sales which grow by about 5 percent to 8 percent per year (see e.g., Vegetarian Research Group 2011). Therefore, in all forms of political consumerism for which over-time data exists, we find a rising trend in participation over the last decades, with some stagnation for boycotts. Still, the evidence so far suggests that the market has increasingly become an arena for political action of citizens in advanced democracies.

POLITICAL ACTION TRANSFORMED?

Political action repertoires in advanced industrialized democracies have been transforming over the last decades to allow for everyday-making, subpolitical engagements, and creative participation that characterize or facilitate individualized responsibility-taking in one way or another. Although evidence suggests that conventional political acts such as voting, joining political parties, and face-to-face organizations have been in decline nearly everywhere, the responsibility collapse of national governments is turning citizen interest in targeting governments through political action to other powerholders and institutions. Some citizens, who experience this vacuum of political leadership, take over the responsibility themselves, and engage in diverse political actions in order to address social and political issues that are important to them and not easily

---

[5] This number includes youth who eat honey.

addressed by conventional means through the parliamentary sphere. Political consumerism is an example of how citizens have turned their attention to the market arena to be able to voice their concern about production, labor, environmental, and other objectionable corporate practices. Most indicators point to the fact that various forms of political consumerism have been on the rise over the last decades. These developments have major implications for how we conceive political participation. They challenge the view that political participation overall is in decline, and they broaden the concept of political participation to include actions that target non-governmental actors and non-parliamentary arenas of political action. Moreover, forms of participation that allow individualized political responsibility-taking often bridge the public and private divide and exhibit different characteristics than conventional political action. These challenges to the research field of political participation have led to debates about the researchability and the true political significance, effectiveness, and equality of these action repertoires. These questions and challenges are addressed in the remainder of this book.

3

Who Are Political Consumers?

INTRODUCTION

Whereas the previous chapter set the stage for viewing political consumerism as a form of political participation, this chapter explores who political consumers are, and by which sociodemographic characteristics, values, attitudes, and behaviors they can be distinguished from other citizens. There is little cross-national research on political consumers. To answer which individual background factors relate to political consumerism and to understand their attitudinal and behavioral profile, this chapter utilizes the *European Social Survey* and two Swedish surveys particularly designed to measure and explore the actions and attitudes of political consumers. The first survey, a cross-national survey conducted in twenty European countries and the United States, was introduced in Chapter 2. One of the Swedish surveys is the SOM (*Society, Opinion and Media*) survey, which is conducted annually as a postal national survey of Swedes between the ages of 15 and 85. The 2003 SOM survey asked 1,816 respondents several questions about political consumerism, probing into their motivations and considerations behind their shopping choices.[1] The SOM data also helps us understand whether political consumers believe that they have a personal responsibility to choose consumer goods on the basis of their ethical, political, or environmental quality,[2] whether they trust political

---

[1] Information about the SOM survey can be found at http://www.som.gu.se/som_institute/-surveys/national-som. The response rate of the 2003 survey was 66 percent. The survey items on political consumerism were developed by the authors for the research project "Political Consumption: Politics in a New Era and Arena" financed by the Swedish Council of Research (Vetenskapsrådet). For more information in Swedish, see http://www.som.gu.se/digitalAssets/1294/1294553_2003_politik.pdf (accessed December 2011).

[2] A similar question was asked in a survey conducted by SIFO, which is a Norwegian governmental institute that conducts consumer research and testing (SIFO 2001, see also http://www.sifo.no/page/English/Meny_Knapper/10237/10281, accessed March 2013).

institutions and labeling schemes currently in use in Sweden, and what kinds of aspects they consider most important when making purchasing choices for themselves and their families. The other Swedish survey is *Consumption and Societal Issues*[3], a mail survey conducted in 2009 with 1,053 randomly selected Swedes aged 18 to 78.[4] The survey was designed to gather broader and deeper information on consumption habits and also includes measures of political participation, acceptance of environmental policy solutions, citizenship norms and ideals, trust in institutions, and perceived environmental risks. At present, these last two surveys are the most comprehensive data sources on political consumerism to date.

ADDRESSING IMPORTANT DEBATES IN THE EMPIRICAL STUDY OF POLITICAL CONSUMERISM

This chapter expands on two important debates from Chapter 2. The first issue concerns the question of who political consumers are and whether this form of political participation exhibits the same or even stronger socioeconomic and gender inequalities as are known from other acts of political participation. The second major issue responds to the critique that this form of individualized responsibility-taking is not sufficiently political in character. The analysis is designed to examine the political values and motivations of political consumers. The theoretical background to these two debates is reviewed in the remainder of this section.

Socioeconomic Predictors and Inequality of Political Consumerism

The study of equality in political participation is not new at all. In a nutshell, there is a widespread demographic though not much of a substantive inequality

---

[3] See more information about the survey and its questionnaire in English here: http://www. sustainablecitizenship.com/survey.html

[4] The response rate was 35% and perhaps appears modest compared with the ones by the Swedish SOM Institute, which reaches a response rate between 60% and 70% after ten reminders by postcard and telephone, and the national election survey (78% response rate in 2006), which involves face-to-face interviews (home visits) administered by the public agency Statistics Sweden. However, for self-administered mail-back surveys, the length of the survey also matters. In 2006, Statistics Sweden received a 47% response rate for its longer questionnaire and a total of 78% when its shorter questionnaire was included. The overall response rate of 35% is still at the same level as other recent academic surveys on environmental matters, such as the Ecological Citizen Survey (2009) with 35% and the SHARP survey (2005) with 30%. The *Ecological Citizen Survey* is administered by Sverker Jagers and Johan Martinsson at the Department of Political Science, Gothenburg University. The SHARP (Sustainable Households: Attitudes, Resources and Policy) program was a research collaboration involving Umeå University and Linköping University and Luleå University of Technology. The response rate is also comparable with surveys of several well-known and reputable Swedish opinion institutes, including Demoskop (40% response rate), and Novus (c. 30%) (Petersson and Holmberg 2008).

in various forms of participation (Verba, Schlozman and Brady 1995, Barnes and Kaase 1979, Verba and Nie 1972). Richer, more educated people, males, and people of older generations are more active in electoral forms of political participation particularly in the United States. Earlier literature emphasized that some European democracies achieve a more egalitarian pattern of involvement because political institutions such as unions and political parties offer the desired resources and mobilization necessary for high levels of participation (Verba, Nie and Kim 1978). Yet, recent analyses reveal that European democracies are dealing with a rising participation gap as well, particularly for voting (Caul 2005, Allego 2007), which is attributed to the diminishing importance of these equalizing institutions such as unions and churches (Kittilson 2005). However, relatively little is known about political inequality in the context of individualized responsibility taking.

As Chapter 2 makes clear, there is some fear that political consumerism, like many other forms of participation, is not all-inclusive. Education, certain values, and predominantly the purse might determine the extent to which it is an accessible political tool. To many, this has truly worrisome democratic implications (Pacheco and Plutzer 2008, Petersson et al. 1998, van Deth, Montero, and Westholm 2007). Although all forms of political and social participation depend on socioeconomic resources, political consumerism might be a case where such resources matter even more. In other words, given the fact that fairtrade and environmentally friendly products are substantially more expensive than regular brands (see Chapter 4), we have to consider the possibility that political consumerism might be even more socioeconomically biased than other forms of political participation.

A closer look, however, reveals that two divergent expectations emerge regarding the potential class-status inequality of political consumerism. On the one hand, most traditional forms of participation are linked to organizations and institutions, which bring with them resources, networks, and opportunities for political action and influence (Verba, Nie, and Kim 1978). Although these institutions are apparently in decline, we still expect them to matter, although less so over time. Yet, individualized responsibility-taking such as political consumerism is by definition disconnected from well-established institutions and thus might be practiced without an established organizational umbrella (Verba, Schlozman, and Brady 1995). In Chapter 5 we explore how newly emerging political consumer organizations potentially nurture and mobilize political consumerism. The lack of established institutions for mobilization, however, might imply that political consumerism requires more resources and skills from the participants to compensate for the missing institutional framework. For instance, education, political knowledge, and cognitive skills are required for the assessment of the various product labels in stores; without this type of practical political knowledge (Stolle and Gidengil 2010) and resources it would be difficult to look beyond the dimensions of price and quality in the assessment of a particular product. That is to say political consumerism is knowledge-intensive. If an individual is to act on the basis of the politics behind the products, she must, of course, be aware of these politics and, furthermore, of the existence of alternative products and potentially of forms of action.

Education, especially tertiary education, can contribute in at least three ways. First, it gives individuals the skills they need if they are to effectively participate in politics. Norris explains: "Education is widely believed to facilitate the acquisition of civic skills, competencies, and knowledge that lead to political participation... [such as] the cognitive skills to make sense of current events in the mass media, the verbal and written skills essential to political communication, and the basic understanding of civics and public affairs that facilitates further learning" (Norris 2002, 91). Second, political consumers necessarily must have relatively high levels of political interest and political information in order to find out about and act upon issues in the marketplace. These are in fact predictors of political participation in general; in addition, levels of political interest and political information rise with education (Verba, Schlozman, and Brady 1995). Thus, we would expect that education would provide individuals with both the desire to participate and the skills to do so effectively. Third, education is positively associated with income and, as political consumerism involves selectively purchasing goods, it also requires significant expenditures. As a consequence, education levels might be extremely important in an indirect way to those who practice individualized responsibility-taking and political consumerism in particular. From this perspective, we expect that particularly education, political interest, and information might be important factors that facilitate political consumerism.

There is some evidence that other emerging forms of political participation, such as checkbook memberships, show a strong relationship with education and income. Verba, Schlozman, and Brady (1995) have shown that – as expected – checkbook activism is heavily dominated by the richest segments of the population, and this inequality is stronger than in traditional forms of participation. Skocpol (2003) too has expressed concern about the fact that the professionalization of political activism could lead to more privileged political access and influence for the wealthiest groups of the population. Of course, active individualized responsibility-taking goes well beyond pure checkbook memberships in that responsibility is not simply delegated to others or to political organizations by writing a check. However, the question arises as to how inclusive these democratic practices actually are with regard to income (Young 2002). Thus, another important aspect here is to understand how much income enables and the lack of income prevents the practice of political consumerism.

Taking the opposite view, one could question whether individualized responsibility-taking actually strengthens patterns of inequality. The argument is that the importance of socioeconomic resources such as education might diminish for participation practices that are more sporadic and do not require a strong commitment: for example, the entry costs for signing a petition or boycotting a product are lower than for becoming an active member of a political party. In order to be engaged politically, people do not need to have the time to regularly go to meetings, and they do not need selective group or leadership skills. As discussed in Chapter 2, individualized responsibility-taking is practiced more sporadically than conventional forms of political participation. This seemingly less taxing approach to exhibiting political views and stances might facilitate a broader recruitment of citizens from diverse and non-traditional backgrounds. Mobilization into individualized responsibility-taking such as political consumerism seems more widely accessible, as the mobilization tools reach more deeply into what has been perceived as private areas of life, and might involve displays in supermarkets, stores, and shops, and often include the Internet and other informal mobilization mechanisms (Jennings and Andersen 2003). Of course, this does not mean that electoral participation or voting are immune from private mobilization (Rosenstone and Hansen 1993, Mutz 2002). Mostly, because of a lower commitment level in terms of time, regularity, and continuity, one could similarly expect that political consumerism requires fewer resources and skills than conventional political participation and therefore might show a diminished importance of socioeconomic resources (Stolle and Hooghe 2011). From this perspective, one could assume that education and other socioeconomic factors play less of a role for political consumerism. In sum, with regard to the inequality of the practice of these action repertoires based on socioeconomic resources, particularly education, two opposing assumptions seem to exist, suggesting that political consumerism might exhibit either higher or lower levels of inequality compared to electoral participation forms. These competing assumptions will be examined below and in Chapter 4.

Another form of inequality is expressed in the gender gap in political participation. Whereas gender gaps for voting have closed in several countries (Conway 2001, Stolle and Hooghe 2011), they remain for several other electoral political activities – even for working informally to deal with a community problem, making campaign contributions, contacting public officials, and affiliation with political organizations (Verba, Schlozman, and Brady 1995, Stolle and Hooghe 2011). For individualized responsibility-taking, we expect less of a gender gap because these activities allow for the merging of public and private spheres, and they relate closely to everyday life activities. Whether it is about the choice of products in the supermarket, lifestyle decisions such as vegetarianism or the fight for animal rights more generally, many of these activities are closely related to the areas of life in which women's involvement is equal to or greater than that of men. Thus, it seems plausible to assume that women are at least equally if not disproportionately drawn toward political consumerism compared to men.

Another dimension of participatory bias to be examined in this chapter is age. Scholars who write about the decline in political participation suspect that the young generation has tuned out of conventional forms of political participation, ranging from voting, to party membership, joining other groups, to contacting politicians and attending group meetings (Putnam 2000, Macedo et al. 2005). Similarly, older people are seen as the model-engagement generation, frequently and eagerly involved in political acts. On the other hand, critics of this perspective put forth that the youngest generation in particular is engaged disproportionately in various forms of political action that have been overlooked, and which the elderly have not taken up (O'Toole et al. 2003, Haste and Hogan 2006, Quintelier 2007). The characteristics of individualized responsibility-taking examined in Chapter 2, and particularly their low entry costs, the sporadic nature of these forms, young people's familiarity with the Internet, and their openness to adopting new lifestyles allow for easier recruitment of younger people into these action repertoires. However, it seems also plausible that the youngest, although inclined to Internet activism and other protest activities, might not be as susceptible to political consumerism because of a lack of resources. Indeed, the middle-age generation, who face mobilizational life-cycle effects such as children, careers, and a general peak of involvement (Zukin et al. 2006), might be more active in political consumerism.

The overall first task of this chapter is to assess these expectations and the validity of the criticisms that participation in emerging action repertoires is more heavily skewed by factors of education, gender, and age than in traditional action repertoires and how this equality has changed over time. At the same time, the chapter assesses the importance of various other sociodemographic and political characteristics for the practice of political consumerism in a cross-national setting, including life in urban or rural areas, religion, political orientation, and others.

Political Attitudes, Values, and Practices of Political Consumers

Several attitudinal and behavioral characteristics of political consumers are examined here as well in order to explore this group of active citizens in more depth and to address some of the skepticism filed in regard to political consumerism as a form of political participation. These analyses include political consumers' 1) political attitudes and practice of other forms of political participation, 2) motivations for political shopping, as well as 3) norms of citizenship and efficacy.

1) *Political Attitudes and Practices of Political Consumers*
The notion of individualized responsibility-taking implies in practice that citizens recognize the limits of national governments and perhaps even

international organizations to solve political problems. This might entail that citizens turn away from national politics and national political institutions. In other words, do citizens adopt these modes of participation because they feel alienated from the political system? As alluded to in the previous chapter, theories of risk society/subpolitics and postmaterialism explain the occurrence of emerging forms of political action by highlighting how citizens have increasingly developed a lack of trust in the capacity of the government (Beck 1999, Inglehart 1997, Welzel and Inglehart 2005). Citizens fear that government either does not understand or cannot control new uncertainties and risks that characterize society today and thus citizens search for new ideas, arenas, and methods to work on these important political problems (Shapiro and Hacker-Cordón 1999). As a result, they choose to take on this responsibility themselves rather than delegating it to professional political actors (Beck 1997). Concerns about governability and ungovernability can motivate citizens to venture into new or simply different forms of political participation. These theoretical investigations offer several hypotheses and research questions regarding the value orientations of citizens who utilize these action repertoires. In the first instance, political consumers might be more disaffected from mainstream political institutions and have developed distrust in electoral political institutions and parliamentary politics. These theoretical insights might also suggest that political consumers place more trust in international or political consumer institutions than nonpolitical consumers. Finally, if notions of individualized responsibility-taking are correct, political consumers should find institutions or actors outside the parliamentary realm and electoral politics more efficacious for solving societal problems. These hypotheses will be tested below.

Turning from political attitudes to practices opens up the question whether political consumerism might crowd out other more traditional forms of participation. This discussion is not new: in the 1960s and 1970s, too, several authors worried that the new unconventional acts that were on the rise in that period (e.g. protesting and marching) would replace or crowd out conventional forms of participation. The *Political Action* study, however, firmly established the fact that people participating in what was then called unconventional action were exactly the same individuals participating in conventional forms (Barnes and Kaase 1979). Sidney Tarrow seconds this conclusion after exploring decades of social movement literature; he states that the repertoire of participation has widened to include both contentious and institutional politics (Tarrow 2000). The underlying question in our analysis is basically the same: are political consumers alienated from society and the political system, causing them to resort to new non-electoral approaches of participation exclusively? Or, do they use various types of participation and voice simultaneously, whereby political consumerism becomes an additional tool in their expanding political-action repertoires? The answer to these questions is of importance in the debate about the link between political action and political democracy and therefore a contribution to emerging scholarship on non-electoral forms of political participation. Earlier studies have found no evidence that engagement in individualized responsibility-taking such as political consumerism actually drives back conventional participation (Micheletti and Stolle 2005, Ferrer-Fons 2004, Tobiasen 2005). Below, we will provide a thorough analysis of this relationship in a cross-national context.

2) *Motivations for Political Shopping*
What are the motivations for political consumerism? As discussed in the previous chapter, political consumerism rarely has political targets as conventionally understood. Indeed, the engagement in what some call subpolitics, creative participation, everyday-making, sustainable citizenship, or individualized responsibility-taking represents a politicization process that blurs the lines between public and private and presents a bundle of new forms of action and responsibilities in politics. Yet, the critics claim that shopping is a private matter and self-interested in character and therefore might not be political in orientation (see van Deth and other chapters in Micheletti and McFarland 2010 for a discussion of these claims). This critique is not completely without empirical verification. Surveys have found, for example, that the highest mentioned motivation for vegetarianism is private health, which is generally viewed as a self-interested concern. Motivations for other forms of political consumerism such as buycotts might also be related to health, e.g., the rejection of antibiotics in meat or a desire for organic food for health reasons (Micheletti and Stolle 2010). Of course, few scholars have devoted time to research the idea that other forms of participation – for instance active membership in political parties or protest groups – might similarly be very self-interested in nature (for an exception, see Bäck, Heinelt, and Magnier 2006). People might join political campaign work because they look for social company and entertainment. They might decide to turn out to vote because they expect some private benefit from a particular candidate or even a free cup of coffee from a fast-food restaurant wanting to reward electoral participation. Rarely has conventional political participation been scrutinized for its public versus private motivations. But the question is asked about these newer acts of participation because they do not explicitly target conventional political actors and thus seem to threaten to water down the concept of political participation to include everything but the kitchen sink (van Deth 2010). The fear is that if indeed private motivations dominate these political acts, this might imply that they do not sufficiently stand for values of the common good and collective concerns as do those that are assumed to characterize forms of participation associated with the duty-based and civic republican model of citizenship (for more discussion, see Micheletti and Stolle 2012, Burtt 1993). The counterclaim is that these forms of citizenship practice emerge because traditional political actors do not or cannot take responsibility for urgent and often transborder political, social, economic, and environmental problems.

Thus, one of the ultimate questions in this debate is about the motivations of political consumers. As discussed in the previous chapter, the worry is that these activities are not sufficiently political, public, and democratic and, therefore, cannot and do not successfully guarantee the link between citizens and the political system. Essentially, this criticism argues that these forms of participation have nothing to do with citizenship ideals and practices. Our research here should help to better understand these different motivations. Are political consumers more driven by self-oriented or more political and other-regarding motivations? Which considerations do they contemplate when choosing a product? In what sense do their motivations reflect that political consumerism is indeed an act of political expression? This discussion has implications for how we view political community-building and the role of private interest and private virtue in politics (Burtt 1993, Micheletti 2010). It should also tell us a bit more about the different nature of citizenship engagement based on motivations as well as elucidate how to better measure, study, and conceptualize various acts of individualized responsibility-taking.

3) Norms of Citizenship

Scholars agree that good citizenship involves a shared set of expectations about the role of the individual citizen in society (Dalton 2008, 78, van Deth 2010). Typically, voting, obeying laws, and putting the collective interest before one's own are seen as examples of what is meant by good citizenship. Some scholars argue that societal changes and global developments must lead to a reconfiguration of what is meant by good citizenship (Micheletti and Stolle forthcoming). They maintain that this reconfiguration must involve more than the traditional relationship between the political individual (the citizen) and government by including decision-making concerning private life, biodiversity, the situation of people in other countries, and even future generations (Dobson 2003, Bullen and Whitehead 2005; see also Dalton 2008). What is good citizenship according to political consumers and non-political consumers?

The next section characterizes political consumers in selected European countries and the United States in terms of gender, demographic, and socioeconomic factors. Who are political consumers in Western democracies, and how do they differ from nonpolitical consumers? Which individual resources are most important for political consumerism? And which conclusions can be drawn from this analysis for the inequality of political consumerism? In the section that follows, special attention is paid to the gender gap in political consumerism, which we call a reversed gender gap, as many more women engage in political consumerism compared to men. Why do women play such a special role in political consumerism? The final section of this chapter looks at the value, attitudinal, and behavioral profiles of political consumers in order to help us understand why they choose this political tool as well as the issues they consider important when choosing among products.

SOCIODEMOGRAPHIC PROFILE OF POLITICAL CONSUMERS

Measuring political consumerism is no easy undertaking. First, there are questions about how the concept of political consumerism can be successfully operationalized. For example, skepticism looms about whether the motivations for buycotts or lifestyle changes are necessarily political (Chapter 2). Not only does this book offer a variety of possibilities for measuring political consumerism, but this chapter will also contribute to analyzing the motivations of political consumers and thus push further the debate about definitions and measurements. The second difficulty is availability of a variety of political consumerism measures. Although Chapter 2 provided some examples of over-time measurements, only a few are available for individual-level and cross-national analysis. Most strikingly, there are no comparative measures for discursive and lifestyle political consumerism. Most cross-national research uses simple survey items of boycotts and buycotts which ask whether respondents have boycotted or buycotted products for political, ethical, or environmental reasons within the last twelve months. These measures are also available in the *European Social Survey* of 2002/2003.

When political consumers are defined as people who state that they have either boycotted or buycotted products for these reasons, about 31 percent of U.S. Americans and Europeans (from twenty countries) between the ages of fifteen and eighty-five years can be said to be political consumers. These people have either (1) participated in a boycott, (2) used a labeling scheme, or (3) both boycotted and buycotted in the past year. About 17 percent of the respondents indicated that they boycotted (4 percent do so exclusively), and 26 percent said that they buycotted (here 14 percent do it exclusively) within the last twelve months. Nearly 12 percent have done both. Now, what are the main sociodemographic characteristics of political consumers?

Table 3.1 presents a bivarite analysis exploring how important sociodemographic characteristics relate to being a political consumer. More specifically, it probes whether gender, age, education, employment status, and religious background affect engagement in political consumerism. It also explores how basic political orientations map onto political consumerism. The bivariate analysis presented in Table 3.1 can be summarized in seven points. First and most importantly, women stand out, although not in all countries. The differences between men and women are particularly strong in Scandinavian countries and in all places where political consumerism is more advanced. In Sweden, for example, 67 percent of women compared with 54 percent of men are political consumers; in Finland, the gender gap is 16 points. In other countries, mostly of Eastern and Southern Europe, women and men do not differ in their levels of political consumerism, which is also the case in the United States. There is not a single country in the available dataset in which women participate significantly less than men. This result has been confirmed in other surveys in Sweden and internationally (Petersson, Westholm, and Blomberg, 1989, Petersson et al.

TABLE 3.1. *Bivariate Results for Political Consumerism in Percentages*

Country	Gender		Age				Education			Employed		Income					Religion				Domicile		Political Spectrum			Political Interest	
	Men	Women	15–29	30–44	45–59	60+	Primary School	High School	Some Post-Secondary	No	Yes	Low	Lower Middle	Middle	Higher Middle	High	Catholic	Protestant	Other	N/A	Urban	Rural	Left	Centre	Right	No	Yes
All countries#	29	33	29	37	33	23	12	28	48	24	36	25	32	38	42	42	21	44	21	36	34	27	42	31	31	20	42
Austria	34	35	35	38	36	27	10	28	48	31	37	32	31	38	45	45	36	22	33	39	37	34	50	35	24	22	43
Belgium	28	34	33	37	33	20	16	25	51	26	35	23	33	38	38	36	30		36	30	35	27	43	30	30	21	43
Czech Rep.	23	30	31	35	29	15		23	45	19	33	33	30	26	36	36	19			28	29	20	28	24	32	22	35
Denmark	44	52	43	55	54	37		41	67	39	53	42	43	58	58	62		36	36	52	50	44	72	48	43	34	56
Finland	39	55	55	54	47	35	26	46	66	39	54	42	47	49	49	58		46	48	49	54	38	49	49	47	39	56
France	36	37	37	42	39	26	18	30	52	31	42	30	33	33	50	59	37	46	34	37	39	32	45	35	33	26	53
Germany	40	50	42	52	49	37	24	41	53	39	51	39	40	50	57	57	45	26	46	45	44	48	59	44	37	30	54
Greece	11	13	14	18	13	5	4	13	25	9	17	5	11	15	17	17	11		12	24	16	8	20	12	10	9	18
Hungary	12	12	14	14	13	7	6	10	30	10	13	6	13	13	13	21	11	11	7	13	14	8	12	11	19	6	18
Ireland	28	29	26	37	31	18	12	26	46	24	32	13	26	34	48	48	11		2	13	33	23	47	30	27	19	40
Italy	8	11	6	15	13	4	4	11	19	8	13	6	11	18	17	17	8	44	54	16	11	9	19	11	6	6	19
Netherlands	27	30	24	33	30	23	13	23	47	24	31	24	30	33	35	35	26	28	32	29	31	25	49	26	23	16	35
Norway	37	46	42	50	44	26		34	58	32	46	32	41	53	53	53		42	36	42	47	34	54	38	41	32	51
Poland	9	12	11	12	13	6	3	8	31	8	15	4	11	17	19	19	10		11	19	14	6	12	11	16	8	15
Portugal	8	8	11	12	8	3	4	14	20	6	10	1	5	12	19	19	7		2	18	11	4	16	8	4	8	16
Slovenia	12	11	13	16	12	6	5	8	17	10	14	6	10	14	20	20	11		17	12	16	9	16	14	10	10	16
Spain	13	14	17	19	14	5	4	13	28	9	19	9	14	14	25	25	12		5	20	17	9	20	13	13	10	26
Sweden	54	67	63	71	61	48	44	62	73	52	66	52	61	68	62	75		65	53	59	62	57	69	58	59	50	68
Switzerland	47	54	33	55	59	48	34	45	68	45	53	49	53	62	58	58	43	56	54	52	57	46	69	47	50	36	60
U.K.	38	43	25	46	46	38		31	60	34	45	26	44	47	47	55	39	48	39	36	38	47	47	41	44	26	53
U.S.	28	28	30	30	27	22	14	21	38	23	31	21	29	34	34	35	30	27	28	28	28	28	46	23	28	13	35

Entries are percentages of respondents indicating that they have participated in these acts.

*** p<0.01; ** p<0.05; * p<0.1; #For income column, "all countries" figure excludes United States.

Source: *European Social Survey* (Jowell 2003) and CID survey (Howard, Gibson, and Stolle 2006)

1998, Stolle and Hooghe 2004, Ferrer-Fons 2004), but also challenged by Baek (2010).[5] We return to the reversed gender gap in a later section of this chapter.

Second, political consumers are not necessarily young people. They are disproportionately middle-aged citizens mostly in the age group of thirty- to forty-four-year-olds. In Sweden, 71 percent of this group engages in ethical and political shopping. In very few countries (Denmark, Poland, Switzerland, and the United Kingdom) do citizens in the next age group (forty-five- to fifty-nine-year-olds) participate as much or more in political consumerism. In Finland, young people from the age group of fifteen to twenty-nine are also very active, but overall they turn out not to be the most active group. The oldest citizens are usually the least involved group in political consumerism with the exception of Switzerland and the United Kingdom, where the youngest generation is least interested in conscientious shopping. Although further analysis is required to substantiate these findings, the results suggest that political consumerism – like many other forms of political participation – is related to the lifecycle and reaches its highest levels at middle age when many people are integrated into the workforce and have families.

Third, and perhaps the most pronounced distinction in terms of gap size, political consumers tend to be more highly educated than non-political consumers, a result also found in a Danish survey on political consumers (Goul Andersen and Tobiassen 2001, 46) and generally in studies on political participation (e.g., Petersson et al. 1998, 89, Brady, Verba, and Schlozman 1995). Citizens with some university and/or college education are on average four times as likely to be political consumers as citizens with only an elementary-school education. In some countries, this difference is even more extreme: in the Czech Republic and Poland, it is ten-fold; in Spain it is seven-fold; and in Austria, Greece, Hungary, Italy, and Portugal the difference is five-fold. It is clear that education plays a crucial role at the individual level as hypothesized in one of the scenarios before. Overall, political consumerism is more evenly spread throughout various education groups in countries that have higher levels of political consumerism; in other words, more political consumerism means that citizens with lower levels of education become mobilized to participate in

---

[5] Baek, drawing from two waves of the 2002 *National Civic Engagement Survey* (United States), separates respondents into four groups: "nocotters," boycotters, buycotters, and "dualcotters." She finds that dualcotters (our political consumers) are actually more likely to be male. Her survey uses different measurements of political consumerism. Boycotting is rejecting a product "because of conditions under which the product is made, or because the respondent dislikes the conduct of the company that produces it" (Baek 2010, 1070). Buycotting, on the other hand, is measured as "buying a certain product or service because the respondent likes the social or political values of the company that produces or provides it" (ibid, 1071). These measures are different from the common use of "ethical, political, and environmental" considerations during the shopping choices, so that different priming might be behind the differences in gender gaps. However, even with the standard wording, the U.S. respondents do not show the reversed gender gap (see Figures 3.1 and 3.3).

this activity. At the same time, political consumerism is also high in countries in which income equality is fairly high, which means that the socioeconomic resources needed for political action are distributed more evenly. In Chapter 4, this distinction will be examined in more detail.

Fourth, employment status matters; in fact, in all countries (without exception) employed respondents were more engaged in political consumerism than those who were not employed at the time of the survey. The differences are not as stark as with education, but they hover around 15 percent in Finland and are as small as 3 percentage points in Hungary. Overall, being employed nearly doubles the likelihood of political consumerism in selected Southern and Eastern European countries, and the effect is smaller elsewhere. There are two main reasons for this relationship. As with education, employment status is one of the socioeconomic variables that turns out to represent important resources for many kinds of political participation (Verba, Schlozman, and Brady 1995). In addition, political consumerism might require additional financial resources, which is a discussion to which we turn now.

Organic food labeled goods and fairtrade goods, as examples of political consumer items, often cost – or are perceived to cost – more than non-labeled goods (Konsumentverket 2004, Rättvisemärkt 2004). The substantial difference in prices for several products leads many to wonder whether political consumers are more often citizens with higher incomes. Table 3.1 shows that household income is indeed important. The respondents of each country are divided into country-specific income quartile groups, and the proportion of political consumers is compared across these four groups. In most countries, with very few exceptions, the highest income respondents are significantly more likely to be political consumers than respondents from lower income groups. In Belgium and Switzerland, it is the second highest income group that tops the ranks of political consumers and in Norway the two highest income groups are similarly engaged in political consumerism. The ratio of political consumerism between citizens in the highest income groups compared to the lowest income group in the overall sample is 1.6:1, which is to say that it is about one-and-a-half times more likely that the respondents in the highest income category are political consumers than those in the lowest income category. The ratio is much higher in Southern and Eastern Europe, mostly in countries with low levels of political consumerism, with 19:1 in Portugal (almost no-one from the lowest income group practices political consumerism), with almost 5:1 in Poland, more than 3:1 in places like Greece, Ireland, Italy, Slovenia, and Hungary, and nearly 2:1 in France. There is no doubt that income does play a substantial role in the purchasing of labeled products, or in the rejection of certain brands.

Fifth, political consumerism is more an urban than a rural phenomenon. People living in large metropolitan areas, in large cities, or even smaller cities are significantly more engaged in political consumerism than people in rural areas and villages with the exception of Germany. This should not be interpreted to mean that political consumerism is not present in the countryside: overall

27 percent of people in the less populated areas are also political consumers compared with 34 percent in urban areas, so the differences are relatively minor.

Sixth, the most interesting part of this analysis relates to political consumerism and its relationship with religion. It is already obvious that conscientious shopping is found more in overall Protestant countries – that is to say, Scandinavia. Overall, Protestants are more frequently political consumers (44 percent) compared to Catholics (21 percent) and other religions (21 percent) and compared to those who are not religiously affiliated (36 percent). However, at the individual level within each country, religion plays out differently and not necessarily uniformly. In the majority of countries though, those who are not affiliated with any religion are significantly more engaged in political consumerism. This is the case in Austria, Denmark, Greece, Italy, Poland, Portugal, Spain, and to a certain extent also Finland and Hungary – basically countries with varying levels of political consumerism. We also find pockets of Protestant or members of other religions who are moving political consumerism forward in other countries. For example, in the Czech Republic (although not significantly so), Sweden, Switzerland, and the United Kingdom, Protestants are more active in political consumerism than those who are affiliated with other religions. In Ireland, and to a lesser degree in Belgium, the Netherlands, and Slovenia, on the other hand, religions other than Protestantism or Catholicism are most important for political consumerism.[6] Only in France do Catholics belong to the group of most practicing political consumers together with those who are not affiliated with any religion. These results reflect that religion is a complex factor for political consumerism, and variations are most certainly based on the differences in the history of these institutions to mobilize for the political consumer agenda. We return to these ideas in Chapters 4 and 5.

In terms of the political nature of the phenomenon, political consumers show more general interest in politics than nonpolitical consumers. In every single country political consumers are more interested in political issues than nonpolitical consumers. Respondents who were interested in political issues were often twice as likely to be political consumers as those who were not. The difference in percentage points ranges from a gap of 27 percent in France and the United Kingdom to 10 percent in Greece.

Finally, the results dispel some common misconceptions about the political views of political consumers. They are not left-wing extremists. The fact that 31 percent of all citizens in Europe and the United States are political consumers, and in Scandinavia and Switzerland that 50 percent or more of the population seems to engage in this activity, show that this phenomenon is much more widespread. It is true that political consumers more often than not have a left-leaning political orientation. In seventeen of the twenty-one countries included

---

[6] For Belgium, these are other Christian denominations and Islam; for Ireland and the Netherlands, other Christian denominations; for Slovenia, Eastern Orthodox religion and Islam.

in this study, respondents who self-identified to the left on a common left-right scale were significantly more involved in political consumerism than people who identified as middle of the road or to the right. There are some exceptions: in Eastern Europe, political consumers are predominantly right-leaning. This is because the right-leaning citizens in Eastern Europe are the ones with mostly Western values, whereas the left in Eastern Europe might at least in part denote the former or now reformed communist camp. Also, according to Baek (2010), in the United States, buycotters are more likely to identify as Republican/conservative, whereas boycotters are more likely to identify as Democrats/liberals. However, question-wording effects need to be taken into consideration before drawing meaningful conclusions about cross-national differences here (see more in Chapter 8).[7]

In order to better understand which of these demographic factors and individual characteristics best relate to political consumerism, they need to be tested in a multivariate model. For that purpose a logistic regression model was created using the ESS which includes all discussed variables except income, which was excluded due to the high number of missing values. The model performs relatively well throughout all countries, indicated by a relatively high Nagelkerke Rsquare ranging from .09 to .27. The model coefficients, their significances, and odds ratios for all twenty-one countries are presented in Table 3.2.

Many of the previous findings were confirmed. For example, gender emerged as an important and robust predictor of political consumerism; in all countries but two, women are significantly more engaged than men when controlling for all other factors. Gender also became an important variable in countries with low levels of political consumerism, which means that given their level of education, employment, political interest, and so forth, women are significantly more engaged than men. The other consistent and robust correlate of political consumerism is political interest, as in all countries but one, politically interested respondents are significantly more active in political consumerism than non-interested ones when controlling for other factors. Another important variable is education; post-secondary education in particular turns out to be an important explanatory variable with the highest impact. In some countries, even controlling for various other factors, people with post-secondary education often have seven to eight times higher odds of being political consumers compared to respondents with only primary-school education. Post-secondary education significantly relates to political consumerism in all but five countries, where the relationship is also strong and positive. Weaker but still mostly positive effects were observed with high school education (compared to primary-school-only education). Also confirmed was the finding regarding the political

---

[7] The finding that generally political consumers self-identify more as left-leaning might have to do with the fact that the survey questions on boycotts and buycotts ask specifically about "environmental" considerations, and these are often located in general left-wing or liberal politics.

TABLE 3.2. *Individual-Level Model – Baseline*

Country	Constant	Gender	Age			Employ	Education		Political Spectrum	Religion			Urban/ Rural	Political Interest	N	Nagel-Kerke
			30-44	45-59	60+		High School	Some Post-Secondary		Catholic	Protestant	Other				
All countries	-3.100***	.471***	.145***	-.027	-.318***	.195***	.575***	1.185***	-.072***	-.569***	.351***	-.588***	-.041***	.601***	33,967	.198
	.045	1.602	1.156	.974	.728	1.215	1.776	3.271	.930	.566	1.421	.555	.960	1.823		
Austria	-2.876***	.216*	.054	.062	-.284	.058	.963	1.558*	-.149***	-.117	-1.088***	.178	.019	.541**	1,887	.141
	.056	1.242	1.056	1.064	.753	1.060	2.619	4.748	.862	.890	.337	1.195	1.020	1.718		
Belgium	-2.595***	.498***	-.021	-.046	-.673***	-.142	.448*	1.300***	-.091***	.140	1.106	.243	-.142***	.605***	1,523	.193
	.075	1.645	.979	.955	.510	.868	1.565	3.67	.913	1.150	3.022	1.276	.867	1.832		
Czech Rep.	-2.480***	.742***	-.139	-.363	-1.020***	.532***	-.456	.052	-.001	-.137	.37	.481	-.166***	.586***	1,153	.160
	.084	2.100	.870	.696	.360	1.702	.634	1.053	.999	.872	1.448	1.617	.847	1.796		
Denmark	-2.630***	.518***	.183	-.003	-.304	.293*	1.257*	1.985***	-.175***	-.422	-.145	-.557	-.078	.553***	1,389	.182
	.072	1.678	1.201	.997	.738	1.34	3.514	7.282	.839	.656	0.865	0.573	.925	1.738		
Finland	-1.871***	.814***	-.511***	-.722***	-.682***	.464***	.424***	1.073***	-.065***	-1.151	-.127	-.007	-.139***	.490***	1,883	.190
	.154	2.257	.600	.486	.506	1.59	1.529	2.923	.937	.316	0.88	.993	.870	1.632		
France	-2.853***	.322**	.224	.157	-.206	.136	.458**	1.208***	-.062**	.101	.115	-.269	-.139***	.674***	1,401	.226
	.058	1.38	1.251	1.17	.814	1.145	1.581	3.346	.940	1.106	1.122	.764	.870	1.962		
Germany	-2.608***	.661***	-.019	-.116	-.497***	-.214**	.138	.605*	-.145***	.129	.040	.204	.074*	.593***	2,681	.145
	.074	1.936	.981	.890	.608	.807	1.147	1.831	.865	1.138	1.041	1.226	1.077	1.81		
Greece	-3.742***	-.498***	.168	-.245	-.806***	.275	.676***	1.029***	-.038	-1.028	-19.644	-.436	-.183***	.625***	1,951	.187
	.024	.608	1.168	.783	.446	1.317	1.966	2.799	.963	.358	0	.647	.833	1.868		
Hungary	-2.966***	.111	-.216	-.447*	-1.170***	-.346*	-.143	.935***	.122***	.037	-.010	-1.324	-.276***	.586***	1,389	.158
	.052	1.118	.806	.640	.310	.707	.867	2.548	1.129	1.038	.990	.266	.759	1.797		
Ireland	-2.505***	.343***	.462***	.224	-.330	-.076	.608***	1.252***	-.130***	-.376**	.539	.374	-.104***	.652***	1,642	.208
	.082	1.409	1.588	1.252	.719	.927	1.837	3.498	.878	.687	1.714	1.454	.901	1.92		

Table (country rows; first line = logistic regression coefficient, second line = odds ratio underneath). Column headers are not printed on this page.

Country															N	R²
Italy	-4.968***	.808***	.821**	.697*	.056	.265	.532	.681	-.205***	-.357	.123	2.686*	-.091	.816***	927	.216
	.007	2.243	2.273	2.007	1.058	1.304	1.703	1.976	.815	.700	1.131	14.673	.913	2.261		
Netherlands	-2.939***	.340***	.248	.195	-.124	.005	.435	1.269***	-.174***	.045	.205	.173	-.031	.604***	2.231	.167
	.053	1.406	1.281	1.215	.883	1.005	1.545	3.557	.840	1.046	1.228	1.188	.969	1.829		
Norway	-1.571***	.503***	-.382**	-.933***	.241*	-.066	.598		-.109***	-.421	.087	-.367	-.124***	.558***	1.984	.171
	.208	1.653	.683	.393	1.272	.936	1.818		.897	.657	1.091	.693	.883	1.747		
Poland	-4.939***	.610***	-.082	.055	-.334	.216	.807**	2.133***	.081**	-.536**	-19.211	-.376	-.073	.453***	1.725	.189
	.007	1.84	.921	1.057	.716	1.241	2.241	8.439	1.085	.585	0	.687	.930	1.573		
Portugal	-4.476***	.448*	.187	-.194	-.820**	.042	.682**	.817***	-.211***	-.367	-.769		-.090	1.026***	1.184	.269
	.011	1.565	1.206	.824	.441	1.043	1.978	2.263	.810	.693	.464		.914	2.79		
Slovenia	-2.306***	-.029	.369	-.223	-.969***	-.247	.249	.959***	-.035	.102	-19.552	.587	-.132	.461	1.174	.090
	.100	.971	1.446	.800	.379	.781	1.283	2.609	.966	1.107	0	1.798	.876	1.585		
Spain	-2.947***	.239	-.144	-.353	-.806***	.249	.365	.959***	-.082**	-.125	.017	-.262	-.103	.612***	1.355	.165
	.053	1.270	.866	.703	.447	1.283	1.440	2.609	.921	.882	1.017	.770	.902	1.843		
Sweden	-1.898***	.726***	.124	-.425***	-.663***	.230	.533	.796***	-.079***	-.230	.341***	-.387	-.016	.512***	1.870	.170
	.150	2.067	1.132	.654	.515	1.258	1.704	2.216	.924	.795	1.407	.679	.984	1.668		
Switzerland	-1.782***	.458***	.723***	.803***	.374**	-.014	.408	.950***	-.135***	-.350***	.056	-.153	-.150***	.528***	1.863	.163
	.168	1.581	2.062	2.232	1.453	.986	1.503	2.586	.874	.705	1.057	.858	.860	1.695		
U.K.	-4.597***	.525***	.689***	.605***	.260**	.301	1.171	.158	.007	-.255	.232*	.074	.107*	.690***	1.849	.207
	.010	1.69	1.992	1.831	1.296	1.351	3.224	1.171	1.007	.775	1.261	1.077	1.113	1.993		
U.S.	-3.435***	.097	.184	-.224	-.396	.155	.436	1.065***	-.132***	.045	.049	.004	-.046	.816***	906	.198
	.032	1.102	1.202	.799	.673	1.168	1.547	2.902	.876	1.046	1.050	1.004	.955	2.261		

*** p<0.01; ** p<0.05; * p<0.1.

Entries are logistic regression coefficients with odds ratios underneath.

Source: European Social Survey (Jowell 2003) and CID survey (Howard, Gibson, and Stolle 2006).

orientation of political consumers: in Western democracies, they are more left-oriented, and in Eastern European countries the effect of right-wing orientations was often washed out by other factors. Other results did not hold or became much weaker in the multivariate analysis. For example, the effect of employment status was overpowered by the inclusion of education and other variables; only in five countries was the employment status a significant predictor of political consumerism. Similarly, the urban-rural division was overpowered by other factors and was only significant in a handful of countries. Also, the effect of age lost some of its bite – the most significant aspect is that in most countries, the older generation is less engaged than the youngest generation, often significantly so. The middle generation of 30–44-year-olds seems to be the one with the highest involvement level, but not always significantly higher than the youngest generation. Finally, the effect of religion washes out completely in the multivariate model, but in the pooled sample (results not shown) Protestants have 1.4 higher odds of being political consumers than nonaffiliated consumers, whereas Catholics and people of religions other than Catholicism and Protestantism have only half the odds of being engaged in this activity. Overall, education, gender and political interest strongly dominate the list of sociodemographic factors explaining political consumerism. The next section explores the role of women in political consumerism more closely.

ENGENDERED SHOPPING

Today, women stand out as more engaged political consumers. What is interesting about this observation is that political participation research has established a persistent gender gap in political interest, political knowledge, and conventional forms of participation (Conway 2001, Delli Carpini and Keeter 1996, Putnam 2000, van Deth and Elf 2000). Despite some persistent gender differences, women at the turn of the twenty-first century are just as likely to vote as their male counterparts, but only in rare cases have women been found to be politically more active than men (Petersson et al. 1998, Steger and Witt, 1989, Stolle and Hooghe 2011). In this section, we further explore women's engagement in political consumerism and we ask why women are at the forefront of this political action repertoire.

A historical look at surveys with questions on boycotts shows that boycotting was a predominantly male activity in the 1970s. This pattern changed gradually over the subsequent decades: in ten out of sixteen West European countries included in the *World Values Survey* (1980–2000), more women participated in boycotts than men (analysis not shown). Women also predominate as boycotters in eleven of the twenty sampled countries included in the 2002 *European Social Survey* (ESS) and 2006 *United States Citizen, Involvement, Democracy* (CID) survey (see Figure 3.1). The gap ranges from a very minor gender difference in Portugal to an 8 percent gap in Finland, though the negative gap still exists in a number of countries, most notably in the United

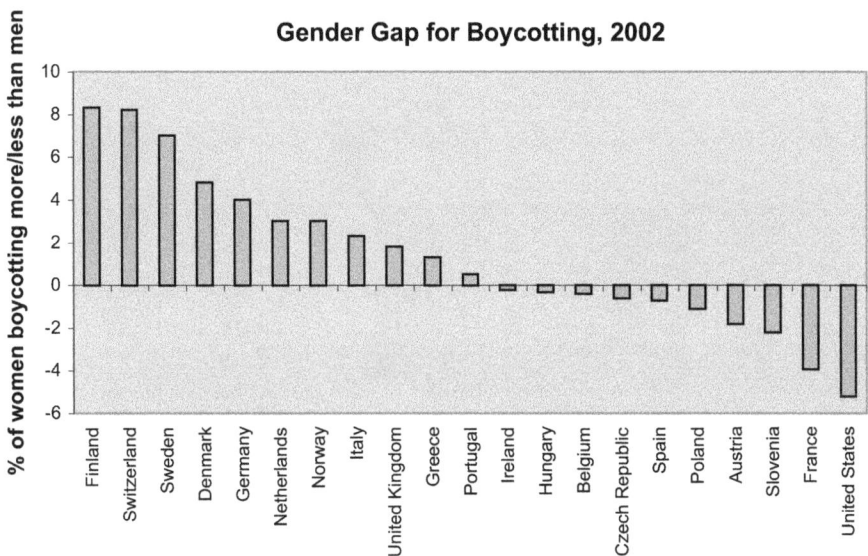

FIGURE 3.1. Gender Gap in Boycotting. Data represent the aggregate percentage for the gender gap for boycotting for each country. A positive gap indicates that more women participate in boycotts than men, whereas a negative gap indicates that more men participate in boycotts than women. *Source*: *European Social Survey* 2002 (Jowell et al. 2003).

States. In fact, boycotting emerged as one of the few political acts in which we find a reversed gender gap at the end of the twentieth century (Stolle and Micheletti 2005, Stolle and Hooghe 2011). In Figure 3.2, we compare the gender gaps in various political acts in the United States and the seven West European countries that were included both in the *Political Action Survey* and the *European Social Survey*. As Figure 3.2 demonstrates, the acts of signing petitions, boycotting, and demonstrations started out with the typical gender gap in the 1970s, but in the 2000s the gender gap had declined, been equalized, or reversed entirely. This means that the "feminization" of boycott actions can be seen as part of a larger societal trend (Stolle and Hooghe 2011). The closing or even reversed gender gap can be found mostly in actions that are on the rise or have remained stable between 1974 and 2002. On the other hand, for acts that clearly show a downward trend (political party membership, contacting a politician, etc.) the traditional gender gap remains present and does not show any visible signs of being reduced. In other words, party membership and contacting politicians have declined in the general population and they remain predominantly male activities. Voting is a special case, as the gender gap here had already been overcome in the 1970s (at least in the selected European countries) and this remained unchanged in 2002. This analysis suggests that women participate predominantly in new and arising forms of engagement

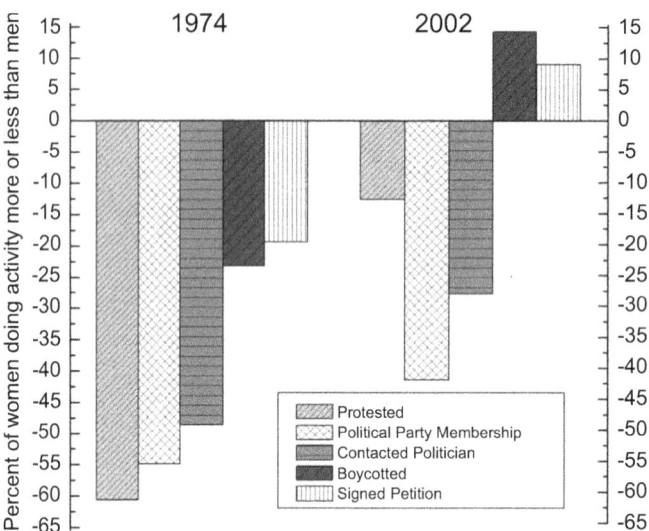

FIGURE 3.2. Gender Gaps Over Time. *Note:* Bars represent relative aggregate gender gaps on various political acts, indicating the percentage that women are more or less engaged than men. *Source: Political Action Survey, European Social Survey* and the 2006 *United States Citizenship, Involvement and Democracy Survey*, Countries Include: Austria, Finland, Germany, Great Britain, Italy, Netherlands, Switzerland, and the United States.

which are located outside the traditional political boundaries. Women's participation in consumer actions, for example, can partially explain the expansion of this form of engagement over the last decades, but more than that, it seems to be a political act favored more by women than by men.

Buycotting in particular has become a near-routine form of engagement for women, particularly in Scandinavia. More women than men in all countries aside from Spain are present as buycotters, as shown in Figure 3.3. However, the use of political consumerism to express political values is not evenly distributed across countries or regions. In Southern and Eastern Europe, buycotting and boycotting are not frequently used as a form of political engagement by women. These differences are most likely linked to the presence of national labeling schemes and other national factors that influence this form of transnational activism (see also Chapter 4). Moreover, the largest reversed gender gap exists in countries where political consumerism is most widespread, which indicates that women are essential in bringing this political tool into mainstream use.

Available market studies from Europe and the United States confirm this gender gap. They show that women stand out as users of organic food labels,

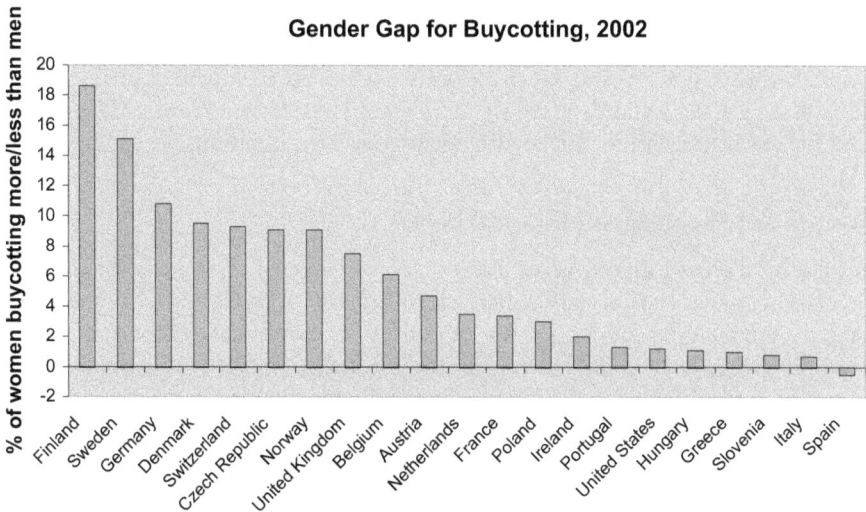

FIGURE 3.3. Gender Gap in Buycotting. Data represent the aggregate gender gap for buycotting for each country. A positive gap indicates that more women participate in buycotts than men, whereas a negative gap indicates that more men participate in buycotts than women. *Source: European Social Survey* (Jowell et al. 2003).

the Max Havelaar Fairtrade label, and eco-labels for seafood, respectively (LUI 1999, 3, Klint 1997, 28, Wessells, Holger, and Johnston 1999, Hunter, Johnson, and Hatch 2004, Brécard et al. 2011). LUI, a Swedish survey institute specializing in consumer research for the farming community, finds that women shoppers also stand out on such aspects as whether food is guaranteed free of salmonella, GMOs, growth hormones, medicines, chemical additives, and chemical pesticides (LRF and Ekologiska LantbrUKarna 2001, 21). The authors of the U.S. study on eco-labeled seafood conclude that "the gender of the respondent has an impact on choice, with women more likely to choose certified products across all species" and that "variables representing age, income, education, and political affiliation are generally insignificant individually and jointly" (Wessells, Holger, and Johnston 1999, 51f). Activists involved in political consumerism also confirm the importance of women, and underscore that middle-class women are the focal group for all new consumerist efforts. They are seen as the people with the interest and means for this kind of political involvement (Dobson 2000).

So, why more women? Perhaps their presence is just a legacy of the past: women have traditionally been family shoppers and have, on certain historical occasions, used their consumer power to change society (Micheletti 2006 for a discussion, Orleck 1993, Young 1994, Hirdman 1983a, 1983b). Another possible explanation is that overall women are still the gender that shops more frequently and, therefore, come into more contact with ethical and political shopping opportunities. A third possibility is that women, unlike men, are particularly motivated to shop ethically and politically. They may, as research on risk thresholds shows, be more sensitive to environmental problems as threats to the health and safety of their communities and families (Davidson and Freudenburg 1996). We briefly review these explanations.

Women and Shopping: A Historical Look

It may be the case that women are drawn to forms of civic engagement that involve activities in everyday spheres traditionally dominated by women and that do not involve the high costs of collective action (see Micheletti 2003). Shopping in grocery and department stores is such a sphere. Historical studies from the United States and Europe show that the market has been frequently used by women as an arena for politics. This research area is still in its infancy, but we find historical cases where women have banded together in neighborhood consumer networks to fight socio-economic injustices (the inability to feed their families properly because of high food prices and poverty, for example) in different countries (Orleck, 1993, Hirdman 1983a, 1983b). Scholars of the American experience consider the activities of these consumer networks "far more widespread and sustained, encompassing a far wider range of ethnic and racial groups than any tenant or consumer uprising before it" (Orleck 1993, 156). Middle-class women have used their purchasing power to help put an end to domestic sweatshop labor in the United States. In the early part of the 1900s, the "white label campaign," an anti-sweatshop labeling scheme appealed to women to buy cotton underwear for themselves and their children that was certified as "sweatshop free" (Sklar 1998). The white label scheme can be understood as having given women access to the political community: it gave them an arena for political action, and their purchasing choices became a tool to exercise moral and political power in a time when men dominated formal civil society and government settings. African-American women have also used the market as an arena for racial politics. They repeatedly boycotted for civil rights, with the role played by women in the Montgomery Bus Boycott being the best-known case (Goldberg 1999, King 1999, Friedman 1999). Not all examples of female involvement in political consumerism are emancipatory. For example, women, as the household's key shoppers, were also particularly mobilized into effective boycotts against Jewish- and Catholic-owned businesses especially in small German cities in the 1930s (Blee 1991).

Even with full suffrage rights, women continued to play a crucial role in political consumerism. The grape boycott in the 1960s, which started in the United States and spread to other countries, would probably not have been successful without women's involvement. The boycott really began to have an impact when the United Farm Workers' Union decided to turn its struggle into an issue of shopping for food for the family. When consumers (who most probably were women shoppers) learned that the pesticides used on grapes were also hazardous to their families and not just to the health of the farm workers, they began to boycott grapes in great numbers (Benford and Valadez 1998, Micheletti 2003). A gendered reading of available historical materials show that the international boycott of Nestlé, for its marketing of infant formula in developing countries, most likely would neither have taken place nor been so successful and effective without the involvement of female health-care professionals and women organized into a variety of civic networks (Bar-Yam 1995, Sikkink 1986).

These patterns are present in more recent years. For instance, we find that women initiated the 1995 boycott of economically sensitive French goods (wine and cheese) (Micheletti 2010). They also, in the late 1980s, played a crucial role in establishing green political consumerism as a priority area, for example, within the Swedish Society for the Conservation of Nature. Noteworthy is that the association's interest in green political consumerism was sparked by one woman's concern about risks involved with purchasing potatoes sprayed with pesticides and her search for pesticide-free potatoes for her family, thus illustrating along with other such reasons for choosing organic over conventional food the claim that women as family shoppers are more sensitive to environmental risks than men (e.g., Lockie et al. 2004, Micheletti 2003). Also, women's groups from different countries have been involved in the fairtrade and anti-sweatshop campaigns to improve the working conditions of women in the global garment industry. Women's groups were some of the first to call attention to women's treatment in outsourced manufacturing, and women individually or in organized fashion have participated in protests and anti-sweatshop fashion shows. Soccer moms joined their high-school daughters in noisy demonstrations outside retail stores (Benjamin 2001, ix). In short, historical and contemporary case studies confirm that women are predominantly active in this area of engagement. But are women of today still the main shoppers?

Today's Women and Shopping

Given these insights, it is entirely plausible that women are more engaged in political consumerism because they shop more often. As the historical examples show, women have traditionally taken on boycotts and buycotts because the purchase of products is one of the daily tasks in which women historically engaged. Of course, the regularity of shopping itself does not successfully explain why women include ethical and political considerations to a higher degree in their shopping decisions than men, but it might explain the extent to which issues related to shopping are on people's minds. So, are today's women more involved in shopping? For the answer we examine the Swedish national SOM survey, which includes questions about the frequency of shopping. Using Sweden as an example here is not just of practical value; it is also a good example because political consumerism in Sweden is particularly pronounced,

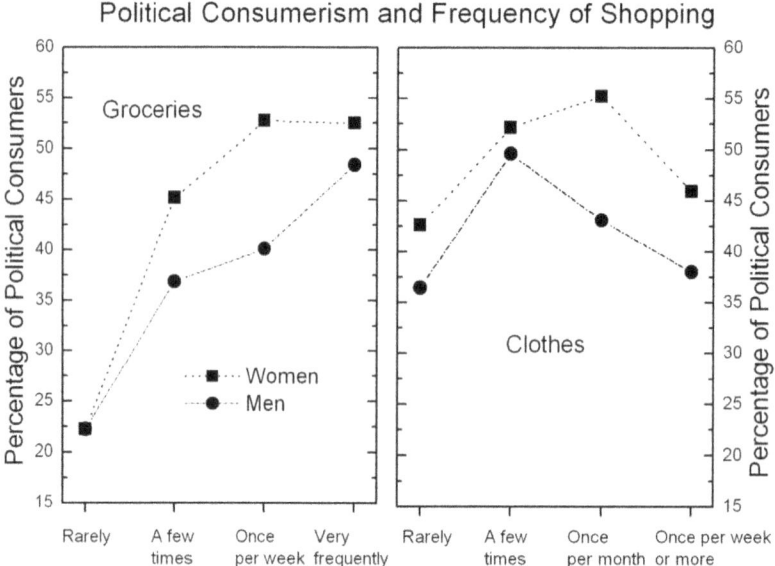

FIGURE 3.4. Frequency of Shopping. *Note:* The data points represent percentages of political consumers per category of frequency of shopping. The number of respondents is 1,748 and 1,754 for shopping of groceries and shopping of clothes, respectively. *Source:* SOM 2003.

and the gender gap is highly significant. Our survey results reveal that women outdo men in frequency of shopping, but not by very much. For example, 29 percent of women indicate that they go grocery shopping every single or almost every single day, whereas only 25 percent of men belong to this group. The differences are small, but statistically significant (results not shown). However, are women, who shop more regularly, more involved in political consumer behaviors than men who shop regularly? Figure 3.4 reveals that women as well as men who shop for groceries more frequently are also more engaged in political consumerism. This difference is statistically significant. However, there is no clear linear relationship between the frequency of shopping for clothes and political consumerism. Rather, both those who shop for clothes very little and very frequently tend to be less aware of the politics of the products they buy than consumers who shop with average frequency. Surely, infrequent clothes shopping contributes to having no clue about labels on clothes; yet it is also true that too much consumption of clothes goes against the ethics of political consumerism. This last point reflects the critical attitude political consumers take toward pure consumer society. Overall, it appears that the predominance of women as political consumers cannot be explained by the fact that they shop more than men, at least not based on the evidence in the Swedish data.

Is it perhaps the case that women know more labeling schemes than men? The SOM data reveal that there is no significant difference between men and women in their knowledge of labeling schemes such as Good Environmental Choice, the Swedish organic food label (Krav), Fairtrade, and the Nordic Ecolabel (Svanen) (results not shown). The only gender difference found is for the eco-label scheme TCO Utveckling which certifies computers and other office equipment, and which more women than men indicated that they have never heard of. However, women have significantly more trust than men in all other mentioned labeling schemes. In other words, women do not necessarily know the labeling schemes themselves better, but once they know them, they believe more strongly in their legitimacy (see also Sønderskov and Daugbjerg 2011).

We are still left with a puzzle. How can we explain women's predominant interest in political consumerism and trust in labeling schemes? We can only find two plausible explanations for the gender differences in political consumerism. First, women are more likely to be members of consumer and animal rights organizations (results not shown). These memberships have several effects, as they connect women through weak ties, and these loose informal contacts are said to spread information more easily (Granovetter 1973, Putnam 2000). In consumer and animal rights organizations, women obviously also receive more information about consumer issues, which can potentially mobilize political consumer behavior. The second explanation is related to gender differences in societal attitudes. From our work with student samples in Belgium, Sweden, and Canada we know that women care significantly more than men about certain issues when it comes to the shopping considerations of food and clothes/shoes (Stolle and Micheletti 2005). Women care especially more about the protection of animals and children than men when they buy groceries and clothes/shoes. This attitudinal difference serves as an additional motivational source which influences women's political and ethical shopping decisions (ibid).

POLITICAL CONSUMERS' POLITICAL ATTITUDES, NORMS, AND BEHAVIORS

Political consumers are among the most resourceful citizens. They are highly educated and affluent. They are also highly interested in politics. They are also often female. But why, given this profile, do political consumers choose the market as an arena of politics to express their concerns about sustainable development and corporate practices? Are they dissatisfied with how established political institutions are dealing with important political problems? Do they, instead, focus on the corporate world and dismiss traditional channels of citizen influence on politics? If this is the case, we should find that political consumers are more distrusting of conventional institutions than other citizens, and perhaps more trusting of newly emerging international institutions that are able to handle cross-border issues of consumption and production practices. They should also engage more frequently in other emerging forms of political engagement and less frequently in electoral politics. Finally, it is important to understand what the driving motivations and citizenship norms of political consumerism are. In short, this section will draw an attitudinal and behavioral profile of political consumers. To probe these issues, we utilize the *European Social Survey* as well as the extended batteries on political consumerism in the SOM survey and the *Consumption and Societal Issues Survey*. This section proceeds in three steps which include the analysis of (1) political attitudes and behaviors of political consumers, (2) considerations behind shopping choices, and (3) citizenship norms and efficacy.

1) Political Attitudes and Behaviors of Political Consumers

Political consumers have a postmaterialist outlook. In the pooled cross-national sample, a unit increase along a question about the approval of gay marriage increases the odds of being a political consumer by 15 percent, indicating that political consumers are significantly more tolerant when it comes to the lifestyles of gays and lesbians. In seventeen out of twenty-one countries, political consumers took on a more tolerant outlook compared to nonpolitical consumers, and in nine of these countries, significantly so (results not shown). Other analyses reveal that political consumers are significantly more worried about environmental problems and climate change but much less worried than nonpolitical consumers about typical issues for materialists, such as the number of immigrants, unemployment, economic crisis, and terrorism (results from the Swedish study are not shown). This strengthens the insights that political consumers exhibit a typical postmaterialist attitudinal profile. But are they also politically distrusting and critical citizens (Norris 2001)?

A bivariate exploration of political consumerism and trust in the parliament, legal system, police, politicians, the United Nations, and even societal trust (trust in other people more generally) reveals that in most countries there is a positive relationship between trust and political consumerism (results not shown). In most longstanding democracies in particular, political consumers are also more trusting of the various political institutions, whereas in Eastern and Southern Europe, the relationship between trust and political consumerism is more varied. What stands out is that political consumers seem to be a bit more skeptical of the police and the legal systems in their respective countries, although trust in the police is absolutely speaking high, still in thirteen out of the twenty-one countries, political consumers trust the police less than nonpolitical consumers, often significantly so. It is also striking that in many countries besides Eastern and Southern Europe as well as the United States, political consumers put more confidence in the international organization of the United Nations than nonpolitical consumers. The most stable and unique finding though is that political consumers are by far more trusting of other people. This is perhaps not a surprise, because political consumers need to believe that other people do their own share of boycotting and buycotting, as it works only as a collective phenomenon and would otherwise not be viewed as an effective tool for engaging in politics.

Going beyond the trust analysis, Table 3.3 presents the results of a logistic regression model including the baseline model discussed above as well as a summated rating scale of institutional trust and two forms of political participation, electoral and innovative. Controlling for other factors though, institutional trust loses some of its positive relationship, indicating that for the high levels of political interest and education that political consumers have, they should be more trusting in these institutions than they actually are. The sign of the institutional trust scale reverses in the majority of countries, but does not reach significance. So, the results of the cross-national analysis tell us that for their sociodemographic background political consumers are less trusting, but not enough in order for institutional distrust to be an important factor in their motivations. This finding does not support the assumption that critical attitudes toward political institutions foster or mobilize political consumerism. However, it does not necessarily contradict the concept of individualized responsibility-taking, which is theoretically linked to the notion that citizens recognize the inability, unwillingness, or inadequacy of governments to solve important political problems. We return to this idea in the conclusion.

Do political consumers engage in other acts of participation compared to nonpolitical consumers? According to the theoretical assumptions, we would expect them more than others to engage in emerging action repertoires. In Table 3.3, we show that in every single country political consumers are by far significantly more engaged in innovative politics. In fact, a unit increase on the emerging action repertoire scale increases the odds of being a political consumer by thirteen times, confirming that political consumers are much more engaged in these innovative repertoires. In the United States, Greece, or Poland political consumers particularly stand out with a high engagement in acts such as petition signing, demonstrating, or illegal protests compared to nonpolitical consumers. At the same time, political consumers are overall also more engaged in electoral political activities, such as contacting politicians, working for a political party or organization, or donating money for a political cause. A one-unit increase along the electoral participation scale increases the odds of being a political consumer by four times. However the effect is visibly smaller and not always significant. This means that although political consumers are more engaged in conventional politics compared to nonpolitical consumers, they really participate more in innovative politics. This finding clearly shows that political consumerism does not crowd out other forms of political participation; indeed, political consumerism is an additional tool of participation for those who are already active, particularly in other new types of participation.

TABLE 3.3. *Individual-Level Model – Trust and Participation*

Country	Constant	Institutional Trust	Forms of Participation According to Factor Solution (Electoral)	Forms of Participation According to Factor Solution (Non-Electoral)	N	Nagelkerke
All countries	−3.520***	.058***	1.458***	2.584***	30,891	.280
	.030	1.059	4.296	13.244		
Austria	−3.443***	−.064**	.871***	2.857***	1,688	.232
	.032	.938	2.390	17.406		
Belgium	−3.578***	.138***	1.411***	2.915***	1,365	.310
	.028	1.148	4.099	18.474		
Czech Rep.	−2.601*	−.094*	2.158***	2.658***	936	.266
	.074	.910	8.654	14.261		
Denmark	−2.542***	.019	.686*	1.516***	1,260	.204
	.079	1.020	1.985	4.555		
Finland	−1.604***	−.013	1.542***	2.089***	1,828	.239
	.201	.987	4.672	8.073		
France	−3.187***	−.097**	1.278***	2.137***	1,346	.307
	.041	.907	3.589	8.473		
Germany	−2.643***	−.035	1.441***	1.945***	2,523	.206
	.071	.965	4.227	6.992		
Greece	−4.064***	−.066*	1.198***	4.161***	1,739	.303
	.017	.936	3.315	64.129		
Hungary	−2.905***	.029	2.009***	3.120***	1,122	.252
	.055	1.029	7.453	22.650		
Ireland	−2.838***	−.001	1.286***	2.654***	1,412	.286
	.059	.999	3.619	14.209		
Italy	−5.481***	.027	.587	3.153***	879	.316
	.004	1.027	1.799	23.412		
Netherlands	−3.050***	.074**	1.836***	3.186***	2,096	.266
	.047	1.077	6.269	24.194		
Norway	−1.970***	.018	1.684***	1.676***	1,936	.240
	.139	1.018	5.387	5.343		
Poland	−4.891***	−.045	2.065***	3.709***	1,462	.277
	.008	.956	7.889	40.822		
Portugal	−4.290***	−.089	2.755***	1.774***	963	.338
	.014	.915	15.724	5.892		
Slovenia	−2.166***	.016	2.030***	2.761***	1,067	.174
	.115	1.017	7.613	15.816		
Spain	−3.867***	−.035	1.387***	2.186***	1,168	.280
	.021	.966	4.002	8.901		
Sweden	−1.720***	−.032	1.211***	1.975***	1,743	.212
	.179	.968	3.358	7.205		
Switzerland	−2.048***	.003	1.720***	2.081***	1,731	.237
	.129	1.003	5.586	8.011		
U.K.	−4.428***	−.030	1.798***	2.361***	1,751	.283
	.012	.970	6.039	10.605		
U.S.	−3.696***	−.066	2.843***	4.361***	876	.438
	.025	.936	17.172	78.312		

*** p<0.01; ** p<0.05; * p<0.1.

Source: European Social Survey (Jowell 2003) and CID survey (Howard, Gibson, and Stolle 2006).

Orientations and Values of Political Consumers

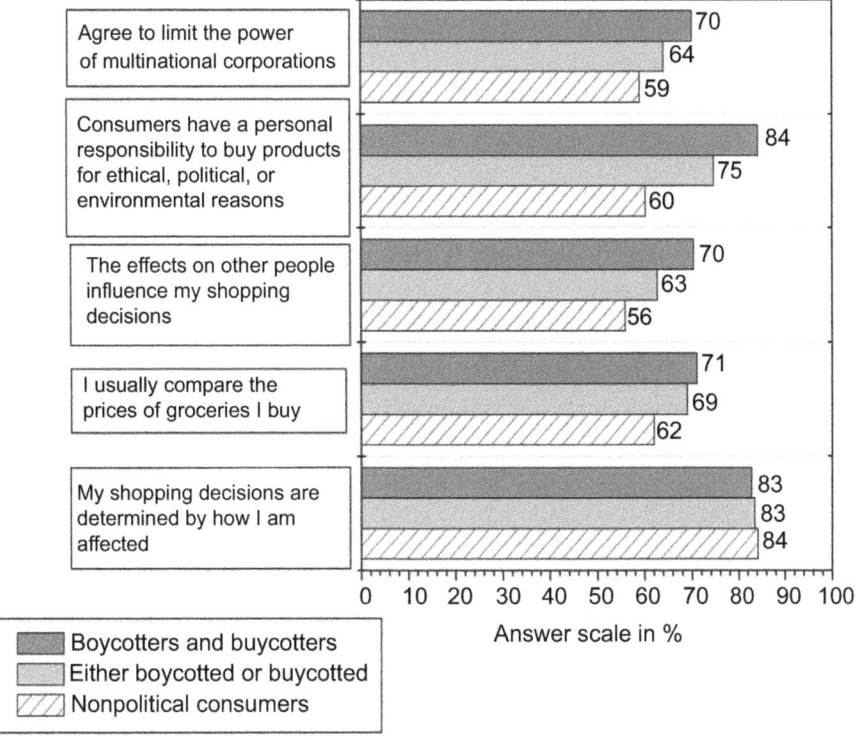

Agree to limit the power of multinational corporations	70 / 64 / 59
Consumers have a personal responsibility to buy products for ethical, political, or environmental reasons	84 / 75 / 60
The effects on other people influence my shopping decisions	70 / 63 / 56
I usually compare the prices of groceries I buy	71 / 69 / 62
My shopping decisions are determined by how I am affected	83 / 83 / 84

0 10 20 30 40 50 60 70 80 90 100

Answer scale in %

▓ Boycotters and buycotters
▨ Either boycotted or buycotted
▧ Nonpolitical consumers

FIGURE 3.5. Values and Orientations of Political Consumers. *Source:* SOM 2003 (N = 1,673).

2) Considerations Behind Shopping Choices

The *European Social Survey* was not designed for the analysis of political consumers; however, some survey items in the two Swedish surveys allow us to dig further into the attitudinal profile of political consumers by asking questions about various aspects of shopping decisions when buying groceries as well as clothes and shoes, or about the responsibility of consumers to watch out for specifics of the production process. Figure 3.5 shows similarities and differences in how political consumers and nonpolitical consumers view several dimensions of consumer products. For this analysis, the Swedish SOM sample was divided into three groups: (1) nonpolitical consumers, (2) people who have either boycotted or buycotted, and (3) people who are both boycotters and buycotters. Several questions about the considerations that go into specific shopping decisions for clothes or groceries were divided into self-regarding (price, quality, and respondent or family's health) and other-regarding (ethical and political considerations, working conditions in the production country, environmental consequences of the production process, animal rights). Figure 3.5 shows the differences and similarities in motivations behind shopping decisions for the three groups of consumers. Interestingly, the three types of consumers consider the price and quality of goods as well as their own and their family's health as the most important factors when making shopping decisions. Political consumerism is, therefore, not a selfless phenomenon; political consumers take into account self-interest when they shop. In fact, Figure 3.5 reveals that political consumers are more often comparative shoppers. This is interesting as it shows that they, generally speaking, are concerned consumers who have reasons to consider the price of goods in their shopping decisions. At the same time, they are other-oriented and give substantially more weight to looking into the "politics of products" than nonpolitical consumers. They look at clothing labels, lists of ingredients on packages, and labeling schemes to see whether the product leaves an undesirable footprint. They wonder whether their consumer choices have hidden environmental consequences and if they have an impact on animal rights as well as on general working conditions in the countries that manufacture consumer goods, and they generally reflect on other ethical and political considerations.

But why do they do this? Why do they care? The survey asked if it is every consumer's personal responsibility to choose between different products and labels on the basis of ethical, political, or environmental considerations. Both groups of political consumers answered affirmatively, significantly more so than nonpolitical consumers. Political consumers who are both boycotters and buycotters are, however, the group most concerned with personal responsibility-taking, as 84 percent of them agree with the statement. Finally, as opinions on multinational corporations are the target of many political consumerist campaigns (as illustrated by the focus on Nike and Nestlé; see Shaw 1999, Baby Milk Action 2011), the survey also asked about curbing the power of multinational corporations. Political consumers were found to be more in favor of limiting their power, with the group of boycotters and buycotters most in favor. In general, political consumers show lower trust in corporate leaders and are more critical about the corporate world than nonpolitical consumers.

In sum, according to the Swedish data, political consumers think about more than just economic and self-interested concerns when they make choices among products. They look beyond the material quality of products and pay attention to how and under what conditions products are made. Political consumers think about the consequences that their consumer choices have on others. But at the same time, they possess the same high degree of self-interest as other citizens. The difference is that they have an elevated sense of personal responsibility-taking for the impact of their choices on others. Clearly, they are not inward-oriented citizens; instead, they express concern for societal debates that focus on the principles of sustainable development. These considerations are tied to policy preferences as illustrated by the proposal to curb the power of multinational corporations and the desire to use subpolitical means to make a political mark.

3) Citizenship Norms and Efficacy

For this part of the analysis, we compare citizenship norms across political consumers and nonpolitical consumers. How do people's citizenship norms relate to the practice of political consumerism? The *Consumption and Societal Issues Survey* asked about several citizenship norms. A factor analysis generated three different citizenship dimensions (results not shown). The *duty norm* contains beliefs about good citizenship vis-à-vis the state and entails obeying the laws of the land and codes of conduct of the welfare state; the *solidarity norm* expands citizenship a bit by involving showing consideration and concern for others in and outside one's own country; the *information-seeking norm* probes citizen views on being prepared to take their own initiative to seek information about societal developments. Bivariate analyses not reported here show that political consumers rate citizenship norms on all three dimensions to be more important than non-political consumers. However, the solidarity norm shows the strongest difference, indicating that political consumers can be distinguished most clearly by this dimension. This is further corroborated by the regression models in Table 3.4 which includes similar controls as in previous models (model 1), and adds citizenship norms (model 2) as well as political trust and external efficacy (model 3). Those scoring high on the more borderless solidarity norm also practice more political consumerism, whereas the duty and information-seeking norms do not relate specifically to practicing political consumerism. As the solidarity norm involves nonreciprocal notions not confined to the nation-state, political consumers, therefore, seem to understand the spatial (that is geographical reach) relationship and material focus of citizenship responsibility vis-à-vis other citizens differently than nonpolitical consumers (for further discussion see Micheletti et al. forthcoming).

A set of values potentially influential on the propensity to engage in political consumerism involves an assessment of sense of personal and institutional efficacy about the sources of societal change. How people perceive government's problem-solving capacity is an important gauge of a citizen's belief in the ability of societal actors to resolve sustainability problems. If citizens fear that government either does not recognize or cannot control new societal uncertainties and risks, they may decide to try new arenas and methods to solve these problems (Beck 1999, Inglehart 1997, Ostrom 1990, Spaargaren and Mol 2008, McFarland 2010). Following scholarship on collective action (Finkel and Muller 1998, Teorell, Torcal, and Montéro 2007), the decision to get more involved can be and has been found to be dependent on whether one believes that people similar to oneself are able to influence societal developments. If this reasoning is correct, political consumers should have more positive views than others about the efficacy or ability of individuals, groups of

TABLE 3.4. *The Socioeconomic and Attitudinal Correlates of Political Consumerism in Sweden*

	Model 1 Socioeconomic N = 975		Model 2 Citizenship Norms N = 975		Model 3 Trust and Efficacy N = 921	
	B	SE	B	SE	B	SE
Socioeconomic position and ideology						
Gender (woman = 1; man = 0)	3.0**	.41	1.9**	.33	2.1**	.33
Age	.04**	.01	.03*	.01	.04**	.01
Education (university studies = 1; else = 0)	1.3**	.44	.32	.35	−.11	.35
Children	−.075	.55	−.38	.43	−.49	.43
Economic situation	.02	.09	−.06	.07	−.09	.07
Living area (large city = 1; else = 0)	.81	.46	.41	.35	.42	.35
Ideology (left = 0)	−.64**	.09	−.25**	.07	−.19**	.08
Citizenship ideals						
Solidarity citizenship			2.2**	.11	2.1**	.11
Duty citizenship			.07	.11	.06	.11
Information seeking citizenship			.01	.14	.08	.14
Trust						
Representative institutions					−.03	.09
International institutions					−.08	.10
Sustainability institutions					.50**	.12
Efficacy						
Institutions					−.13	.09
People					.39**	.09
Constant	22.9**	.9	7.4**	1.13	5.1**	1.28
Model fit						
Adjusted R²	.12		.47		.50	
Standard Error of Regression	6.3		4.9		4.8	

* p<.05; ** p <.01.
Notes: Cell entries are unstandardized b-values (B), standard errors (SE), and model performance statistics.
Source: Consumption and Societal Issues Survey.

individuals, and nongovernmental actors to influence society. In contrast, individualized responsibility-theorizing suggests that political consumers should be less convinced about the efficacy of political institutions to contribute to change in society. To analyze this, we included perceptions of efficacy that distinguish the efficacy of *political institutions* and of *people* (and *corporations*). The political institutions efficacy dimension includes questions about politicians, public authorities, and international organizations (European Union, United Nations, World Trade Organization). The nongovernmental dimension includes oneself, people more generally, and corporations. The perceived efficacy of institutions and of people is positively correlated with political consumerism in a bivariate analysis,[8] but controls for other variables show that the general perceptions of political institution's capacity is not important. Rather, what stands out are the strong beliefs of political consumers in the capacity of other people and corporations to initiate social change and transform current practices and institutional orders (see Table 3.4). That is, political consumers believe more strongly than nonpolitical consumers in the efficacy of people and other such actors, whereas they cannot be distinguished in their beliefs in the efficacy of traditional institutions.

That is also true (as in the cross-national data in Table 3.3) for institutional trust in Sweden. Factor analysis revealed three different trust dimensions, which were captured in scales. The first is a summated rating scale measuring trust in mainstream political institutions (parties, the parliament, the national and local government), whereas the second measures trust in institutions of the European Union (the Commission and the European Parliament). The third scale measures trust in organizations that have a consumer profile, that is the Swedish Consumer Agency and independent consumer organizations, thus offering an institutional alternative to political consumers.[9] Including these scales in a logistic regression model with socioeconomic controls indicates that all else being equal, political consumers are not distinguished from nonpolitical consumers by their trust in mainstream or international political institutions, but by their higher trust in consumer-oriented organizations. Thus, political consumers do not take much more of a critical stance on traditional political institutions (cf. Norris 1999), but they are more trusting of institutions that have the issues of transparency and accountability of consumer goods and the corporate world on their agenda, as exemplified by international and domestic consumer organizations and public consumer agencies (see also Berlin 2011).

CONCLUSION

This chapter reviews and examines political consumerism as a form of political participation. Analysis of available survey data shows that a substantial

---

[8] Correlation for institutional efficacy = .14 p<.01; for people efficacy = .27 p<.01
[9] All three scales showed a Cronbach's alpha around .80.

group of citizens fuse citizenship with their shopping routines. More than half of the population in Sweden (57 percent) was found to have undertaken at least one form of political consumerism. Buycotting (deliberately purchasing goods for political, environmental, or ethical reasons) is practiced by 51 percent of all adult Swedes. Outside Sweden as well, political consumerism has become more widespread. Most importantly, this chapter attempts to explain and understand individual acts of political consumerism. This cross-national analysis found that political consumers are most of all educated, politically interested, female, middle-aged, and somewhat more left-leaning, richer, and urban than nonpolitical consumers. Women are more engaged in political consumerism than men, thus leading to what we call the reversed gender gap. The historical role of women in political advances related to food and other types of consumption and their openness to shopping motivations related to protecting children and animals are possible explanations for the rise of this phenomenon. Political consumers are not necessarily less trusting of electoral political institutions as some theories would expect, but they do believe more in the trustworthiness of consumer agencies.

Overall, political consumerism is, like many other forms of participation, related to inequality in participation. Women, who are usually less represented in several forms of participation, have caught up here, but this mode of activity is still nevertheless dominated by the highly educated, the rich, the middle-aged, and urban professionals. So, although some previously excluded groups are more engaged in political consumerism, others are still not included. However, taking the evidence of Chapters 2 and 3 together, there is reason to believe that political consumerism is on the way to becoming a mainstream phenomenon.

Other findings about the values, attitudes, and behaviors of political consumers are noteworthy. First, most political consumers (but not all) generally engage in several forms of political participation, but mostly in non-electoral ones. They are, therefore, active citizens who like to use means beyond voting to express their political voices. Second, they are like other citizens with regard to belief in law and order (duty citizenship) but differ from other citizens because they are more solidarity-oriented and, therefore, adhere more to borderless solidarity citizenship than other citizens. This finding clearly refutes the criticism that political consumerism is solely self-oriented in nature. Although self-interest plays a role in political consumerism, as political consumers are just as interested in the quality and price of the products as nonpolitical consumers, they mention more frequently other-regarding motivations that include for instance labor conditions and environmental effects (see Figure 3.5).

Furthermore, political consumers believe more in the ability of ordinary people and corporations to solve political problems. At the same time, they are similar to other citizens in their faith in the role of government institutions to solve problems, but when background characteristics are included, political consumers are less confident than others in similar categories in the abilities of institutions to solve problems (though not significantly so). These results on external efficacy are very interesting given the theoretical expectations. On the one hand, political consumers seem to recognize political power exercised by actors, institutions, and arenas not traditionally part of the representative democracy realm. This result fits with the general ideas about the market as an arena of politics and its ongoing politicization process globally. It also verifies the theory of individualized responsibility-taking in that political consumers believe that ordinary individual citizens have the ability and responsibility to make a difference. On the other hand, political consumers still have faith in national and international governmental institutions to solve societal problems. However, they also have higher trust than nonpolitical consumers in the "sustainability institutions" included in the survey. Thus, their belief in consumer-oriented institutions is quite strong.

An important question is whether these findings invalidate the theory of individualized responsibility-taking? Not necessarily. Although it is surprising that political consumers do not favor more the information-seeking citizenship ideal than nonpolitical consumers, their strong focus on solidarity as a citizenship norm does confirm one of the linking mechanisms of responsibility-taking. Also, although political consumers maintain a certain level of efficacy in governmental organizations, this does not mean that they are ready to rely on them completely to solve societal problems, whether they be local, national or global in nature. Political consumers, in this regard, are similar to aware citizens who decide to participate in politics through a variety of venues and degrees. They most of all believe more than nonpolitical consumers in the efficacy of people and corporations and in the responsibility of individual consumers to make responsible choices – and that is an essence of individualized responsibility-taking. At the same time, they appear to place demands for better policies and practices on the conventional institutions of representative government and on other consumer-oriented institutions.

The skeptics of political consumerism summarized earlier in this chapter and the previous one have also warned that political consumerism is not truly political and can lead to a flight from politics. The survey results do not support such claims. Once again, political consumers are active citizens who use different modes of participation to make their mark on politics. The conclusion is that it does not crowd out other forms of political engagements. Rather it makes politics a more all-round and everyday activity that includes venues other than traditional civil society and the parliamentary sphere. Our investigations show that only a small group of political consumers is solely involved in its practice to the exclusion of other forms of political action. These few political consumers are not so different from nonpolitical consumers.

Without a world government and the accountability mechanism of political citizenship (suffrage and running for political office), concerned individuals must find other ways of affecting change on global institutions – whether they are governmental or corporate in nature. Turning to the market as an arena of politics appears to be an additional venue open for impatient citizens wanting to join together with citizens cross-nationally in taking responsibility in transborder political issues of solidarity. Political consumerism may be one of the few available mechanisms that let them stand up and be counted on matters concerning the political and economic imbalances between the North and the South.

In sum, political consumerism might be only within reach for those groups of the population who already are (because of their cognitive, financial, and other resources) highly active in social and political life. Consumer activities, therefore, might have limits in the way that they can directly substitute for traditional channels of political participation. However, the more citizens shop for eco-labeled products or products that guarantee safety and respect for workers who produce the products, the greater their market share and the more such products would be found to be affordable and in reach of larger groups of the population. From this perspective, the still rather exclusive nature of political consumerism has the potential to become an inclusive form of involvement that should not be forgotten in the debate about our current state of civic behavior.

4

Mapping Political Consumerism in Western Democracies

With Jean-François Crépault

INTRODUCTION

Individual consumers are taking individualized responsibility in that they think about and act upon the consequences of their purchasing decisions for global common pool resources, the environment, and human rights. The analysis of Chapter 3 showed that personal resources, socioeconomic characteristics, solidarity values, and a strong belief in the efficacy of citizens all enable individuals to take responsibility. It became clear that despite the supranational reach of political consumerism, there are wide variations across countries in the potential of such actions. Most likely, the context in which political consumerism is embedded shapes the general resources and opportunities that empower, sensitize, and mobilize political consumers.

The first goal of this chapter is to explore the national variations in behavioral political consumerism across Europe and North America. To be sure, all forms of political consumerism are difficult to quantify, let alone compare cross-nationally. For example, as discussed in detail in Chapter 2, there is no cross-national account of discursive political consumer actions. Rarely either have lifestyle-related political consumer activities made it into any national surveys or other statistics. Thus we have to rely – once again – on existing research that measures the cross-national spread of the two most common forms of political consumerism among citizens –boycotting and buycotting. The *European Social Survey* (Jowell et al. 2003) combined with the *Citizenship, Involvement, Democracy* (CID) survey of the United States (Howard, Gibson, and Stolle 2006) offer the most detailed source of self-reported individual political behavior across a wide variety of democracies – these measures simply remain the best approximations of cross-national political consumerism to date. However, additional market share data of labeled products is added to this analysis, as it allows us to understand the quality of cross-national measurements of political consumerism.

The second purpose of this chapter is to examine why this form of individualized responsibility-taking varies across countries. The combination of survey material and other measures of political consumerism with a variety of economic and political country-based statistics builds the analytical material for the second part of this chapter. Since this chapter includes a wealth of empirical material, many of the measures and data sources are explained in detail in the Appendix and notes.

NATIONAL VARIATIONS IN POLITICAL CONSUMERISM

Comparative results of boycotts and buycotts across twenty-one democracies in Europe and the United States are presented in Table 4.1. The first thing that is immediately noticeable here is that in all but two countries (Greece and Italy) buycotting is more common than boycotting – in many cases twice as common or more. Different reasons might account for this. It might be that the boycotting activity depends on campaigns and mobilization on the basis of current issues, while buycotting is a more regular behavioral pattern in everyday life (Ferrer-Fons 2004). As discussed in Chapter 5 and again in Chapter 8, boycotting is also an activity that is not promoted by most political consumer activist networks anymore because of its adverse effects and outcomes. At the same time, there is a highly significant correlation between these two forms of political consumerism in all studied countries, ranging between 0.36^{***} and 0.57^{***} with an average of 0.49^{***}.[1] This suggests that the two activities are complementary (see Neilson 2010 for a different view). There is no pattern here, however; both high- and low-political consumer countries are among those with the strongest correlations between boycotting and buycotting.

When trying to distinguish countries with high and low levels of political consumerism (using the percentage of individuals who boycott and/or buycott), it becomes noticeable that countries with similar geographic, economic, and political characteristics are clustered together to a remarkable extent. The top five political consumer countries are Sweden, Switzerland, Denmark, Finland, and Germany, while the five lowest are Portugal, Italy, Poland, Hungary, and Greece.

Geographically, then, the top political consumer countries are all in North-western Europe, with Southern and Eastern Europe lagging behind. To be fair, these findings might be due to our limited abilities to measure political consumerism cross-nationally. Research on Italian political consumerism for example shows a different focus, on lifestyle commitment, slow food, worldshops,

---

[1] These stars stand for the p value of the significance test, usually indicated by *** $p < 0.01$, ** $p < 0.05$, * $p < 0.1$.

TABLE 4.1. *The Cross-National Spread of Political Consumerism*

Country	% Not Active at All in 2002	% Boycotting in 2002	% Buycotting in 2002	% Boycotting and/or Buycotting in 2002	% Doing Both in 2002	Correlation between Boycott and Buycott
All countries	69.2	16.8	26.5	30.8	12.4	0.49***
Austria	65.5	21.5	29.7	34.5	16.4	0.54***
Belgium	69.2	12.8	27.0	30.8	9.0	0.37***
Czech Republic	73.7	10.8	22.6	26.3	6.8	0.34***
Denmark	52.2	22.9	43.8	47.8	18.8	0.42***
Finland	52.9	26.8	41.8	47.1	21.6	0.47***
France	63.5	26.6	28.0	36.5	18.2	0.54***
Germany	54.7	26.1	39.2	45.3	20.0	0.46***
Greece	88.0	8.5	6.6	12.0	3.1	0.36***
Hungary	88.3	4.8	10.5	11.7	3.5	0.46***
Ireland	71.5	13.6	24.6	28.5	9.5	0.42***
Italy	89.9	7.6	6.5	10.1	3.9	0.53***
Netherlands	71.6	10.4	25.7	28.4	7.6	0.37***
Norway	58.6	20.3	36.7	41.4	15.5	0.42***
Poland	89.2	3.6	9.8	10.8	2.6	0.40***
Portugal	91.8	3.4	6.9	8.2	2.0	0.39***
Slovenia	88.3	5.1	9.6	11.7	2.8	0.36***
Spain	86.5	8.0	11.6	13.5	5.7	0.57***
Sweden	39.7	32.5	55.1	60.3	27.2	0.40***
Switzerland	49.6	31.4	44.6	50.4	25.6	0.50***
United Kingdom	59.8	26.1	32.3	40.2	18.2	0.48***
United States	71.9	18.2	22.9	28.1	13.0	0.55***

*** $p < 0.01$; ** $p < 0.05$; * $p < 0.1$.

Table entries from columns 1 to 5 represent percentages of political consumerism practiced per country. Column 6 represents Pearson correlation coefficients between individual-level buycotts and boycotts.

Source: European Social Survey (Jowell 2003) and *Citizenship, Involvement, Democracy Survey* (of the United States) (Howard, Gibson, and Stolle 2006). See Appendix for more information.

etc. (Forno and Ceccarini 2006, Sassatelli and Davolio 2010). These different types of lifestyle involvements are simply not measured in the *European Social Survey*, so admittedly our analysis here does not capture all the facets of political consumerism that are perhaps more prevalent in some regions of Western democracies (see more in Chapter 8).

Of course, geography is not the only variable along which these countries are clustered, however. At a glance, it seems that higher-income countries have higher levels of political consumerism than their less wealthy counterparts. It would also appear that the countries with the highest proportion of political consumers are consolidated democracies[2] (that is, democracies that have contested free, fair, and regular elections since at least 1950), while most of the low political consumer countries have fairly recent (postwar) communist or authoritarian legacies. Finally, countries are clustered by religion too, but to a lesser extent, with the top five being either predominantly Protestant (the Scandinavian countries) or mixed Protestant-Catholic (Switzerland and Germany) and the bottom five being Catholic (Portugal, Italy, Poland, Hungary) or Orthodox (Greece).

Again, these numbers are gleaned from the *European Social Survey* and represent respondents' claims to have purchased, or refrained from purchasing, a particular good or service at least once in the past year, based on ethical, environmental or political considerations. These measurements in themselves remain limited because they do not indicate the frequency with which consumers engage in these activities, and might thus misrepresent the extent to which political consumerism is able to capture important market shares (Stolle and Hooghe 2004). So, the question that arises is how these measurements translate into actual market activity.

As discussed in Chapter 2, some forms of buycotting provide an opportunity to observe actual, as opposed to reported, political consumer behavior. The sale of fairtrade[3] goods and in part organic foods has been recorded (see Chapter 2). While no official statistics on organic consumption are kept and it is difficult to gauge demand directly, organic food sales have been estimated for most countries in this study. Figures for sales of other political consumer products such as eco-labeled goods, products certified under forest or marine stewardship programs, "clean" or "no sweat" clothing, socially responsible investment, ethical banking, and other ethically or sustainably produced goods and services are either unavailable or insufficient for cross-national comparison.

For these reasons, this section uses fairtrade coffee and organic foods data from the time period when the surveys were taken to examine cross-national variation in actual (as opposed to reported) buycotting activity, see Table 4.2. Of course, these results represent only two instances of political consumer buycott activity and do not show how much political consumerism or buycotting actually occurs per country – only how much these particular *activities* occur. In addition, the numbers might not solely be a result of individual-level consumption; institutions and governments might also be purchasers of such labeled products (see more in this chapter). Nevertheless, the data analysis shows that there is a correlation between the percentage of people who indicate that they have buycotted and actual market shares and sales of fairtrade coffee and organic foods.

Consumption levels of these "socially responsible" goods range widely. Coffee is by far the highest-selling fairtrade good, though bananas, cocoa, tea,

---

[2] See the use of the term "consolidated democracies" in Inglehart 1997.
[3] About the use of the term fairtrade, see Chapter 2.

TABLE 4.2. *Consumption and Market Share of Labeled Products*

	Fairtrade Coffee: Average Per Capita Consumption in Grams, 2000–6*	Fairtrade Coffee: Average Market Share, 2000–6**	Organic Food: Average Per Capita Consumption in USD, 2002–5***	Organic Food: Market Share, 2001****
Austria	58.55	0.85%	$51.71	2.7%
Belgium	73.51	0.99%	$34.81	1.0%
Canada	26.69	0.41%	$28.82	1.5%
Denmark	120.34	1.34%	$66.60	3.5%
Finland	26.00	0.23%	$38.54	1.0%
France	46.00	0.86%	$36.00	0.7%
Germany	38.43	0.56%	$49.45	2.1%
Ireland	30.52	1.36%	n.a.	0.5%
Italy	5.09	0.09%	$39.88	0.7%
Japan	0.42	0.01%	$3.35	n.a.
Netherlands	186.54	2.88%	$29.97	1.2%
Norway	66.17	0.72%	$8.16	0.2%
Sweden	46.13	0.56%	$57.22	1.7%
Switzerland	194.19	2.94%	$122.22	3.7%
United Kingdom	52.06	2.27%	$36.22	0.9%
United States	23.29	0.56%	$40.51	1.5%

Table entries from column 1 represent domestic sales of Fairtrade coffee in grams, divided by the total population of each country. Column 2 represents the percentage of total national coffee sales that is Fairtrade. Column 3 represents domestic sales of organic food, divided by the total population of each country. Column 4 represents the percentage of organic food that is sold in supermarkets. For sources and methodology, see Appendix.

  * This measure captures individual as well as some institutional purchases of Fairtrade coffee. See more on government procurement policies later in the chapter.
 ** Belgium data includes Luxembourg. Data from 2005–2006 are estimates; see Appendix for methodology.
*** Belgium data from 2001–2003; Finland data from 2003–2005; Norway data from 2004–2005.
**** Canada data from 2002; United States data from 2003.

and other commodities are becoming increasingly popular. Global sales of fairtrade coffee were approximately 10,000 metric tons in 1996 and reached just over 50,000 tons by 2006 (see Chapter 2). Growth was especially impressive between 2005 and 2006 when global sales expanded by more than 50 percent fuelled mainly by skyrocketing sales in the United States. The United States has rapidly increased its share of global fairtrade coffee consumption, rising from 5.5 percent in 2000 to 18.5 percent in 2003 to a remarkable 45.2 percent in 2006 (FLO 2007). At this rate, the majority of fairtrade coffee consumption will soon occur in the United States.

Looking first at per capita consumption of fairtrade coffee in Table 4.2, we find Switzerland and the Netherlands far ahead, and Denmark also near the top. These three countries lead by a wide margin, with Denmark's per capita consumption nearly twice as high as that of Belgium, the country with the next highest rate. Italy and Japan bring up the rear. But coffee consumption rates vary greatly from one country to another; for example, Finland's annual per capita consumption of coffee is more than five times that of the United Kingdom or Ireland. For this reason, it is also useful to look at market share data, which indicates the portion of the total national coffee market captured by fairtrade. Using this measure, the ranking shifts a bit: the top two remain unchanged, but the United Kingdom rises to third, just ahead of Ireland and Denmark. Fairtrade coffee consumption has spiked sharply in the United Kingdom since 2005, when it surpassed Switzerland as the top global consumer of this product in terms of market share. This share reached an estimated 4.51 percent in 2006. By both measures, Japan and Italy rank lowest.

As detailed in Chapter 2, data on the sales of organically labeled goods exhibit similar trends. In 2005, global sales of organic food totaled 33 billion USD (Willer and Yussefi 2006). The United States was responsible for 31 percent of this consumption. Regarding the annual average consumer expenditure for organic food, Table 4.2 reveals that Switzerland leads by far while Denmark and Sweden follow; Norway and Japan lag far behind. These numbers may be somewhat distorted by differences in relative food prices. Market share data might be more useful here. Recent information on the latter is patchy and often contradictory,[4] but evidence suggests that in 2005 Switzerland had the highest organic market share at about 4.5 percent, with most West European and North American countries ranging between 1 percent and 2 percent (Willer and Yussefi 2003, 2004). To have a wide spectrum of cross-national data that includes all of the countries in the survey sample, we must go back to 2001. These estimates suggest that Switzerland, Denmark, and Austria have the highest organic market shares. Norway, Italy, Ireland, and France lag behind.

Beyond fairtrade and organic foods, it is possible to get a partial glimpse of national markets for other political consumer goods and services. One such indicator is socially responsible investment (SRI). This indicator is problematic because it taps into not only individuals' banking and investment decisions but also those of NGOs, churches, and particularly institutions managing pension and mutual funds. In this way, it is an indirect measure of the role of individuals in globalized responsibility-taking: SRI may rise in response to demand for increased corporate social responsibility but those directly involved are more often institutions rather than individuals.[5] For our purposes, a study of retail

[4] This is because estimates of overall food sales are difficult to obtain and differ a great deal from one source to the next.
[5] Another challenge is that most SRI studies are national in scope and, given the wide range of benchmarks used to calculate SRI, are usually not comparable cross-nationally.

SRI in fifteen European countries will be used (Avanzi 2003, 2006).[6] According to this study, the largest SRI market in Europe between 1999 and 2006 was the United Kingdom, with an average size of over 8 billion USD per year. As of 2007, the authors of this study found no SRI funds in Denmark, Finland, Ireland, Norway, or Poland. Measured per capita, the largest retail SRI markets were Switzerland (285 USD per person), Sweden (282 USD per person), and Belgium (218 USD per person). The absence of SRI funds in Scandinavia outside of Sweden is difficult to explain, given high levels of other types of political consumerism in those countries.

Finally, very limited sales data are available for Forest Stewardship Council (FSC)-certified timber (see more on FSC certification in Chapters 5 and 8). The FSC estimated in 2005 that global sales of certified sustainable timber had reached 5 billion USD (FSC 2005). The top consumer of FSC-certified timber that year was the United Kingdom with more than 1.7 billion USD in sales. Meanwhile, it was estimated that fully 12 percent of the Dutch market for timber had been captured by FSC-certified products, a total of 420 million USD. These measures are too partial and too indirect to allow for inferences about cross-national variations in political consumerism, but they certainly give a glimpse of the geographic variance in actual political consumer activities.

The best cross-national overview of actual market behavior of political consumers is thus captured by the sale of fairtrade coffee and organic foods. How well do rates of reported political consumerism match up with actually observed market shares in these two areas? Taken together, there are a few interesting surprises in this first direct comparison of fairtrade and organic sales data as well as survey data on self-reported buycott activity. Switzerland and Denmark are among the leaders in all categories of buycotting, both self-reported and observed; however, other countries with top percentages of self-estimated buy-cotters such as Sweden and Finland are not; Sweden has high consumption rates of organic foods but is a relatively low purchaser of fairtrade coffee (see more in Micheletti et al. forthcoming). Meanwhile, Finland and Germany rank low for both types of political consumerism while the United Kingdom ranks highly, which its survey results would not have led us to expect. It may be that in some of the countries with the highest rates of reported buycotting, consumers prefer activities such as buying eco-labeled goods or ethically-sourced clothing, or other political consumer products over buying fairtrade coffee or organic foods. Alternatively, it could be that these goods are not widely available in

---

[6] It should be noted that the authors of the study count socially responsible funds according to where they are based – not where they are bought. That is, if an Austrian organization purchases a Germany-based SRI fund, the fund counts toward the German SRI figure. Funds have been converted from Euros to U.S. dollars at a rate of 1 € = $1.28. These figures represent the median of daily Bank of Canada exchange rates (251 opening days) for 2006. Available at "10 year currency converter," Bank of Canada, http://www.bankofcanada.ca/en/rates/exchform. html (accessed December 14, 2007).

these countries. The survey data also does not capture the regularity with which political consumers actually do make ethical or political shopping decisions, which might also explain some mismatch between survey and market/sales data (see more on this in Chapter 2).

However, when relating the measures of political consumer activity to each other, the percentage of individuals per country who claim to buycott correlates with fairtrade coffee per capita sales at 0.576*** (N = 21), with Fairtrade coffee market share at 0.503** (N = 21) and organic food sales per capita at 0.698*** (N = 15), and with organic market share at 0.684*** (N = 18). This means that the claimed engagement of citizens in our survey data and the actual market share of organic and fairtrade-labeled products do indeed correlate relatively strongly to each other, despite the few irregularities we found. This lends substantial validity to our survey data, though the actual percentage of people who claim to participate in political consumerism is by far higher than the actual market share or sales of certain labeled products. This discrepancy is addressed in Chapter 2.

EXPLAINING WEAK AND STRONG POLITICAL CONSUMERISM

This book investigates political consumerism as a way citizens can take personal responsibility for global developments. As discussed in Chapter 1, citizens involved in political consumerism realize that their national governments are not able or willing to solve globalized problems that relate to the association of consumption and production with sustainable development. They have been sensitized to take their own individualized responsibility, and thus engage in more DIY (do-it-yourself) activism, spontaneous and sporadic forms of responsibility-taking. Buying labeled products, rejecting others that are not consistent with their basic values or discussing consumer issues with others, and generally targeting markets with their political and social values, are only a few ways for consumers to act as responsible citizens. Although it is difficult to correctly measure the extensiveness of the variety of people's market-based political actions, the examples given above show clearly that political consumerism varies cross-nationally and across a number of measures; at the same time, countries with similar characteristics tend to be clustered together. A more penetrating analysis is necessary to answer the question of which country characteristics might best be able to explain this cross-national variation.

Indeed, we have argued earlier that the "burden" of individualized responsibility-taking might be stronger in Western democratic countries where socioeconomic resources and affluence as well as civil and political rights are most developed. This is so because responsibility-taking requires high levels of information access and abilities of analysis, which are related to high levels of socioeconomic and educational resources. Democracy offers a framework within which such individual capacities can be realized and relatively freely acted upon. Furthermore, within democratic countries the responsibility-taking claim on individuals might be stronger where the social rights of citizenship (that is, a welfare state that provides employment, good education, health care, and so on) are well-developed and thus provide resources as well as the abilities to access and accumulate information necessary to take "consumer social responsibility." Some of these aspects have also been important in explaining conditions that foster postmaterialism, a value change that seems conducive to individualized, unconventional and so-called elite-challenging forms of political participation and responsibility-taking (Inglehart 1997, Welzel and Inglehart 2005). Furthermore, we expect that in countries with more mobilizational resources such as political consumer activist groups and networks, citizen-consumers are more sensitized to issues of consumer social responsibility, and perhaps more motivated to follow through with responsible action.

Accordingly, three sets of factors that potentially explain the rather stark country variation in political consumerism are investigated in this section. As will become clear, they resemble factors that underlie the logic of individualized responsibility-taking, as well as those that are important for political participation generally, for unconventional or creative participation more specifically, and also include a set of factors targeted uniquely at political consumerism. First, typical country characteristics that explain differences in political participation, such as level of democracy, GDP, social capital, religion, education, and socioeconomic equality are explored. The second set of factors are country characteristics related to processes of postmodernization and various resulting forms of unconventional, extra-parliamentary, and nonhierarchical political action. In this context, the employment in the service sector, again GDP per capita, education, and expansive welfare states in particular will be highlighted. Finally, specific country characteristics solely related to political consumerism (and not all forms of emerging political action repertoires) are explored. They include price premiums of labeled products (that is, the difference in price between conventional and labeled products), political consumer infrastructures with conducive institutional arrangements (such as legacy of neo-corporatism or market responsiveness to political consumer issues), and political factors such as left party power and green party success, economic openness and density of multinational corporations, all of which might foster market-based political actions. These general factors have been grouped into seven areas of inquiry, which are discussed and examined below. The analysis will shed light on the macro-level contexts in which political consumerism thrives. In the following, unless otherwise indicated, the dependent variable to be explained is the national percentage of individuals who boycott and/or buycott according to the ESS (Jowell 2003) and CID survey (Howard, Gibson, and Stolle 2006) (see Table 4.1 of this chapter).[7]

---

[7] Although more recent versions of the *European Social Survey* exist, they did not ask a question regarding buycotting; for this reason, ESS 2002 is used.

TABLE 4.3. *The Role of Socioeconomic Resources and Postmodernization for Political Consumerism*

	Political Consumerism Entire Sample	Political Consumerism Western Democracies
GNI per capita, (constant 2000 international $ PPP), average 1990–2003	0.660***	0.075
	N = 21	N = 14
Employment in services (% of total employment), average 1994–2003	0.706***	0.337
	N = 21	N =14
Years of continuous democracy, 2003	0.738***	0.277
	N = 21	N = 14
Labor force with tertiary education (% of total), latest available year	0.616***	0.481*
	N = 20	N = 13

*** p < 0.01, ** p < 0.05, * p < 0.1.

Table entries represent Pearson correlation coefficients between aggregate-level political consumerism and the variables listed in the first column. For sources and methodology, see Appendix.

1) Socioeconomic Resources and Postmodernization

The first set of factors captures socioeconomic resources that generally enhance citizens' ability to gather and analyze information. In Ronald Inglehart's post-modernization thesis, industrial societies that achieve a high degree of economic security tend to experience a shift in values and belief systems – from "materialist" values, which emphasize economic and physical security, to "postmaterialist" values, which privilege quality of life and self-expression. As discussed in Chapter 3, political consumers tend to hold postmaterialist values. Since postmaterialist societies are wealthy countries, with a high gross national income (GNI) per capita, and where the citizens benefit from high levels of tertiary education (defined as the percentage of individuals with some university or college education, whether a degree was completed or not)[8] and a large majority of the labor force is employed in the service sector (that is, jobs outside of the agricultural and manufacturing sectors), it is plausible to assume that these characteristics also relate to high levels of political consumerism (Inglehart 1997, Welzel and Inglehart 2005). Postmaterialist countries also have a long tradition of continuous democracy. Table 4.3 below shows correlations between these indicators and political consumerism (the national percentage of individuals who boycott and/or buycott).

As shown in the left column of Table 4.3, all of these variables correlate very highly with political consumerism – consolidated democracies, wealthy

---

[8] Trade or professional certifications were not included.

countries, and those with high levels of employment in services and tertiary education are all countries with high rates of political consumerism. In this sense, there seems to be a preliminary confirmation of the association of political consumerism with postmaterialist societies. But to state that political consumerism occurs more in Western democracies is to confirm what was already known, whether these societies are called postmaterialist or not. What is more interesting is whether the broader distinctions between Western democracies and the rest of our cases may obscure significant patterns within the group of countries with high political consumerism. The inclusion in our analysis of formerly communist countries in particular, with their very divergent histories and specific economic and institutional characteristics, may hide other characteristics that matter beyond democratic legacy and economic development. The formerly communist countries score lower on economic indicators, length of democracy, the employment in services, employment with tertiary education, and also political consumerism. Therefore, a new analysis strategy will be employed, which first presents the results of all selected factors within the entire sample of twenty-one European democracies and the United States and then again for the reduced sample of only fourteen Western democracies.[9] Since the democracies of Western Europe and the United States have enjoyed an uninterrupted period of democracy since 1945, as well as similarly high levels of economic development and a rise in the service industry, this two-step procedure effectively controls for these factors, helping to uncover other relevant country characteristics facilitative of political consumer action beyond democratic experience and economic development.[10] This separate focus is also appropriate given the fact that Western democracies account for the majority of global production and consumption, and thus the majority of the global problems associated with these activities.

As shown in the right-hand column of Table 4.3, most of the postmodernization indicators are no longer as relevant when controlling for continuous democracy and economic development, confirming that these differences between the twenty-one Western countries may overpower our analysis. Education is an important exception of these indicators of postmodernization:

---

[9] It should be noted that the seven countries being temporarily removed from the second analysis step (Czech Republic, Greece, Hungary, Poland, Portugal, Slovenia, and Spain) are not only democratic laggards, but also the least wealthy in terms of GNI per capita and have the lowest percentage of employment in services.

[10] This group comprises fourteen countries with the longest period of continuous democracy, which also rank highest in terms of GNI per capita and employment in services. They are: Austria, Belgium, Denmark, Finland, France, Germany, Ireland, Italy, the Netherlands, Norway, Sweden, Switzerland, the United States, and the United Kingdom. (Canada and Japan are also included when the dependent variable is something other than reported political consumerism, for which we have no Canadian or Japanese data.) Methodologically, though, it needs to be pointed out that the analyses in the smaller groups of countries render the focus on significance tests in correlational analyses meaningless. Therefore, the sole strength of the correlation is examined and compared in this smaller sub-sample.

even within the group of Western democracies, higher national levels of tertiary education are associated with more political consumerism. Chapter 3 already discussed the major role education plays at the individual level in terms of political engagement and acquiring knowledge about political consumer issues; clearly, this holds for the national level as well: countries with higher levels of education also provide more resources for their citizens to engage in individualized responsibility-taking. This analysis gives strong evidence of this relationship and future chapters discuss how university campuses in particular are important facilitators of political consumerism (see Chapters 5, 6, and 8).

Furthermore, the percentage of employment in the service industry as well as the years of democracy still show reasonably large correlations to political consumerism, although they have lost statistical significance because of the reduced sample size. This means that even within the group of Western democracies, the development of the service industry and the length of democratic experience still correlate fairly well with the level of political consumerism. In sum, political consumerism is more prevalent in postmodern societies – that is in countries with long democratic experiences, higher economic development, and higher levels of education.

2) Economic Openness

Political consumerism clearly targets transnational corporations. Thus it is plausible that in countries with higher levels of economic globalization and a higher density of multinational corporations, citizens have more information about the corporate world. Such information might include media discussions about corporate activities, scandals, or simply awareness about national historical examples. This information in turn might mobilize consumer activists and consumers to express their (dis)pleasure with corporate activities, which may provide overall more opportunities for citizens to put political consumer demands on corporations (Bennett 2004a, 2004b). Therefore, measures of manufacturing abroad, and specifically the spread, density, and size of transnational corporations, might also correlate with levels of political consumerism. In brief, economic openness might provide further opportunities for action by those concerned with the negative effects of production and consumption on common pool and human resources.

For this study, economic openness is measured by foreign direct investment flows, trade dependence, the number of Fortune 500 corporations based in the economy, and the number of transnational corporations either based in the economy (parent corporations) or having subsidiaries there (foreign affiliates). These indicators are measured as a percentage of GNI or per capita when appropriate in order to control for the size of the economy or society (see Appendix). Table 4.4 presents correlations between various indicators of economic openness and political consumerism.

TABLE 4.4. *Does Economic Openness Foster Political Consumerism?*

	Entire Sample	Western Democracies
Foreign direct investment, average net inflows (% of GDP), average 1993–2003	0.118	−0.071
	N = 21	N = 14
Foreign direct investment, average net outflows (% of GDP), average 1993–2003	0.330	0.049
	N = 20	N = 14
Economic openness (exports + imports as % of real GDP in constant prices), average 1990–2003	−0.022	−0.096
	N = 21	N = 14
Number of corporations ranked among the world's 500 largest, 2003	0.083	−0.206
	N = 21	N = 14
Number of non-financial TNCs ranked among world's top 100, 2002	0.200	−0.155
	N = 21	N = 14
Number of parent corporations based in the economy (per capita), latest available year	0.501**	0.455
	N = 21	N = 14
Number of foreign affiliates located in the economy (per capita), latest available year	−0.085	0.326
	N = 21	N = 14

*** $p < 0.01$, ** $p < 0.05$, * $p < 0.1$.

Table entries represent Pearson correlation coefficients between aggregate-level political consumerism and the variables listed in the first column. For sources and methodology, see Appendix.

The results for the entire sample in Table 4.4 show that only the number of parent corporations is significantly related to political consumerism. This variable indicates the number of *domestically based* transnational corporations for each country. Expressing this variable in per capita terms allows us to control for the size of the economy and get a sense of the concentration of domestically based transnational corporations in each country. The relationship with political consumerism holds in the smaller sample of Western democracies, although the reduced sample size explains the loss of statistical significance.[11] The outflows of foreign direct investment also relate fairly strongly to political consumerism, but here the relationship disappears altogether in the smaller sample of Western democracies. These results might suggest that a high concentration of transnational corporations in a country may indeed promote actions

---

[11] As Denmark appears to be an outlier here, we tested the relationship without Denmark, as a result the coefficient rises to 0.668*** for all countries (N = 20) and 0.646** for Western democracies (N = 13).

on issues surrounding political consumerism. It is curious, however, that this relationship does not hold for the two measures of the countries' share of the world's largest transnational corporations. Although it might be surmised that the dominance of the United States – one of the countries with lower levels of political consumerism – in these categories might explain the result, excluding the United States does not lead to different results. Overall then, these economic openness factors appear to be less associated with political consumerism than originally assumed.

3) Price Premiums

Another important economic factor for the macro cross-national investigation of political consumerism is the price premium. Socially responsible and ethically sourced goods and services are almost always characterized by a price premium for consumers, meaning that they are more expensive because they reflect the higher costs of production that firms incur when they take corporate responsibility and "internalize the externalities" created by conventional production and distribution methods. This is the case for fairtrade coffee (Giovannucci 2003), organic food (Hamm et al. 2002), and eco-labeled goods (Ferraro, Uchida, and Conrad 2005).

The causes of the price premium vary depending on the product. For fairtrade goods, the explanation for the price premium is relatively straightforward. The essence of fairtrade as practiced by FLO is that its national affiliates in the North and producers in the South[12] agree to pay a contractually stipulated minimum price that is substantially higher than the world price, as well as a premium designated for local economic development. By its very nature, a fairtrade product costs the importer more than its conventional equivalent (see more in Chapter 7); in addition, importers and retailers often place their own price premium on fairtrade goods, according to their perception of their customers' willingness to pay (Giovannucci 2003). Higher prices for organically labeled goods are poorly understood. On the consumer's end, the price of organic goods generally carries a premium.[13]

---

[12] Although there are FLO-certified producers in the North, these are few in number.

[13] Most observers agree that organic agriculture involves higher labor costs and lower yields (which offset savings on pesticides and fertilizer), as well as higher transportation and distribution costs due to less-developed supply chains and infrastructure (Wier et al. 2003). These costs should be reflected in wholesale and retail prices. In many markets, an excess of demand over supply also may play a role (Oberholtzer, Dimitri, and Greene 2005). Finally, the higher price may also reflect consumers' willingness to pay for a product that they consider healthier, better-tasting, and/or more environmentally friendly. These factors seem to be the main components of the price premium; together, they make organic agriculture a potentially profitable venture. The role and relative importance of each of these factors is the subject of much debate. The issue of higher costs, for example, should diminish in salience as organics rise in popularity, since market expansion should lead to economies of scale and streamlining of the supply chain. In addition, some conventional farmers should theoretically be drawn to enter the market, converting to organic methods in order to capture higher profits. Eventually, this would cut

The value of the fairtrade coffee premium paid by consumers is unfortunately unknown for most countries. The organic premium, meanwhile, is better measured, and there is some knowledge of its variation between foods and across countries. According to a 2001 study, European consumer price premiums on organic tomatoes ranged between 10 percent (France) and 225 percent (Netherlands) while those on organic milk varied between 0 percent (Slovenia) and 186 percent (Portugal) (Hamm et al. 2002). In terms of average national premiums on the highest-selling organic foods (produce and dairy/eggs), premiums range from lows of 14 percent and 16 percent (Slovenia and the Czech Republic) to highs of 117 percent and 107 percent (Portugal and the Netherlands), with an average of 64 percent. Premiums on different foods vary widely within countries as well.

Price is the number one reason given by non-purchasers to explain their motivation not to buy organic – this is true for 53 percent in the United Kingdom and 70 percent in the United States , according to two separate studies (Dimitri and Greene 2002, Hallam 2003).[14] This trend is also evident for Fairtrade products.[15] Less is known about premiums in the ethical garment

into the part of the premium that results from undersupply. Many observers see this as a logical outcome of the rise in organics: the costs of organic agriculture relative to conventional (and thus the price premium) will decline, leading more consumers to buy organic. The question of whether organic premiums will remain in the long term, according to this analysis, is largely a function of whether demand will catch up with supply. Analysts agree that the industry is too young and data insufficient to forecast these developments. But a recent study in the United States, the world's largest organic market, suggests that organic premiums for produce remain stable and high – with premiums on some products well over 100 percent (Dimitri and Greene 2002). Even more controversial is the question of who benefits from the consumer premium. Many argue that at its core, the organic premium should be a reward received by the farmer for stewardship of natural resources (Hamm et al. 2002). But despite hefty premiums at the consumer's end in supermarkets and specialty shops, it is not uncommon for organic farmers to receive very small premiums, or even none at all. Studies in Australia and Canada have shown that this is sometimes the case for farmers who sell directly to consumers, and others state that the same is true for organic coffee producers in developing countries (Parsons 2005, Halpin 2004). In addition, as organic markets expand and the involvement of big business increases, large portions of the premium may be absorbed between consumer and farmer. In a much-publicized case in 2001, U.S. firm Horizon Organic Dairy implemented plans to cut farmers' contractually established premiums, resulting in an average decline in income of 15,000 USD per farming family. Later that year, Horizon announced a 200 percent increase in profits, on sales of 160 million USD (Sligh & Christman 2003). While these cases may not be typical, they are indicative of the murkiness of the premium's distribution throughout the organic supply chain.

[14] The same is true in Australia; moreover, a 2001 study there found that 15 percent was the highest premium retailers and farmers could reasonably hope to command, and 28 percent of consumers said they were unwilling to pay any kind of premium (see Halpin 2004, 66–67).

[15] In Belgium, a group of researchers found that willingness to pay a premium for Fairtrade coffee was low, with just 10 percent of their respondents willing to pay the then-current price premium of 27 percent on Fairtrade coffee (de Pelsmacker, Driesen, and Rayp 2005). Dividing respondents into four categories based on personal values and sociodemographic characteristics – Fairtrade lovers, Fairtrade likers, flavor lovers, and brand lovers – they found that 50 percent of Fairtrade lovers were willing to pay the 27 percent premium; this group, however, represents only about 10 percent of the population. Fairtrade likers, who make up about 40 percent of the

industry.[16] Another reason consumers may not wish to pay a premium is if they consider the ethical or sustainable good to be of lesser quality than its conventional counterpart. Giovannucci has noted that quality (along with price) is the primary reason why a large number of buyers are reluctant to purchase fairtrade coffee (Giovannucci 2003, 39, 46).[17] Our own research (see Chapter 3) shows that political consumers pay just as much attention to quality and price as conventional consumers, but in addition they care about the consequences of their products for others, including workers, animals, children, etc. (page 87). What is less understood is how these values are traded off in the actual purchasing decision and which additional factors might influence such a decision.[18] Generally though, there seems to be sufficient concern about the high prices of socially responsible goods that might contribute to the fact that some consumers refrain from buying them, or conversely, when such premiums are low, more consumers are encouraged to buy them. According to these concerns, we expect particularly higher buycotting of fairtrade and organic foods to be associated with lower average national premiums.[19] Table 4.5 examines the relationship between price premiums and market shares for organic produce, as well as buycotting survey data, as this is the form of

Belgian population, are interested in buying Fairtrade but have a weak willingness to pay the premium, while flavor lovers and brand lovers are mostly indifferent. Based on their results, the researchers conclude that Fairtrade likers represent a potential market for Fairtrade coffee, and are amenable to buying Fairtrade if premiums decline or disappear. They suggest that tax incentives could help accomplish this, for example lower value-added taxes for Fairtrade coffee. Similarly, in a study of Swedish consumers' willingness to pay for sustainable coffee, one researcher claims that "the monetary attribute has a significant impact for the experienced utility of the consumer... an environmentally friendly and socially fair choice has to come at a minor cost for the consumer" (Wikström 2003, 29). Wikström also argues that individuals who consume a lot of coffee are less likely to buy Fairtrade and concludes that the market share of Fairtrade coffee would increase if premiums declined.

[16] However, some manufacturers of such clothing acknowledge the higher costs of ethical business and have found creative ways of adjusting. Clothing manufacturer *No Sweat*, for instance, notes that it offers its union-made apparel at a price comparable to other clothing of similar quality by refraining from advertising, relying on word-of-mouth and press coverage, and selling its goods online instead of operating shops (No Sweat 2007). Meanwhile Adbusters, makers of the union-made and eco-friendly Blackspot sneaker, points out that the sneakers are in fact costly to make and thus expensive relative to comparable shoes, but that higher-than-expected sales indicate strong demand for socially responsible goods and "demonstrate the hollowness of the old corporate argument that business necessity compels them to use sweatshops" (Adbusters 2007).

[17] Giovannucci also states that this view may be outmoded, as many fairtrade coffees have performed well in taste competitions vis-à-vis conventional coffees.

[18] See Giovannucci (2003). Fairtrade coffee is a good example here; given its high cost, it is often compared by consumers to similarly priced but allegedly superior-quality conventional coffees. More research is needed into the conditions and circumstances in which consumers either choose perceived quality or instead let their ethical concerns speak.

[19] This could be argued in two ways: that at lower prices, there are more individuals willing to pay the premium; or that as demand for these goods increases, the premium declines due to maturing markets. The latter explanation applies more for organics than fairtrade. Either way, we expect negative correlations. A possible counterargument would be that in the short term, high consumer demand would actually be reflected in high price premiums.

TABLE 4.5. *Do Price Premiums Discourage Political Consumerism?*

	Market Share Entire Sample	Market Share Western Democracies	Buycotting Entire Sample	Buycotting Western Democracies
Average price premiums (%): organic produce, bread, and dairy/eggs, 2001	−0.123	−0.068	−0.064	0.056
	N = 16	N = 13	N = 17	N = 13

*** p < 0.01, ** p < 0.05, * p < 0.1.

Table entries represent Pearson correlation coefficients between aggregate-level political consumerism (market share and buycott) and the average price premiums for organic produce, bread, and dairy/eggs. For sources and methodology, see Appendix.

political consumerism that should be most influenced by price premiums. As mentioned above, reliable data on premiums for fairtrade coffee are unfortunately unavailable.

The results show a weak negative relationship between premiums and organic market share, however, it is not statistically significant. Reducing the sample to Western democracies in column 2 excludes Slovenia and the Czech Republic, which have the lowest premium levels while also having low levels of organic food consumption (despite them being major exporters of organic goods). Yet, even without those cases, the relationship between buycotting and price premiums is nonexistent; the conclusion is that the evidence of an association between organic price premium levels and organic market maturity is weaker than expected. This in itself is an important conclusion, as critics of political consumerism often cite price premiums as the number one obstacle to ethical purchasing decisions. However, future studies should take the importance of price premiums for individuals into account.

4) Political Consumer Infrastructure

The fourth category focuses on political consumer infrastructure, also referred to as nudging or choice architecture in other chapters. Buycotting, for example, is facilitated by the sheer availability of labeled products, and by the existing labeling schemes certifying that specific goods were produced according to a set of well-defined and independently assessed standards. Both the existence of and information about these labeling schemes are crucial here. For an incipient political consumer, a desire to purchase goods that are sustainably produced and traded is not enough. Even with in-depth knowledge of the environmental issues surrounding, say, paper towels, a consumer may have a difficult time finding a green or eco-friendly alternative on store shelves. Labeling schemes seek to provide this information. Ideally, embodied in the label – whether organic, Fairtrade, or an eco-label – is a promise that the good has been produced according to well-defined, transparent criteria relating to environmental sustainability and/or just labor practices and that this has been verified and confirmed by an independent third party. Thus, the label provides information that helps the consumer distinguish between products. Where these labeling schemes are created or backed by governments, they might bestow greater visibility and legitimacy (Sønderskov and Daugbjerg 2011). As in the case of organics, governments may even pass legislation setting labeling standards. The point here is that it is not enough for these schemes to be known; they must also be considered credible and trustworthy by consumers. Third-party auditing or accrediting of labels (as in the case of eco-labels) or third-party verification (as in the case of fairtrade and organic products) are important elements that support the credibility of a labeling scheme (Giovannucci and Ponte 2005, Morris 1997; see also Chapter 5 for a brief discussion on different kinds of labeling schemes).

In discussing political consumer infrastructure, a distinction should be made between nongovernmental and governmental infrastructure. The former consists of labeling schemes and other initiatives undertaken by nongovernmental actors in order to facilitate political consumerism, while the latter involves actions by government actors such as consumer agencies and competition bureaus that support or encourage political consumerism by providing information on various labeling schemes, regulating labeling claims, or promoting ethical or sustainable consumption more broadly. It seems likely that in countries with a developed and mature chain of labeling schemes, a variety of participating actors, and strong institutional settings, we will find a better atmosphere for the spread of relevant information and more opportunities for mobilization, and thus high levels of political consumerism. Moreover, we would also expect that a higher level of government support might reflect a conducive, sensitizing atmosphere for this form of individualized responsibility-taking, signaling that consumer issues and roles are politically important in this national context.

In Table 4.6, we show the international spread of three types of well-known, third-party-verified, market-based labeling schemes, revealing the extent to which the nongovernmental infrastructure for these political consumer goods is developed. The first column indicates the existence of national fairtrade initiatives, recognized and certified by FLO International and selling fair trade products domestically. The second indicates the number of product categories covered by eco-labels recognized and certified by the Global Ecolabelling Network (GEN). Eco-labeled goods are sorted by category – for instance, batteries, home appliances, office supplies, etc. In 2005, GEN eco-labeling programs covered forty product categories; by 2007, this number had reached sixty-one. Here, the number of product categories is used rather than GEN membership because some countries are members through regional organizations such as the European Union or the Nordic Council of Ministers, in which case membership alone may or may not signal commitment to

TABLE 4.6. *The International Spread of Market-Based Political Consumer Labeling Schemes*

	FLO-Affiliated National Fairtrade Initiative (Existence as of 2005)	GEN-Recognized Eco-Labeling Programs (Number of Product Categories Covered, 2005)	FSC National Initiative (Existence as of 2007)
Austria	Yes	19	No
Belgium	Yes	19	Yes
Canada	Yes	39	Yes
Czech Republic	No	24	Yes
Denmark	Yes	40	Yes
Finland	Yes	40	Yes
France	Yes	28	No
Germany	Yes	40	Yes
Greece	No	19	No
Hungary	No	19	Yes
Ireland	Yes	19	Yes
Italy	Yes	19	Yes
Japan	Yes	27	Yes
Netherlands	Yes	31	Yes
Norway	Yes	40	Yes
Poland	No	19	No
Portugal	No	19	No
Slovenia	No	19	No
Spain	No	26	Yes
Sweden	Yes	40	Yes
Switzerland	Yes	0	Yes
United Kingdom	Yes	19	Yes
United States	Yes	19	Yes

Source: Fairtrade, FLO 2005b; eco-labeling, GEN 2005; Forest Stewardship, FSC 2007.

eco-labeling.[20] Looking at the number of product categories gives us a better idea of the depth of this facilitating institutional factor. Finally, the last column shows whether countries have an FSC-accredited national initiative. Much like FLO, the FSC accredits national initiatives, which in turn are the organizations that issue certifications guaranteeing compliance with the FSC's Forest Management and Chain of Custody[21] standards. Both certificates must be earned before a producer can sell products as FSC-certified.

[20] Strictly speaking, countries themselves are not GEN members; the organizations operating the eco-labels are. In some cases, however, this organization may in fact be a branch of government.

[21] "Chain of custody" refers to "the path taken by raw materials from the forest to the consumer, including all successive stages of processing, transportation, manufacturing, and distribution." (See www.fsc.org.)

Four countries – Denmark, Finland, Germany, and Sweden – have national initiatives for fairtrade and forest stewardship as well as the highest number of GEN product categories. These are four of the five countries with the highest rates of reported political consumerism; the other, Switzerland, a country outside the European Union, does not participate in all European or global initiatives, and thus is not a member of GEN eco-labeling programs. It is important to note that Switzerland has various regional and canton-level labels in different product sectors, some of which go beyond current EU level or international specifications. Also ranking highly are Canada and the Netherlands, which have initiatives in all four areas but have slightly less extensive GEN programs.

Infrastructure promoted by the government is also measured in multiple ways. One is whether a country has legislation defining the conditions under which goods may be labeled organic – that is, regulations pertaining to the production, processing, and importing of organic goods. It has been argued that government regulations on organic standards have helped expand the organic industry by increasing consumer awareness, consumer confidence, and product visibility (Willer and Yussefi 2004). However, there is not much variation between the countries in our sample here: as of 2005, Canada was the only member of our sample that had not implemented a regulatory framework for organics (Willer and Yussefi 2004). Canada finally rectified this issue late in 2009, creating the mandatory Canada Organic label (CFIA 2009). Because of this lack of variation, this factor will not be included in the analysis.

Thus, the first factor related to governmental infrastructure is the presence of governmental agencies for consumer affairs. These demonstrate a country's political interest in the question of private consumption and can provide impartial information to consumers that possibly aid their search for information about ethical sourcing. While consumer agencies are traditionally more concerned with issues of consumer protection and consumer rights, many have begun to offer information on political consumer issues. The Canadian government's Office of Consumer Affairs web site, for instance, features a section on "sustainable consumption," which offers advice on how to shop sustainably, tips on eco-labels, and more. Similar information has been available from the Swedish Consumer Agency. These agencies and/or the government branch dealing with fair competition and advertising may also set guidelines regulating environmental or ethical marketing claims. In response to the increased number of companies making "green" claims on labels or in advertising, many governments have set specific guidelines for such claims in order to clarify the application of competition and advertising laws to this particular area. These guidelines are meant to prevent vague, misleading, or false claims (Consumer International 1999). Although no comprehensive list of countries with such national guidelines exists, as of 2007, Austria, Canada, Denmark, France, Norway, Sweden, the United Kingdom, and the United States were among those that had established guidelines for environmental claims; the Nordic Consumer Ombudsmen have gone further, implementing guidelines on ethical claims as well for Denmark, Finland, Norway, and Sweden.

TABLE 4.7. *Conducive Political Consumer Infrastructure?*

	Buycotting Entire Sample	Buycotting Western Democracies
Existence of FLO-affiliated national Fairtrade initiative as of June 2005	0.719***	No variation between countries
	N = 21	
Number of product categories covered by local GEN-recognized eco-labeling programs as of July 2005	0.467**	0.397
	N = 21	N = 14
Existence of FSC-accredited national initiative as of June 2007	0.264	0.056
	N = 21	N = 14
Existence of governmental agency for consumer issues as of July 2005	0.236	0.534**
	N = 21	N = 14
National or regional eco-labeling program created by governments as of June 2005	0.482**	0.466*
	N = 21	N = 14
Government participation in international environmental collaborative efforts, 2005	0.728***	0.636**
	N = 21	N = 14

*** $p < 0.01$, ** $p < 0.05$, * $p < 0.1$.
Note: Table entries represent Pearson correlation coefficients between aggregate-level political consumerism and the variables listed in the first column. For sources and methodology, see Appendix.

Next, some governments have created or facilitated national or regional eco-labeling programs. These labeling schemes allow firms that follow best practices to advertise their adherence to sustainable production practices and thus tap into consumer demand for such products. By launching such programs, governments help create institutions that promote political consumerism. Governments can also promote political consumerism through their own purchasing policies and practices, a topic discussed further in Chapter 7.

Finally, a general governmental atmosphere of attention to environmental and labor issues might be important for fostering citizen involvement in political consumerism. For measurements here we capitalize on the fact that some governments are more active than others in joining environmental intergovernmental organizations and signing international environmental agreements.

Table 4.7 shows the correlation between these aspects of a conducive infrastructure and the percentage of buycotters in each country, as once again, this form of political consumerism has the potential to be most influenced by the political consumer infrastructure.

Nearly all of these aspects of a conducive infrastructure – whether non-governmental or governmental – show relatively significant correlations with levels of citizens' political consumerism. There is only one exception: the presence of FSC national initiatives. Among nongovernmental infrastructure, the existence of a FLO national initiative in particular correlates very strongly with buycotting. As for governmental infrastructure, the existence of government agencies dealing with consumer issues does not correlate significantly to buycotting in the sample as a whole, but the correlation is relatively high in the smaller sample of stable Western democracies. Government-created eco-label programs and especially government participation in international environmental collaborative efforts correlate very highly with buycotting, indicating their positive association with high levels of political consumerism. This is confirmed in comparative research, which shows that an active government is a necessary but not sufficient condition for the establishment of successful national eco-labeling schemes, whether run by government or nongovernmental organizations. What is also necessary is an environmentally aware citizenry, which is mobilized into awareness through an active civil society and a pro-environmental policy atmosphere among politicians and civil servants (Jordan et al. 2006).

In sum, political consumerism is clearly higher in countries with a strong supportive infrastructure. However, our findings seem to be an example of the proverbial chicken and egg problem. Do these institutions arise in response to demand by political consumers, or do they arise somewhat independently perhaps also as a reaction to social movement activism and then promote citizens' political consumerism?

For the answer, we may refer to the analysis in Chapter 5 that discerns roughly two ways of how political consumer activist organizational settings bring about infrastructural change. Some institutions arise due to the efforts of a small vanguard of committed activists. Examples include the alternative trade organizations that gave rise to the fairtrade model, now championed by FLO, and the local organic movements that eventually formed the International Federation of Organic Agriculture Movements (IFOAM). In these cases, the institutions preceded, nurtured, and supported the broad citizen engagement on these issues. Though they began as grassroots alliances between small producers and concerned consumers, the creation of institutions such as FLO and IFOAM has helped raise awareness, disseminate information, and expand the political consumer cause. However, generally both types of labeling institutions were formed by major global actors reacting to business and environmental concerns over sustainability of current production practices, and less so as a reaction to direct consumer demand for sustainable goods, confirming that in these cases institutions probably precede widespread political consumerism.

Nevertheless, disentangling the pivotal roles of institutional aspects of the infrastructure for the rise of political consumerism is problematic. The above discussion suggests that once labeling schemes are established, governments can play a role in providing impartial information to consumers and protecting them from false claims. They can also go further in institutionalizing political consumerism by launching voluntary labels, or even promoting it through government procurement, as the European Union has begun to do by passing a "green procurement" policy and serving fairtrade coffee in the European Parliament (European Commission 2009, EFTA 2007). More research is needed to assess the role of governments in the rise of political consumerism (see also Chapters 7 and 8), but so far our analysis has shown that both nongovernmental and governmental infrastructure might potentially have an enabling and possibly mobilizing role for people to become responsible consumers.

5) Political and Institutional Factors

Next in our discussion are political and institutional factors. As described in Chapter 3, individuals who identify with the political left are over-represented among political consumers. The left is traditionally concerned with labor issues, regulation of the market, and social justice more broadly (Inglehart 1997). If political consumers are more often than not leftists, we would expect to find more of them in countries not only with a tradition of support for left-wing political parties but also in countries with more left-leaning governments. Again, old and new left parties are generally more sympathetic to labor and environmental issues than their counterparts in the center and to the right, and may thus be more likely to create an atmosphere that fosters citizens' engagement in political consumerism.

This may be measured by using both macro-level and survey data, which are mostly longitudinal averages of the twelve years preceding the ESS data. The first macro variable is the percentage of left party vote in national elections between 1991 and 2003 (see Appendix for methodology). Second, we include measures of how strongly left parties were represented in government, as measured by the share of left seats between 1991 and 2003. Third, we add the number of years in which a left party has been in power – that is, in control of the executive branch of government – between 1991 and 2003. The association of political consumerism with the political left may appear to be complementary to the postmaterialist explanation, but a closer inspection suggests that they may potentially be rival hypotheses. As discussed above, postmodernization involves a transition from scarcity values to security values. Inglehart claims that support for state ownership, government responsibility, and leveling of income inequality – all traditionally left-party goals – are actually scarcity values; postmaterialists are said to be more skeptical of big government and prefer to scale it down in favor of private ownership, personal responsibility, and competition over state-mandated income equality (Inglehart 1997, chapter 8). The personal responsibility aspect in particular describes well how this book has conceived political consumerism. Thus, postmaterialists are unlikely to be classical leftists; in fact, Inglehart states that postmaterialists are

more likely to be drawn to the green party or other postmaterialist alternatives to the New Left; or they might also vote for other parties of the left that
include postmaterialists values. So, in addition, green party votes, seats, and
their presence in government cabinets are also included as potential factors
here.

It can also be assumed that beyond the political background of the government and parliaments, certain governmental institutions and policies are
important facilitators of political consumerism. We examine here three institutional aspects that can be considered as facilitative and supportive of political consumerism: presence of an encompassing welfare state, neo-corporatist
legacy, and official development assistance (ODA) as a percentage of national
income is also included.

ODA is a typical proactive policy often supported by left-leaning governments and citizens, which symbolically signals that development issues are of
concern within a particular national context. Although often criticized for its
limitations and the conditions that are frequently attached to its distribution
("tied aid"), as well as the continued presence of Northern trade barriers that
may negate the beneficial effects of aid (Stiglitz and Charlton 2005, Watkins
and Fowler 2002), strong ODA commitment is likely to precede commitment to
fairtrade solutions, both of which are targeted at Southern poverty reduction.
Recently, fairtrade has been seen as a way of replacing at least partially foreign aid because it is viewed as the more empowering alternative for Southern
farmers and workers (more in Chapter 7).

Whereas ODA is sometimes viewed as an international extension of the
solidaristic universal welfare state, the welfare states are important factors
in themselves. Often, traditionally supported by left-wing governments, well-
developed welfare states ensure that all citizens enjoy a basic social safety net,
and thus citizens are able to live and think beyond their personal material
well-being. The social safety net and socioeconomic equality that come with
well-developed welfare states guarantee basic socioeconomic resources for all
citizens, which in turn might help in the process of information-gathering and
offer the basic resources necessary for participation (Kaariainen and Lehtonen
2006).

Welfare states have also been theorized as ensuring that citizens think beyond
their own material needs and focus on the needs of others (Inglehart 1997).
Since political consumerism does include other-regarding values and needs
effort to promote a caring sensitivity, well-developed welfare states should be
expected to foster political consumerism. Welfare state strength is measured by
social spending as a percentage of GDP.

Finally, neo-corporatism (also called societal or democratic corporatism) has
historically been associated with the left-oriented welfare state. More importantly, neo-corporatism, though now diminished in political importance, fostered collaboration, trust, and peaceful relations between interest groups of

labor and business and the government as well as created a consultative nature between these actors that helped solve important national problems of national economic and sociopolitical importance (Cameron 1984, Lijphart and Crepaz 1991, Rothstein 1987). These experiences or institutional legacies of trustful cooperation can now be transferred to the collaboration of business with other societal actors, as well as to other issue areas, that include, for example, environmental and labor concerns (see also discussion on varieties of capitalism in e.g., Hall and Thelen 2009). Thus, we include a cross-national measure of neo-corporatism in our analysis. This measure, created by Siaroff (1999), gives a comparative classification of twenty-four countries by standardizing the measures of twenty-three scholarly analyses to create an average neo-corporatism score.

First, Table 4.8 shows that left party vote, seats, and years in power show no association in the whole sample but a high association for all three within Western democracies, though this association is only significant for left vote due to the small sample size. Green party results show the opposite trend, correlating very highly with political consumerism for the sample as a whole but not for the wealthy-country sample.

These results remind us that positions on the political spectrum have different meanings depending on a society's history, culture, and level of economic development. When these are controlled by examining only wealthy Western democracies, left party vote is more robustly associated with political consumerism than green party vote. For the latter, the high correlation with political consumerism in the large sample seems to simply reflect that, in keeping with Inglehart's postmodernization thesis, green parties are more common and more popular in wealthy democratic countries. Once economic development and historical/institutional differences related to how long the country has been democratic are controlled, the relationship between green party and political consumerism weakens.[22]

Meanwhile, it is notable that the vast majority of left parties of the high-political consumerism countries are social democratic as opposed to socialist. In fact, France is the only country with relatively high levels of both political consumerism and support for socialist parties. This macro-level correlation between moderate left leanings and political consumerism may reflect the fact that social democrats generally combine support for economic equality with

---

[22] The performance of this green party variable also depends to a great extent on the inclusion of Denmark's Socialist People's Party (SF), which as its name implies is not a typical green party. Representing virtually all of Denmark's green party support, the party has participated in the European Greens alliance as an observer since 1994, when it split with the Nordic Left Alliance. As such, it is the only party not officially a member of the Global Green Network to be included in this data set. Without this party, the correlation between green party vote and political consumerism is 0.487** for the entire sample and 0.089 for the wealthy-country sample.

TABLE 4.8. *Political and Institutional Factors that Promote Political Consumerism*

	Political Consumerism Entire Sample	Political Consumerism Western Democracies
Left party vote (% of total vote), average 1991–2003	0.166	0.571**
	N = 19	N = 13
Left party seats (% of total seats), average 1991–2003	0.088	0.353
	N = 21	N = 14
Left parties: Years in power from 1991–2003	0.223	0.441
	N = 20	N = 13
Green Party vote (% of total vote), average 1991–2003	0.602***	0.236
	N = 21	N = 14
Green Party seats (% of total seats), average 1991–2003	0.509**	0.166
	N = 21	N = 14
Green Party members in cabinet, average 1991–2003	−0.218	−0.433
	N = 21	N = 14
Government social spending as % of GDP, average 1990–2003	0.502**	0.458*
	N = 21	N = 14
Neo-corporatism (mean score of 23 studies conducted between 1981 and 1997)	0.725***	0.599***
	N = 17	N = 14
Official development assistance, net, as % of donor state's GNI, 1996–2003	0.640***	0.443
	N = 21	N = 14

*** $p < 0.01$, ** $p < 0.05$, * $p < 0.1$.
Table entries represent Pearson correlation coefficients between aggregate-level political consumerism and the variables listed in the first column. For sources and methodology, see Appendix.

an acceptance of more free economic markets – a combination that points to political consumerism as an effective avenue for the expression of political beliefs (see Chapter 3 for individual-level analysis of the relationship between left-leaning political ideology and political consumerism.)

Neo-corporatism and social spending are strongly and significantly correlated in both groups, and ODA only in the whole sample. The results for social spending by government suggest that political consumerism occurs more frequently in welfare states. Neo-corporatism in particular may set a pattern for cooperation between government, industry, and labor as well as acceptance of political involvement in the market, and this legacy may facilitate the creation of the caring sensitivity and mobilization of political consumers. In conjunction with the results for ODA, these results suggest that political consumerism is higher in countries with proactive governments. It is also possible that left parties in Western democracies are more ideologically open to institutionalizing political consumerism, for example by mandating the use of fairtrade coffee in national legislatures, or creating eco-labels. Although data for the former is insufficient for analysis, information on eco-labels is easier to find. Eleven countries within the "wealthy-democracy" sample have created eco-labels. Seven were indeed developed by left parties, but the involvement of center and three right parties suggests that ideology may not be a crucial factor. In fact, the more convincing pattern is chronological: with the exception of Germany's Blue Angel, all these labels were created between 1988 and 1993. Thus, in a six-year period, half of the governments in our wealthy-country sample launched an eco-label, regardless of the ideology of the party in power (see Chapter 5 for additional explanation). Equally important is the fact that the six countries in our sample that did not create eco-labels during this time had parties in power that were all over the spectrum – left, center, and right. In sum, green party strength contributes to the explanation of the variance in people's engagement in political consumerism within the entire group of countries (but not for developed democracies alone); once more we seem to be seeing a spurious effect in which Green parties appear strongest in developed long-term democracies, which also score high in political consumerism. However, left party vote and to a degree power helps us distinguish why some developed democracies have more political consumerism than others. In other words, left party governments might have a facilitative effect on political consumerism for the reasons discussed above. Institutions and institutional legacies such as that of neo-corporatism are more promising in their ability to explain the overall cross-national differences in the rates of political consumerism. Institutions set the tone for cooperation between various societal actors, and thus better enable them to solve the globalized problems they face. Neo-corporatism and expansive welfare states offer such institutional conditions.

6) Social Capital

Social capital theory offers another point of entry into explaining why political consumerism differs cross-nationally (Neilson 2010, Neilson and Paxton 2010). Proponents of social capital theory suggest that embeddedness in voluntary associations makes it easier for citizens to learn to overcome collective

TABLE 4.9. *Social Capital as a Resource for Political Consumerism*

	Entire Sample	Western Democracies
Generalized trust (%), 2002	0.814***	0.617**
	N = 21	N = 14
Membership in humanitarian, peace, environmental, or animal rights organizations (% of population), 2002	0.659***	0.343
	N = 19	N = 11
Membership in consumer/automobile organization (% of population), 2002	0.687***	0.464
	N = 19	N = 11
Membership in any voluntary organization (% of population), 2002	0.868***	0.740***
	N = 19	N = 11

*** p < 0.01, ** p < 0.05, * p < 0.1.

Table entries represent Pearson correlation coefficients between aggregate-level political consumerism and the variables listed in the first column. For sources and methodology, see Appendix.

action problems (Hooghe and Stolle 2003, Putnam 1993, 2000). Networks and associations facilitate recruitment for political participatory acts (Almond and Verba 1963). If this observation holds for political consumerism, this would imply that political consumers are better integrated and embedded in such associations and networks, particularly traditional face-to-face associations that have been at the heart of social capital theories (Putnam 2000). This hypothesis can be juxtaposed to the claim of other social capital scholars that the effects of passive or checkbook activism can be just as strong (Wollebæk and Selle 2003). Furthermore, an important aspect of social capital theory relates to attitudes. Generalized trust, the willingness to give the benefit of the doubt to abstract others (Stolle and Nishikawa 2011), is an important societal ingredient that is widely known to facilitate collective action problems, such as for environmental issues such as recycling (Putnam 2000, Sønderskov 2009). Globalized problems such as sweatshops, environmental damage, and treatment of animals are other examples of free riding on responsibility-taking and collective action problems that need to be addressed at least in part through citizen cooperation. Even if seemingly individualized, concerned, and responsible citizens with a caring sensitivity need to come together in order to use their political consumer power and address these issues, they may do so in loosely coordinated and online ways and in the belief that others follow suit. Societies high in generalized trust, then, should be better able to engage in these other-regarding activities and, therefore, help address the structural injustice problems discussed in Chapter 1.

The results in Table 4.9 are impressive, providing as a group of variables the highest correlations so far. Membership in any voluntary organization and generalized trust, in fact, have the strongest correlations with aggregate polit-ical consumerism at 0.868*** and 0.814***, respectively. All four indepen-dent variables' correlations with the dependent variable decline for the smaller group of developed democracies, with two falling just below statistical sig-nificance (membership in a consumer/automobile organization by just 0.01). Clearly, membership in peace, environmental, and other such organizations distinguishes long-term democracies from other European countries, but the strength of these organizations is not powerful enough to explain variations of political consumerism in stable democracies. On the other hand, generalized trust and the density of associations more generally seem to be powerful factors in relation to the strength of political consumerism. Thus, it seems that a trust-ful citizenry and robust civil society helps socialize individuals into political consumerism. These results have also been confirmed in other cross-national and multivariate analyses (Neilson and Paxton 2010).

7) Religion

As seen in Chapter 3, at the individual level, political consumers tend to be Protestant rather than Catholic. This is far from groundbreaking news. Protes-tants have been found to have higher rates of political participation and civic voluntarism than Catholics and members of other religions in the United States by numerous observers, from Tocqueville (2000 [1848]) to Verba et al. (1995) to Wuthnow (1999). This trend has also been identified in cross-national studies as well (Curtis et al. 2001). At the individual level, it has been linked to Protes-tant churches' apparent individualism and egalitarianism vs. Catholic churches' hierarchy and elitism. Indeed, there is a historical legacy of non-Catholic reli-gious engagement in political consumerism. As discussed in Chapter 5, Quakers played a vital role in the antislavery movement in the 1600s to 1800s and estab-lished the important fairtrade advocate Oxfam, and Quakers and Methodists formulated early ideas about socially responsible investing. Thus, rather than relying on the state or the church establishment to provide for the needs of the community, Protestants are encouraged to join together voluntarily as free individuals to fulfill various societal functions, including philanthropy and the preservation of public morality (Curtis et al. 2001, 785).

While there is also a Catholic tradition linked to worldshops and fairtrade activism, for example in Italy (Forno and Ceccarini 2006), some writers have derived a national-cultural argument from the Protestant legacies. Drawing on Weber's Protestant ethic thesis, Inglehart argues that in post-Reformation Protestant (especially Calvinist) countries, these individual qualities led to a culture more favorable to economic achievement. Protestant Europe – here Inglehart includes Sweden, Germany, and the Netherlands, the latter two of which are in part mixed Protestant/Catholic but are considered by him to be culturally Protestant – proceeded to modernize, rationalize, and become wealthy over the next few centuries. For these reasons, he argues, Protestant

TABLE 4.10. *Religiosity and Political Consumerism*

	Political Consumerism Entire Sample	Political Consumerism Western Democracies
Level of religiosity, 2002	−0.471**	−0.653**
	N = 21	N = 14
Church attendance, 2002	−0.573***	−0.598**
	N = 21	N = 14

*** p < 0.01, ** p < 0.05, * p < 0.1.
Table entries represent Pearson correlation coefficients between aggregate-level political consumerism and the variables listed in the first column. For sources and methodology, see Appendix.

countries have also been the first to move into postmodernization, de-emphasizing economic needs as they move away from scarcity values. In this he differs from scholars who see church attendance and involvement as being at the root of Protestants' higher rates of voluntarism.

While they may disagree on the causes, most observers agree that Protestants have higher rates of political participation (Wuthnow 1999). If these writers are correct, we would expect to see these trends reflected in our country analysis as well. Given the disagreements here, we examine several hypotheses. First, whether religiosity in itself is a factor here, and second, whether Protestant countries have indeed higher rates of political consumerism. Table 4.10 gives a first indication that religiosity and church attendance per se are negatively related to political consumerism. Religious involvement within a country and in itself does not foster political involvement in the market arena. This does not mean that religiosity in itself prevents political consumerism.

For better readability, the analysis in Table 4.11 is presented differently than before; it groups countries by their predominant religion and shows political consumerism averages for all groups of religious countries. In order to control for economic development and historical experience, the seven less wealthy, ex-authoritarian countries (six Catholic and one Orthodox) have been dropped. This leaves seven majority Protestant countries, three mixed Protestant/Catholic, and five majority Catholic. A religious split seems clear.

Table 4.11 shows that Protestant countries do indeed have the highest number of political consumers and most socially responsible investors. Only for organic and fairtrade food and coffee consumption do we see that mixed religious countries indicate a higher rate. On the flipside, in Catholic countries, all measured types of political consumerism are considerably lower. But beyond this, other facilitative factors for political consumerism also vary by dominant religion. Protestant countries seem to have an extensive political consumer infrastructure and also score high on social capital indicators such as trust, whereas Catholic countries have a less facilitative infrastructure and lower

TABLE 4.11. *Religion and Political Consumerism*

	Protestant	Mixed	Catholic
Political consumerism measures			
Boycott, 2002	24.5%	22.6%	16.4%
Buycott, 2002	38.8%	36.5%	23.1%
Boycott and/or buycott, 2002	44.2%	41.4%	28.1%
Fairtrade coffee: Average market share (% of total coffee sales), 2000–2006	0.87%	2.13%	0.83%
Organic food: Average per capita consumption ($USD), 2002–2005	$44.65	$67.21	$40.60
Socially responsible investment, retail ($USD), average 1999–2006	$209.17	$143.16	$102.04
Factors that foster political consumerism			
Median number of product categories covered by local GEN-recognized eco-labeling programs as of July 2005	39	31	19
Existence of FSC-accredited national Forest Stewardship standards as of June 2007 (proportion of countries)	6 of 7	2 of 3	0 of 5
Generalized trust (%), 2002	72.4%	60.2%	48.7%
Membership in a humanitarian, peace, environmental, or animal rights organizations (% of population), 2002	12.8%	17.1%	10.2%
Membership in any voluntary organization (% of population), 2002	77.1%	77.5%	59.8%

For sources and methodology, see Appendix.

levels of trust and association membership. Even when controlling for country-level economic indicators, we still see the influence of Protestant and mixed religion. Thus, the conclusion is that the Protestant and, to a degree, mixed-religion countries in Europe are ahead on political consumerism, as measured in this analysis, and they are ahead on some of its facilitative conditions.

Multivariate analysis is better able to disentangle the various competing country-level factors that are related to political consumerism. In a multilevel model, which includes the individual factors covered in Chapter 3 as well as baseline socioeconomic controls at the country level, we tested one by one all significant aggregate factors introduced in this chapter. The results indicate that societal trust and associational memberships, some aspects of the facilitative government infrastructure, and Protestant religion are the strongest and most robust correlates of political consumerism in this setting (results not shown, but available from the authors). Thus, above and beyond the many socioeconomic, demographic, and other differences within and between countries, social capital, religion, and government facilitation might matter most for political consumerism.

POLITICAL CONSUMERS ACROSS COUNTRIES

The practice of political consumerism varies across countries. The lion's share of political consumerism is practiced in Scandinavia, Switzerland, and Germany; whereas in Southern and Eastern European countries only a small share of the population engages in this fashion. Interestingly, countries with high levels of political consumerism are usually also the ones in which there has been little decline in voter turnout. Generally, these are countries characterized by active citizenship. As Chapter 3 has demonstrated, this relationship also holds at the individual level: political consumers are more involved in various forms of political participation.

In this chapter, we have attempted to lay out which country-level factors including economic conditions, political institutions, political constellations, civic traditions, and specific aspects of a political consumer infrastructure might account for this variation in political consumerism. Clearly, political consumerism is more frequently practiced in long-term democracies with relatively high levels of economic development. These are also predominantly countries with higher levels of postmaterialism, green parties and by association countries with higher levels of practice of various other emerging forms of political participation. Within the group of long-term democracies, we found that a political consumer infrastructure provided by the government and non-governmental actors including a high density of and initiatives for labeling schemes, legacies of neo-corporatism, strong and expansive welfare states, high levels of social capital, and Protestant religion are characteristics of countries with high levels of political consumerism, but some of these factors such as social capital, religion, and government infrastructure stand out as some of the most robust ones. It is the challenge of future comparative work to understand better which of these characteristics simply accompany political consumerism and which serve as causal factors that facilitate, shape, or hinder it.

Clearly, long-term democracies, a certain level of economic development, social capital, and postmaterialism and its consequences seem to lay the groundwork for political consumerism to develop at all. However, once these foundations exist, there are still differences between the stable advanced industrialized democracies. Surprisingly, these differences cannot be explained by standard economic factors of foreign direct investment or the character of companies and not even by price premiums for labeled goods. What this chapter has uncovered is a facilitative role of institutional and governmental factors that shape or at least embed political consumerism in a national framework of caring sensitivity for environmental and social justice concerns. Although individualized responsibility-taking is in important ways a consequence of government inaction or inability to address globalized problems (Chapter 1), this chapter has refined this insight to show that certain levels of government interest in consumer issues and conducive institutional conditions go hand in hand with high levels of political consumerism. We return to this role of institutions and government actions in the conclusion of this book.

APPENDIX

All Variables

For each variable, data were gathered for the following twenty-three countries, unless otherwise indicated:

Austria, Belgium, Canada, the Czech Republic, Denmark, Finland, France, Germany, Greece, Hungary, Ireland, Italy, Japan, Netherlands, Norway, Poland, Portugal, Slovenia, Spain, Sweden, Switzerland, the United Kingdom, the United States.

For all variables that are longitudinal averages, 1990–2003 was the desired period. Where data are not available, this period was shortened in order to avoid losing cases. This explains the variation in time periods between variables. The reason for choosing 2003 as the most recent year in the period was consistency with our dependent variables measuring reported political consumerism, which are from the 2002/2003 round of the *European Social Survey*.

THE CROSS-NATIONAL SPREAD OF POLITICAL CONSUMERISM

Percentage of individuals who boycott
Percentage of individuals who buycott
Percentage of individuals who boycott and/or buycott

Methodology:
The first two variables are derived from variables in the *European Social Survey* 2002/2003, "bctprd" and "bghtprd," respectively. The former asks respondents whether they "boycotted certain products last 12 months," while the latter asks whether they "bought product for political/ethical/environment reason last 12 months." In order to derive an aggregate measure for each country, we obtained the percentage of respondents in each country who answered "yes" to these questions. The third variable is a composite, derived by obtaining the percentage of individuals in each country who claimed to boycott, or buycott, or both.

Countries excluded:
Canada and Japan were not included in the ESS; any statistical procedure involving one of these political consumerism variables automatically excludes these two countries.

CONSUMPTION AND MARKET SHARE OF LABELED PRODUCTS

Fairtrade coffee: Per capita consumption in grams, 2000–2006

Methodology:
Fairtrade coffee sales in metric tons converted to grams (1 MT = 1,000,000 G), divided by population.

Sources:
Coffee data 2000–2003, FLO 2005a, 2004–2006, FLO 2007. Population data, World Bank 2007.
   Note: Belgium data includes Luxembourg.

Fairtrade coffee: Market share (% of total coffee sales), 2000–2006

Methodology:
Fairtrade coffee consumption per capita divided by total coffee consumption (that is, fairtrade + conventional) per capita, multiplied by 100. (See previous entry for methodology and sources of fairtrade coffee per capita consumption.)

   For source of total coffee consumption per capita between 2000 and 2004, see below. Figures from 2005–2006 are estimates; they are simply the average yearly per capita coffee consumption from 2000–2004.

Sources:
Total coffee consumption per capita 2000–2004, all countries except Canada, International Coffee Organization (ICO) 2006. Total coffee Canada, ICO 2005.
   Note: Belgium data includes Luxembourg.

Organic food: Average per capita consumption ($U.S.), 2002–2005

Notes:
Some funds have been converted from Euros to U.S. dollars. This conversion was carried out using exchange rates prevalent during the years in question (2002: $1 = 1.03€; 2003: $1 = 0.88€; 2004: $1 = 0.81€). These figures represent the median of daily exchange rates (251 opening days) throughout the specific calendar years according to the Bank of Canada. These rates are available at http://www.bankofcanada.ca/en/rates/exchform. html and were accessed July 20, 2005 (2002–2003) and October 18, 2007 (2004).

Methodology: Sales of organic food divided by population.

Sources:
Retail sales data for 2002: Willer and Yussefi 2004, 23–24, 100.
Retail sales data for 2003: Willer and Yussefi 2005, 19–23, 108.
Retail sales data for 2004: Willer and Yussefi 2006, 69–72, 143–144.

Retail sales data for 2005: Willer and Yussefi 2007, 52–55, 143–147. Population data: World Bank 2007.

Organic food: Market share (% of total food sales), latest available year

Note: Data from 2001, except Canada (2002) and the United States (2003).

Sources:
All countries except Canada, United States: Hamm, Gronefeld, and Halpin 2002: 124. Canada: United States Department of Agriculture 2002. United States: Organic Trade Association 2004.

SOCIOECONOMIC RESOURCES AND POSTMODERNIZATION

GNI per capita (purchasing power parity, current 2000 international $), average 1990–2003

Source: World Bank 2006.

Methodology:
To obtain an average for 1990–2003 for each country, the sum of GNI per capita for every year in the period was divided by the number of years.

Employment in services (% of total employment), average 1994–2003

Source: World Bank 2007.

Methodology:
To obtain an average for 1994–2003 for each country, the sum of the percentage of employment in services for every year in the period was divided by the number of years.

Years of continuous democracy, 2003

Source: Inglehart 1997, 358. Note that Inglehart's data include "the number of years of continuous democracy since 1920 (as of 1995), with a maximum score of 75 years." For our purposes, these numbers have been updated to 2003.

Labor force with tertiary education (% of total), latest available year

Source: World Bank 2005. Note that 2001 is the latest available year for all countries except Belgium and Denmark (2000) and Norway (1998). Japan and the United States were excluded due to insufficient data.

ECONOMIC OPENNESS

Foreign direct investment, net inflows/outflows (% of GDP), average 1993–2003

Source: World Bank 2005.

Methodology:
To obtain an average for 1993–2003 for each country, the sum of net inflows/outflows for every year in the period was divided by the number of years. Countries excluded due to insufficient data (FDI outflows only): Greece.

Economic openness (exports + imports as % of real GDP in constant prices), average 1990–2003

Source: World Bank 2005.

Methodology:
This variable was derived by adding exports and imports, both expressed as % of GDP, for each country. To obtain an average for 1990–2003 for each country, the sum of this new "economic openness" variable for every year in the period was divided by the number of years.

Number of corporations ranked among the world's 500 largest, 2003

Source: *Fortune* 2003

Number of non-financial TNCs ranked among world's top 100, 2002

Source: UNCTAD 2004

Number of parent corporations based in the economy (per capita), latest available year

Number of foreign affiliates based in the economy (per capita), latest available year

Sources:
Parent corporations/foreign affiliates, UNCTAD 2006. Population data, World Bank 2005.

PRICE PREMIUMS

Average price premiums (%): organic produce and dairy/eggs, 2001

Source: Hamm et al. 2002.

THE INTERNATIONAL SPREAD OF MARKET-BASED
LABELING SCHEMES

Sources:
Organic food, Willer and Yussefi 2005. Fairtrade, FLO 2005b. Eco-labeling, GEN 2005. Forest Stewardship, FSC 2007.

POLITICAL CONSUMER INFRASTRUCTURE

Existence of FLO-affiliated national Fairtrade initiative as of June 2005

Coding: 0 = No; 1 = Yes.

Source: FLO 2005b

Number of product categories covered by local GEN-recognized eco-labeling programs as of July 2005

Source: Global Ecolabelling Network 2005

Note: Some countries are covered by two and, in the case of Sweden, even three different programs (i.e. a national one, a regional Scandinavian one, and the EU one). The product categories often overlap. In these cases, individual product categories were counted once per country; they were not double-counted.

Existence of Forest Stewardship Council-accredited national initiative as of June 2007

Source: FSC 2007

Existence of governmental agency for consumer issues as of July 2005

Coding:

0 = No

1 = No, but the central government does provide financial support for certain nongovernmental consumer organizations

2 = Yes

To be included, agencies 1) must be funded and run by the state, and 2) have consumer protection and education as their central mandates. Competition bureaus were not included.

For Portugal, no consumer agency was found; however, due to language limitations, it is possible that one exists but was missed.

National or regional eco-labeling program created by government as of June 2005

Coding: 0 = No; 1 = Yes.

Government participation in international environmental collaborative efforts, 2005

Source: Esty et al. 2005, 375.

POLITICAL AND INSTITUTIONAL FACTORS

Left party vote (% of total vote), average 1991–2003
Left party seats (% of total seats), average 1991–2003
Left parties: Years in power between 1991–2003

Note: Parties were coded as left if they were members of Socialist International.

Methodology (vote and seats):
To obtain national averages for 1991–2003, the sum of the percentage of the overall vote received by left parties in parliamentary elections (presidential in the case of the United States) / total parliamentary seats (House of Representatives in the case of the United States) occupied by left parties for every year in the period was divided by the number of years. Years between elections were assigned the result from the previous election.

Methodology (years in power):
This variable indicates the number of years, for each country, in which a left party was at the helm of the executive (whether as the majority party or senior partner in a coalition) on December 30.

Sources:
Election data, Inter-Parliamentary Union 2007. Left party coding, Socialist International 2008.
   Countries excluded due to missing data: Italy (party vote) and Switzerland (years in power).

Green party vote (% of total vote), average 1991–2003
Green party seats (% of total seats), average 1991–2003
Green party members in cabinet, average 1991–2003

Note: Parties were coded as green if they were members or observers of the Global Greens and/or European Greens networks.

Methodology (vote and seats):
To obtain national averages for 1991–2003, the sum of the percentage of the overall vote received by green parties in parliamentary elections (presidential in the case of the United States) / total parliamentary seats (House of Representatives in the case of the United States) occupied by green parties for every year in the period was divided by the number of years. Years between elections were assigned the result from the previous election.

Methodology (cabinet):
This variable indicates the average number of green party members who were part of a government cabinet in each country, for each year in the period.
   Note: Figures for Belgium and the Netherlands are for two green parties. For Portugal 1990–2003 and Hungary 2002–2003, data are for the percentage of green party seats.

Government social spending, as % of GDP, average 1990–2003

Source: OECD 2008

Methodology:

To obtain an average for 1990–2003 for each country, the sum of government social spending (as a percentage of GNI) for every year in the period was divided by the number of years.

Neo-corporatism (mean score of 23 studies conducted between 1981–1997)

Source: Siaroff 1999

Countries excluded due to missing data: the Czech Republic, Hungary, Poland, Slovenia

Official Development Assistance, net, as % of donor state's GNI, average 1996–2003

Source: World Bank 2006

Methodology:
To obtain an average for 1996–2003 for each country, the sum of net ODA (as a percentage of GNI) for every year in the period was divided by the number of years.

SOCIAL CAPITAL

Generalized trust (%), 2002
Membership in humanitarian, peace, environmental, or animal rights organizations (% of population), 2002
Membership in consumer/automobile organization (% of population), 2002
Membership in any voluntary organization (% of population) 2002

Methodology:
The first variable is a composite, derived from three variables in the *European Social Survey* 2002/2003 that ask respondents to place themselves on a scale (0–10) with respect to the following questions: 1) Do you think that most people would try to take advantage of you if they got the chance, or would they try to be fair? 2) Most people can be trusted, or you can't be too careful? 3) Most of the time people are helpful, or they're looking out for themselves? In order to derive a composite, aggregate measure for each country, we merged the three trust variables to create a generalized trust variable, then obtained the percentage of respondents in each country whose trust levels were above 5 (higher trust).

The second variable is a composite, derived from two variables in the *European Social Survey* 2002/2003 that ask respondents whether in the last twelve months they have been members of 1) a humanitarian organization or 2) a peace, environmental, or animal rights organization. In order to derive a composite, aggregate measure for each country, we obtained the percentage of respondents in each country who answered "yes" to either of these questions.

The third variable is derived from a variable in the *European Social Survey* 2002/2003 that asks respondents whether in the last twelve months they have been members of a consumer/automobile organization. In order to derive an aggregate measure for each country, we obtained the percentage of respondents in each country who answered "yes" to this question.

The fourth variable is a composite, derived from twelve variables in the *European Social Survey* 2002/2003 that ask respondents whether in the last twelve months they have been members of 1) a sports/outdoor activity club, 2) a cultural/hobby activity organization, 3) a trade union, 4) a business/profession/farmers organization, 5) a consumer/automobile organization, 6) a humanitarian organization, 7) an environmental/peace/animal rights organization, 8) a religious/church organization, 9) a political party, 10) a science/education/teacher organization, 11) a social club, and 12) an other voluntary organization. In order to derive a composite, aggregate measure for each country, we obtained the percentage of respondents in each country who answered "yes" to any of these questions.

Source: Jowell et al. 2003

Countries excluded due to insufficient data: the Czech Republic and Switzerland

RELIGION

Church attendance, 2002
Level of religiosity, 2002

Methodology:
These are derived from two variables in the *European Social Survey* 2002/2003. The first asks respondents how frequently they attend church; the second asks "How religious are you?" In order to derive an aggregate measure for each country, we obtained the average country response for each variable.

5

The Organizational Setting for Political Consumerism

INTRODUCTION

Where do the individuals who engage in Buy Nothing Day, dive into trash to salvage and eat discarded food, or decide to look for an organic or a fairtrade cup of coffee get these ideas? How do the large numbers of people who boycott and buycott for political, ethical, and environmental reasons decide which products to look out for? More generally, what makes an increasing number of individuals, groups, and even business leaders aware of the politics of products? For some, friends might be the important source of information, inspiration, and participation. Others might come into contact with political consumerism in their local community, through holiday and sports events, civic groups and networks, or different media sources. But most likely all the ideas in one way or another find their origin in political consumer market campaigns (cf. O'Rourke 2005) run by the groups and institutions that form the organizational setting for political consumerism. Efforts by political consumer labeling schemes and activist groups involve a span of campaign activities that attempt to change what scholars identify as the "register of responsibility" embedded in the complex role of the consumer (Malpass, Barnett, Clarke, and Cloke 2007, 240). Scholars identify activism developing in the "new geography of globalization from below" (Cravey 2004, 204), which involves less conventional ventures and venues and, as illustrated in the sections below, is envisioned to have the ability to connect people locally and worldwide with globalized political problems.

This chapter contributes to the discussions in the previous chapters by investigating the informational and choice architecture prerequisites for reasonable choice theorized in Chapter 1.[1] It discusses how civil society actors and other institutions promote public awareness about the politics of products, attempt in different and at times creative ways to cultivate a caring sensitivity for shopping choices on the part of individuals and others, and to mobilize people into practices of a more individualized responsibility-taking character. It focuses on important developments, strategies, and even problems in eight identified organizational settings for political consumerism historically to the 2000s and examines how and why each setting has played a critical role in the rise of political consumerism. The discussion of the organizational settings employs previous research to identify and map involved actors, mobilizing events, and actions. Its focus is primarily "third-party" or "type 1" labeling schemes. Unlike business-led labeling initiatives, third-party schemes certify products more independently from business and at times even government; they have been found to have a high degree of transparency, quality control, and accountability (cf. Cashore, Auld, and Newsom 2004a, 2004b, 2004c, Boström and Klintman 2011, Appleton 1997, Cook, Downes, van Dyke, and Weiner 1997). In this vein, the chapter highlights organic food, fairtrade, and eco-labeling schemes and discusses briefly third-party certification in the field of forestry and seafood. Special attention is devoted to how these organizational settings mobilize citizens into buycott political consumerism, the most practiced form (see previous chapters). However, universal or global labeling schemes are only part of the political consumer organizational story. Anti-sweatshop activism is also a crucial development for the theorizing on new models of political responsibility (Chapter 1) and new venues for political action (Chapter 2). In order to map the settings for political consumerism more fully, three other organizational fields must be explored: socially responsible investing, farm animal activism, and lifestyle political consumerism. The concluding section discusses some common developments in the organizational settings and efforts towards

---

[1] For this chapter, a deductive and inductive research strategy has been employed. Deductively we have used previous research to identify the organizational settings. This scholarship has identified an organic food movement, a fair trade movement, an anti-sweatshop movement, "ecological modernization" driven eco-labels, and socially responsible investing as distinct fields of activism. We use this scholarship in identifying these movements as forming certain political consumer organizational settings. Other organizational settings have been identified by collating scholarship on activism with a similar focus, e.g., animal rights and animal welfare into farm animal activism. Theoretical insights from previous research on political consumerism and emerging forms of activism helped to identify lifestyle political consumerism as a particular organizational setting. Our theoretical focus on choice architecture as well as previous research on environmental stewardship was employed to identify the organizational setting of forest and marine stewardship. More inductively we have scrutinized activist networks and labeling schemes (both primary and secondary literature) and allowed our findings to help map and sort out these main organizational settings. This methodology helps us address certain elements of the concept of individualized responsibility-taking empirically (that is, to demonstrate and explain how individuals are informed, sensitized, and mobilized into political consumer practices through choice architecture and choice editing) and to systematize activism historically to contemporary times.

collaboration and harmonization on the political, ethical, and environmental politics of products.

LABELING SCHEMES FOR POLITICAL CONSUMER CHOICE

Labeling schemes provide simple and categorical information about consumer products. Some schemes just include information on product content on their packaging. Others, such as many business self-certifying or self-declaring schemes, have developed as a reaction to third-party labels in wood certification (Cashore, Auld and Newson 2006, Boström and Klintman 2011, 52–53), fairtrade (e.g., Utz Kapeh, see Chapter 7 in this book), or consumer activism. Large retailers – Marks & Spencer, Tesco, Carrefour, Whole Foods Market, Woolworth, and others – have developed their own private labels (cf. Kumar and Steenkamp 2007). Such labels address GMOs (see Oosterveer 2007, 125 for a listing), carbon footprinting, or their products' general social and environmental impact (*New York Times* 2009b, *Guardian* 2009, Carbon Trust 2011). Other private labels bundle together different standards under one heading and simplify complex food information for consumers (Schurman and Munro 2009, 182).[2] Governments participate in third-party schemes (e.g., USDA Organic and the German eco-label Blue Angel) or devise ones similar to private labeling strategies, as with the Keyhole Symbol which was started by the Swedish National Food Administration in 1989 as a voluntary label without certification procedures for business to use to help Swedish and now Nordic consumers identify healthier food options (Nordic Council of Ministers no date).

ORGANIC FOOD ACTIVISM AND LABELING SCHEMES
FOR AGRICULTURAL PRODUCTION

Organic food is one of the oldest organizational settings for political consumerism. It is also the largest and most institutionalized and continues to grow and spread around the globe (see Chapter 4). A large span of activists with somewhat different goals, values, and opinions are involved in what is often called the organic movement. They include advocates of the principles of small-scale organic farming, community-supported agriculture, and animal welfare, religious communities, lifestyle and health consumers, groups focusing on public procurement of organic food, and activist networks demanding that transnational corporations in agri-businesses take more responsibility for their commodities and production. Support for organic farming has also come

---

[2] For instance, the "ICA I love eco" label developed by the large Swedish supermarket chain ICA bundles together third-party labeled fairtrade and organic food, is used on products with one label (e.g., the EU organic label), or alternatively even designates certification by labels that are not fully third-party in character (e.g., UTZ, Rainforest Alliance) (http://www.ica.se/ICAs-egna-varor/Vara-egna-varumarken/Vara-egna-varumarken/ICA-I-love-eco/).

from nationalist and far left political groups and agricultural interests favoring protectionism from foreign competition (Reed 2001, Conford 2001, 215, Dimbleby 2001, 13, Winter 2004). Today, the International Federation of Organic Agriculture Movements (IFOAM, founded in 1972) coordinates and attempts to create agreement among these diversified groups that form the global organic movement (Reed 2001, Raynolds 2000, 2004, Conford 2001, Boström and Klintman 2011, Kristiansen, Taji, and Raganold 2006, Oosterveer 2007). IFOAM is the only global organic NGO in existence and has, as such, accredited status in global governmental and nongovernmental forums on food policy and safety (IFOAM 2011).[3] Today, the IFOAM-led organic movement globally includes more than half the countries in the world; its organic labeling schemes certify a growing number of goods that now include animal food, plant food, aquaculture farmed fish and shellfish, wild produced food from forest, natural lands, pastures and uncultivated land, processed food, cotton products, and certain other goods such as gardening soil and seeds. It has shown resiliency since the 2008 economic crisis.

The organic food movement started as an alternative lifestyle for farmers and others concerned with soil life, food good for human health, and small-scale biodynamic or alternative farming. Its origins can be traced at least to the mid-1800s when ideas were brought to Europe from colonies in Asia. Cultural and societal elites have played a role in its promotion, importantly Austrian philosopher Rudolf Steiner whose publications and support facilitated the establishment of the Demeter biodynamic label in 1928 (a very strict form of organic farming) and Lady Eve Balfoul whose book on experimental organic farming, *The Living Soil*, helped pave the way for the British Soil Association (founded in 1946), the foremost actor in the British organic movement and an influential one globally. The term "organic farming" is attributed to an English baron who compared it to "chemical farming."[4] Early-on organic agriculture was regulated informally through loosely developed codes of conduct and informal inspection (Courville 2006, 202). An important turning point for the movement was the publication of Rachel Carson's bestselling book *Silent Spring* (1962), which sensitized the public to pesticide use in agriculture. The book caused a heated public controversy involving chemical and seed companies (including Monsanto, later to become a central target of contentious food

---

[3] IFOAM is a member or accredited participant in eight UN bodies, including the Food and Agricultural Organization, Environmental Program (UNEP), and Framework Convention on Climate Change (UNFCCC), and participates in the two large umbrella institutions for harmonizing and standardizing voluntary certification and labeling, International Organization for Standardization (ISO) and International Social and Environmental Accreditation and Labelling Alliance (ISEAL).

[4] Demeter later developed an international labeling scheme network with about 3,500 products sold mainly in health and natural food stores in more than fifty countries globally (http://www.demeter.net, accessed March 14, 2011). For more information on the origin of the term organic farming, see Reed (2010, 70).

activism), and is credited with galvanizing support for the U.S. governmental ban of the pesticide DDT in 1972, as crucial for the creation of the postwar environmental movement (an important proponent and mobilizer for organic food), and the reason for the British Soil Association's decision to establish its national labeling scheme in 1967 (Smith 2001, Oreskes and Conway 2010, chapter 10, Kroll 2001, Conford 2001, 214, Kristiansen 2006, 6).[5] Sensitized consumers in other countries either followed sub-national labeling schemes (e.g., those in California and Vermont that started up in the early 1970s) or shopped for so-called natural foods directly from smaller farmers or at such stores as Safer Way Natural Foods (later to merge into Whole Foods Market in 1980) (interview with Friström 2001; also Harbin and Humphrey 2010). These groups and others, and particularly the French Nature et Progrès, would later become important advocates for a more universal certification of organic food and strong opponents of genetic engineering (Schurman and Munro 2006, 1, Buttel 2000, 5).

The late 1960s and 1970s have been identified as the beginning of the organic movement's new activist era (Conford 2001, 211, Raynolds 2004, Kristiansen 2006, Courville 2006). By 1980, IFOAM issued its first common definition of organic farming (focusing on food produced from renewable resources, without antibiotics and growth hormones, that conserved the soil and water and enhanced biodiversity), and alternative farmers campaigned side by side with societal elites, scientists, consumer and environmental activists and even political parties to raise public awareness about what they believed were problems associated with large-scale agriculture. The movement's complexity and "series of interwoven values" (Torjusen, Sangstad, O'Doherty Jensen, and Kjærnes 2004, 13) is demonstrated by the issues on its globalized agenda: pesticide use, farm animal welfare, transnational agri-business, and now the relationship between climate change and global poverty. Both self-interest (personal health and lifestyle) and other-oriented interest (climate change, environmental, and animal stewardship) play a role in the organic movement (see also Chapters 3 and 8).

More food activism, consumer concern, media attention as well as governmental and business responses were triggered by the so-called food scares in the 1980s and the 1990s. Particularly, the intense public controversy and news reporting on genetic engineering (GE) and genetically modified organisms (GMOs), with catchy British newspaper titles like "Mutant Crops" and "Terrifying Tampering," mobilized greater interest in organic food. Activism soared with the emergence of networks and groups to mobilize for the cause: the U.S. Pure Food Campaign founded in 1992 and the Organic Consumers Association founded in 1998 are two examples. National and global environmental

[5] See also: "Our Achievements," Soil Association, http://www.soilassociation.org/aboutus/ourhistory/ourachievements/tabid/71/default.aspx (accessed August 9, 2012).

organizations became involved or intensified their involvement. Scholars under-score the importance of Greenpeace International's decision in 1996 to dedicate key organizational resources to campaign against GE (Schurman 2004, 252). In this period, organic food advocates also started to emphasize the personal health angle over their traditional natural scientific arguments to mobilize sup-port. They framed their message as the need for "pure" and "natural" food and played off popular culture when they called GE food "Frankenstein food" from "terminator seeds" (cf. West and Larue 2005, Lockie, Lyons, Lawrence, and Mummery 2002, Buttel 2000, Conford 2001, 211).

Activism targeted national government and involved litigation, for example in 1997 when the Sierra Club, Greenpeace, IFOAM, and others filed a legal petition to the U.S. Environmental Protection Agency for approving genetically modified crops. It also involved extensive efforts in mobilizing people globally to sign petitions and engage in protest demonstrations, boycotts, and letter-writing campaigns directed at both industry and government (e.g., West and Larue 2005). In 1992, the Pure Food Campaign coordinated a NGO-supported international boycott against GE and demanded mandatory labeling of all GM food products. Greenpeace activists engaged in spectacular and theatrical political performance that even involved stripping naked at the 1996 World Food Summit in Rome, blockading the ports of destination for the first delivery of Monsanto GMO seed for the European market (Schurman and Munro 2006, 25) and then in 1999 chaining themselves to gates in Spain as part of the broad 1999 European campaign "Take the GM out of Animal Feed." Some celebrities – including the Prince of Wales, TV actors, celebrity cooks, and rock stars – came out to support and publicize the organic food and anti-GMO cause (Charles 2001, chapters 14, 16).[6] Local and national newspapers in the United States were targeted with letter-writing campaigns, and The Sierra Club, Greenpeace, and about sixty other groups collaborated on financing three full-page *New York Times* advertisements titled "Globalization vs. Nature" shortly before the 1999 WTO summit in Seattle. Later, groups in France, Spain, and India started so-called "bio-sabotage" that involved destroying GM crops in open fields (Schurman 2004, 253), illustrating that "eye-catching gimmicks" (Sun 1997, 6) and performative actions are growing in importance within political consumerism (see Chapter 8).

The strategy of anti-GMO activists was to use corporate competitiveness as agri-business' Achilles' heel by targeting well-known brands in seed and chem-icals, food processing, fast-food, and supermarket retailing, and mobilizing food consumers cross-nationally to boycott certain popular brands (e.g., Ger-ber, Kraft, Kellogg) and several fast-food chains (Schurman and Munro 2009). McDonald's was the main target for the well-known activist and politician José

[6] See Josie Clarke (September 1, 2001), "Celebrities Strike a Pose Against GM," *New Zealand Her-ald*, http://www.nzherald.co.nz/nz/news/article.cfm?c_id=1&objectid=213079 (accessed August 9, 2012).

Bové.[7] In the United Kingdom, Friends of the Earth, the British Soil Association, the Women's Environmental Network, and others passed out leaflets to food shoppers to pressure large supermarkets to stop stocking GM foods (Schurman 2004, 253). More than any other business, the Monsanto Company was the target of aggressive campaigning. It was brought to court, antibranded and culture jammed (see Chapter 6 for definitions) into "Muntanto," "Monsatan," and "Global Leader Cereal Killer" (Smith 2010, Robin 2010, see picture slide of a culture jam in chapter 8 of Charles 2001). It was Greenpeace International's main target in its large 1996 campaign and the focus of the 1999 international grassroots groups' effort "GE-Global Day of Action against Monsanto." In 2006, the Organic Consumers Association started its now annual "Millions against Monsanto" campaign. Greenpeace also drew on scare tactics relating to personal health when it proclaimed "No need for condoms – GE corn can do the job" to publicize a report linking a Monsanto produced strain of transgenic corn with lower levels of fertility in mice.[8] This example is important because it demonstrates how scare tactics have, in one way or another, been part of political consumerism and particularly farm animal activism (see section below in this chapter and discussion in Chapter 8 of this book, Micheletti and Stolle 2012).

Activist campaigning and the ensuing public debate created a caring sensitivity (see Chapter 1) on the part of many consumers, who then demanded a GM label. Public attitude changed particularly in some countries previously less critical of GMOs in food. Eurobarometer polls showed that U.K. opposition to GMOs in food increased from 33 percent in 1996 to 53 percent in 1999, Greek opposition from 51 percent to 81 percent and in Luxembourg from 44 percent to 70 percent (see Schurman 2004, 255). Even consumer trust in agri-business and science is reported to have dropped, and citizen distrust in governmental agricultural policy and government's role in assuring food safety to have increased (Torjusen et al. 2004, 117, Moore 2001 174–175, Roff 2007; see other sources in Raynolds 2004). Some scholars maintain that heightened public awareness about mad cow disease led consumers, at least temporarily, to panic and stop purchasing beef in many Northern nations (Oosterveer 2007, chapter 5, Pfannhauser and Reichhart 2003). Boycotts were called, and in the late 1990s some large food corporations (e.g., Marks and Spencer, Nestlé, Heinz, Frito-Lay, McDonald's, and the Japanese beer brewers Sapporo and Kirin) decided to eliminate certain GMO food products from their lines (see Schurman 2004 for more listings). Some of the corporations

---

[7] José Bové has been a candidate for the French presidency and has been involved as an activist against GMOs and globalization. He is the spokesperson for the Confederation Paysanne and now member of the European Parliament.

[8] See more at Greenpeace (2009), "No need for condoms: GE corn can do the job," Greenpeace Indian web site, http://www.greenpeace.org/india/en/news/no-need-for-condoms-ge-corn (accessed December 2011).

decided to go further and create their own private GM labels as a way to satisfy more fully consumers' concerns. Interestingly, Kellogg rejected activist demands because it did not find sufficient consumer interest for non-GM food products (Schurman and Munro 2009, 178). IFOAM's engagement in the anti-GMO debate involved advocacy for the introduction of mandatory and comprehensive labeling for genetically engineered agricultural products; whereas a more comprehensive labeling was not a controversial issue in Europe, it divided sentiments in the United States.

While European food activism has become less confrontational due to governmental and corporate action (see note 9 to this chapter), U.S. groups still agitate against Monsanto, continue to demand a mandatory GM label, and campaign for the right of consumers to know and choose what is in their food. The Millions against Monsanto campaign has formed local chapters in all 435 federal congressional districts, and rallies support at World Food Day (which has become its nationwide action day) and at green festivals throughout the United States. The GMO campaign has led to multiple mobilization efforts for organic food more globally but particularly in the Northern world. Consumers are, for instance, asked to promote community-supported agriculture and use both organic labels and green food guides (e.g., the Organic Consumers Association's GreenPeople directory). Activist groups even run awareness and caring sensitivity information and mobilization campaigns close to major gift-giving and food-eating holidays (e.g., Thanksgiving, Christmas, Mother's Day) and, in so doing, create additional market venues or "new geography" for the practice of political consumer individualized responsibility-taking. The Organic Consumers Association's Valentine's Day campaign is interesting because it relies on both solidarity emotions and guilt when it claims that "by purchasing organic and fairtrade chocolate and flowers... your consumer dollars will no longer be going towards toxic pesticides, child slavery, and farm worker exploitation" (Organic Consumers Association 2011). In Europe, mainstream supermarkets stock a growing assortment of organically labeled goods, feature them in their advertisements, and discuss their benefits on their web sites. The Walt Disney Company even campaigns for organic milk. These efforts increase the availability of organic food. Governments have also provided support for organic production and consumption.[9] This support tends to legitimate the organic movement. It bolsters the authority of organic certification systems, consolidates the world market for certified products, and aids international organic trade. Interestingly, critics note that organic production has also benefited

---

[9] Governments in the United States, European Union, and Sweden have legislated on a common standard for organic certification. Denmark, the United States, and the EU have established and operate organic food labeling schemes. Sweden, the United Kingdom, and other governments encourage public authorities to procure organic food (see Micheletti 2010, epilogue). In South Korea and Sweden, governments are guiding farmers to participate in organic farming. The Organisation for Economic Co-operation and Development (2003) has formulated certain policy regulation and enforcement that has promoted organic labeling.

from free-trade doctrines and even neoliberal deregulation (Courville 2006, Raynolds 2004, 731).[10]

While mobilization has created more caring sensitivity and demand for organically labeled goods, it has also had certain consequences for the organic movement itself. IFOAM is, for example, continually forced to mediate the diverse interests that make up the organic food movement and particularly the two important factions of the ideological small-scale farming "movement" and the large-scale labeling mainstream "market" segments. One such important mediation process from 2003 led to the formulation of four general mission principles – "health," "ecology," "fairness" and "care" – that aim at promoting widespread individualized responsibility-taking in the food and agricultural sector for current and future generations and the environment (IFOAM 2009; for criticisms of these principles, see Roff 2007, Pollan 2006). Moreover, given the increasing importance of mainstreaming organic food labeling, there is concern among scholars that the corporate world increasingly tends to dominate national organic labeling schemes because it has been successful in getting its products certified as organic (Boström and Klintman 2011, 170). Certain activist mobilizing groups now advocate what they call "beyond organic" that focuses more on eating fresh and locally produced organic food and slow food (Thompson and Coskuner-Balli 2007, Nijhius 2007; see later section on lifestyle political consumerism and Chapter 8). Dealing with the rise in consumer demand for organic food reveals, therefore, the complex series of interwoven and at times conflicting values that challenge the future of political consumerism in regard to food.

FAIRTRADE LABELS FOR GLOBAL SOCIAL JUSTICE

A second organizational setting of political consumerism with a well-developed global choice architecture in the form of a universal labeling scheme is fairtrade. Its roots can be found in the struggle against slavery in England when activists

---

[10] In 1997, the European Commission required that every EU member state enacts a law mandating the labeling of all new products containing GMOs. In 2001, the U.S. Department of Agriculture established a voluntary label for business to use to identify if their products did or did not contain GM ingredients (Gruere and Rao 2007). In 2007, the European Council of Agricultural Ministers established a European organic label (EU-organic, now "EU Leaf") that can be used separately or together with national organic labels (European Commission no date). The important organic food actor, the British Social Association, has been a particularly harsh and vocal opponent of the EU Leaf's establishment. Its policy director has declared that it "runs completely counter to the spirit of the pioneers of the organic movement, which grew from the grassroots, prioritizing local distinctiveness, care for the environment and animal welfare" and "mimics the agribusiness model of globally competitive, freely traded commodity production" (Melchett 2007). The Swedish case demonstrates that the EU-label can lead to a loss of market share for more stringent certification criteria. This happened when the large Swedish meat producer SCAN AB decided in 2008 to change its certification for its meat products from the national KRAV organic label to the EU Leaf. Consumer and retailer pressure, however, forced it to change this general decision but it has retained the EU Leaf for some of its products, most notably the Falu sausage (a big seller) that cannot receive KRAV certification (SCAN 2009, KRAV 2010).

called consumers into large boycotts and even some buycotts of "slave-grown" cotton, sugar, and tea after the British parliament voted down an abolition bill in 1792 (Micheletti 2007, 128). Contemporary fair trade is commonly dated to the 1940s and 1950s and to the efforts of religious, charity, and third-world solidarity groups. Since its start it has focused mainly on buycott political consumerism (see Low and Davenport 2005). Oxfam, the important contemporary fair trade organization established by the Quakers in the early 1940s for famine relief, sold crafts produced in third-world countries in its charity shops (first opened in Oxford in 1948) that later developed into world-oriented shops. In the 1960s, 1970s, and 1980s growing concern about the effects of international trade on developing countries mobilized other interests to the cause. More world-oriented solidarity shops were opened, with some run by the U.K. workers cooperative Equal Exchange and Traidcraft, now the largest British fair trade organization.

The early fair trade movement used commodities, including again cane sugar, to educate about third-world solidarity (Low and Davenport 2005, 145). The solidarity stores became special geographic venues of activist mobilization for a new international economic order that focused on "trade not aid" and involved responsibility-sharing between the North and Southern producers. Voluntary supporters worked in the solidarity stores, which unlike contemporary fair trade sold mostly non-food products of poorer material quality (Davies, Doherty, and Know, 2010, Reed 2009, 5). Scholars emphasize how early fair trade, though a marginal political and economic force, created a political community of likeminded individuals that involved cooperative movements in India and Southern Europe (see Low and Davenport 2005, Livraghi and Pappadà 2009). Fair trade burgeoned in the late 1980s to early 1990s when new organizations were established (e.g., the European Fair Trade Association founded in 1987, the International Fair Trade Association in 1989 – now the World Fair Trade Organization – the U.K. Fair Trade Foundation in 1991, the Network of European Worldshops (NEWS!) in 1994, and the U.S. Equal Exchange in 1986, which was the first U.S. business to adopt internationally recognized fairtrade standards).

The establishment of labeling schemes began to popularize the fair trade mission, broaden its list of commodities, and facilitate its entrance into mainstream supermarkets. The first scheme, the Dutch Max Havelaar (founded in 1988), has been considered an "immediate success" (Reed 2009, 5) because it helped to solve the problem of protecting small coffee farmers once coffee prices declined after the governmental regulating body, the International Coffee Organization, had difficulty in negotiating a new agreement that regulated the price of coffee. Other national fairtrade labeling schemes were rapidly established in the first half of the 1990s (see Chapter 4).

Targeting brands is another characteristic that fair trade political consumerism has in common with other organizational settings. Starbucks has, for instance, been used to mobilize support for the cause. The U.S.-based Global Exchange and other groups conducted a series of campaigns against its well-known brandscape (see Chapter 6) of coffee shops and even planned a national day of protest that was cancelled when the company agreed to sell fairtrade coffee. This effort inspired activists in other countries to pressure Starbucks and other well-known national large coffee shops (Fridell 2004, 146). Global Exchange uses coffee and other fairtrade goods (particularly chocolate) in discursive campaigns for public education-for-action (e.g., summer 1999) and in its speaking tours. It has even attempted to get Procter & Gamble's shareholders to use shareholder activism to persuade the corporation to offer fairtrade coffee (Global Exchange 2008, James 2002; see Chapter 8). Market-based activism is also revealed in the establishment of cooperatives and ethical businesses (e.g., Cafédirect founded in the United Kingdom in 1991) to sell fairtrade (and even organic coffee) on a larger scale and in the shop directories posted on activist group web sites. Examples include Green America's "Fairtrade Your Supermarket" web site that encourages consumers to order action kits to test their supermarkets' fairtrade profile and suggests a variety of discursive actions (leaving messages on shelves, contacting the store manager, etc.) to pressure stores to stock more fairtrade goods. The tactic of pressuring stores in this fashion has been used by other fairtrade groups; Christian Aid (founded in the 1940s) carried out a campaign in which hundreds of thousands of supporters handed in their receipts to stores as a way of voicing a demand to produce goods under better labor standards.

Large public institutional consumers – universities, legislatures, public agencies, and so on – are also targeted to procure fairtrade coffee (see also Chapter 7). First in the United States, then Canada and Europe, student activists have attempted to mobilize fellow students to choose fairtrade coffee and pressure their university administrators to do likewise. Global Exchange and others have assisted students in coordinating fairtrade coffee campaigns and have been joined by United Students Against Sweatshops (see section on anti-sweatshop political consumerism below), campus environmental groups, and others to raise awareness, create caring sensitivities, and mobilize support for fairtrade. Although they followed the same strategy as anti-sweatshop political consumerism, they were initially less successful in influencing university procurement policy (for discussion, see Fridell 2004). Even in Global Exchange's own San Francisco surroundings, Rick Young, fresh out of the University of California, Berkeley's Boalt Hall School of Law, ran up against local business opposition to his citizen's initiative mandating that all coffee sold at the university and the city of Berkeley must be fairtrade labeled, organic, and/or shade grown. Perhaps his initiative was too forerunning for the local community, his advocacy too confrontational in tone, or there were simply too many coordinating problems within the American fairtrade movement (Interview with Young 2002, Linton, Liou, and Shaw 2004, Jaffee 2010, Reed 2009). However, today, similar ideas in the form of fairtrade universities and towns are spreading throughout Europe and North America (see Chapter 7). A large spectrum of actors globally (including many from the organic food, eco-labeling, anti-sweatshop, and lifestyle political consumer settings), businesses, conventional supermarkets, public institutions, and national governments now play a role in providing information and mobilizing buycotting support for fairtrade-certified goods. For instance, in the late 1990s, the Belgian government created the Belgian Fair Trade Center and began to contribute economically to fairtrade activities directed at development cooperation (Huybrechts 2010, 220, 234). Funding institutions also support fairtrade activism, as illustrated by a grant to Oxfam in 2001 for "Promoting Ethical Consumer Choice in the United States" that involved student coffee organizer training and led to the creation of United Students for Fair Trade in 2003 (usft.org/history).

These developments led to fairtrade developing institutionally and, therefore, gaining stability. Fairtrade Labelling Organisations International (FLO-I, now Fairtrade International, FLO), founded in 1997, presently coordinates and represents a total of twenty-one labeling schemes operating in fifteen countries. In 2002, it launched the international Fairtrade Certification Mark after the main coordinating groups agreed on a common definition of fairtrade in 2001 (cf. Low and Davenport 2005, 149). Worldshops, that is retail shops that specifically sell fair-traded goods, have been affected by the general fair trade developments. They now must compete with supermarket chains and are forced to professionalize their activities considerably (Becchetti and Castantino 2010, Gendron Bisaillon and Rance 2009).

Some scholars argue that the development of fairtrade represents a general political transformation in social movement activism from targeting the parliamentary to targeting the economic sphere. They maintain that this turn can lead to innovative new geography (venues) for the movement to mobilize for responsibility-taking in the current period of globalization and ongoing reassessment of public institutions' role in solving complex problems (cf. Gendron, Bisaillon, and Rance 2009, Wilkinson 2007). Others argue that fair trade as a movement is at a critical juncture (Hudson and Hudson 2009, cf. Jaffee 2010). Of particular interest is that mainstreaming the cause appears to imply that a number of involved groups, especially the labeling schemes, seek to de-emphasize the political ideological roots of fairtrade and to avoid identifying it a political lifestyle choice or community (Davies, Doherty, and Know 2010, 130). Perhaps this apparent flight from ideology is an attempt to balance the fairtrade mission- and money-driven forces (cf. Fridell 2009) or an example of the trade-offs involved in creating a global governance framework for new farmers' politics (cf. Rice 2001). If so, it parallels developments in other political consumer settings and particularly the eco-pragmatism found in the eco-labeling movement.

ECO-LABELING FOR ENVIRONMENTAL CONSUMER CHOICE

Eco-labels are the third highly institutionalized organizational setting for political consumerism. They aim at offering citizens clear and simple information that certified consumer goods and now even some services are rated as less harmful for the environment. This example of organized political consumerism grew out of the new green activism of the 1960s, which redirected attention from nature conservation to consumption's and production's role in environmental pollution. Generally, eco-labels have a rather low-key presence in political consumerism, and, unlike the organic and fairtrade movements discussed above, this organizational setting does not really have long historical roots. Nor has it advanced in popularity by using emotionally charged messages and highly contentious political consumer activism. The civil society and even governmental initiators of eco-labels have from the start sought to work together with industry and reflect, therefore, the eco-pragmatism of ecological modernization, that is, the necessity of coordinating economic growth with protection of the environment through a pragmatic green governance policy framework involving the state, civil society, science, and the market in responsibility-taking endeavors (Mol 2000, Boström and Klintman 2011, 20–21, 123). However, before the schemes were institutionalized, boycotts were called on paper, mercury batteries, disposable diapers, and other goods. Activists still hold yearly special green shopping and discursive events and offer online green shopping guides (see e.g., O´Rourke 2005, Micheletti 2010, chapter 4). Green consciousness-raising on consumption's environmental effects and consumer mobilization into green shopping has, to large degree, also been part of general environmental activism supported by governmental efforts to promote greener practices (e.g., recycling, less energy use, etc.). Its early acceptance by government and business perhaps explains why it differs from the other organizational settings.

Much previous research on eco-labels focuses on explaining their emergence rather than on the activism behind them. This scholarship identifies disappointments in governmental policy-making and changes in political climate as the main reasons for their creation. Along the lines of individualized responsibility-taking and challenges to the conventional model of political responsibility, green activists in the 1980s and 1990 began to reevaluate government as the main agent and arena for environmental protection. Scholars find that green groups believed that the parliamentary sphere favored infrastructural projects (highways, airports, approval of certain locations for industrial development, etc.) that they opposed adamantly or, as in the case of Sweden, were highly dissatisfied with how government managed anti-nuclear power sentiment (Mol 2000, Micheletti 2010, chapter 4). These groups also realized that their effectiveness depended on working in the political climate of policy deregulation (neoliberalism, free trade) that favored competitive market forces and gave priority to economic development (Jordan, Wurzel, and Zito 2003). Well-established environmental associations cross-nationally were also influenced by ideas included in *Our Common Future* (the so-called Bruntland Report from 1987) for the World Commission on Environment and Development, which argued that economic growth and environmental protection should and could go hand in hand. Thus, they began to devise ways to bring consumers and corporations (the two main market actors) into "beyond compliance" green governance arrangements (Mol 2000, 49, 2001, Chapter 5). Scholars also point out that the European Union aided the establishment of eco-labeling schemes when it simplified its public regulation rules and developed more sensitive tools for sustainable development (Jordan, Wurzel, and Zito 2003). Today eco-labels are quite prevalent and widely used in Europe, which has several national and two large supra-national schemes. As discussed in Chapter 4, the spread of these schemes are an important explanation for the high rise in "buycott" activity particularly in Northern Europe.

Campaigning for more environmentally friendly and reasonable consumer choice (see Chapter 1) became part of the green action repertoire and problem-solving strategy in this period. Older nature conservation organizations, such as the Sierra Club (founded in 1892) and the Swedish Society for the Conservation of Nature (founded in 1909), began to appeal to consumers and engage in market-based activism. They followed the path of newer global environmental organizations, for instance Greenpeace, established in the early 1970s, and World Wildlife Fund for Nature (formed in the early 1960s and now known simply as WWF), attuned to the importance of more individualized political responsibility-taking and the role that market forces could play in protecting and promoting the environment (Mol 2000). Interviews with green activists in different countries confirm how they felt that eco-labeling let them offer consumers positive advice and problem-solving alternatives rather than just discouraging them from certain consumer practices (see Micheletti 2010, chapter 4, Piotrowski and Kratz 1999). Older consumer advocates even joined the green consumption cause: well-known U.S. consumer advocate Ralph Nader traveled to Europe to teach environmental organizations about working together with corporations on consumer issues and voiced early ideas on the consumer power of governments. In so doing, he foreshadowed later activist efforts to target governmental public procurement policy (see Chapter 7, Micheletti 2010, 125, Nader, Lewis, and Weltman 1992).

The first eco-labeling scheme, the Blue Angel, was established in West Germany in 1977 as a response to German public pressure on the need to create trustworthy opportunities for green shopping. Today, it certifies about 11,500 products and services in roughly ninety product categories.[11] Other eco-labeling schemes followed in the 1980s and 1990s: Canadian Environmental Choice (1988); Nordic Swan, now called the Nordic Ecolabel in English (1989), and the European Flower, now the EU Ecolabel (1992), and several other national schemes. The Nordic and EU labels were initiated by two supra-national governmental bodies, the Nordic Council of Ministers and European Commission, respectively. Today, a global nonprofit association, the Global Ecolabelling Network (GEN, established in 1994) coordinates eco-labeling ideas and practices, includes twenty-six third-party eco-labeling schemes

---

[11] http://www.blauer-engel.de/en/blauer_engel/index.php (accessed April 18, 2011).

worldwide and has members from twenty-two countries.[12] GEN's members certify many different commodities – household chemicals, detergents, personal-care products, paper, office furniture and equipment, computers and cell phones, batteries, heavy electrical consumer durable goods or white goods such as refrigerators, washing machines, and the like, paint, building materials, motor vehicles, public transportation, tourist accommodations, restaurants, supermarkets, and energy.[13] Specific labeling schemes that promote more sustainable energy efficiency are also growing in number (Banerjee and Solomon 2003, Boström and Klintman 2011, 58–60).[14]

Eco-labeling's proliferation globally is often considered to be a success story for political consumerism (Boström and Klintman 2011, Rubik 2005, Jordan, Wurzel, and Zito 2003). Eco-labels are frequently used by individual consumers and within public procurement. However, as with some other organizational settings, the activist groups promoting eco-labeling have been criticized for selling out the green "small is beautiful" and alternative lifestyle cause by integrating mainstream consumption into environmental practice. Initially, the schemes found it difficult to mobilize consumer support for downsizing consumption by purchasing less or buying secondhand and have thus been viewed as a mechanism for promoting rather than reducing private consumption (interviews with Eiderström 2000, 2002). They have also been accused of supporting a governance framework that gives business considerable influence in the setting of certification criteria. Recently, for instance, the Nordic Ecolabel admitted that it lowered its standard on the use of a chemical in soft paper bleaching to accommodate business interests but also emphasized that it is ratcheting up other standards on paper certification (Nordic Swan no date).

LABELING SCHEMES FOR FOREST AND MARINE
STEWARDSHIP CERTIFICATION

Two additional universal labeling schemes focus on common pool resources. Along with the words sweatshop, slow, and responsibility, the term "stewardship" has become important in the political consumer organizational settings. Stewardship is "the responsible use (including conservation) of natural resources in a way that takes full and balanced account of the interests of society, future generations, and other species, as well as of private needs, and accepts significant answerability to society" (Worrell and Appleby 2000, 263).

[12] The countries include Australia, Brazil, Canada, Croatia, Czech Republic, Germany, Hong Kong, India, Indonesia, Japan, Korea, Luxemburg, New Zealand, the Philippines, Singapore, Sweden, Taiwan, Thailand, Ukraine, the United Kingdom, and the United States.
[13] GEN Information Paper, *Introduction to Ecolabelling*, http://www.gen.gr.jp/pdf/pub_pdf01. pdf (accessed August 14, 2009); GEN, *Product Category List of Ecolabelling Programs Worldwide*, http://www.gen.gr.jp/product_list.html (accessed August 14, 2009).
[14] See also Blue Angel 2008, http://www.blauerengel.de/_downloads/publikationen/english/press_ release_Eco-label_Climate_protection_perspectives.pdf.

The environmental activists behind the establishment of Forest Stewardship Certification (FSC) in 1993 and Marine Stewardship Council (MSC) in 1997 were concerned about the lack of sufficient national and international governmental regulation on and even governmental agreement about resource depletion and habitat degradation in the forestry and fishery industries (Guldbrandsen 2006, 48off, 2009, Boström and Klintman 2011, 50, 77, Cashore, Auld, and Newton 2004ab, Tamm Hallström and Boström 2010).

   To raise public awareness and create a caring sensitivity about what they identified as deforestation caused by practices of the forestry industry, Greenpeace, Friends of the Earth, the Rainforest Action Network (RAN, founded in 1985 to call attention to deforestation), WWF, and several national environmental organizations called consumer boycotts of tropical wood furniture that targeted some of the vulnerable buyer-driven units in the long and distant global forestry commodity chain. Activists reasoned that these well-known and popular brand corporations could be persuaded to send demands about sustainable forestry practice to the less visible and less consumer-oriented units in their commodity chain. In the late 1980s for instance, they mobilized consumers to boycott IKEA's tropical timber furniture, Home Depot's wooden products, and Burger King for its role in the clear-cutting of rainforest to graze beef cattle. They also ran a Boycott Mitsubishi Campaign that mobilized teenagers to send letters to Mitsubishi's CEO to end the company's trade in tropical timber. These campaigns produced information on the politics of wooden products and attracted media interest, which increased dramatically in the late 1980s to the early 1990s (Bartley 2003, 442, figure 2), and involved celebrities from popular culture. Friends of the Earth published its *Good Wood Guide* in 1987 to inform about purchasing choices and even raised the idea of wood certification. Activists also learned from the organic food labeling schemes in place (Gale 2002). In 1989, RAN launched its SmartWood program, considered to be the world's first sustainable forestry certification program.

   But even with heightened public awareness about rainforests and deforestation, FSC and business-initiated forestry certification schemes in place, activism continued. RAN conducted its "Destroying Old Growth" and "Lumbering toward Extinction" campaigns throughout most of the 1990s. However, to underscore the effectiveness of one of its market-based campaigns, it called off its Home Depot boycott in 1999 because the company had changed its practices and even purchased a full-page ad in the *New York Times* to urge U.S. consumers to start shopping at Home Depot again. While large paper campaigns in the 2000s targeted Staples, OfficeMax, and Office Depot, Forest Ethics (a Canadian environmental association founded in 2000) ran its "Do Not Mail" campaign to reduce junk mail paper consumption. Other efforts targeted large public and private consumers including local governments and urged them to refrain from purchasing tropical forest products (Gulbrandsen 2006, 682, Domask 2003). North American–based forestry corporations also took notice by either seeking FSC certification or developing less stringent business-led certification (for information, see Auld, Gulbrandsen, and McDermott 2008, Cashore, Auld, and Newton 2004, Boström and Klintman 2011, Sasser, Cashore, Prakash, and Auld 2006, Prakash and Potoski 2006).

The third-party FSC label certifies all wooden products from the forest to the point of consumer sale, that is, so-called "chain of custody" certification from forestry material's growing and harvesting, to their processing at lumber and paper mills, packaging, furniture manufacturing, distribution, and retailing. Along with its green criteria, it includes social considerations that aim to protect indigenous people, workers' rights, and community relations (Meidinger 2003). FSC has made inroads in countries where losses of forests occurred in the early to mid-2000s and has received considerable support from governments, including the World Bank. In 2011, it had slightly more than 1,000 forest area certificates in about eighty countries (mostly Europe, North America, and Brazil) and has global chain of custody certifications (about 21,000) in 107 countries, with the majority representing Europe, North America, and Asia (Forest Stewardship Council 2011). However, its certification density remains generally low, with only 2.4 percent of the world's forest covered in 2007 (Auld, Gulbrandsen, and McDermott 2008, 193). Therefore, campaigns to inform consumers and mobilize them into different shopping practices continue to be important. A 2010 FSC-commissioned survey found, for example, that almost 80 percent of the responding corporations (about 3,500 from twenty-nine countries) stated that consumer demand was their reason for initially seeking FSC certification (Forest Stewardship Council 2010, 23).

Like the other labeling schemes discussed in this chapter, FSC has its critics. It has been criticized for letting Northern members, ideas, and interests dominate its governance structure (Dingwerth 2008). More recently, a loose group called FSC-Watch criticized FSC for its decision to certify plantations and allow corporate interests more say (FSC-Watch 2008, Tamm Hallström, and Boström 2010). Some initial FSC supporters, such as the Swedish Society for the Conservation of Nature (the operator of the Good Environmental Choice eco-label) have left FSC entirely because they believe that its certification functions badly (Swedish Society for Nature Conservation 2010). Greenpeace and RAN express similar criticisms but in a different way (Greenpeace 2008, Rainforest Action Network 2008). In response, FSC has, like Fairtrade International, attempted to improve its governance structure. Its decision-making body now includes an economic, environmental, and social chamber and each is subdivided into a Southern and Northern part to ensure more equal voice of Southern members. It also works together with FLO on dual labeling as a way to further promote social concerns in its principles and criteria for responsible forest management, which are undergoing reevaluation (Forest Stewardship Council 2010). However, efforts are still necessary to convince former supporters about the functioning of its certification procedures and its democratic legitimacy.

MSC is patterned on FSC's experience but differs from it in important ways. It is a foundation rather than a membership-based organization, its governance structure does not include tripartite chambers, and social criteria are not specified (Tamm Hallström and Boström 2010, chapter 5). MSC certifies seafood caught in the wild through sustainable practices and ensures that they are identified as such in chain of custody procedures. Its certification process aims at prohibiting overfishing, marine ecosystem misuse, and fisheries' avoiding international and national agreements. Marine certification has its origin in green activist concern for dolphins caught in tuna fishing and sea turtles in shrimp nets. Environmental groups called large tuna boycotts in the 1980s, which included targeting Heinz with ads in the *New York Times* and *Wall Street Journal*, to inform and mobilize consumers. Even children were recruited into the cause. This led large tuna procuring companies to purchase only tuna caught in a dolphin-safe way. Civil associations and governments established dolphin-free tuna labeling schemes, and the U.S. Congress passed the Dolphin Protection Consumer Information Act. Environmental groups continued to campaign for seafood awareness with such efforts as "Give Swordfish a Break" and WWF's Endangered Seas Campaign. Then, WWF contacted the global corporation Unilever PLC (the large British-Dutch food conglomerate, at that time the largest purchaser of frozen fish and well aware of green activism in the field) to help launch its MSC label. Both actors viewed the labeling scheme, built on the UN Food and Agriculture Organization (FAO)'s code of conduct for responsible fisheries and other international fisheries agreements (Gulbrandsen 2006, 2009), as "a way to harness market forces and consumer power in appropriate ways," (Short 2003, 181) – that is to say without direct public confrontations between consumers outraged over conventional fishing practices and the fishing industry (Constance and Bonanno 2000).

MSC originated, therefore, in a trustful and constructive relationship between activists and industry. Scholars conclude that MSC demonstrates how green activists and business entrepreneurs – "sandals and suits" – can work together in problem-solving ventures to safeguard the future (Constance and Bonanno 2000, 131). In 2001, it became a fully independent nonprofit organization funded and supported by European and U.S. trusts, charitable foundations, NGOs, some governmental bodies, and even a few corporations. As of summer 2011, more than 250 fisheries were part of MSC's program; the MSC labeled more than 10,000 seafood products, and MSC-labeled goods could be found in sixty-six countries worldwide. However, certified fisheries accounted for only about 6 percent of the annual global harvest of wild capture fisheries. Wal-Mart, Safeway, Marks & Spencer, Tesco, Sainsbury, McDonald's Europe, the large transnational food and service provider the Sodexo Group, and other large seafood procurers (including governments) sell, buy, and/or promote MSC-labeled goods. MSC also makes product information available to consumers online, including local sellers and sustainable seafood recipes, and gives consumers ideas about initiating national sustainable seafood days (see msc.org/).

Although widely supported, MSC has also been criticized by green activists, developing countries, environmental scholars, and competing labeling schemes (e.g., Jacquet et al. 2010, the Danish Society for a Living Sea and the Swedish organic label KRAV; see Tamm Hallström and Boström 2010 for details). MSC is aware of these complaints and, as with other criticized labeling schemes discussed in this chapter, has taken steps to remedy them (Marine Stewardship Council 2010). But criticism remains that capitalist logic has too much influence over its certification decisions and that its efforts to support Southern farmers are insufficient. Importantly for discussions in Chapter 7, it has been criticized for not taking sufficient responsibility for climate change (e.g., by including fishing vessel energy use in its certification criteria) and for not solving the problem of certification for fishers meeting most MSC criteria but who catch fish in waters also used by fishers who do not follow sustainable procedures. These and other difficulties characterize the complex, multi-problem issues involved in many political consumer organizational settings. They also point to the necessity of sector-wise collaborative solutions that involve businesses, civil society, and government and even for more harmonization among the labeling schemes addressed in this chapter (also see Chapter 8).

ANTI-SWEATSHOP POLITICAL CONSUMER ACTIVISM

Anti-sweatshop activism is one of the youngest, most dynamic, and creative organizational settings for contemporary political consumerism. Like most other organizational settings, it has a historical root: with the metaphor "sweatshops" from the 1800s, Christian socialist agitation in the United Kingdom in the 1850s, and activism and a national labeling scheme in the United States since the early 1900s (see Micheletti 2010, 50f, Sklar 1998, Boris 2003, Kingsley 1850). However, unlike the previously discussed organizational settings, it lacks a global labeling scheme and has generally not striven to develop one. Activists have reasoned that the industry's highly complex character, the scarcity of worker garment cooperatives to base a labeling scheme, corporate opposition to third-party certification, and even potential negative consumer reaction to labeled apparel make the establishment of a labeling scheme too risky a venture and too big an investment (Sluiter 2009, 202, 204, Lindefors 2004, 2005, Merk 2008; see more in Chapter 8). Nevertheless, by the mid-2000s, anti-sweatshop political consumerism had become an influential political claim-maker, transnational advocacy network, and innovative institution-builder. Over the years, many anti-sweatshop groups began to focus more on lesser-known brands and even other industries (e.g., fast-food services, the beverage industry, and particularly Coca-Cola, farm labor, electronics, toys, mining of diamonds and other minerals). They have also started to pressure large heterogeneous discount retailers (e.g., Wal-Mart, Aldi, Tesco, Carrefour) that advertise bargain apparel and other manufactured goods to join multi-stakeholder initiatives (MSI) and offer employers in their entire supply chain a "Better Bargain" (Sluiter 2009; see also CCC 2009). But even with this broader focus, the network has retained its mission of consciousness-raising and involvement in creating and supporting global mechanisms to promote a living wage and deal with the problems of overtime and long working hours, unsatisfactory working environment, sexual harassment, lack of unionization, and other related issues. This section discusses activism to improve the manufacturing of apparel and footwear in the globalized garment trade.

Anti-sweatshop political consumerism can be divided into a European and North American branch. As with most other political consumer organizational settings discussed in this chapter, the North American branch has pitted itself more aggressively against corporations by calling boycotts, offering bitingly negative criticism of popular brands' production practices, and using the court system (e.g., lawsuits for false advertising as in *Nike v. Kasky*). The lack of trust between activists and corporations (see Smith, Verrilli, Carpenter, and Maynard 2003, DeWinter-Schmitt 2007; see Chapter 3) partly explains this confrontational stance. Another important reason has been the organizational setting's focus on garment worker unionization, an idea not particularly favored in corporate America, and its tendency to oppose outsourced manufacturing, which has been viewed as labor protectionism in North America (Mandle 2000). North American efforts to improve both the domestic and globalized garment industry have forged alliances with humanitarian, anti-globalization, and ethnic and minority groups (Liebhold and Rubenstein 1998) less apparent in Europe. In Europe, unionization has been more accepted in the corporate world; activist groups have perceived European business as more trustworthy, cooperative, and forward-looking, and labor protectionism not such a hot issue (cf. Greathead 2002). European anti-sweatshop activism, with the Clean Clothes Campaign (CCC founded in 1989, with an international secretariat and branches in fifteen European countries) as the main anti-sweatshop organization is more homogenous in composition. Early on, the CCC was able to call corporate attention to problems in outsourced garment manufacturing and exchange information, expertise, and even personnel with European-based garment corporations (as demonstrated in the case of H&M, C&A, and the newer Swedish ethical jeans brand Nudie). Unlike its American counterparts, CCC has not officially called boycotts and supports them only if workers sanction them, but has admitted that boycotts called by others have benefited its goals (Interview with Lindefors 2004, 2005). Most likely, its less confrontational style helps explain why the anti-sweatshop cause has been less publicly visible in Europe than North America, where aggressive street, shopping mall, university campus, antibranding campaigns and honing of celebrities who market brands (e.g., Michael Jordan's and Tiger Woods's Nike ads, see also Chapter 6) continued to make news in the 2000s. Lower levels of anti-sweatshop awareness and activism among students have been found in the high political consumer setting of Sweden when compared to Canada and continue to be low in Sweden (Stolle, Hooghe, and Micheletti 2005, 256; see also publications on www.sustainablecitizenship.com).

Contemporary anti-sweatshop activism is usually dated to the end of the 1980s. In 1988, European and particularly Dutch activists picketed a C&A store in Amsterdam to protest working conditions and the firing of protesting workers in this market leader's supplier in a Philippines' free-trade zone. On International Women's Day (March 8), 1990, activists mobilized for a second action against C&A that included the performance of an anti-sweatshop fashion show in a central city square and police confrontations at the public burning of clothes at a C&A store. In the United Kingdom, fair trade activists, unions, and women's solidarity and other groups targeted William Baird, a large European garment corporation associated with C&A and publicly asked retailers "how clean their clothes are" (Sluiter 2009, 15). Similar developments occurred in North America when, for example, the Coalition for Justice in the Maquiladoras (the Mexican-Spanish term generally referring to a manufacturing plant) mobilized 120 religious, labor, women's, and community organizations from Mexico, the United States, and Canada in 1989 to oppose corporate globalization and workers' treatment in outsourced manufacturing (Bandy 2004). Other important anti-sweatshop groups emerged – Jeff Ballinger's Press for Change (1993), Canada's Maquila Solidarity Network (1994), People of Faith Network congregational campaign (1994), and so on – and began to collaborate on actions against well-known transnational brands. The National Labor Committee's (NLC, founded in 1981, now the Institute for Global Labour and Human Rights) invested in the anti-sweatshop cause and, among other efforts, held a U.S. testimonial tour with global garment workers and produced the TV documentary "Zoned for Slavery: The Children Behind the Label." In these early activist years, anti-sweatshop groups on both sides of the Atlantic pressured well-known brands and their retailers to take more responsibility for their supply chain; concentrated on educating consumers and caring sensitivity consciousness-raising; targeted government and politicians to regulate garment production, pricing, and corporate transparency; and supported domestic and globalized garment workers.

Scholars consider August 1995 to August 1996 to be the "year of the sweatshop" (De Winter-Schmitt 2007, 201, Ross 1997, Sluiter 2009) because it marked a period of heightened general awareness of and more communicative action on the hidden politics of apparel. In 1995, the media reported extensively on a police raid at a Southern Californian garment factory where illegal Thai immigrants had been forced to sew in virtual captivity. NLC's testimony at the U.S. Congressional hearings on problems in the outsourced manufacturing of garments included information on popular talk-show host Kathie Lee Gifford's Wal-Mart apparel line and generated public debate. Unions became more active and focused on well-known brands in their large consciousness-raising effort "Come Shop with Me" in which activists targeted the iconic brand (see Chapter 6) Disney, and in particular, its Pocahontas pajamas, to draw families into the cause, and *Life* magazine featured a story about a 12-year-old boy making footballs for Nike (National Museum of American History no date, Hemphill 2002). Also in this year U.S. politicians submitted a congressional bill to end sweatshops; the U.S. Department of Labor initiated a three-pronged strategy consisting of a) consumer education and heightened labor enforcement, b) recognition of garment corporations pledging to help eradicate U.S. sweatshop practices, and c) the establishment of the Apparel Industry Partnership, a voluntary task force to improve the situation in outsourced garment manufacturing (Hemphill 2002). In Europe, CCC held workshops and used EU support to improve its mobilization skills and for better collaboration with Southern partners. Anti-sweatshop activism emerged in other parts of the world as well.

"Sweatshops" was becoming a household word (see Chapter 6). Among other examples of the word's diffusion into everyday life, Gary Trudeau drew in the Doonesbury series a Nike Comic Strips, which is credited with raising consciousness among college students and graduates (Shaw 1999, 56ff) who then became important activists for the cause. Pollsters found broad general support for paying more for clothing manufactured by workers guaranteed better wages, boycotting certain targeted brands, and the idea of a labeling scheme to guarantee so-called "no sweat" clothing (see Elliot and Freeman 2000, 2, No Sweat 2004; for further media analysis, see Greenberg and Knight 2004, 158ff).

Although the issue was on the governmental agenda, anti-sweatshop activism continued to develop. In summer 1997, the AFL-CIO offered anti-sweatshop training to college students who then organized a national "back-to-school boycott" of Guess Jeans, also targeted in the NLC's "Holiday of Conscience" campaign. As time went on, anti-sweatshops groups targeted well-known brands manufacturing apparel and footwear in different price ranges: Nike, Gap, Sears, Marks & Spencer, H&M, Benetton, Tommy Hilfiger, Mulberry, Louis Vuitton, Armani, Prada, and others. But globally their central target was Nike (for reasons, see Chapter 6). New organizations specializing in anti-sweatshop advocacy also emerged – e.g., Behind the Label, Ethical Threads, Sweat Gear, the Oxfam Australia's "Just Stop It" campaign. Additionally, the United Students Against Sweatshops and other groups such as Global Exchange, which is skillful in consciousness-raising (Bullert 1999), joined the cause. More contacts were also established with Southern garment workers and NGOs and later with groups in Eastern Europe and Turkey.

The diversity of activist groups engaged in anti-sweatshop advocacy gives some indication of the complexity of the anti-sweatshop cause.[15] Scholars

---

[15] They include unions, youth associations, international humanitarian, human rights organizations, church and local community groups, consumer associations, women's organizations, third-world solidarity groups, fairtrade groups, new social justice networks, the academic community, governments, policy institutes, museums (e.g., Smithsonian Institution), and "no sweat" companies (e.g., Blackspot shoes formed in 2004, No Sweat Apparel formed in 2000, Ethical Threads from the late 1990s or early 2000s).

have used anti-sweatshop activism to develop ideas about the "new geography of globalization from below" discussed earlier in this chapter and responsibility-taking in globalized politics (see Chapter 1). They focus on how anti-sweatshop groups have furthered their cause without a labeling scheme by successfully inventing new tactics and venues for consumer consciousness-raising and actions and finding innovative ways to pressure corporations to change their production practices (cf. Lipschutz 2004, 202, Merk 2008, cf. Johns and Vural 2000, Micheletti and Stolle 2007; for criticisms, see Greenberg and Knight 2004). The North American branch called, for instance, consumers into antibranding discursive actions against many popular North-American headquartered brands. CCC cooperated with other activist groups on globally dispersed publicized urgent alerts informing about specific current problems such as deaths and injuries in fires in outsourced garment manufacturing factories, structural problems with factory construction, chemical use in manufacturing, poor working conditions, and the garment trade's violation of core aspects of the International Labour Organization's (ILO) conventions (e.g., freedom of association and collective bargaining) (Merk 2008, 20, Sluiter 2009). Interestingly and reiterating a criticism of political consumerism generally, the CCC and its Southern partners could at times disagree on when to call off an urgent alert (see Sluiter 2009, 198f for details). National CCC branches also targeted brands popular in their home countries and together with others started to utilize concerts and festivals as new venues for activism (Sluiter 2009, Balsiger 2010, Merk 2008; see Chapter 6). Other innovations in activism include publicizing do-it-yourself activist guidebooks for concerned consumers to perform local anti-sweatshop fashion shows (MSN no date; for a picture, see Micheletti and Isenhour 2010). These efforts aimed at creating more caring sensitivity and drawing consumers into different discursive actions and even new shopping practices that do not rely on a universal labeling scheme (e.g., by seeking out small businesses that certified "no sweat" apparel or reconsidering fast fashion's role in one's lifestyle).

Universities became an increasingly central activist venue, with student activism growing in a "sudden and sharp" manner (Elliot and Freeman 2000, 12) on campus after campus in the late-1990s to mid-2000s United States. Union training efforts, network groups' consciousness-awareness, and even these educational institutions' latent consumer power and the corporate presence in academic life explain the heightened importance of this particular geographical space for anti-sweatshop political consumerism (Cravey 2004, Silvey 2004, Featherstone and United Students Against Sweatshops 2002). Campuses hosted a wide variety of activities including the innovative Nike e-mail exchange discussed in Chapter 6. Student activism targeted both brand corporations (and most prominently Nike, who supplied many college teams with apparel and equipment) but also university administrations for not sufficiently taking responsibility to protect workers when they procured sports uniforms and university logo apparel (t-shirts, baseball caps, etc.). Among other things, campus activism led college administrators to change their procurement policies, raised student and public consciousness, led to the establishment of the MSI Workers Rights Consortium (WRC), and encouraged CCC to target public procurement in Europe.

Many activist groups began to target the popular globalized venue of big international sporting events to advocate and mobilize for their cause. Since 1998, CCC has utilized every large sporting event, the promotional visibility and vulnerability of sportswear brands at these events, and even the spirit of sportsmanship. These activities have mobilized new groups (e.g., team supporter organizations and youth groups) into the cause but otherwise have had marginal effects (see Sluiter 2009, 139–143, 195, Merk 2008 for a discussion).

Furthermore, without a universal labeling scheme buycotting political consumerism functions differently in this organizational setting. Activist groups have tended to focus more on proactive, forerunning "no sweat" ethical businesses (examples in note 15 to this chapter and Chapter 7), the creation of clean clothes or "sweatfree" communities, MSIs, and, because of difficulties in advancing legislation and litigation on national and EU governmental levels, adoption of ethical procurement policies by public bodies (Sluiter 2009, 21ff). Unlike other organizational settings, anti-sweatshop activism has even begun to target citizens to put demands on how their tax money is spent and to pressure government "to stop tax dollars from subsidizing sweatshops and abusive child labor" (Sweatfree Communities no date a, no date b) and purchase sweatshopfree workwear for their uniformed employees. U.S. activists have driven this message home with culturally resonating slogans like "Conduct Unbecoming: Fighting for Freedom in Sweatshop Uniforms" (Behind the Label no date). By 2010, nine American states, forty cities, fifteen counties, and 118 school districts had adopted "sweatfree" procurement policies (Sweatfree Communities no date). European activists have followed suit with CCC campaigns on community involvement and public procurement policy.[16]

Finally, activists increasingly believe that the entire globalized garment industry, government, civil society in the North and South, and all consumers must be part of problem-solving. Different reasons other than the complexity of the globalized garment trade explain this development. They include current problems with mobilizing groups into the cause, perhaps due to the individualization trends discussed in Chapter 2, successes in raising consumer consciousness about the cause and getting the issue on the public agenda to the extent that, as stated by a CCC founder, activists do not need to explain "anymore that Clean Clothes is not the name of a dry-cleaner" (Ineke Zeldenrust as quoted in an interview in Sluiter 2009, 263), and even more open and

---

[16] Two examples are the French campaign that led to 250 communities adopting a clean clothes resolution and becoming clean clothes communities and the Swedish CCC campaign "My tax money" (Mina skattepengar) in election year 2006.

positive responses from transnational garment corporations. Activists generally view MSIs as an innovative problem-solving mechanism (see also Chapter 8). However, there are some opposing views on different sides of the Atlantic on the ability of MSIs to solve complex problems in globalized manufacturing, thus demonstrating again general differences between the European and North American political consumerism on finding solutions together with business. What unites most groups is their conviction that problem-solving must involve governments and consumers.

SOCIALLY RESPONSIBLE INVESTING TO PUSH FOR CORPORATE SOCIAL RESPONSIBILITY

Socially responsible investing (SRI) aims at giving both positive and negative financial advice on the basis of the political, ethical, and environmental values. Individual and institutional investors including community development banks, mutual funds, financial institutions, investment consultants, institutions, and retail investors, and NGO pension funds seek and use SRI advice. SRI's long roots in religious political activism can be traced to Quaker George Fox in the 1600s, Quaker involvement in the anti-slavery struggle in the 1700s and 1800s, and Methodist John Wesley who, in the 1700s, formulated directives about how to invest money in an ethical fashion (Schueth 2003). Much later in the 1920s, other religious groups decided to boycott what they called "sin stocks" in the alcohol, tobacco, gaming, and weapons industries. SRI was again important in the 1960s as a less confrontational way to protest the Vietnam War, e.g., by boycotting investments in Dow Chemical which manufactured napalm used in bombing raids in Vietnam. SRI gained more publicity in 1970 when Ralph Nader succeeded in an unprecedented way in getting the U.S. Securities Exchange Commission to approve two socially responsible resolutions (that is, shareholder activism, see below) on the General Motors annual meeting proxy ballot (Michael Jantzi Research Associates 2003, 2). SRI was even important for the anti-apartheid movement and in RAN's Global Finance Campaign (2000) primarily against the large financial institution CityGroup for its involvement in tree cutting. Increasingly, labor unions and even Amnesty International and other established civic associations employ it as a tool for their causes. SRI even entered the American electoral arena for a short time in the mid-2000s in the form of the "Buy Blue" campaign that attempted to mobilize voters to use their purchasing power to either promote or scold companies for their position on the (blue) Democratic Party.

SRI is well institutionalized in North America, Europe, and Asia in the form of umbrella nonprofit trade associations such as Social Investment Forum (SIF, founded in 1985) and European Social Investment Forum (EUROSIF, founded in 2001). The associations offer readily available information and arguments for not investing in certain corporations (negative screening, a kind of boycott) and investing (positive screening, a kind of buycott) in others. The American SIF uses two additional investment activism forms. First, community investing focuses on investing in local and global communities so that they can provide affordable housing, child care, health care, and jobs that pay a living wage. Second, shareholder activism, which can be viewed as discursive political consumerism, is used by various activist groups, and also at times by everyday citizens, to influence corporate behavior. SRI has grown dramatically in the 2000s and even in Europe and North America after the 2008 financial crisis. Important contributing factors for its rise are the presence of professional organizations, more employed middle-class women and therefore a larger pool of SRI-prone investors (60 percent of all investors in the early 2000s were women), Internet browsing for stock shopping, and increased SRI institutional success in convincing investors that "responsibility can now walk hand-in-hand with prosperity" (Schueth 2003, 192, Zwick, Denegri-Knott, and Schroeder 2007). Public discussions about inappropriate corporate dealings that triggered the 2008 financial crisis are also credited with heightening awareness about the role that SRI can play in globalized governance (EUROSIF 2010, Green Money Journal 2011; for more information on SRI, see Logsdon and van Buren III 2008, 524, Sjöström 2008, O'Rourke 2003, Lee and Lounsbury 2011, Monks, Miller, and Cook 2004, Reid and Toffel 2009).

ORGANIZATIONAL SETTING FOR FARM ANIMAL ACTIVISM

Increases in public interest and activism in farm animal treatment have been noted over the past two decades. A public debate on the role of farm animals in human consumption and the responsibility of consumers has been spurred on by different concerns. They include the mad cow disease, swine and avian flu, public revelation of animals' force-feeding (especially geese for foie gras), farm animals' confinement and slaughter (particularly for chickens and pigs), meat-eating's impact on health and climate, and large farming's environmental pollution and use of antibiotics. All segments of society have in one way or another been drawn into farm animal activism. Today, this political consumer organizational setting involves environmental, agricultural, animal rights, consumer-oriented, women's and religious groups, humane societies, academics, politicians, pop culture celebrities, governments, and certain corporations. While involved actors generally agree that "caring people" should adopt "increasingly compassionate lifestyles that give evidence of their personal, ethically driven commitment not to abuse those who have the capacity to suffer" (Kullberg 2002) and that "the treatment of farm animals is a marker for the entire industrial system's attitude towards farmers, communities, consumers and the environment" (Sierra Club 2006), they disagree about whether it is ethically defendable to use animals for human consumption.

Animal activism has long roots. In the early 1800s, humane societies and societies for the prevention of cruelty to animals (SPCAs) began establishing themselves. In 1906, Upton Sinclair's publication of his undercover investigation of slaughterhouses in the book *The Jungle* led to a public outcry and the enactment of the U.S. Federal Meat Inspection Act. Ruth Harrison's 1964 book *Animal Machines: The New Factory Farming Industry* triggered an official British inquiry on farm animal treatment, and Peter Singer's 1975 book *Animal Liberation* has been attributed with the same force as Rachel Carson's *Silent Spring* in forging activism – but this time in England and through the emergence of generally rather small animal rights' groups. The important exception is People for the Ethical Treatment of Animals (PETA), founded in the United States in 1980, now in operation in Europe and the Asia-Pacific region, and viewed as the most energetic and highest-profile animal rights group globally (Simonson 2001). These animal rights groups advocate a complete non-animal consumer lifestyle.

Although some animal activist groups increasingly promote vegetarianism and reduced animal-based food consumption, their main goal has been to make it easy for consumers to avoid what they see as food from unacceptable production systems (e.g., battery cage eggs) and to make responsible and reasonable "humane" food choices that should "be significantly influenced by an ethical concern for animals" (Pacelle 2005). To help consumers, farm animal welfare associations with this focus – e.g., the Humane Society for the United States (HSUS, founded in 1954), Compassion in World Farming (founded in 1967), the British Royal Society for the Prevention of Cruelty to Animals (founded in 1824) – support and sponsor animal-welfare labeling, award companies with good animal welfare practice, and promote community-supported agriculture. They also ask governments to regulate agriculture. Animal rights groups ask consumers to go further by participating in the "ultimate boycott" (Munro 2005, 87) and become what they term "compassionate consumers" who align their complete lifestyle with these values by changing their diet drastically, following "non-violently produced" and "cruelty-free" shopping guidelines for apparel and household products, and investing socially responsibly in "cruelty-free" companies and organizations. For these groups, "the best way to help animals is to stop eating them" (Caring Consumer no date). To generate more caring sensitivity, animal rights activists have performed guerilla street theater, "cage-ins" and "die-ins" (cf. "sit-ins") replicating farm animal treatment and including fake bloody farm animal slaughters and the burning of effigies. Media has also reported on their sabotage of fur farms and furriers and their raids against the science community for testing pharmaceuticals on animals. Their use of undercover surveillance (similar to Sinclair's method) has involved trespassing and spying on farms and the public release of films on alarming farm animal treatment at strategically important business seasons, for instance in the high food-consumption holiday season (Munro 2005, Cherry 2010, Farm Animal Rights Movement Underground no date). Activists also establish national and international action days that target specific brand corporations (e.g., Procter & Gamble), promote specific food habits (e.g., meat-free Mondays), and receive support from governmental leaders and school systems. Meat-free Mondays are even being discussed at the parliamentary level in several countries.

Popular culture in the form of celebrity support (e.g., Paul McCartney) and YouTube videos have also become a vehicle for publicizing the animal activism cause, demonstrating a turn to discursive action in political consumerism (see Chapter 6). Free Range Studios (founded in the early 2000s) has innovatively adapted the music and theme of the blockbuster movies *The Matrix* and *Star Wars* for its animated films *The Meatrix* (from 2003 onward) and *Grocery Store Wars* (2005, produced for the Organic Trade Association), which hit hard at agri-business, factory farming, fast-food restaurants, and GMO products and then direct viewers to vegetarian, Meatless Mondays, and buycott action web sites. Activist networks use the Internet to publicize videos that offer disturbing visual evidence of slaughterhouse practices (e.g., film clips on Animal Equality's web site, or HSUS's "Cage vs. Cage-Free") that can involve antibranding (e.g., McCruelty campaign), action tools and tips for the four general forms of political consumerism (boycotts, buycotts, discursive actions, and lifestyle change), and for collecting donations and selling activist merchandise. Concern about farm animal treatment has reached the governmental agenda in different ways: the U.S. Congress has debated the proposed Farm Animal Stewardship Purchasing Act, and the Party for the Animals was voted into the Dutch Parliament. Animal welfare groups have developed Internet platforms to help fulfill their humane eating's boycott/buycott three Rs plan (reducing meat and other animal-based food consumption, refining food consumption to avoid worst practices, replacing animal-based foods with plant-based foods). They promote labeling schemes and private labels that either ensure "humane" animal treatment or mobilize consumers into veganism. Animal use for entertainment purposes (circuses, zoos, etc.) and in sports (e.g., the fox hunt in Britain) has also engaged them.

Many people associate animal activism with a particular rhetoric that challenges the traditional relationship between humans and animals and, therefore, society and nature (cf. Buller and Morris 2003, Cherry 2010). Activists have also attributed animals with unique personality traits (see Micheletti and Stolle 2010, 147 for more discussion) and adapted the discourse of human rights, civil rights, and even the Holocaust to advocate their cause. Telling examples of the latter are the early 2000s PETA campaign "Holocaust on Your Plate" and French activists' comparison of factory farms and slaughterhouses with concentration camps. But equating animal confinement with murder and human slavery is more common. For instance, PETA generated media attention by initiating a lawsuit against Sea World Marine Park in San Diego, California, for what it argues is a violation of the Thirteenth Amendment to the U.S.

Constitution, which abolished slavery.[17] Many U.S. and European animal rights activists call butchers and meat-eaters murderers. The phrase "meat is murder," which originated in England in the 1970s, has been sprayed on fast-food restaurants and is used in PETA antibranding campaigns that target McDonald's, Kentucky Fried Chicken, and Burger King (called Murder King[18]) (see also Cherry 2010).

This characteristic rhetoric leads some social movement scholars to identify animal activism as a moral protest (Jasper and Nelkin 1992) that aims at creating "disgust sensitivity" (Herzog and Golden 2009, cf. Chapter 1's discussion on caring sensitivity) by alerting consumers about certain ethical issues associated with contemporary conventional farm animal rearing. Noteworthy, given this morality discourse, is the increased emphasis on taste, personal health and at times personal appearance in animal activism campaigns and advocacy. HSUS gives consumers information about how good vegetarian alternatives can taste; Farm Animal Rights Movement's (FARM) Live Vegan proclaims that a vegan diet is not only good for animals and the planet but also for personal health; PETA has a "Eating for your health" web site focusing on the relationship between eating animal food, heart disease, obesity, cancer, diabetes, and strokes. This campaign also mentions impotence, the focus of an aggressive campaign video in the early 2000s, and the PETA UK (no date) web site features an ad with the glamorous British TV celebrity Chantelle Houghton asking "Eating Meat Got You Down?" and showing a drooping hot dog in a bun to get the point across. Thus, along with more stress on popular culture, performative participation and personal appearance, sex appeal, and nakedness are ways PETA and others choose to mobilize for plant-based diets (for a critical discussion, see Deckha 2008, Micheletti and Stolle 2012, 2010, 147, see more about sexualization in mobilization in Chapter 8).

LIFESTYLE POLITICAL CONSUMERISM

World leaders at the 2002 UN World Summit on Sustainable Development ("Earth Summit") declared that fundamental changes in the way societies produce and consume are indispensable for achieving global sustainable development. These ideas have been reiterated at other Earth Summits that emphasize the need for a less consumption-congested private life (e.g., UNEP 2010). The organizational setting for lifestyle change engages in considerable discursive

---

[17] See David Crary and Julie Watson (October 25, 2011), "PETA lawsuit seeks to expand animal rights," *Yahoo! News*, http://news.yahoo.com/peta-lawsuit-seeks-expand-animal-rights-222219887.html (accessed December 16, 2011), International Animal Rights Organisation, http://www.animalequality.net/ (accessed December 16, 2011).

[18] See PETA's McDonald's campaign, http://www.mccruelty.com (accessed December 16, 2011); PETA's campaign against KFC, http://www.kentuckyfriedcruelty.com (accessed December 16, 2011).

political consumerism but also boycotting and buycotting to mobilize consumers into lesser and alternative consumption (Nelson, Rademacher, and Paek 2007). This section briefly highlights three important developments in this organizational field: slow food, simplicity, and Buy Nothing Day (see also Chapter 8).

Slow food is emerging as an important and dynamic lifestyle community network (cf. Cooper 2005). It began in the mid-1980s as a protest against fast food (thus, its name) and plans to establish a McDonald's restaurant near Piazza di Spagna in Rome, Italy (Ritzer 2004, Petrini 2006, Sassatelli 2006). Now, it is a global phenomenon and includes an international non-profit organization with foundations and many national branches that promote farmers markets, biodiversity, and education. Globally it has more than 100,000 members in 1,300 local chapters or "convivia" in 150 countries and a network of 2,000 food communities that practice small-scale and sustainable production of what they consider quality foods. Slow food advocates local food heritage, tradition, and culture (Pietrykowski 2004), aims at bringing together responsibility and pleasure, opposes GMOs in food, foreign ownership of farm land in developing countries, and what it identifies as the standardization of taste and culture and the unrestrained power of the food industry multinationals and industrial agriculture (slowfood.com). It promotes better eating in schools and on university campuses and fair prices for farmers. Thus, it combines issues from several other political consumer organizational settings. Scholars view it as a new business model (Nosi and Zanni 2004), also including a new market-based activism paradigm that considers consumers as "co-producers." It is closely associated with Slow City or CittaSlow (Knox 2005), which aims at uniting people into a community of slow food ideology and practice.

Another important market-based lifestyle activism now more firmly institutionalized within political consumerism and sustainable consumption is simplicity (also called voluntary simplicity and downsizing consumption). This cause promotes "voluntary, long-term lifestyle changes that involve accepting significantly less income and consuming less" (Hamilton and Mail 2003, vii, UNEP 2010). Scholars have defined simplicity as consciously chosen "voluntary poverty" (Wilks 2008) particularly among the well-off who deliberately choose "to limit material consumption in order to free one's resources, primarily money and time, to seek satisfaction through nonmaterial aspects of life" (Huncke 2005, 528). Simplicity's roots go back at least three centuries in religious and secular concern about the immorality of acquired money and material goods (Ski 1985, Thoreau 1854). Today, it involves various activities including more sustainable household management, the three Rs discussed above, and even "slower" or less scheduled and commodity-cluttered child rearing. Individuals are even encouraged to leave fast-track careers, slow down their private economic development by working less, and choose cohousing and eco-living communities over traditional household lifestyles (for further listings, see Huneke 2005, 531–532, 539–540). An important contemporary downsizing advocate is the U.S.-based New American Dream (a nonprofit organization founded in 1997) that strives to popularize simplicity by helping consumers to find balance in life. Today, environmental groups, climate change activists, and slow food support some aspects of simplicity.

Finally, Adbusters Media Foundation has as its mission the empowerment of consumers so that they can build "a brave new understanding of living" (adbusters.org/about/submissions) primarily through its now internationally observed "Buy Nothing Day" (first organized in Vancouver, Canada, in 1992) (Vinken and Diepstraten 2010). This event starts at the beginning of the Christmas season and asks consumers to boycott all shopping on one particular day of the year, for instance Black Friday in North America. The UK branch calls on consumers to challenge themselves, their families, and friends to "detox" and "switch off from shopping and tune into life" (buynothingday.co.uk). Buy Nothing Days have involved performative activities in malls and shopping streets in South and North America, Europe, and Asia. The 2011 Buy Nothing Day was labeled "#OCCUPYXMAS" in hashtag-style to highlight the spirit of the Occupy Movement as well as the importance of social networking and media sites like Twitter (see Chapter 8). In 2012, the founder of Adbusters, Kalle Lash, published the book *Meme War – The Creative Distruction of Neo-Classical Economics*, which he hopes will change how economics is taught in university classrooms (see review in *Guardian* 2012). These different activities demonstrate how Adbusters use the four forms of political consumerism to attempt to change consumer lifestyles.

COMMON DEVELOPMENTS AND TRENDS

Consumer choice is now in large part acknowledged by politicians and policy makers as a part of politics in developed countries (e.g., Lazzarini 2007) and increasingly so in developing ones (see Chapter 8). Information about the politics of products given in choice editing campaigns and the new mechanisms for enabling such choices (labeling schemes, MSIs, etc.) are thus important topics for scholarly attention. As shown in this chapter, they engage consumers, civic networks, governments, and corporations. The Sustainable Development Commission in the United Kingdom (2006) maintains that these different actors form the "triangle for change" with shared responsibilities to promote more environmental and socially just consumption and production. This chapter points out that these ideas are not really new. Therefore, the history of political consumerism is interesting as it identifies the actors, developments, and challenges involved in market-based politics. Some organizational settings were started by groups dedicated to morally oriented causes. A good example is the faith-based groups wanting to end slavery, live more in accordance with nature, or curb sinful consumption. Faith-based groups collaborated with scientific, humanitarian, and other associations. The Nestlé boycott referred to briefly earlier in this chapter is a good case in point. It also involved the medical profession and women's and humanitarian groups, all of which put in great effort to raise public awareness about problems associated with the use of infant formula in developing countries. This long-running boycott, along with the Greenpeace boycott of Shell Oil over the Brent Spar oil platform and the South African anti-apartheid boycott and divestment campaign (Bromberg Bar Yam 1995, Sikkink 1986, Rask Jensen 2003, Klotz 2002), have taught mobilizing skills and gave arguments for why the market could be an effective arena for politics. Other early political consumer actors were labor unions, which particularly in the United States turned to consumers and the market venue in historical boycotts for recognition as legitimate representatives of workers (for other examples of early users, see Cohen 2003, Glickman 2009, Micheletti 2010, chapter 2). This chapter discusses how contemporary political consumerism has learned from its history.

Political consumerism has generally evolved from targeting corporations in boycott actions (with the exception of farm animal activism) to buycotting through labeling schemes and the shopping choices of individual and institutional consumers. This development helps explain the finding in Chapter 3 that consumers engage in buycotting more regularly than boycotting. The examination of the organizational settings reveals, moreover, that unlike much of its history, contemporary activist mobilization's final goal is not always legislation or governmental regulation. The reason is the character of complex political problems and the current period of the ongoing reassessment of public institutions as mechanisms of political authority, regulation, and change (cf. Gendron, Bisaillon and Rance 2009, Wilkenson 2007). Contemporary political consumerism thus aims more at cultivating a caring sensitivity in order to convince them to shop strategically, that is, individualized responsibility-taking. This reflects their understanding of new spheres of authority with evolving new models of political responsibility that do (at least some of) "the work once reserved for governments" (Spar and La Mure 2003, 92, O'Rourke 2005, 119). While other chapters in this book demonstrate how individual consumers are taking these responsibilities and believe more that other people will do the same (see Chapter 3), this chapter maps the activist awareness-creating and choice-motivating architecture of political consumerism. Contemporary political consumerism has developed somewhat differently than its historical predecessors, whose goal frequently was framed in the traditional model of political responsibility. It has integrated the logic of market transactions more fully in its mission, strategy, and action repertoire.

Not all mobilizing groups, as discussed in this chapter, view this development in a positive light. They believe that it legitimates business influence over movement commitment by giving prominence to mainstream marketing and opening up certification to goods produced by transnational corporations. For them this development threatens the original cause because it transforms political consumerism into a conventional market. The infusion of more market logic has, for instance, led to declines in worldshops and, as discussed regarding eco-labeling, gives corporations the possibility of influencing certification criteria by threatening to certify their products elsewhere. Importantly, this demonstrates that corporations too can use market competition to leverage change over political consumer institutional developments and is a development worth following in future research.

It also appears that political consumerism's increased market orientation also fits well with the Internet age, DIY activism, and the more creative forms of participation that characterize the current global political situation. The organizational settings have had success in convincing individual and institutional consumers to become part of the circle of responsibility, given them options to design their own register of responsibility, and have even created new venues and spaces for political action. They have, in other words, been innovative in "appropriating and using public and quasipublic places for purposes other than those for which they were designed or intended" (Lipschutz 2006, 7).

Another important general finding also examined in Chapter 4 is the importance of political context for political consumerism. Clear differences in particularly organic food, fairtrade, and anti-sweatshop activism can be found in North America and Europe. While the mutual distrust that tends to characterize the relationship between corporate America and civil society has prompted confrontations and hampered finding common ground for "triangle of change" solutions, involved European actors have generally showed more readiness and willingness to engage in cooperative endeavors (cf. Boström and Klintman 2011, 183–185). But even given these political cultural differences, most organizational settings include more ideologically radical or confrontational activist groups as well as those of a more reformist or pragmatic vein. The diverse groups tend to offer different reasons for why and how individuals should be mobilized into the politics of products. Some scholars employ the metaphor of the "good" and "bad" cop to analyze the dynamic relationship between these two kinds of activist groups and to understand how they depend on each other to keep the fire of the cause burning, open up space for discussions with corporations and others and, thus, to advance the general goals of political consumerism (cf. Linton, Liou, and Shaw 2004, 232, Cherry 2010).

A third general finding is that all organizational settings use simplifications to inform about and mobilize for their cause. As discussed above, they have in several cases put more emphasis on framing their message with more emotional and market-oriented messages and employed popular culture, antibranding and moral panics to create guilt, disgust sensitivity, peer pressure, and personal desire (sex appeal and potency, good health[19]). Political consumer campaigning can, therefore, appear quite similar to much commercial marketing. Some scholars fear that the move to simpler and less scientific information and

---

[19] Scholars have found that a change to the personal health frame was also important in mobilizing consumer support for the grape boycott in the 1960s (for a discussion, see Micheletti 2010, 53f).

mobilization campaigning can hamper what they consider to be necessary deeper analysis and deliberation on the complex problems involved in political consumerism (see Boström and Klintman 2011 and Chapter 8 for more discussion). They even fear that nudging choice architecture in the form of labeling schemes can limit deliberation and value change because it simplifies consumer choice too much (John et al. 2011).

Fourth, the activism identified in this chapter points to the mid-1900s and early 2000s as important formative years for the surge of contemporary political consumerism. New groups and activism emerged in all settings, and older civil society associations joined the cause. Together, they coordinated large national and transnational campaigns (e.g., for unionization in outsourced manufacturing and global human rights). They encouraged consumers to boycott targeted corporations, edit their shopping choices and, thereby, form a critical mass of market demand for political consumer labeled goods (see discussion on carrotmobs in Chapter 8). They mobilized consumers to engage in antibranding discursive actions to spearhead corporate change and to reconsider their general level of consumption or particular forms of consumption (e.g. meat-eating) in their lifestyles. More national and global labeling schemes were established in these years; they became important new regulatory tools that created a stable infrastructure for cause advocacy and activism that could be used as a basis for triangle of change initiatives to solve the complex problems of production and consumption.

Finally, attempts have been made to deal with political consumerism's complex problems in harmonization efforts. Two general forms of harmonization – standardization and integration – have been alluded to in different chapter sections. The first involves efforts in standardizing definitions and goals. Governments have also been involved in leading some international and regional efforts here, e.g., the EU's efforts in harmonizing the national eco-labeling and organic food schemes within Europe (European Commission DG Health and Consumers no dates ab, Kern et al. 2001). Standardized definitions generally tend to set a minimal level that must be met for all labeling certification while allowing regional or national labeling schemes the opportunity to place higher certification demands. On occasion, corporations have decided to "comparatively shop" among labeling schemes and choose the less demanding one (see the Swedish sausage case in note 10 to this chapter). More stringent national eco-labeling schemes have also feared that this development can force a ratcheting down of criteria (interview with Eiderström 2002). The second form of harmonization involves integrating the different political consumer causes. Activist groups have taken some piecemeal steps when they coordinate boycotts and discursive actions, for instance in joint efforts against Starbucks and fast-food chains, through slow food which bundles up the causes of several organizational settings when it calls for good, clean, and fair food, and downsizing that asks people to consume consciously by, among other things, following the different labeling schemes discussed in this chapter. Even some labeling schemes have engaged in this form of harmonization. Since the 1990s, IFOAM has included animal welfare and workers' treatment in its organic criteria, fairtrade labels emphasize environmental considerations, and animal activism voices concern about agri-business's environmental impact on common pool water resources. FSC and FLO's dual certification pilot project is mentioned in this chapter. Noteworthy is that scholars argue that this bundling of criteria has potential negative effects, for example the inclusion of animal welfare criteria into organic certification has been found to lead to more large-scale farming in certain countries because it both offsets production costs and satisfies increased consumer demand (Verhoog and de Wit 2006).

Infrastructural harmonization efforts are also underway. All the universal labeling schemes in this chapter follow ISO (International Organization for Standardization) management standards that aim at ensuring transparency and openness in criteria selection, prohibiting financial conflicts of interest, and promoting sound scientific methods and accepted test procedures. Here the general goal is to improve the institutional credibility and legitimacy of voluntary regulatory tools such as labeling schemes. Another attempt seeks to mobilize what International Social and Environmental Accreditation and Labelling Alliance (ISEAL) (founded in 1999 by FLO, IFOAM, MSC, and FSC) identify as the voluntary sustainability standards movement that it hopes will strategically transform global markets by using its market share (about 10 percent in forestry, fisheries, and key agricultural commodities) to encourage additional institutions and actors to achieve sustainable development at the operative level. This grand effort, now underway, implies broadening political consumerism's reach to countries with strong emerging economies (e.g., China, Brazil, India), focusing more on public procurement and financial institutions, addressing criticisms of political consumerism by making it easier for small-scale producers and enterprises to participate, and finding ways for the labeling schemes to collectively promote sustainability. Time will tell whether political consumerism is sufficiently established, legitimate, and popular to rise to the challenge of affecting "greater social, environmental and economic impacts" (ISEAL Alliance and AccountAbility 2011, 1) and play a more strategic role in reconfiguring global market trade.

6

Discursive Political Consumerism

INTRODUCTION

Political consumer activism aiming at revealing the politics of the products is evolving beyond the strict practice of boycotting and buycotting by using labeling schemes. A development that has received considerable activist, media, and scholarly attention is the employment of well-known brands as platforms and spaces (new geography) to create and convey political messages. Scholars consider this development part of the discursive turn in political action and use so-called antibranding and particularly culture jamming (terms explained later) to illustrate how market-oriented political consumer action is becoming more reliant on the creation of innovative, communicative, performative, and humorous political messages. The term "discursive political consumerism" has been coined to identify this phenomenon; it signifies a particular form of political consumerism beyond boycotting and buycotting. This chapter addresses the discursive turn in political consumerism theoretically and studies an important case of it empirically. It starts with a brief section on more general scholarship to explain the discursive turn in collective action and discusses how it applies to political consumerism. Then, it turns to a particular form of discursive political consumerism, namely antibranding, and follows up with a separate section that explains why political consumer activists target well-known brands, and also why Nike, the topic of the chapter's empirical investigation, has been a central focus in this and other forms of political consumer activism. The heart of the chapter is an extensive empirical analysis of the Nike e-mail exchange (NEE), a well-known culture jam that scholars have frequently used to discuss the impact of "e-communicative" and political consumerist participation, and to illustrate and theorize the discursive turn in political consumer action (Bennett 2006, Greenberg and Knight 2004, Häyhito and Rinne 2008, Sherrod 2006; see other sources later in the chapter). This is the first time that the e-mail responses generated by the Nike e-mail exchange have been investigated empirically. Albeit an older culture jam from a period when social media was not as developed as today, the NEE from 2001 is still of current interest for how and why it in different ways relied heavily on brand discourse and digital platforms. Moreover, as scholars have noted, research on culture jamming has been lacking a solid empirical basis. Most culture jams are studied because they are brought up in conventional media and, therefore, do not involve an examination of the motivations of their activists and how they are received in general society. This chapter concludes with a summary of the effectiveness of the NEE culture jam and follows up with a more general chronological discussion of how anti-sweatshop activism has targeted Nike and how Nike has changed its policy and practices.

DISCURSIVE TURN IN POLITICAL CONSUMERISM

Social scientists generally agree that political action repertoires are influenced by the character of their target, the political context in which they operate (the political opportunity structure), and the public discourse on problems of the day (Kitschelt 1986, Kriesi 1995, Rootes 1997, Tarrow 2005). Many scholars find that political action has taken a discursive turn and argue that it reflects the reconfiguration of political responsibility and citizenship now occurring due to the shift in power from government to governance, the role of the economy in globalization and the enhancement of the choice mechanism generally as well as a potential problem-solving mechanism (see references in Chapter 1 and 2, Spar and La Mure 2003, Argenti 2004, Burchell and Cook 2008, Chapman 2010, 128, Harvey 2007, Steinberg 1998, Aronczyk and Powers 2010, Jacobs, Cook, and Delli Carpini 2009, Macedo 1999). A discursive turn can also be said to be taking place in political consumerism. Unlike the more traditional boycotting and buycotting market-based action alternatives investigated earlier in this book, discursive political consumerism (see definition in Chapter 2) focuses on using communication and deliberation – not the stick of boycotts or the carrot of buycotts – to change how the people view consumption and how corporations assess their social responsibility. It also differs in three distinct ways from the other forms of political consumerism. First, it is more reliant on creative communicative civic skills and frequently a sense of humor and consumer cultural criticism on the part of its users but neither the monetary resources necessary for buycotting nor the need to boycott (see more in this chapter). Second, it uses the market as an arena for politics while avoiding the harmful unintended effects of consumer boycotts (see Chapters 5 and 7) and the ethical dilemmas facing conscious consumers when buycott or reasonable choice opportunities are lacking. It is, thirdly, also more highly reliant on digital tools to craft and communicate its political message than the other forms.

Like the other forms of political consumerism, discursive political consumerism has deep historical roots. While antibranding evolved from the street-theater-like medieval carnival, as a form of activism it primarily is related to the strong reactions vis-à-vis the role of commercial life found in different Western societies. It is a more performative means of political action that attracted for instance the performative anti-Vietnam War and countercultural political group the Yippies in the 1960s, whose member Tom Hayden later became a fairtrade activist. Counter-art groups like the Dadaists, Fluxus, and most importantly the French Situationalists are considered to be its artistic forerunners because they gave different meanings to commercial objects. Noteworthy is that the activities of the Situationalists even triggered French students in 1968 to protest and, therefore, lie behind the 1968 student revolution in the Northern world, thus indicating again that young people can be drawn into political action by unconventional political sources. In 1984, the San Francisco rock band Negativland coined the term "culture jamming" after the radio terminology of "jamming" to mean illegally interrupting a signal. Within a few years, mainstream media took note when a journalist described culture jamming as "artistic 'terrorism' directed against the information society in which we live" (Dery 1993). Ten years later, Naomi Klein praised culture jamming as a "brand boomerang" in her widely read book *No Logo* as a way to protest the spread of global corporate capitalism, and Kalle Lasn, founder of Adbusters Media Foundation, wrote the manifesto *Culture Jamming* which sought to mobilize consumers into protesting the further commercialization of society. Legal scholars assess the broader phenomenon of antibranding and the narrower one of culture jamming as a form of "semiotic" (that is, discursive) warfare and "guerilla" marketing, and study whether and how it is trademark violation (Katyal 2010).

ANTIBRANDING AS DISCURSIVE POLITICAL CONSUMER ACTIVISM

Although discursive political consumer actions appear in multiple forms and include for example cooperation with corporations (such as shareholder activism and active dialogue between business and NGOs to create common ground, see Chapters 5, 7, and Arts 2002), it is the more humorous, confrontation, and antibranding examples that are the general focus of this chapter. Most confrontational discursive political consumerism uses brands and corporate imagery as its source and platforms for political consciousness-raising and mobilization. Antibranders utilize well-known brands to create textual, audio, visual, and performative messages about what they consider to be the negative effects of globalized production and consumption (see Chapter 8 for a discussion on weaknesses of the brand focus for political consumerism). Some examples serve as illustrations for the diverse character of antibranding or culture jams.

For example, the activist actor Bill Talen created the "Reverend Billy" persona for his fictive "Church of Stop Shopping." Reverend Billy offers a live performance, staged since the "Seattle-WTO winter of '99–'00," in shopping malls, on street corners, and outside the Disney Store, Starbucks, Niketowns and Wal-Marts. These are all very well-known, expressive, and popular brands that scholars identify as "powerful devices of economic power and market domination" (Katyal 2010, 797). Talen calls his actions 'anti-consumption shopping interventions' and, like some historical acts of political consumerism (see Chapter 5), they evoke the idea of sinful consumption. His public stunts on Buy Nothing Days, arrests, cash register "exorcisms," film, and book have an online following and are reported on in the mass media (Dee 2004). Reverend Billy also participated in the Occupy events of fall and winter 2011 and has interested the academic world (e.g., as a keynote speaker at the 5th Popular Culture and World Politics conference in 2012). In comparison, the Nike e-mail exchange, which was also conceived of and conducted by one individual, was a low-key online alteration of Nike's brand image that "jammed" high-tech marketing and was then publicized highly globally. A third example of more loosely organized antibranding is "shopdropping" (the reverse of shoplifting) where individuals alter the meaning of brand commodities and leave them in stores. Barbie dolls, Coca-Cola bottles, brand-name clothing, and food products have been altered to include political messages and then dropped in stores to make a political statement (*New York Times* 2007a, Lambert-Beatty 2010).

More established political consumer groups and networks also engage in antibranding. Anti-sweatshop activists have in the past, for instance, altered the brand imagery (logos, slogans, etc.) of Nike, Gap, and other well-known garment brands to call attention to the hidden politics of clothing. They have turned the popular brand Gap's logo into the "Income Gap. An American Classic" for a postcard campaign, they have clothed a man with money stuffed in his mouth in a T-shirt advertising "the true colors of Benetton," they have altered the Levi's jeans patch to "Evil Strauss & Co. $$$," and, importantly for the discussion below, played with Nike's swoosh and slogans.[1] As some anti-sweatshop groups expand their cause to other sectors, they adopt the spectacular language of murder and killer in order to be able to communicate further. For example, some groups work together with the labor rights group Killer Coke Campaign, which employs the Coca-Cola Company's imagery to make political statements about Coke's operations in Colombia, the Philippines, India, and other countries. Its culture jams alter the Coke slogan to "Murder, it's the real thing" (Gill 2007, killercoke.org), and designate the Coke logo as the source of the message. Noteworthy for this book's theme is that former union activist Ray Roger, who heads the Killer Coke Campaign, consciously chose antibranding and culture jamming as an activist tool because, as he puts it, Coca-Cola has too many products to keep track of, and it is not easy to mobilize and retain large unions as boycott supporters (Zaitchik 2003; see Chapter 7

---

[1] For more examples of culture jamming, see "Center for Communication and Civic Engagement: Culture Jamming," University of Washington, http://depts.washington.edu/ccce/polcommcampaigns/CultureJamming.htm (accessed January 9, 2012).

on the effectiveness of boycotts). Thus, current developments both within markets and activism have influenced the decision to give priority to culture jamming and antibranding in the political consumer action repertoire.

Well-known political consumerist activist groups from other organizational settings also engage in this form of discursive political consumerism. The public attention created by PETA's "Murder King" campaign has even been attributed as leading Burger King, the campaign target, to invite PETA and the Humane Society of the United States (HSUS) in 2007 to discuss a different procurement policy (*New York Times* 2007b). However, PETA's "Kentucky Fried Cruelty" campaign only led Kentucky Fried Chicken to challenge PETA's claims (Seijts and Sider 2006). Finally, special antibranding and culture jamming groups have emerged and actively supported ideas about how individuals on their own can engage in confrontational discursive political consumerism. Adbusters Media Foundation has, for instance, aided the anti-sweatshop cause as well as actions focused on downsizing and anti-consumption (see Chapter 5 for explanations) and was an important initiator of Occupy Wall Street (see Chapters 5 and 8). Billboard Liberation (formed in 1977) has received publicity for its altering of perfume, cigarette, automobile, and gas and oil companies' large outdoor (that is, billboard) advertisements (billboardliberation.com, Katyal 2010). The Yes Men, a group of anticorporate pranksters, chose a different route. Instead of altering ads, slogans, and logos, the group concentrated on publicly performing the role of altered spokespeople for the brands McDonald's, Dow Chemical, Exxon Oil, BP, and even the WTO (Ramsey 2010). Parenthetically, it is noteworthy that this kind of activity even targets activist groups; PETA has been the target of brand manipulation by the web site PETA (People Eating Tasty Animals) (mtd.com/tasty; for discussion, see Katyal 2010, 819f).

These examples demonstrate in a general way how discursive political consumerism seeks to alter brand imagery or rebrand it in order to raise consciousness about "the latent psychological, socioeconomic, and environmental implications of consumer choice" and to mobilize people into market-based activism (Rumbo 2002, 143, Arvidsson 2005, Katyal 2010). Researchers who study this political consumer activism classify it as creative resistance (Atkinson 2003), civil disobedience (Rumbo 2002), a critical public pedagogy (Sandlin 2007), rhetorical protest and sabotage (Warner 2007, Harold 2004) that "'talk[s]' back' to and through popular culture" (Sandlin 2007, 80), a reflexive form of action (Binay 2005, 15), and a new social movement fit for the market-oriented contours of post-Fordist, do-it-yourself modernity (Sandlin 2007, Hynes, Sharpe, and Fagan 2007). Because of its humorous and prankish adaptations of brand imagery, these researchers hypothesize that it is an ideal venture for everyday citizens to develop the capacity for more independent thinking and individualized action (Handelman 1999) because this kind of political activism makes it appear natural, familiar, and even cool (Kubal 1998). Scholars believe, therefore, that it should function as an important stepping stone to other forms of political participation by multiplying "the tools of intervention for contemporary media and consumer activists . . . [and] embracing the viral character of communication, a quality long understood by marketers"(Harold 2004, 208; see also Duncombe 2002, cited in Sandlin 2007). Whether and how antibranding and culture jamming are powerful rhetorical symbolic tools requires empirical investigation. This chapter's case study offers an empirical investigation into the soundness of some of these theoretical hypotheses and evaluations.

POPULAR BRANDS AND POLITICAL CONSUMERISM

Why do political activists turn to popular buyer-driven brands to promote their cause? Part of the reason as covered in this book is, of course, their need to develop an action repertoire to address their dissatisfaction with the environmental and ethical performance of transnational brand corporations. A second reason for targeting popular brands is simply that they have a large market share and are highly visible in consumer society; therefore, changing their practices can make an imprint on environmental and social justice matters. Not surprisingly, large brands have traditionally been an important focus of boycotting actions (e.g., the decades-long Nestlé boycott) because they are well-known among consumers and easily identified on store shelves; more recently, well-known brands' interest in labeling schemes has been hailed as crucial for the "certification revolution" (Conroy 2007) and considered important for the mass marketing of more environmentally and social justice-friendly goods. However, global brands play a different role in the more confrontational forms of discursive political consumerism. Not only are they the *target* of activism, they are its *source, medium,* and *political message board*. Thus, more so than the other forms of political consumerism, antibranding has developed from the realization that brand imagery is important for communicating with consumers. Activists use brand imagery to inform about their cause because this kind of imagery is easily manipulated in the age of Photoshop, cutting and pasting, and YouTube. Scholars argue, moreover, that brand imagery is of central importance in contemporary capitalism (Clifton and Maughan 2000) and that buyer-driven corporations are highly dependent on it to produce "particular immaterial use-values; an experience, a shared emotion, a sense of community" (Arvidsson 2005, 248) so that they can compete successfully with other similar brands. Brand marketing helps them create "culturally resonant stories and images" (Holt 2005) that, scholars maintain, have "an irresistible form of cultural authority" (Holt 2002). It is claimed that this makes consumers believe that brands are gathering places for social identities.

This may sound far-fetched, and although reliable information on corporate investments in brand marketing is difficult to get, in 1994, around the time when the anti-sweatshop public discourse was starting up, more than 3,000 new companies in the United States together spent an estimated 120 million USD to create and implement a new logo to compete in consumer society (van

Riel, van den Ban, with Heijmans 2001, 428); between 1977 and 1991, Nike spent more than 300 million USD on advertising its brand, and in 2001 it created a new executive position: vice president for brand communication. In the advertising world, the swoosh, Nike's logotype, is seen as having success-fully communicated the lifestyle that Nike wants to promote. Its marketing slogan "Just Do It," launched in 1980 to convince "Americans that wearing Nikes for every part of your life was smart... and hip" is considered the "most famous and easily recognized [slogan] in advertising history" (CFAR, 1999). Nike's investments in brand imagery have paid off; aggregate sales of "Just Do It" Nike products had, as of 1993, exceeded 15 million USD. According to Phillip Knight, former Nike CEO, marketing made his company: "We've come around to saying that Nike is a marketing-oriented company, and the product is our most important marketing tool. What I mean is that marketing knits the whole organization together.... We used to think that everything started in the lab. Now we realize that everything spins off the consumers" (quoted in Lury 2004, 49). Other transnational corporations focused on discursive polit-ical consumerism also invest highly in brand imagery to convince consumers that only their products – and not similar ones – are necessary for everyday life. For the Coca-Cola Company, for example, "'the ideal outcome... is for consumers to see Coca-Cola as woven into their local context, an integral part of their everyday world'" (quoted in Arvidsson 2005, 90). Some transna-tional corporations have even invested in what scholars term "brandscapes" (Sherry 1998) – that is, specific brand-building commercial locations dedicated entirely to creating a shopping experience for particular brand commodities. Such brandscapes as McDonald's restaurants, Niketowns (ibid),[2] Disney Stores (Wickstrom 2006), Starbucks coffee shops (Thompson and Arsel 2004), and Ikea stores give what scholars call an "iconic" quality to brands (Holt 2005), and as such, many have been the focus of political consumer activism.

   Yet, no matter how successful large and iconic brands are, they continue to want to develop their marketing and commodities in order to maintain or advance their position in consumer society. They now also employ digital platforms to bring consumers who desire enhanced choice directly into product development and innovative Internet shopping. We highlight one example, Nike iD, because of its importance to the NEE case study below. In 1999, Nike launched so-called "market for one shopping" (Gilmore and Pine 2000, Story 2005), which further developed both its direct relationship with consumers and its brand image – the Nike spirit of individual empowerment through sports. The Nike iD, created by web developer Critical Mass[3], was considered an

---

[2] See also http://www.crito.uci.edu/noah/NOAH/CMC%20Website/CMC%20PDFs/CMC2_4. pdf#page=6.

[3] For information on this online service, customized and personalized customer service and the received award, see *Critical Mass Wins Grand Prix at Cyber Lions in Cannes*, available

immediate success. Estimates by Interbrand (2001), which publishes annual listings of the best global brands, put Nike's brand value at 70 percent of its total market value (that is, public consensus on the value of its brand equity) in 2001.

However, Nike and other brands must constantly monitor their brand imagery for plagiarists, pirating activities, "brandjacking" (Ramsey 2010), and antibranding. In fact, most big brands have attempted to sue activists and other businesses for patent violations and trademark infringement[4] but generally speaking the judicial system does not offer them complete protection from brand parody and hoaxing.[5] Thus, the importance of brand imagery for buyer-driven transnational corporations along with the state of law opens up opportunities for people to poke fun at corporations and use their brand imagery in political and social criticism. Brands easily become prey for market-based discursive activism.

As discussed in Chapter 1, Nike was a particular target for anti-sweatshop activism. Given the problem with boycotts and buycotts in the globalized garment sector as well as frustrated attempts at encouraging government to take more regulatory responsibility over outsourced garment manufacturing, it is

at http://www.criticalmass.com/about/news/view.do?article=nike_062001_p&year=2001, accessed February 4, 2006) and Business Wire, Critical Mass Grabs Best Web Site Award for NIKE iD at @D:TECH Awards, December 5, 2001. Available at http://wires.vlex.com/vid/critical-mass-grabs-nike-id-d-tech-56451137 (accessed December 21, 2012).

[4] Nike, Coca-Cola, Red Bull, Unilever PLC, Walt Disney Productions, Seven-Up, Campbell's Soup Corporation, Colgate Palmolive, and other large corporations have taken culture jammers to court for tampering with their brand imagery. Rimmer, Matthew, "The Black Label: Trade Mark Dilution, Culture Jamming and the No Logo Movement," *Scripted* 5(1) April 2008: 71–138. Regarding Nike see, for instance, "Intellectual Property Protection in China, Nike Wins Compensation for Trademark Infringement Case," August 24, 2007, at http://english .ipr.gov.cn/ipr/en/info/Article.jsp?a_no=109546&col_no=127&dir=200708 and Los Angeles Intellectual Property Trademark Attorney Blog, "Los Angeles Patent Attorneys For Nike Filed Design Patent Infringement, Trade Dress Infringement, and Lanham Act 43(a) Unfair Competition Lawsuit Over Sales Of Allegedly Copycat Air Jordans – 15 U.S.C. 1125, May 6, 2008, http://www.iptrademarkattorney.com/2008/05/patent-design-shoes-trade-dress-air-jordan-attorney-lawsuit-lanham-act-43a-15-usc-1125.html. See also "6 F.3d 1225: Nike, Incorporated, an Oregon Corporation, Plaintiff-appellee, v. Just Did It Enterprises, a Business of Unknown Legal Character, and Michael Stanard, an Illinois resident, Defendants-appellants," https://bulk.resource.org/courts.gov/c/F3/6/6.F3d.1225.92-3303.html (accessed December 21, 2012).

[5] For instance, in the 1993 U.S. Court of Appeals, Seventh Circuit court case Nike Incorporated v. Just Did It Enterprises, judges dismissed Nike's suit against an artist for designing and selling apparel with a "swoosh" design identical to Nike's but with the word "Mike" instead of "Nike." The court declared that "[n]o one likes to be the butt of a joke, not even a trademark. But the requirement of trademark law is that a likely confusion of source, sponsorship or affiliation must be proven, which is not the same thing as a 'right' not to be made fun of." Available at http://law .justia.com/cases/federal/appellate-courts/F3/6/1225/576886/ (accessed February 18, 2013).

not surprising that it became, for different reasons, a prime focus for anti-sweatshop political consumerism. First, Nike's brand image power and name recognition helped to ensure that any market-based activism that targeted it would get attention. Second, since Nike has proclaimed publicly that it was taking the lead in social responsibility in outsourced garment manufacturing, it was monitored closely to see whether it kept its word (Clean Clothes Campaign 1998). Third, activists have argued that Nike, as an industrial leader, must take responsibility to solve the so-called "race to the bottom" problems that it helped to create when it decided to outsource its manufacturing globally (see Chapter 1). Among other things, anti-sweatshop and social justice activist groups have pointed out that, in the past, more workers and local labor groups had filed labor-related complaints about Nike with the AFL-CIO in Indonesia than about other similar garment corporations. They also claim that Nike can easily afford the cost of improvements without increasing its retail prices, and as the largest sports apparel company in the world, its initiatives would have industry-wide effects that "other manufacturers will have to follow" (Global Exchange 2003, 1). Finally, when compared to other garment brands, it was easier for anti-sweatshop activists to mobilize support against Nike. Not only was Nike an iconic brand desiring to have a good image in consumer society, the corporation's initial comments about sweatshop abuses being out of its sphere of responsibility and its early policy of responding to all activist accusations gave anti-sweatshop activists a good rhetorical device to mobilize support for their cause (De Winter-Schmitt 1997).

Anti-sweatshop activists declared what some scholars like to call a "semiotic war" on Nike and employed altered versions of the Nike swoosh and its "Just Do It" marketing slogan to publicize their cause and claims. Over the decades, Nike has been bombarded with consumer messages, criticized at shareholder meetings, forced to answer critical press questions, sued for falsely marketing its advances in corporate responsibility-taking, used to market Adbuster's "no sweat" shoes (see Chapter 8), and borne the brunt of anti-sweatshop antibranding and culture jamming.[6] Due to its well-known corporate status, what came to be known of as "Nike's sweatshop woes" (see Miller no date) received considerable public attention in mainstream media and popular culture. Examples include Jay Leno's joke in his *Tonight Show* monologue in 1998 ("It's so hot out I'm sweating like a 10-year-old Malaysian kid in a Nike factory"), and

<hr/>

[6] Anti-sweatshop groups purchased stock in the Nike Corporation to gain access to shareholder meetings. See for instance "Beware The Coming Corporate Backlash," February 4, 2001, *Industry Week*, http://www.industryweek.com/CurrentArticles/asp/articles.asp?ArticleID=1006 (accessed March 8, 2004) and "Church Pension Fund Uses Clout to Effect Change," April 22, 2002, *Worldwide Faith News*, http://www.wfn.org/2002/04/msg00285.html (accessed March 8, 2004). See also Philip Knight's special presentation at the National Press Club in May 1998.

numerous news stories. A few headlines from these news sources illustrate the media discourse: "Nike: The New Free-Trade Heel" (*Harper's Magazine* 1992), "Sweatshop Christmas" (*US News & World Report* 1996), "Nike is a Four Letter Word" (*San Francisco Examiner* February 1997), "Sweatshop King. Nike Exec Reneges on $30 Million Pledge" (*New York Times* April 25, 2000), "Making Nike Sweat" (*The Village Voice* 2001), "Is Nike Still Doing It?" (*Mother Jones* 2001), and "Sweatshops: Finally, Airing the Dirty Linen" (*Business Week* 2003) (see Greenberg and Knight 2004 for graphs on media attention to the anti-sweatshop cause). Nike was, in a manner of speaking, an open target for discursive political consumer activism.

THE CASE OF THE NIKE E-MAIL EXCHANGE

As demonstrated in the brief discussion above, the Internet is now an important communication and marketing tool in the corporate world. The Nike e-mail exchange shows how an individual consumer found a way to use an Internet business platform to "jam" corporate brand imagery. What is interesting about this particular effort is that it spread rapidly around the world. The entire Nike e-mail exchange (see textbox) began on January 17, 2001, when Jonah Peretti, a master's student at the prestigious MIT media lab, decided to order a pair of customized Nike shoes from Nike iD. Normally, this would not have been difficult. However, Peretti, who was sympathetic with the anti-sweatshop cause and who had experience with antibranding, wanted them customized with the word "sweatshop." He placed his order at a time when the word sweatshop was peak news and Global Exchange had publicly identified Nike as the poster child of the new age sweatshop company. Nike's customer service repeatedly sent Peretti canned-response e-mails that explained why his request and queries about it were denied. Peretti persisted in his request and evoked Nike's brand imagery when he wrote this e-mail:

Your web site advertises that the NIKE iD program is "about freedom to choose and freedom to express who you are." I share Nike's love of freedom and personal expression. . . . My personal iD was offered as a small token of appreciation for the sweatshop workers poised to help me realize my vision. I hope that you will value my freedom of expression and reconsider your decision to reject my order.

Nike terminated e-mail contact; Peretti revised his customization request but never received his shoes. He then sent the e-mail exchange to a few politically aware friends who decided to forward it to other people (Peretti and Micheletti, 2006, 131). Because of its antibranding prankishness, and a bit of Peretti's own legwork, it soon entered the global public sphere. It is estimated that within three months, the exchange reached up to 11 million people globally (Macken 2001). Of these, 3,655 people e-mailed Peretti within three months.

Textbox: The Nike E-mail Exchange

From: "Personalize, NIKE iD" <nikeid_personalize@nike.com> To: "'Jonah H. Peretti'" <peretti@media.mit.edu> Subject: RE: Your NIKE iD order 016468000

Dear NIKE iD Customer,

Your NIKE iD order was cancelled because the iD you have chosen contains, as stated in the previous e-mail correspondence, "inappropriate slang".

If you wish to reorder your NIKE iD product with a new personalization please visit us again at www.nike.com

Thank you, NIKE iD

From: "Jonah H. Peretti" <peretti@media.mit.edu> To: "Personalize, NIKE iD" <nikeid_personalize@nike.com> Subject: RE: Your NIKE iD order 016468000

Dear NIKE iD, Thank you for your quick response to my inquiry about my custom ZOOM XC USA running shoes. Although I commend you for your prompt customer service, I disagree with the claim that my personal iD was inappropriate slang. After consulting Webster's Dictionary, I discovered that "sweatshop" is in fact part of standard English, and not slang. The word means: "a shop or factory in which workers are employed for long hours at low wages and under unhealthy conditions" and its origin dates from 1892. So my personal iD does meet the criteria detailed in your first email.

Your web site advertises that the NIKE iD program is "about freedom to choose and freedom to express who you are." I share Nike's love of freedom and personal expression. The site also says that "If you want it done right... build it yourself." I was thrilled to be able to build my own shoes, and my personal iD was offered as a small token of appreciation for the sweatshop workers poised to help me realize my vision. I hope that you will value my freedom of expression and reconsider your decision to reject my order.

Thank you, Jonah Peretti

Dear NIKE iD Customer,

Regarding the rules for personalization it also states on the NIKE iD web site that "Nike reserves the right to cancel any Personal iD up to 24 hours after it has been submitted".

In addition it further explains:

"While we honor most personal iDs, we cannot honor every one. Some may be (or contain) others' trademarks, or the names of certain professional sports teams, athletes or celebrities that Nike does not have the right to use. Others may contain material that we consider inappropriate or simply do not want to place on our products.

Unfortunately, at times this obliges us to decline personal iDs that may otherwise seem unobjectionable. In any event, we will let you know if we decline your personal iD, and we will offer you the chance to submit another."

With these rules in mind we cannot accept your order as submitted.

If you wish to reorder your NIKE iD product with a new personalization please visit us again at www.nike.com

Thank you, NIKE iD

From: "Jonah H. Peretti" <peretti@media.mit.edu> To: "Personalize, NIKE iD" <nikeid_personalize@nike.com> Subject: RE: Your NIKE iD order 016468000

Dear NIKE iD,

Thank you for the time and energy you have spent on my request. I have decided to order the shoes with a different iD, but I would like to make one small request. Could you please send me a color snapshot of the ten-year-old Vietnamese girl who makes my shoes?

Thanks, Jonah Peretti

{no response}

Investigating Culture Jamming as Individualized Responsibility-Taking

Peretti has given the authors of this book privileged access to the entire collection of this e-mail exchange. This unique material builds the base for the Nike e-mail exchange data (NEED)[7] which allows for the case study analysis reported in this chapter. This study entails a content analysis of all e-mail messages, a discourse analysis of selected e-mails,[8] and discussion of a

[7] The entire collection of e-mails received by Peretti as a result of his culture jam was provided to the authors for content and discourse analysis. The Research Ethics Board at McGill University approved the content and discourse analyses of the NEE e-mails as well as the follow-up survey. The e-mails were coded on the basis of a codebook containing more than 100 variables formulated by the authors. Barbara Hobson offered useful comments on the codebook. The variables include the sending date, content, sender's characteristics, and several other aspects. We are extremely grateful to Matthew Wright for coding all the NEE e-mail responses, to Laura Nishikawa for conducting a careful discourse analysis on the selected e-mails, and to Cesi Cruz for designing the online survey and keeping track of data. Without the help of these former McGill University students, the analysis in this chapter would have been impossible.

[8] Two types of messages were selected for the discourse analysis: those containing more than ten lines and, therefore, deliberative in character (267 in number and 11.2 percent of the NEED

follow-up online survey conducted in the fall of 2004.[9] The combination of
these unique materials is then merged with qualitative data on anti-sweatshop
political consumer activism. The case study with its multifaceted data sources
represents an isolated instance of antibranding via e-mail that engages a high
number of people in different discussions on sweatshop issues and therefore
serves as a microcosm in which individuals engage in discursive political consumerism. The combination of materials enables the analysis of the participants, their main political messages, the mobilizational potential of the NEE
culture jam and, finally, how the Internet is used to communicate sweatshop
issues broadly and globally.

Who Took Part in the Continued NEE Culture Jam?

To our knowledge, there is no ample data source that attempts to measure who
engages in discursive political consumerism more broadly and antibranding
more specifically, which makes the following analysis unique. While the e-mail
messages give certain insights into the microcosm of antibranding discursive
political consumerism and individualized responsibility-taking in general, it
should be kept in mind that the sample of NEE corresponders is clearly not
representative of the entire group of NEE participants (estimated at about 11
million; see previous section). Most likely, millions of people forwarded and
perhaps continue to forward the prank e-mails without leaving a footprint
for our research purposes. Nevertheless, singling out the group of corresponders gives us an insight into one important sub-group of recipients, namely
those who actively corresponded with Peretti. This study offers, therefore, a
sociodemographic profile of these corresponders, including their characteristics, activities, and views about sweatshop issues.

   Table 6.1 sketches a brief profile of this sub-group of culture jam corresponders. Although the culture jam is assumed to have reached people globally,
the NEE corresponders come mostly from the Anglophone world. Around 50
percent were American, and another 40 percent hailed from other Anglophone
countries. Whereas Chapters 3 and 4 find boycotters and buycotters to be

---

data) and 101 message items that the coder flagged for their discursive content. The two message
   types overlap considerably.
[9] The invitation to take the online survey was sent to a total of 2,383 original NEE responders.
   As the survey was sent three years after the original NEE, 42 percent of the sample was lost
   due to undeliverable e-mails. Of the remaining 1,377 original e-mailers, 21.2 percent answered
   the survey. This response rate compares well to those in other online surveys, despite the fact
   that the survey invitation was sent three years later. Still, because the rate is nevertheless on the
   low end, the worry might be that the respondents are anti-sweatshop activists and, therefore,
   highly motivated to answer this survey. However, a comparison between the distributions of
   sociodemographic characteristics in Table 6.1 (especially city and gender) shows that the survey
   respondents are very similar to the e-mailers. In addition, the types of messages in the NEE are
   similar to the distribution of types of messages in the survey. Thus, survey respondents seem
   representative of the entire NEE.

TABLE 6.1. *Who Are the Discursive Political Consumers?*

	NEE	Online Survey
Country	37.3% not identifiable Of the remaining 1,494: United States: 49.8% United Kingdom: 15.9% Australia: 12.0% Canada: 9.3% New Zealand: 2.1% Other Europe: 3.9% Other developed countries[a]: 6.1% Developing countries[c]: 2.5%	United States: 52.7% United Kingdom: 15.2% Australia: 7.9% Canada: 11.9% New Zealand: 1.4% Other Europe: 6.0% Other developed countries[b]: 4.1% Developing countries[d]: 1.9%
Gender	12.2% not identifiable Of the remaining 2,384: Male: 62.7% Female: 37.3%	Male: 61.1% Female: 38.9%
Employment Sector	64% not identifiable Of the remaining 858: media/arts/entertainment: 36.8% business/finance/marketing: 10.3% high-tech/IT: 10.0% academic/education: 8.9% student (university/college only): 7.5% non-profit: 6.3% other: 19.4%	Student: 4,4 Full-time employed: 55.6% Part-time employed: 5.1% Self-employed: 25.8% Unemployed: 1.1% Retired: 6.2% Other: 1.8%
Education Level		Less than high school: 0% High school: 2.9% Some college: 17.0% Undergraduate degree: 37.0% Master's degree: 31.9% Doctoral degree: 11.2%
Age		Below 18: 1.1% 18–23: 2.5% 24–29: 13.7% 30–35: 19.5% 36–41: 17.7% 42–47: 12.6% 48–52: 10.8% Over 52: 22%

[a] Includes: Austria, Belgium, Belarus, Switzerland, Germany, Denmark, Spain, Finland, Greece, Hungary, Israel, Japan, Korea, Malaysia, the Netherlands, Norway, Portugal, Romania, Sweden.
[b] Includes: Germany, Japan, the Netherlands, Poland, Spain, Switzerland.
[c] Includes: Afghanistan, Argentina, Brazil, Chile, China, Egypt, Guatemala, Honduras, Indonesia, India, Kenya, Lebanon, Lesotho, Mexico, Namibia, Thailand, East Timor, Vietnam, South Africa.
[d] Includes: Argentina, Brazil, Lebanon, Mexico.

disproportionately Scandinavian and European, the Anglophone dominance can perhaps be attributed to language proficiency, the pervasiveness of the Nike brand in these countries, the culture jam's U.S. origin, and the higher profile of confrontational anti-sweatshop activism in North America than in Europe (see Chapter 5). The NEE discursive political consumers are also predominantly (57 percent) from large metropolitan areas (with populations of 1 million or more) and more often men than women. The NEE corresponders are also overrepresented in higher education and professions. From the sample of online survey respondents we know that nearly all of them have some college education and, it is particularly striking that more than 40 percent hold a graduate degree, a level far above any national average. The survey also provides information about the NEE corresponders' ages and indicates that surprisingly few are very young people, thus putting into question theorizing on the role of antibranding and culture jamming in drawing youngsters into politics. Most importantly, they are regular Internet users, and a disproportionate number (about 85 percent) are regularly online for an hour or more per day. Here, it should be recalled that the events took place in 2001 and the survey in 2004, when computers were expensive purchases and before the Internet had penetrated home living and ordinary people's lifestyles. This analysis confirms results from Chapter 3 and elsewhere about boycott and buycott political consumers being Internet-users, highly educated, middle-aged, and urbanites (Tobiasen 2005, Strømnes 2005). However, an important difference is the prevalence of men, which reflects gender gaps that were earlier found in Internet use for certain countries, though not notably in the United States.[10] It is possible that women might have participated in the other antibranding activities against Nike or reacted to the NEE in other ways than choosing to respond directly to Peretti electronically. Moreover, the participants' sociodemographic distribution may have been influenced by Peretti's background (a male graduate student in Boston, information revealed in his e-mail address); it cannot, therefore, be known whether this result holds for other antibranding activities. Within the microcosm of this particular culture jam and the circle of e-mail correspondents, it can with certainty be said that they are more likely to be male, educated, and socioeconomically resourceful people than the average population and even other political consumers.

The NEE's Political Messages

Most important for understanding the purpose and consequences of this case of antibranding discursive political consumerism is the analysis of the messages' content. The NEE corresponders shared different thoughts with Peretti in their e-mails. The content analysis (see Table 4.2) shows whether the NEE corresponders: (1) offered judgments on the NEE or Jonah Peretti's culture

[10] Own calculations from ESS data 2002/2003. See also Cooper and Weaver (2003).

jam; (2) sought or offered information; (3) directly indicated having taken political action on sweatshop issues, and (4) offered suggestions about how to deal with the Nike customer service unit. Whereas an e-mail can contain all of these contents or only one of them, Table 6.2 indicates both how many times a selected content was mentioned overall and measures the distribution of main messages. Even though the e-mails cannot truly reflect the distribution of opinions on sweatshop issues in general and the NEE in particular, they do convey the nature of opinions, attitudes, and viewpoints in the discourse on anti-sweatshop political consumerism.

Roughly two-thirds of the NEE corresponders offered judgments about the culture jam and anti-sweatshop issues. Most of them contained positive evaluations of Peretti's action; only about 10 percent are critical. About 56 percent of all e-mails contained supportive comments about the culture jam. While some are very short, for instance: "Well done, Jonah," others included comments covering several pages. About 13 percent commend his use of humor, which scholars believe contributed to its rapid spread globally. One sender wrote: "[I]f one email, slightly humorous in its irony but memorable for it's [sic] ingenuity catches people's attention and leaves them primed to bother to watch the next late night documentary on such a subject or take 15 minutes out of their day to read the next newspaper article on exploitation, then that email has done some good!" About 11 percent acknowledge the importance of the Internet and 6 percent are impressed by Peretti's ingenuity in using brand vulnerabilities to raise political awareness about global problems.

From all the messages sent, several can be identified as dealing with the sweatshop issues directly; most often addressing concerns about exploitative labor conditions, corporate ethics and the power of transnational corporations, and child labor. Similar concerns have also been found in surveys that ask about transnational corporations and political consumerism (Tobiasen 2005). Many messages reveal insights into the senders' ideological focus but, surprisingly, the discourse analysis reveals little trace of culture jamming's ideological opposition to the pervasiveness of brands in consumer society (cf. Lasn 2000, Klein 2000). Rather, the e-mails generally frame the central problem as the existence of sweatshops and the exploitation of developing countries and (child) workers and, thus, correspond more with the dominant discourse about reforming free trade and making corporations more socially responsible that is found in most political consumer causes (see Chapter 5; Micheletti, Follesdal, and Stolle 2006). The NEE material reveals an implicit hope that political consumer activism can effectively combine capitalism and social justice: that people just need to "keep up the pressure," and corporations will "change from within." Hope is also placed in socially responsible corporations; The Body Shop and New Balance are commonly cited examples (see Chapter 7 for a discussion of ethical corporations).

The NEE corresponders' focus is also directed at the global economy and transnational corporations as political targets. Both the content and discourse

TABLE 6.2. *Themes Addressed in E-mail Responses to the Nike E-mail Exchange*
(percentages)

Topic Category Mentioned Overall	Main Message	Sub-Category Illustrations and Percentages in Relation to Main Message
Judgment 65%	45%	59% Messages with judgments on culture jamming: explicit support for Peretti's actions acknowledging the importance of raising awareness this way, the power of the Internet, or humor. 50% Messages with judgments on anti-sweatshop issues: explicit or general support for anti-sweatshop movement (e.g., against child labor, corporate ethics/behavior, exploitive working conditions, human rights and justice) 12% Messages with critical judgments: offered an explicit critique of Peretti's actions 8% Messages with critical judgments: offered an explicit critique of the anti-sweatshop movement
Information 45%	25%	42% Info – culture jamming messages: seek or share information about this case of culture jamming 12% Interview request by media 23% Info – corporate practice messages: seek or share information about Nike practices, other corporate practices in other countries, or even provide personal testimonies of own experiences in factories. 29% Info – truth messages: try to confirm whether the jam has actually happened or not.
Mobilization 40%	21%	27% Conventional mobilization: indicated that would contact or has contacted the media, politicians, written about the culture jam, published on it. 80% Sharing with others: talking to others, forwarding to others, posted the culture jam on a list or web site. 33% Political consumerism: indicates that will boycott or has boycotted Nike, will watch or has watched out for better companies, contacted Nike, followed similar campaigns, etc.
Suggestion 13%	8%	40% Messages with alternative suggestion: offered advice on how one could get around the Nike censors 21% Alternative types of activism 19% Suggestions regarding or directed at Nike 20% Suggestions to further publish this episode

Note: The actual number of e-mails analyzed was less than 3,655 because many of them came from the same author. Multiple messages from the same author were collapsed into one e-mail. The final e-mail database contains 2,384 e-mails. The percentages in the first column are results from the content analysis; column percentages do not add up to 100 percent because multiple themes are possible. Results in the second column stem from the coder assessment about the main message of each e-mail – only one theme can make up the main message. Percentages in the third column are distributions within each of these categories based on content coding of each e-mail. All categories were part of the initial codebook.
Source: Nike e-mail exchange data (NEED), Quantitative Content Analysis.

analyses reveal that government is not viewed as a key actor to solve sweatshop problems, and there is also little direct mentioning of conventional forms of political participation. In line with this attitudinal profile, the survey respondents reveal fairly strong postmaterialist values: nearly 90 percent are either mixed or pure postmaterialist types (Inglehart 1997), who have been found not to trust mainstream political institutions and who refrain from conventional political participation (see also Chapters 3 and 4 on postmaterialists and their values).

As indicated earlier, critical voices are present in the e-mail responses. A significant number who worry about sweatshops also oppose Peretti's approach and call for other forms of involvement. Even though Peretti was never able to buy the customized shoes, many e-mailers support consistency in value expression and shopping decisions. For them, corporations should either be punished (boycotted) or rewarded (buycotted). This group is interesting because it represents a unified political consumerist approach including the two prominent forms of market-based activism. Other messages illustrate general criticism of political consumerism by including attacks on Peretti's white, middle-class status and Northern, MIT-elitist, and educated view of global production conditions that lose track of the actual benefits of inexpensive labor and foreign investment in developing countries (see Chapter 7 for a discussion of these critiques).

The NEE's Mobilizing Potential

Can an Internet culture jam, as theorized by scholars, be a stepping-stone for further political action? The study's answer is that this appears to be the case. The content analysis distinguishes three mobilization types: (1) requesting, discussing, or sharing related information (45 percent); (2) mentioning related direct political action in other contexts (36 percent) and (3) discussing of suggestions and ideas of further actions (13 percent). The largest share of the mobilization entailed discursive actions as information-sharing and information-seeking about the culture jam or corporate labor practices. More than a fourth of the responders asked whether the message was spam.

The NEE analysis also offers a good overview of the kinds of political involvement that can be triggered by culture jamming campaigns and antibranding events. This addresses important issues in the academic literature about potential spillover effects from Internet-based political mobilization to participation in other media types or arenas (Vissers, Hooghe, Stolle, and Mahéo 2011). The hope is that Internet mobilization can stem the tide of diminishing political engagement in part caused by declines in certain types of associational life (Putnam 2000). The question emerges whether online mobilization might primarily trigger online engagement or also other forms of engagement in the offline world as well. For the purposes of this analysis, it is important to understand whether and which types of political consumer or

TABLE 6.3. *The NEE's Political Mobilization Effects*

Forms of mobilization mentioned by 857 responders or 36% of the entire sample	Number	Percentage of People Mobilized	Percentage of Entire Sample
Conventional			
Published e-mail offline	207	24.1	8.6
Posted e-mail online	88	10.2	3.7
Contacted media	37	4.3	1.6
Contacted a politician	5	0.6	0.2
Contacted an organization	3	0.4	0.1
Joined a demonstration against sweatshops	3	0.4	0.1
Exchange with Others			
Contacted other people	717	83.6	30.1
Forwarded the e-mail	430	50.2	18.0
Talked to individuals offline about the e-mails	38	4.4	8.6
Explicit Political Consumer Strategies			
Contacted Nike	206	24.0	8.6
Boycotted Nike	68	7.9	2.8
Sent Nike a request for "Sweatshop" shoes	48	5.6	2.0
Participated in similar campaigns	22	2.6	1.0
Changed to more responsible shoe manufacturer (buycott)	4	0.5	0.2

Note: The final e-mail database contains 2,384 e-mails. The first column presents results of the content coding of all responders who mentioned this form of mobilization as a likely or already performed activity which directly follows as a consequence of the original culture jam. Column 2 mentions percentages calculated based on those who mentioned some form of mobilization (36 percent of entire sample = 100 percent). Column 3 mentions percentages of entire sample. The data in the second and third columns do not add up to 100 percent because many e-mails mentioned more than one form of political mobilization. All categories were part of the initial codebook.
Source: Nike e-mail exchange data (NEED).

other action repertoires might have been facilitated or triggered based on the NEE (while actual percentages play less of a role because of the small sample of NEE receivers – they are used here comparatively). Our results in Table 4.3 show that 36 percent of the NEE corresponders explicitly and voluntarily mentioned that they had or planned to engage in various political acts as a consequence of the NEE. Most of them focus on further discursive actions in the form of communication and exchange on sweatshop issues; a smaller group also mentions the use of conventional political methods (see Chapter 2) and another group, explicit political consumer tactics. Communication in the form of contacting others and forwarding the NEE or posting it on a web site was the activity most frequently mentioned. Corresponders also said that they used the NEE as an opportunity for personal conversations, indicating a spillover effect from Internet to face-to-face involvement. As a result of the NEE, some claim that they are motivated to or will become boycotters or buycotters, while fewer became or plan to be involved in conventional forms of participation targeted at politicians or government institutions. This also shows that concern about sweatshop conditions does not necessarily lead to calls upon government.[11]

The discourse analysis reveals the contemporary importance of consumer identity and consumer power, thus indicating a specific direction of mobilization and giving weight to the importance of market-based individualized responsibility-taking. Whether praising Peretti for helping people understand consumer society better ("reflect on their behavior as consumers") or arguing that consumers have a role to play in sweatshop practices ("the accusing finger should be pointed at the mirror"), they consistently identify themselves in the role of consumer more explicitly than as citizens. "Consumer" is both a collective and individual identity. Peretti is the empowered individual consumer – the "David" in the David and Goliath struggle against Nike and garment sweatshops as it has been understood in media and research accounts – whose innovative and strong underdog struggle appeals to feelings of frustration, powerlessness, and isolation. One woman thanks him for "voicing what myself and I am sure many others feel"; another corresponder remarks that "now I know that I'm not the only one who questions Nike's methods." Mobilizational e-mails typically express the sender's craving to be part of a larger and public community more critical of consumption choices. While some senders advocate simply choosing "good" over "bad" corporations, many others emphasize that if action is to be effective it must be collectively mobilized. They reflect the importance of the discursive turn in political action when commenting about communication's empowering nature and its being, as one corresponder said, "a link in a chain of CHANGE which will lead to ACTION... It's about US creating the communities that we wish to live in." A common response to the e-mail was, "I will forward it to everyone I know," and many asked Peretti how many people in how many countries had received the Nike e-mail exchange. Several e-mails refer to the NEE's rapid spread as "a movement" and ask "may I forward it to everyone I know so that it will become a movement? I want it to be on the news." Some suggest that "many of us should get together and make the same request." A widespread concern is how to be "counted" in this so-called movement. Some go so far as to state that enhanced consumer choice is "the greatest power" we have against corporations and that "if *you don't like it, don't buy it* is how a person applies *real* power and gets things to change" and that "If more people could only realize how much power we consumers have... our choices as consumers... Which give us ultimate power, IF WE ONLY USE IT!"

---

[11] Moreover, as this finding relies on responses volunteered in the e-mails, this analysis may have underestimated (but not overestimated) or missed some aspects of the political mobilization of this culture jam. However, again, the small sample given the large population of NEE receivers precludes any direct claims about mobilization.

Corresponders also want to solve sweatshop problems, and 13 percent offer suggestions, including additional discursive action ideas about how to further the culture jam by getting important words stitched on Nike shoes without being stopped by censors (6 percent), alternative actions like sweatshop watch, demonstrations against unacceptable corporate practices, or public debate (3 percent of the sample) and media contact (3 percent). There is an interesting tension in the discourse about the responsibility-taking of individual consumers, which reflects the role of active and more habitual choice in theorizing on how structural injustices emerge and how they can be resolved (see Chapter 1). Some point to consumers as an important cause of sweatshop problems ("[W]e all spend a lot of time criticizing the 'bad' companies that dominate our society and often miss the bigger point about the individuals that make them up (us)"), others view consumer values and choice as a way of solving sweatshop problems. These e-mails emphasize that individual responsibility-taking by consumers can form a critical mass to hold corporations accountable and, thus, challenge prevailing structural injustices.

Long-Term Impact of the NEE

Of course, there is no real way to successfully estimate the full impact of the Nike e-mail exchange on the people who received and discussed it. However, a powerful analytic way to examine the effect of an innovative antibranding Internet campaign is the use of longitudinal data, which we have created with the help of the survey that asked original NEE correspondents three years later about their political involvements during the previous twelve months (in 2004). Assuming that the survey sample can be seen as a fairly representative sample of the original correspondents (see note 9 to this chapter), the results will help us understand more about this jam as a microcosm. The results reveal that the 2001 correspondents are a predominantly active bunch: nearly 90 percent voted in the last national elections or signed petitions; and more than 90 percent visited political web sites. This finding indicates that the respondents are highly participatory in both conventional and less conventional ways. What we do not know for sure is whether they were already more politically active before they engaged with this culture jam. Yet, when asked specific questions about how best to address the sweatshop issue, they do not seem to believe in the power of conventional political action. Rather, they appear to be politically active citizens who widely use more individualized political action repertoires, including different forms of political consumerism – more than 80 percent have also boycotted, buycotted or forwarded messages with political content.

Two analytical avenues are pursued in order to investigate more fully whether the NEE shaped responsibility-taking in a more lasting way. A first step involves the analysis of direct survey questions about the NEE's

TABLE 6.4. *Direct Effects of the NEE*

Did Jonah Peretti's e-mail Exchange with Nike...	Yes	No	Do Not Remember
...give you more information about the issue?	43.8%	23.7%	32.5%
...affect the way you view Nike?	53.8%	40.7%	5.5%
...prompt further action on your part?	48.5%	43.8%	7.7%

Forms of action inspired by Jonah Peretti e-mail (analysis of open-ended question)	
Spread information	65
Forwarded e-mail	21
Discussion	19
Media (e.g. wrote article)	15
Classroom	8
Other Internet (blog, etc)	2
Boycotted Nike	51
And other companies	4
Contacted Nike	11
Conducted further research into issue (including other companies)	9
Reinforced commitment to issue (renewed preexisting course of action)	5
Changed general lifestyle (more conscious, greatly reduced spending on consumer goods)	5
Launched a new anti-sweatshop campaign (No Sweat sneakers; legal action)	2
Total	138

Note: The first table presents the distribution of answers to the questions in Column 1. The second table presents a quantitative analysis of an open-ended question that was a follow-up to the question "Did Jonah Peretti's e-mail exchange prompt further action on your part?" This was worded as: "If so, please specify what type of political actions."
Source: Nike e-mail exchange survey with 293 respondents.

mobilizational effect. The second step is an examination of which participants are most affected by the NEE.

The survey included direct questions about the effect of the NEE on its participants. Table 6.4 shows that 44 percent thought they received more information on Nike and sweatshop issues through the NEE, 54 percent remember that it affected the way they view Nike, and nearly half indicate that the NEE spurred further action on their part. An analysis of the open-ended questions about types of further actions provoked by the NEE shows the prominence of discursive actions, such as the spreading of information about anti-sweatshop issues, thus indicating the growing importance of communication as political activism (see earlier discussion on the discursive turn). Some respondents described their informational role in specific offline settings such as school and university classrooms. Others referred to their boycott of specific Nike products and/or related companies. This result indicates again that discursive political consumerist actions and political communication on the Internet can spill over into face-to-face settings. Some respondents noted effects on lifestyle more generally. Two respondents even initiated a new anti-sweatshop campaign. Overall, the results of this analysis demonstrate that an active Internet campaign of the caliber of the NEE might be able to shape political engagement in multiple ways, including further antibranding activities and other creative innovative actions.

Finally, who are the corresponders most affected by the NEE according to their own judgment? For this final step of the analysis, a simple ordered logit regression model was developed using the items that measure the effect of the NEE (from Table 6.4) as a summated rating scale. In other words, the dependent variable distinguishes respondents who indicated that the NEE gave them more information about sweatshop issues, affected their view of Nike and/or prompted further action on their part from those who did not feel affected by the NEE.[12] Ideally, most of the typical sociodemographic predictors such as education and political interest should not matter here, as there is no evidence that education and political attitudes foster the mobilization process in itself. This analysis (not shown but available from the authors) reveals that this is indeed the case; none of the typical sociodemographic variables really explain the mobilization process. However, women claim to be more affected by the NEE than men, and older people twice as affected as middle-aged responders; young people indicate half as much of an effect compared to older folks. This finding shows that, although the prominence of culture jams is higher among young people, the long-lasting influences seem to be more significant in the older generations, who generally had probably experienced fewer of them.

As earlier scholarship on culture jamming has theorized and argued, the NEE gives insights into how community around consumer issues is built and how it sets into motion a spiral of awareness raising, creation of a caring sensitivity, and mobilization. This first systematic empirical investigation into the structure of a culture jam reveals that the people involved with culture jams are more male, educated, Internet-savvy, and of younger age than the general population. Most importantly, the NEE seemed to have had consequences, not all of which could be measured in this analysis. However, when asked about the NEE, the majority of corresponders indicated that it did affect them; particularly women and older people, two groups of citizens not most commonly active in these forms of participation, were affected. While generalizations to everyone who received the culture jam cannot be made, those whom we studied indicated heightened awareness and potential of mobilization into further action repertoires.

---

[12] Thus, the dependent variable is a scale ranging from 0 to 3, indicating 0 = no effect of the NEE; 1 = one effect; 2 = two effects; 3 = all three effects. This variable divides the sample into four about equal groups of respondents and requires ordered logit analysis.

The Effectiveness of Targeting the Nike Iconic Brand

"Every Joke is a Tiny Revolution,"[13] the title of a master's thesis on culture jamming, is one way of summarizing the responsibility-taking goals and potential consequences of the Nike e-mail exchange and its aftermath. The Nike e-mail exchange was, for example, brought into school classrooms, family and friendship circles, and larger public settings. It was cartooned by Doonesbury and reported on in national and even international newspapers. Its originator, Jonah Peretti, granted numerous interviews about it and appeared together with Nike's Director of Global Issues Management on the NBC morning program *The Today Show* (February 28, 2001) to discuss the sweatshop problem in the globalized garment industry and the personalization of his order of Nike shoes. Peretti understood clearly the public relations value of his endeavor. His collected e-mails show that he initiated contacts with journalists and promoted the spread of the NEE. He even wrote an article, "My Nike E-mail Adventure," for *The Nation* (March 22, 2001). The Nike Corporation and Peretti communicated about media inquiries about the event, and Peretti informed us that Nike assigned a public relations person to deal with media questions on the culture jam (Peretti, personal correspondence). However, in an interview conducted for this book, Nike did not admit the need to take direct action because of the culture jam, even though it acknowledged that the corporation should have dealt with Peretti's request for personalized shoes in a much different way (Nike Interview 2004).

Nevertheless, what is clear is that the NEE pushed Nike once again in public settings to discuss its "sweatshop woes." Nike even attempted to manage the publicity damage that it caused by including culture jamming in its advertisements; other corporations have reacted in similar fashion (see Katyal 2010).[14] The publicity from the NEE encouraged mainstream civil society organizations to post it on their web sites and incorporate aspects of culture jamming in their campaigns, thus showing both how activist groups emulate successful events, tools, and examples as well as the importance of the discursive turn for political action repertoires (Meyer 2006).

Clearly, culture jamming and antibranding more generally are highly dependent on the Internet as an infrastructure and technological tool. They are also, of course, highly dependent on the presence of iconic and well-known global brands, which they can use as their political message boards. But how effective has anti-sweatshop activism been generally? To begin to answer this question, Figure 6.1 constructs a timeline of Nike-targeting activism from the early 1990s to 2011. It also chronicles Nike's responses and corporate changes (for more detailed examples of activism, see DeWinter-Schmitt 2007, appendix 3,

---

[13] S. Woodside (2001), "Every Joke is a Tiny Revolution – Culture Jamming and the Role of Humour," master's thesis, University of Amsterdam, The Netherlands.

[14] For Nike's own use of culture jamming see "Jamming the Jammers," Antimedia Network, http://www.antimedia.net/nikesweatshop/ (accessed December 15, 2009).

Early Years of Awareness and Mobilizing (early to mid 1990s)

Consciousness-raising activism & boycott calls	Sweatshop issue on government agenda	Nike responses: Defensive but changes in manufacturing policy
Indonesian workers protest against treatment in manufacturing sector. European campaign tours with protest leaders for the Indonesian workers' cause (1993)	U.S. government signals awareness of the sweatshop problem in Cabinet reports and legislation (1992)	Justifies its outsourced manufacturing (1992)
Press for Change's critical report of Nike's manufacturing in Indonesia (1993)		Follows Levi Strauss' lead and formulates Code of Conduct and Memorandum of Understanding for its offshore contractors (1992)
Sneaker campaigns in the Netherlands and Italy (1993)		Signs Athletic Footwear Association "Guidelines on Business Practices of Business Partners" (1993)
German Nike boycott launched (1993)		Creates NEAT (Nike Environmental Action Team) (1993)
New anti-sweatshop groups emerge, e.g., Coalition for Justice in the Maquiladoras (1989), European Clean Clothes Campaign (1990), Maquila Solidarity Network (1994)		

"Year of the Sweatshop" Surge in Consciousness-Raising and Mobilization to Force Nike into Responsibility-taking (1995–1996)

More coordinated & intensified activism	Government responses	Publicity around Nike	Nike responses: Defensive but efforts in policy innovation
Californian garment factory raid becomes formative event for North American anti-sweatshop movement (1995)	Clinton administration initiates Apparel Industry Partnership (AIP) (1996)	Receives award as one of the "Ten Worst Corporations of 1994"	Nike CEO Phil Knight & Donald Katz defend Nike book at book-signing event in Portland, Oregon (1995)
Release of *Just Do It!*, a book favorably portraying Nike, becomes an anti-sweatshop mobilizing event (1995)		International NGO Forum on Indonesian Development rates Nike as worst U.S.-based multinational in workers' rights (1995)	Adopts the Natural Step and Re-use-a-Shoe programs, hires prominent accounting firm to do its social audits (1995)
Launch: Just Do It! The Boycott Nike Campaign (1996)		Media interest surges. Nike and Kathie Lee Gifford singled out for close investigation; CBS news show *48 Hours* focuses on Nike; anti-sweatshop stories run in major U.S. newspapers and magazines (1996)	Becomes AIP charter member (1996)
			Creates its first department (Labor Practices) specifically responsible for managing supply chain partners' compliance with labor standards (1996)
			Joins Business for Social Responsibility after turning down two years of invitations (1996)

FIGURE 6.1. Rise and Effect of Anti-Sweatshop Activism against Nike

International Day of Action against Nike (1996)

More anti-sweatshop groups founded (1996)

Sweatshop Watch premiers its Faces Behind the Labels photo exhibit in San Francisco (1996)

Activist Pressure, Nike Denials, Nike Moves to Make Corporate Responsibility Core Business Value & Practice (1997–2001)

Surge in activism, creative protests, media interest & consumer reactions	Governmental & institutional responses	Nike responses: Focus on policy changes
Creative political consumerism (1997): Postcard campaigns, worldwide protest days, petition signing events, community organizing, Niketown sit-ins, protests in Nike's home state, holiday targeting, anti-sweatshop fashion shows, culture jam of Nike's "If You let Me Play" campaign, shareholder activism	U.S. national politicians call on Nike to change its manufacturing practices (1997)	Announces Indonesian subcontractors are to receive newly raised minimum wage; steps being taken to make improvements in Vietnamese factories and declares corporate punishment in its Vietnamese factories is "appalling" and "simply not allowable" (1997)
Students and unions unite in unique effort (1997)	UN consultant releases critical report of working environment in Nike's Vietnamese factories (1997)	Former UN ambassador Andrew Young's favorable report on working conditions in Nike's Asian factories used in full-page ads in every major U.S. newspaper (1997)
Joint women's organizations efforts (1997)	Sweatshop exhibit featured at Smithsonian Museum of American History (1998)	Amends Code of Conduct for contractors (1997)
Global trade unions' International Confederation of Free Trade Unions denounces Nike operations in Indonesia and Vietnam (1997)	Duke University, all eight University of California schools, and others adopt code of conduct on workplace standards for manufacturing products bearing university logo (1998)	Letter from Director of Labor Practices explains that Nike cannot ask its contractors to raise wages to "living wage" level because it would drive all companies out of business and destroy jobs, letter used in Kasky lawsuit to establish false advertisement
Anti-sweatshop messages in popular culture (1997–1998); important examples: Doonesbury comic strip, TV series *Beverly Hills 90210*, *Today Show*, *Life Magazine*; Michael Moore's film *The Big One* ridiculing Nike's CEO premieres at the Sundance Film Festival		Pulls out of Thai factory after workers stage sit-in; union organizers fired (1998)
		CEO holds press conference, refers to himself rhetorically as "the great Satan," details Nike's progress in dealing with sweatshop allegations (1998)

FIGURE 6.1 (*continued*)

Global Exchange publicizes Nguyen's critical report commissioned by Nike (1997)	U.S. governmental "No Sweat U" conference for schools (1998)	Files motion for dismissal of Kasky's lawsuit on First Amendment grounds. ACLU of Northern California supports Nike (1998)
Student activism increases (1997): school protests, United States Student Association and University of California Student Association pass resolutions condemning Nike (1997)	AIP releases Charter Document including provisions for internal and external monitoring (1998)	Establishes Corporate Responsibility department (1998)
United Students Against Sweatshops initiated (1997)	UN General Secretary Kofi Annan launches UN Global Compact (1999)	Focuses on factory work environment: certifies all subcontract factories in ISO 14000 environmental standard, formulates six major commitments to change manufacturing practices to meet U.S. Occupational Safety and Health Administration's standards in indoor air quality (1998)
Unique sales drop; business analysts state that bad publicity is one reason. Nike stocks drop 39 percent while market as a whole rise 20 percent (1997)	Stop Sweatshops legislation reintroduced in U.S. Congress (1999)	Amends Code of Conduct for contractors (1998)
Marc Kasky files lawsuit accusing Nike of false advertising and violating Californian truth-in-advertising laws. Retains well-known lawyer Alan Caplan who successfully sued Camel cigarettes. Sierra Club, California Labor Federation/AFL-CIO, state Attorney General and others file amicus curiae briefs (1998)	President Clinton announces formation of the Fair Labor Association (FLA); students react with sit-ins (1999)	Initiates corporate responsibility training programs (1998)
	San Francisco Superior Court dismisses Kasky's lawsuit (1999)	Raises minimum age for specified Nike factory workers (1998)
AFL-CIO's call for national Nike boycott (1998)	President Clinton's National Economic Advisor not able to convince USAS to join FLA process (1999)	Focuses more on transparency by including NGOs in factory monitoring, releasing report summaries publicly (1998)
NGO-hosted Living Wage Working Summit; NGOs conduct worker testimonial tours (1998)	Several universities threaten to terminate licenses with manufacturers who do not identify their factories (1999)	Funds creation of Global Alliance for Workers and Communities (1999)
Training camps for WTO meeting in Seattle 1999 (1998)	Brown University first to join Workers Rights Consortium (WRC) (1999)	Improves transparency by launching new web site "Correcting the Record" to counters activists' claims that it states are based on past incidents (1999)
Anti-sweatshop demonstration outside midtown Manhattan Niketown (1998)		Opens for more dialogue with activists, claims common goal of improving global manufacturing; VP of CSR to work with core of individuals designated by activist groups to represent their collective interests (1999)
		More transparency: First large apparel company to disclose its manufacturing factories; announces names and location of forty-one of its contractors in eleven countries producing collegiate apparel for ten universities (1999); NYT journalist (Oct. 8, 1999) calls this "one of the biggest victories thus far by the campus anti-sweatshop movement." Earlier Nike considered this information a trade secret.

FIGURE 6.1 (*continued*)

Continued activist and investigative journalist reporting on workers' treatment in Nike's offshore factories, sportswriters report on Nike labor problems, journalists criticize sports' celebrity endorsements of Nike and Nike's university sponsorships (1998)

Naomi Klein's book *No Logo: Taking Aim at the Brand Bullies* criticizes Nike, receives intensive media coverage, and becomes political manifesto for young people (1999)

Student activism intensifies: Sit-ins, violence at universities (1999)

Global Exchange's holiday season campaigns targets Nike in culture jams (1999)

Violent protests at WTO Summit, so-called "Battle of Seattle" (1999)

Nike Truth Tour with worker testimonials in U.S. cities (2000)

Niketown demonstrations (2000)

Activists target Nike at Sydney Olympics, Play Fair in Europe campaign launched for World Football Cup (2000)

Joint activist report "Sweatshops Behind the Swoosh" on conditions in Nike's Chinese factories made public (2000)

Nike e-mail exchange (2001)

Continued activist monitoring of Nike's progress with corporate responsibility, critical statements and reports, worker testimonial tours (2001)

Lessening of pressure on Nike after 9/11; activists focus on promoting peace (2001)

Several universities leave FLA and join WRC (2000)

University of California issues stronger code of conduct, including provision for living wage, collective bargaining, women's rights, full disclosure (2000)

Schools hire PricewaterhouseCoopers to investigate factories (2000)

Dear Colleague letter asking members of Congress to endorse the WRC circulates in U.S. House of Representatives (2000)

U.S. Department of Labor issues a study on meeting workers' needs in apparel and footwear industries in twenty-six countries (2000)

U.S. congressional member introduces House Resolution on Corporate Code of Conduct Act for businesses operating abroad (2000)

California Attorney General releases statement supporting Kasky's right to sue Nike (2000)

FLA's University Advisory Council votes to require public disclosure of licenses' factory locations (2000)

Offers to sponsor ten students to audit its disclosed factories with PricewaterhouseCoopers (PWC) monitors. (USAS calls this a publicity stunt) (1999)

Fired union organizer at Nike Indonesian factory reinstated after U.S. speaking tour (1999)

Announces another wage increase for Indonesian workers (2000)

Withholds 30 million USD from University of Oregon, cuts funds to Brown University and University of Michigan for joining the WRC (2000)

Joins Coalition for Environmentally Responsible Economies (CERES) (2000)

Initiates "Transparency 101!" web site, promises to release information on PWC-audited factories, agrees to share its internal SHAPE (safety, health, attitude of management, people investment, and environment) audits; issues press release on increasing its transparency by releasing its PWC audits "warts and all" because "we have nothing to hide" (2000)

Refuses to disclose names and locations of all its factories (2000)

Cooperates with several U.S. schools to investigate factory working conditions (2000)

Endorses UN's Global Compact Principles. Nike's CEO only representative from a U.S. company to attend its launching (2000)

Corporate responsibility (CR) performance becomes one of six corporate strategic goals, all job descriptions adjusted to include CR work, production managers on location in producing regions graded in part on their success in fulfilling CR, including demonstrating improved labor practices in contractors. Grade affects pay levels and bonuses (2000)

Publicizes audit reports on twenty-two South and Central American factories (2000)

FIGURE 6.1 (*continued*)

USAS expands agenda to oppose corporate globalization, begins new era campaign in support of workers (2001)

Shareholder resolution at Nike's Annual General Meeting voted down (2001)

New York City mayor vetoes city council resolution to require city to purchase sweat-free uniforms (2001)

U.S. congressperson visits Nike's Kukdong factory, circulates Dear Colleague letter asking other congressional members to support newly founded union there (2001)

U.S. congressperson sends letter signed by fifty members to Nike CEO criticizing conditions in its Asian factories, compares them to CEO's personal wealth, high price of Nike's products, Nike's advertising budget (2001)

Nike's VP of corporate responsibility asks Kukdong management to reinstate fired workers and drop charges (2001). NYT journalist calls this "the biggest success thus far" for the WRC. Nike-contracted workers gain recognition of their independent union, negotiate collective bargaining agreement. Nike immediately announces its plans to place a 2.5 million USD order with the factory; responds to collegiate letter writing campaign that it will resume placing orders at Kundong (2001)

Nike admits that CR is a process: VP of corporate responsibility responds to criticisms by stating that "there is no finish line and improving the lives and working conditions of workers who make Nike products is no exception" (DeWinter-Schmitt 2007, 392, footnote 546)

Releases second installment of Transparency 101 initiative with monitoring summaries of Central and South American factories; criticized for not releasing entire report and disclosing factories (2001)

Launches web site for virtual tour of Vietnamese factory (2001)

Nike and Gap release Global Alliance report on Indonesian working conditions. Nike releases remedial plans to address specific issues uncovered in talks with workers (2001)

Director of Global Issues Management admits that Nike was "arrogant" to think it did not have to respond to public scrutiny, admits that as a large supply chain, mistakes will be made (2001)

Begins grading system of all suppliers to register inspection and other factory information (2001)

Releases first Corporate Social Responsibility Report (2001)

Claims that shareholder resolution is redundant due to its efforts (2001)

Changes view on WCR and begins working with it and FLA to solve problems at Kukdong

FIGURE 6.1 (continued)

Anti-sweatshop activists & others credit Nike with progress; Multi-stakeholder platforms flourish	Ethical businesses arises from activism	Government reactions (important examples)	Nike responses: Learning responsibility-taking
FLA reports membership success at U.S. schools and new standardized reporting (2002)	Kalle Lasn & Adbusters announce plans to manufacture no-sweat "Blackspot" sneaker market venture as way of "kicking Phil's [Nike's President] ass," criticizing Nike's marketing strategy of selling ideas and identity (2003)	California Supreme Court rules that Nike can be sued in the Kasky v. Nike case since it deals with commercial, not protected free speech (2002)	Kasky lawsuit leads Nike to enter less public phase; decides not to release second CSR report, states that it will evaluate its "ability to engage in public debate and to publish further reports on corporate responsibility initiatives" but remain committed to integrating "corporate responsibility into the heart of its business" (quoted in DeWinter-Schmitt 2007, 427–428) (2002)
WRC works with Nike, factory management, workers, and union to address code violations in Indonesian factory (2003)		Kasky v. Nike heard and dismissed by U.S. Supreme Court, sent back to California state courts (2003)	Nike involved in FLA efforts to reinstate fired workers at Dominican Republic factory; *New York Times* reports that Nike's collective bargaining agreement at Dominican Republic factory is "unheard of among the country's 5,000 foreign-owned plants" and "first formed in a free [trade] zone in five years" (quoted in DeWinter-Schmitt 2007, 418) (2002)
WRC, Clean Clothes Campaign, Nike, and other global garment corporations push for agreement at Thai factory to reinstate workers fired illegally (2004)		Better Work partnership programme between the ILO and International Finance Corporation (IFC) to improve compliance with labor standards and competitiveness in global supply chains launched (2007)	Nike donates 5.1 million USD to Global Alliance (2002)
FLA accredits the compliance programs of Nike and five other companies (2005)		ILO unanimously adopts the ILO Declaration on Social Justice for a Fair Globalization (2008) and holds forms and other activities to implement the goals (2007)	Nike hesitant about further transparency because of Kasky case (2003)
KLD announces it will add Nike to its Broad Market Social Index and Large Cap Social Index, decision based on second CSR report and Nike's decision to disclose factories. TUAA-CREF and Calvert add Nike as acceptable socially responsible investment outlet (2005)			Nike and union request FLA to resolve dispute at a Sri Lankan factory (2003)
			Nike settles Kasky case for 1.5 million USD without admitting any liability. Kasky donates settlement to FLA (2003)
			Nike implements responsibility-taking measures (2003): Majority of code compliance staff located directly in production regions to ensure close contact with factory management, management training of contractors on implementing code standards
			Aftermath of Kasky case: Nike's legal counsel again permits detailed public statements on its CR efforts (2004)

FIGURE 6.1 (*continued*)

Nike contributes to initiative campaign in California (Prop. 64) to make it more difficult to sue companies for deceptive advertising and other fraudulent practices (2004)

New VP for corporate responsibility, President of the Nike Foundation, Phil Knight, steps down from posts as CEO and president (2004)

Nike issues second CSR report, acquiesces to activist demands to disclose names and location of all its (700+) factories in more than 50 countries employing around 650,000 employers; calls on other corporations to do the same (2005)

Nike and others agree to source from Cambodia as part of International Labor Organization's multi-stakeholder Better Factories Cambodia project (2005)

Nike VP of corporate responsibility states that Nike sees corporate responsibility as strategic opportunity, bringing benefits far beyond that of risk management (2005)

CSR report states that it needs to understand better how its business decisions may contribute to negative impacts on workers; formulates the goal of affecting positive systemic change in working conditions and driving multi-stakeholder partnerships and industry change (2005)

Corporate responsibility department takes on central role in Nike's operations. VP of corporate responsibility states: "For the first time our team doesn't feel like we are salmon swimming upstream, we actually feel like we are swimming in tandem with the business towards business excellence" (DeWinter-Schmitt 2007, 436)

UK Responsible and Accountable Garment Sector Challenge Fund (RAGS), funded by UKaid from the Department for International Development, is fully operable (2010)

Canadian anti-sweatshop groups' transparency report card ranks Nike high (2005)

Joint Initiative on Corporate Accountability and Workers' Rights launched through collaboration involving FLA, WRC, SAI, Nike, and seven other companies. Pilot project to run in Turkey (2005)

Continued collaboration and joint involvement in innovative responsibility-taking collaboration with Nike (2007)

Activists and Nike establish projects to undertake skills development for workers, trainings for managers on improved labor-management relations, increased efficiency of production process, etc. (2007)

Innovest/Corporate Knights Inc. identify Nike as one of 100 Most Sustainable Companies (2009)

The Ethisphere Institute named Nike as one of the World's Most Ethical Companies for 2010

FIGURE 6.1 (*continued*)

Ceres and the Association for Chartered Certified Accountants gave Nike the award for best sustainability reporting (2011) conference in Oakland

Corporate Responsibility Magazine lists Nike as number 10 on its "100 Best Corporate Citizens List" (2011)

Nike takes out large CSR advertisement in *New York Times* (2005)

Nike helps Bono launch brand Product Red (2006)

Nike becomes member of The Fair Factories Clearinghouse since 2007 and working actively with them to enhance brand collaboration on sweatshop and other issues

Begins offering human resources management training and other support to its contract factories (financial year 2007)

Starts its sustainable business and innovation team (2009)

Further work on creating its sustainable supply chain that it claims is "lean, green, equitable, and empowered" across all Nike brands

Began work to define the actions it expects for contract factories to make progress toward better wage systems with wages that meet the FLA definition of "fair wage" (financial year 2011)

More multi-stakeholder efforts with other leading apparel and footwear brands, retailers, manufacturers, NGOs, academics, and the U.S. Environmental Protection Agency to launch Sustainable Apparel Coalition to help create industry-wide common performance indicators and index for ensuring and evaluating product sustainability (2011)

Sources: The information presented in this figure has been collected from different secondary sources appearing in this book, particularly DeWinter-Schmitt 2007 and Shaw 1999, as well as from Kendall, Gill, and Cleneyl 2007 and directly from news reports, Nike, and the activist groups.

Ballinger no date).[15] The Nike-targeting activism listed in the figure has been collated and generalized from numerous primary and secondary sources. Chapter 7 offers a more detailed discussion of where it is important to begin the assessment of the effectiveness of broad political activism. Following this model, the timeline begins with activists attempting to create public awareness about the problem of working conditions in particularly offshore garment manufacturing and ends with more general responses by the Nike Corporation on its social responsibility policy and practices. The timeline also follows how activist groups lodged complaints with government which tried to solve the sweatshop problem, undertook efforts to collect and communicate factual information to raise public and media awareness of the sweatshop problem, and then once they had mobilized more support began to diversify their tactics in performative market-based and popular cultural ways (see also Chapter 5). The timeline highlights the crucial role played by U.S. students and universities, a development duly noted in theoretical scholarship on political responsibility (cf. Chapter 1) and analyzed as a new geography of activism (cf. Chapter 5). Noteworthy in the timeline is the escalation of more confrontational anti-sweatshop activism from the mid-1990s to the early 2000s, including boycott calls, student activism (pressure on their universities, sit-ins, and ensuing violence), Niketown demonstrations, antibranding, and rude remarks about Nike's CEO to personalize the struggle. Interviews with activist group leaders identify frustration with governmental efforts as an important explanation for this more confrontational action repertoire (Micheletti and Stolle 2007). The character of this activism contrasts greatly with developments after 9/11. From 2002 onward, cooperative forms of discursive political consumerism, primarily explained by changes in Nike's social responsibility-taking, are more observable.

CONCLUDING REMARKS

The discursive turn in political consumerism and the Nike e-mail exchange case study give a clear indication about how political activism is emerging in the current age of globalization, Internet communication, a more open and fragmented media environment, individualization, and enhanced consumer choice. This activism has multiple targets and appeals to various groups, organizations, and individuals in society in its advocacy for more environmental and social justice responsibility-taking in production and consumption. It also borrows ideas from popular culture and adopts a more performative and humorous approach to consciousness-raising and the making of public opinion. The chapter also

---

[15] Several web sites document Nike timelines:

"Nike Timeline," American Studies at the University of Virginia, http://xroads.virginia.edu/~CLASS/am483_97/projects/hincker/timeline.html (accessed December 2009), John's Swoosh Page, http://www.trizera.com/jsp/nikehist.html#tl (accessed December 2009).

underscores the importance of digital technology for the crafting and communication of political activism and indicates in the Nike timeline how particularly discursive political consumer activism has been able over the long run to affect the policies and practice of well-known transnational corporations. Moreover, it addresses the enhanced role that brands play in public and corporate life. In discursive political consumerism, brands are not only the target but also the source, medium, and political message board of activism. Thus, although antibranding and culture jamming activists criticize the commercial branding of the public sphere, they are dependent on the cultural resonance of well-known popular brands in consumer society to create awareness, mobilize supporters, and forge political communities and identities. Noteworthy is that although discursive political consumerism tends to offer harsh criticism of corporate policies and politics it too is dependent on the logic of capitalism to publicize its cause.

7

Does Political Consumerism Matter? Effectiveness and Limits of Political Consumer Action Repertoires

With Jean-François Crépault

INTRODUCTION

One of the most persistent criticisms of political consumerism has been its effectiveness as a form of participation and as a solution for problem-solving. There has been some fear that it is a type of activism that requires minimal and infrequent effort and does not lead to any major outcomes or effects. Even worse, it might imply that people do something for politics, while in effect they do not reach any goals, and get distracted from the main political issues by focusing on their shopping choices (Patel 2007, 312). In sum, the question is whether individualized responsibility-taking, in the form of political consumerism, is as equally effective as electoral or other forms of participation focusing on the parliamentary realm in bringing about political and social change. Moreover, how does its effectiveness compare to the traditional political responsibility model discussed in Chapter 1 and its top-down models of policy-making? Can political consumerism compensate for the lack of government action? Few studies have examined this issue explicitly. Indeed, little research has been undertaken to compare the effectiveness of various conventional and important emerging forms of political participation. This chapter offers a first more comprehensive analysis of political consumerism's effectiveness. One of its main findings is that measuring political consumerism's effectiveness is not a straightforward task. Whereas the question of effectiveness for conventional forms of political participation focuses primarily on the analysis of public policy change (e.g., as a result of pressure on parliaments to pass legislation) or direct political change (as after an election campaign leading to different parties taking office), the assessment for political consumerism is more complex because its actions are not solely or ultimately concerned with changes in government action. Determining its influence in bringing about change therefore must rely on expanding the general view of political effectiveness to include not only how government is influenced, but also how political consumerism affects other individuals, raises general public awareness for its cause, and how it shapes the values and behaviors of corporations – its main targets. In addition, the effectiveness investigation needs to focus on how political action addresses and solves real-life political problems. In other words, how close do political consumers and activists come to reaching their goals? What is the degree to which political consumerism solves environmental problems, issues of child labor, and the actual problems of the life and rights of farmers and workers in developing countries (one of its main goals)? Thus, insights from this first study of effectiveness also urge and challenge scholars to include considerations about the effectiveness of all forms of participation on delivering the public goods, policies, or societal innovations and solving the problems that these actions intend to address (see also Chapter 8).

The chapter is structured in three major sections. The first section presents critical views of political consumerism's effectiveness. In the second section, a more nuanced view of effectiveness is presented that develops a model and measures which capture "effectiveness as a process." We then examine these processes in the third section and present empirical evidence that allows for a first evaluation of the strengths and limits of political consumerism as an example of political engagement. Here, the focus is the effectiveness of political consumer activism (1) on other consumers, (2) on both business and government, and (3) on solving problems associated with production and consumption.[1]

DOUBTING EFFECTIVENESS

Critical observers across the political spectrum claim that political consumerism is not and cannot be an effective mechanism for globalized political responsibility-taking. This section reviews five main critiques of political consumerism's effectiveness.

Consumers Are More Self-Interested than Other-Regarding

Here, the claim is that consumers cannot be trusted with the responsibility for solving global problems. By being focused predominantly on individualism (see Chapter 1) they are not capable of other-oriented actions, or at best much less so. The argument is that consumers are mostly price-oriented (and thus not political) agents, and even if certain consumers take social and ethical values into account, political consumerism is still primarily a self-regarding personal risk-management activity involving the purchase of products that mostly benefit consumers themselves. This claim is substantiated by surveys in the United Kingdom, the United States, France, Germany, and Canada, which found that

---

[1] Because of limitation of space, we do not discuss how the political consumer organizational settings affect the media.

health and nutrition were consistently given as the top reasons for buying organic (Dimitri and Greene 2002, Hallam 2003, Halpin 2004, Kortbech-Olesen 2004, Leifert and Bourlakis 2004). Critics argue that the simple fact that consumers might also get a personal benefit from their politically oriented choices shows that this form of participation is not an "effective vehicle for advancing or expressing social goals" (Vogel 2006, 97). For them, the predominantly self-regarding nature of consumers implies that political consumerism 1) distorts the logic of politics because most consumers cannot think and act as citizens, and 2) will remain a niche market, unable to capture the commitment of a sufficient critical mass of consumers and thus powerless to establish itself as a market-based vehicle for political and social change. Of course, this criticism can also be directed against representative democracy itself, as economic self-interest has been one of the basic assumptions about voting behavior. Anthony Downs' statement in his seminal book *The Economic Theory of Democracy* that "each citizen casts his vote for the party he believes will provide him with more benefits than any other" (1957, 37) formed the foundations for theories of "pocketbook voting," which have influenced rational choice and collective action theory in the social sciences (cf. Olson 1969, Tuck 2008).

Not only are the self-interested motivations of Northern consumers questioned, but critics argue that political consumerism gives consumers an easy way out of real political responsibility-taking by buying, boycotting, and talking themselves out of guilt. They are, so to speak, let off the political hook and do not personally need to take many financial and political risks to rectify the North-South power balance in the global economy. Thus, their radius and degree of actions contrast greatly with the situation of Southern workers who must, for instance, find ways to finance and monitor their fairtrade or organically certified goods and struggle "against political and economic inequalities" (Lyon 2006, 457).

Political Consumerism Goes Against Core Market Principles

Another forceful criticism takes the opposite approach and argues that political consumerism distorts the logic of markets, thus making it unsuitable as a mechanism for changing corporations (Friedman 1963, Lindsey 2003). It is claimed that corporate social responsibility and corporate citizenship (the adding of concerns for the environment and human rights into the business bottom line) and the voluntary regulation of the market, especially through labeling schemes, contradict the basic capitalist principle and activity of profit-making. In 1970, Milton Friedman argued that "the social responsibility of business is to increase its profits." Corporate executives are to place profitability above all other considerations since any reduction in profits is equivalent to using stockholders' money in an irresponsible way. The same claim is said to apply to socially responsible investing, which Friedman called a "fundamentally subversive doctrine" in a free society (Friedman 1970).

These critics also argue that because political consumers ignore basic economic truths, they frequently harm the people they want to help. Two forms of political consumerism – boycotts and buycotts – are the focus here. For instance, buying fairtrade coffee is criticized because of its negative effects on farmers. The argument is that the minimum price ensured by selling beans to certified roasters is in essence a price floor that skews economic signals and encourages farmers to artificially increase production, thus causing excess supply in a market where overproduction is already the main cause of low world prices (*Economist* 2006, Lindsey 2003, Booth and Whetstone 2007). Thus, well-meaning fairtraders unwittingly contribute to the further impoverishment of coffee farmers because their actions lead to overproduction. Boycotting results in other economic problems. Northern consumers may, for example, boycott targeted goods or corporations to express their opposition to the use of child labor. However, their actions may just put the child workers back on the street and foster their employment in other uncontrolled sectors (Basu and Zarghamee 2005). Even political consumer groups oppose boycotting in some circumstances; many anti-sweatshop groups, including the Swedish Save the Children Foundation, have publicly asked consumers not to boycott certain corporations for just this reason.

Political Consumerism Is Neoliberalism-Friendly

Other critics claim that market-driven activism cannot fundamentally change the business practices that have developed along with neoliberalism. Political consumerism's "laissez-faire" approach to solving social and political problems generates choice-oriented soft-law approaches (labeling schemes, codes of conduct, etc.) that are too weak to combat complex globalized economic and political problems. Thus, political consumerism feeds rather than starves political deregulation of the market, which has been shown to perpetrate many production and consumption-oriented problems concerned with global human rights and common pool resource stewardship (see Chapter 1). Critics maintain that soft-law political consumer voluntary regulatory tools are strategically used as "window dressing" (greenwash, sweatwash, etc.) by businesses to improve their goodwill in order to make profits and point to evidence that they promote corporate economic development (e.g., by certifying plantation produced products, see Chapter 5) and discourage unionization, which has been an important anti-sweatshop and Fairtrade goal.[2] Corporations running their own ethical or sustainable business product lines or adopting CSR policies to

---

[2] See the e-mail conversation between Jeff Ballinger (founder of the anti-sweatshop group Press for Change) and Tim Connor (coordinator of the Oxfam Australian Community Aid Program and Nike Boycott) on the role of unionization in the goals of anti-sweatshop political consumerism that took place in 2005. On file with authors. For a discussion of the problematic relationship between labeling schemes and unions, see Boris 2003.

ensure a better sourcing of commodities are also said to do so to placate, offset, or preempt activism while avoiding true social responsibility for their production practices (Newell 2008). Critics distrustful of market-based mechanisms for responsibility-taking accuse these businesses of "minimalism," arguing that corporate ethical lines and labels have lower environmental and social standards than, and therefore, compete unfairly with, those run by more transparent and multi-stakeholder ones such as Fairtrade (FLO) International or USDA organic labeling (Fridell 2007, Jaffee 2007). Corporations have also on occasion been able to force political consumer labeling schemes to lower their certification standards (see Chapter 5).

In sum, these critics argue that political consumerism does not go far enough in revamping the role that production and consumption play in environmental and human rights harms. It accepts the unfettered geographic mobility of capital, does not forcefully contest neoliberal globalization and business-driven models of free trade (Fridell 2007, Newell 2008), and, for many critics, its approach to problem-solving also lets governments off the hook. It diverts social movements from pressuring national governments and international organizations to take political responsibility by reregulating trade in order to subordinate markets to politics and socially determined objectives (Jaffee 2007, Utting 2008). Similarly, political consumer campaigning and nudging into alternative shopping practices is said to personalize global problems and even leave "little room to ponder institutions, the nature and exercise of political power, or ways of collectively changing the distribution of power and influence in society" (Maniates 2002, 45, cf. Katz 1998, 52, John et al. 2011).

Generally, critics maintain that corporations cannot be trusted to change their production practices unless required to do so by hard law or governmental regulation. All political consumer activism does is force them into a defensive position to dodge political activism. Here, critics give as examples cases of how corporations have shifted their country of operation to rid themselves of problems, decided not to reveal where they manufacture goods abroad to avoid activist scrutiny, found loopholes in international agreements, made "window dressing" promises that they did not keep, shifted the composition of their local workforce to include a greater proportion of contract and migrant workers who do not benefit from the improved work conditions that are a part of CSR policies (Barrientos 2008), and made their operations less transparent in order to avoid lawsuits and negative monitoring evaluations. Given the logic of the market, critics claim that voluntarism doesn't and can't work. Instead of mobilizing citizens into consumers who shop, activists should be pressuring for more governmental regulation to reassert political control over markets (see Utting 2008). In this view, political consumerism may have some positive effects, but ultimately governments must play the central role. Thus, overemphasizing political consumer activism is ineffective and counterproductive and impedes the development of governmental mechanisms for corporate accountability.

Political Consumerism Is a Northern Project with a Northern Agenda

Here, the claim is that Northern consumer society is political consumerism's point of departure and that it lacks a good understanding of the lives and worlds of producers and workers in developing countries. Some critics go so far as to characterize it as a new imperial formation and "left-over colonialism" (Wedding as quoted in Constance and Bonanno 2000, 134) that tells the South how to manage its resources and thus reconfigures earlier colonial power relations and economic dependencies. Political consumer initiatives are accused of undermining local cultures and communities as much as commercially driven globalization (e.g., Dholakia and Dholakia 2001), and of operating in a top-down manner, with little or no input from Southern stakeholders (Lund-Thomsen 2008). As discussed in this book, this charge is levied against the labeling institutions for fairtrade, organic food, FSC, and MSC. Their operations, standards, and certification procedures are criticized as lacking necessary transparency and proper channels for effective Southern voices, and as too costly and bureaucratic for Southern small producers. Political consumer campaigns are even criticized for relying on traditional stereotypes of third-world people as disempowered victims in need of Northern help to sensitize consumers and mobilize them into action (cf. Brooks 2007).

Political Consumerism Has Limited Reach

Finally, certain critics applaud political consumerism's ability to target and tarnish the public image and reputation of well-known (and thus vulnerable) brands, which reply by changing their policies and practices. However, they find that it has no effect on corporations without Northern consumer brand appeal. Thus, political consumerism's ability to mobilize brand-aware consumers is also its Achilles' heel. These critics find that political consumerism is limited by its boundaries of reach (see Chapter 8 for more discussion).

In sum, political consumerism is criticized in four major ways: (1) as an unrealistic project because it cannot influence consumers, citizens, corporations, or government into true responsibility-taking and problem-solving; (2) as lacking effective governing tools, which makes it an inadequate substitute for strong regulatory government on different levels; (3) as a distortion of core market principles and, therefore, a dysfunctional and potentially harmful mechanism for change; and (4) having limited reach, meaning that it cannot really make societies more sustainable and help people in the South sufficiently. It is, therefore, ineffective on several fronts: it cannot inform, sensitize, and mobilize sufficiently to make a mark globally and has, therefore, no lasting or long-term positive impact. The remainder of this chapter evaluates these criticisms.

DETERMINING EFFECTIVENESS

How can political consumerism's effectiveness be studied? A look at how other sub-fields or disciplines examine effectiveness might be a helpful start. Political scientists study the political influence of individuals through voting, membership in organizations, and other participation channels and use survey data to establish whether citizens find different forms of participation effective. Social science more generally penetrates the framing, mobilizing, and agenda-setting skills of social movements, political parties, and interest groups to establish how successfully they "define problems, propose solutions, aggregate citizens' policy preferences, mobilize voters, make demands of elected officials, communicate information about government action to their supporters and the larger public...make relatively coherent legislative action possible" and change social values (Burstein and Linton 2002, 1–2, Rochon and Mazmanian 1992).

While the focus of participation scholars is still exclusively on the accumulated impact of pressure on legislative policy-making, the social movement literature has established the most subtle discussion of effectiveness to date. The claim is that the effects of social movements outside of the direct policy realm are often overlooked (Giugni and Passy 1998, Meyer 2006). Furthermore, since movements' goals can be broad and vaguely defined, the consequences of their actions can often be unanticipated (Giugni, McAdam, and Tilly 1999). For instance, although the U.S. feminist movement's failure to bring about the passage of the Equal Rights Amendment is often considered a movement defeat and therefore a sign of ineffectiveness, it was nevertheless successful in changing prevailing public attitudes and cultural values about women's roles in society (Meyer 2006). Thus, the ability of social movements to influence public opinion is a relevant measurement of their effectiveness. This broadened view of effectiveness is a good first step in addressing political consumerism's role as a problem-solver. Scholars of public policy also find that they need to broaden their assessments of effectiveness and now consider implementing public policy, not as a straightforward "assembly job" but rather as a negotiating, trial-and-error, and incremental process whereby involved actors may even revise their initial (policy) goals to better address the problem at hand (Barrett and Fudge 1981, 23).

The lessons from this short review of accumulated research are that there is no tested or agreed-upon model for assessing the effectiveness of participation and even public policy. Rather, effectiveness is increasingly viewed as a complex process that cannot be reduced to one simple measurement or even a clear yes or no answer. Effectiveness involves the actions and learning curves of a variety of actors in different arenas as well as the maturity and legitimacy of the issue at hand. It involves defining and creating skills as well as convincing people individually and in collective settings to take responsibility for problem-solving tasks. This means that the process of effectiveness can have its ups and downs. Each component or task in the effectiveness process should, therefore, be evaluated separately before a more comprehensive judgment of overall effectiveness can be rendered. For scholars of participation and social movements, this means in particular that political action cannot be seen as the gun that shoots a magic bullet cutting through the whole of society and all relevant institutions with a simple and straightforward impact that leads to effective resolution of societal problems and ills (cf. Keck and Sikkink 1998, 25–26, 1999, 98–99, Micheletti 2010, appendix).

Since a complete investigation of all components of political consumerism's effectiveness process is impossible here due to its magnitude, a few important questions have been chosen for closer investigation.

1. Effectiveness of political consumer activism on consumers. Do activist campaigns convince people that there is a problem that needs solving? Do people see the political, ethical, global social justice, and environmental problems associated with production and consumption? Do they get mobilized to think and act on these issues? Here, we summarize our findings from Chapters 2, 3, 4, 5, and 6.
2. Effectiveness of political consumer activism on business. Does business feel pressured by this activism? How do corporations respond to the problems that activism raises? Do they recognize the problem as part of their responsibility? Do they design and make policy that addresses political consumerism's concerns?
3. Has political consumerism reached the governmental level in terms of agenda-setting and policy making? Although an important reason for the emergence of political consumer activism has been governmental inactivity, the question is whether and how governments have recognized problems and been sensitized into taking action.
4. Effectiveness in solving problems in real-life situations. Does the implementation of corporate changes that have been formulated in response to political consumer concerns have an effect on the life quality of farmers and workers in the South as they are an important target of political consumer campaigns?

The conclusion offers a first assessment of how effective market-based consumer and corporate activism can be in solving the complex global problems associated with production and consumption.

How Effective Is Political Consumerism to Date?

In this empirical section, certain components of the effectiveness process model are applied to political consumerism. Most notably, it examines how the organizational settings have mobilized citizens, and how they and citizens have pressured corporations and even governments to respond to their concerns. Finally, it takes a look at how political consumerism has affected the lives of people in developing countries and addresses directly the criticisms and doubts about political consumerism. This analysis cannot give an overall verdict because the effectiveness process is ongoing and changing. However, it will help to set an example for the future evaluation of forms of individualized responsibility-taking and their economic, political, and social consequences.

Political Consumer Activist Effects on Consumers

Chapter 5 discusses the effort that the organizational settings of political consumerism have put into sensitizing and mobilizing Western consumers. Has it done so effectively? There is a wide variety of evidence that Northern democracies have seen a steep rise in political consumerism over the last decades. As discussed at length in Chapter 2, survey respondents indicate that their engagement in consumer boycotts has quadrupled over the last three decades, and many citizens are "buycotters" and show considerable awareness of and trust in labeling schemes. Overall, when asked whether they had deliberatively purchased products for ethical, environmental, or political reasons (that is, "buycotted"), about 24 percent of respondents of all countries included in the *European Social Survey* in 2002 said they had done so in the previous twelve months. In Scandinavia, about two-thirds of citizens buy products based on labeling schemes, or ethical, political, or environmental considerations (our own calculations from the ESS). In the United States, political consumerism is less widespread, with about 19 percent of consumers boycotting and about 23 percent buycotting as of 2005 (our own calculations). In many Southern and Eastern European countries, such forms of engagement have not taken off to the same extent, although also here about 7 percent to 12 percent of the respondents indicated to have been engaged in this activity (see more Chapter 4).

In short, survey data clearly finds that citizens feel increasingly drawn into acts of political consumerism and, therefore, express a heightened sensitivity and awareness of the political meaning of their purchasing choices. Even when going a step further to determine behavioral change independently, we find a rise in political consumer behavior. Chapter 2 reports that the sales of fairtrade food products, especially of coffee, bananas, sugar, cocoa, tea, and honey, was nearly eight times higher in 2005 compared to 1997 (Fair Trade Federation 2005) and that most certified fairtrade products and even organic products experienced a growth in sales despite the struggling economy. However, whereas behavioral change is visible and citizens appear to be more open to choosing these kinds of items over conventional ones, their actual market share is still fairly low.

There is no doubt that mainstream products dominate the markets around the world. The point though is that the phenomenon of political consumerism is spreading and that there is a substantiated interest and potential among

Northern citizens to engage in political consumer-oriented shopping. However, some doubts linger. First, are these citizens really able to think beyond their own interests? Our evidence so far shows that political consumers are, just as ordinary consumers, interested in the product quality and price, but when it comes to other-regarding values, they really stand out (see Chapter 3). However, mobilization into political consumerism frequently appears to work best when issues of ordinary consumption and even self-oriented concerns are blended with the political consumer political, ethical, and environmental messages. This also reflects the success of the recent strategies of the political consumer organizational settings, which now try to focus on the personal-health and appearance value of their products (e.g., regarding organic food and vegetarian meals) as well as on triggering emotional reactions and self-interest (Micheletti and Stolle 2010, Boström and Klintmann 2011, Herzog and Golden 2009, Benford and Valadez 1998, Micheletti 2010, 53; see more in Chapters 5 and 8).

Secondly, consumers might be fickle and, therefore, not a reliable or regular source for durable political change. Moreover, because many labeled goods are more expensive, consumers' purchasing choices might even be influenced by economic ups and downs. If this happens, political consumerism becomes a "fair weather product" rather than a stable or reliable political practice and, as a consequence, a risky venture for the South because its engagements with labeling schemes depend on a stable and preferably growing consumer demand in the North. The fear is that when consumers have less money, they must economize and perhaps begin to think more about price than politics. Furthermore, political consumerism must rely on NGOs that continuously engage in consciousness-raising and consumer mobilization campaigns and that also need donations to fund their work. The general criticism is, therefore, that political consumerism is too dependent on the Northern pocketbook. If the economy takes a dive, political consumerism is potentially doomed as an activist cause and market share. Corporations might even have fewer resources to address ethical issues of corporate responsibility in economically hard times.

The claim that citizens will flee political consumerism in economic bad times has not yet been verified empirically. Perhaps the 2008 financial crisis can offer some initial thinking on this matter. There is evidence that NGOs have suffered from the 2008 financial crisis and have been forced to reconsider their strategies in periods of declining donations.[3] Some of the most important NGOs for the political consumer organizational settings are old established civil society

---

[3] See several articles on this topic at: http://abcnews.go.com/Business/Economy/story?id=6123902 &page=2; Jamieson, Alastair (2008), "Charity donations hit by financial crisis," *The Telegraph*, November 8, http://www.telegraph.co.UK/finance/financetopics/financialcrisis/3405594/ Charity-donations-hit-by-financial-crisis.html; "Mixed Picture on Private Donations as Financial Crisis Bites" (2008), *Global Policy Forum* (November 28), http://www.globalpolicy.org/ component/content/article/176/31501.html (all accessed on December 4, 2009).

organizations, such as unions, Oxfam, and other humanitarian associations, that have survived economic slumps in the past. Others, for instance, Global Exchange, have always been low staffed and rely on the Internet, which cuts the costs of activism and mobilization. At the individual level, the situation may be different. Indeed, looking at the relationship between economic means and political consumerism we find that income and political consumerism are clearly related, and the poorest in Northern societies are not as frequently active as political consumers (Chapter 3). Still, the general trend of political consumerism has gone up over the last three decades, despite earlier economic ups and downs (see Chapter 2). Yet, it is not clear what will happen to political consumerism in a situation similar to the oil crisis in the 1970s or the 2011 financial crisis. Some reports after the 2008 crisis indicate that the steady growth of political consumer behavior might plateau a bit during financial downturns, for example, organic milk sales have slowed (*New York Times* 2009a). Research still needs to fully verify how political consumer behavior actually continues under prolonged and recurrent financial restraint and crisis.

Some political consumer actions do not depend on money and should thus be independent of economic fluctuations. Boycotting certain products and choosing an alternative product should be a financially viable course of action, despite economic downturns, if the alternative products are in a similar price range. And, of course, voluntary simplicity, a form of lifestyle political consumerism, as well as discursive political consumerism, can be practiced by people with very limited economic means. Therefore, it is not so surprising that citizens are increasingly interested in and mobilized by the issues pushed by the political consumer organizational settings and that at present, expressed attitudes and values on political consumer issues (as measured in surveys) appear to be stronger than actions. In other words, while political consumer values have taken root in Northern societies, they have not yet been fully translated into regular political consumer practices.[4] Does this prove that the critics are right? Further research is necessary to establish whether the political consumer values that have been found to take root will weather the more recent economic storms. Thus, more studies are necessary to answer questions about if and how financial crisis affects consumers' actions and whether or not they feel a sense of frustration about the need to make a trade-off between economic necessity and the purchase of labeled goods.

Political Consumer Activist Effects on Corporations

To further investigate political consumerism's effectiveness and its criticisms, we need to elucidate how corporations respond to complaints and campaigns. How aware are corporations of the ethical, political, and environmental

---

[4] Research on racism and sexism suggests that societal change begins at the attitudinal level (Light, Vincent, and Kalev 2011, Steffens 2005).

demands placed on them, and how do they integrate these claims into their corporate practices?

Several corporations have responded to political consumer campaigns, and in many cases their ways of dealing with activism have evolved over the years. Chapter 6 discusses the case of Nike, arguably the most important corporate focus of anti-sweatshop activism in the 2000s. Nike's reactions have been an important focus for modeling how corporations develop responses to activist demand.[5]

The question, of course, is whether political consumer activism is an important force behind the corporate changes in new ethical or environmental directions. When asked, corporate executives often first answer that activism played only a minor role in their decision to change corporate practices but then admit that it played a variety of roles in bringing the issues into corporate settings (Nike interview 2004). Sometimes, corporate leaders acknowledge that they have listened to and learned about the politics of their products from consumers, political consumer activists, and the media. The *Australian Financial Review* (June 14 2002) as quoted in DeWinter-Schmitt 2007 (footnote 481, p. 332) cites Nike's former vice-president of corporate responsibility Maria Eitel as stating: "I don't think Nike would have made the kind of progress that it has made if we hadn't been attacked.... There are not a lot of companies making progress on social issues that haven't been forced to. The probability of a company voluntarily taking on a social issue if they haven't been forced to by activists or legislation is very low." Similarly, in 2007, Dominique Reiniche, the president and chief operating officer of the EU Group Coca-Cola, acknowledged that consumer awareness prompted his company in the area of CSR: "We believe consumers do care that we use as little water as possible... that we treat wastewater whenever we discharge into natural bodies of water" and declared the need to involve NGOs and government in

---

[5] On the basis of the Nike development, Simon Zadek (2004) formulated a model that identifies five stages in the process of corporate citizenship responsibility-taking; similar stages are identified in other research (e.g., Mirvis and Googin 2006). The first stage is "denial" of responsibility and involves using corporate "activism management" communication skills to avoid responsibility-taking (see citation of Nike officials on pages 16 and 17 in chapter 1). Corporations enter a second stage, identified as initial compliance, if activism and public targeting persists. Activists targeting the corporation often view this form of compliance as "window dressing" and "white washing." If activism persists, business leaders realize that problems cannot be "swatted away with attempts at compliance or a public relations strategy" (Zadek 2004, 2) and, therefore, involve core corporate divisions (managers of production, etc.) to play an operative role in responsibility-taking (third stage). Resource investments of this kind trigger new thinking and can evolve into the fourth stage that involves the realization that deepened commitment is good business strategy and can generate corporate goodwill and long-term financial success. Corporate leaders begin to "champion" the CSR-cause (Mirvis and Googins 2006, 108) by increasingly committing themselves to solving problems. If they enter the final and fifth stage, they may even promote visionary unconventional business commitments – public education, industry-wide collective action, new institutional mechanisms (e.g., partnering with nongovernmental organizations, voluntary or third-party controlled labeling schemes, monitoring institutions, their own ethical lines), and even governmental legislation.

their efforts.[6] The same reaction pattern is evident in the fast-food restaurant industry. McDonald's vice-president of corporate relations Karen van Bergen openly revealed her company's reactions to the aggressive 2006 Greenpeace campaign "McAmazon" that charged the hamburger chain with "eating up the Amazon" by purchasing chickens fed on soya from deforested lands. She admitted that Greenpeace "had so much information and brought concrete facts, so there was only one way to address it" (Goldberg and Yagan 2007, 8). Although these quotes may be exceptionally open statements, they demonstrate, nevertheless, corporate acknowledgement of activist pressures (see also Figure 6.1 in Chapter 6 of this book).

While it is extremely difficult to causally link particular political consumer events and corporate actions, the following sections focus in multiple ways on the evidence of how these activists shape corporations to act ethically and environmentally. First, a brief overview of the development of corporate social responsibility is provided. Second, the effects of boycott actions on corporations are examined. Third, we establish through examples that there has indeed been a rise in worldwide ethical business. Finally, it is explored that large retailers have developed ethical lines while also highlighting the weaknesses of this process. Overall, this section probes into the questions of how the political consumer organizational settings and individual consumers have succeeded in pushing corporations into better ethical business practice in order to draw conclusions about its effectiveness.

1) Is There a Rise in CSR?

Since the 1990s, a rising number of transnational corporations have taken the idea of CSR into consideration. More corporations acknowledge that they cannot "shirk social responsibility" and that CSR must inform every aspect of their business (Barner 2007, 59–60). A Nike vice-president told shareholders at a 1998 meeting that CSR is a consideration throughout "every part of the company" and not "a separate function that can be put into a box" (DeWinter-Schmitt 2007, 376). Some large global brand corporations that have been the primary target in political consumer campaigns even state that they have the "ability and responsibility" to lead their industry in CSR (Nikebiz 2007) and that global problems are their problems (Wal-Mart CEO H. Scott Lee, cited in Barbaro and Barringer 2005). Michael Kobori, Levi Straus & Company's vice-president of social and environmental sustainability, said, "If we are going to ask ourselves anything, it should be: What's the business case for *not* doing CSR?" thus seemingly indicating that the time for debate is over (Langert 2008).

---

[6] Dominique Reiniche, president and COO, European Union Group, Coca-Cola, "Corporate Citizens Serving Individual Consumers" remarks at InnoBev, Madrid, Spain, July 3, 2007, http://www.wbcsd.ch/Plugins/DocSearch/details.asp?DocTypeId=35&ObjectId=MjMzNDI& URLBack=%2Ftemplates%2FTemplateWBCSD2%2Flayout.asp%3Ftype%3Dp%26MenuId %3DMzc4%26doOpen%3D1%26ClickMenu%3DRightMenu%26CurPage%3D11%26Sort Order%3DPubDate%2520DESC (accessed December 19. 2012).

This trend is reflected in the increasing inclusion of CSR themes into corporate codes of conduct. (See Smith, Bhattacherya, Vogel, and Levine 2010, Vogel 2005, Hassel 2008 for an overview of the emergence of corporate codes of conduct.) A study of changes in the codes of conduct of the largest Canadian corporations between 1992 and 2003, for instance, found that the number of corporations that included environmental issues in their codes rose from 9 percent to 25 percent (Singh 2006). Although quantitative, longitudinal work on changes in the content of codes of conduct is rare (see Kaptein 2004; for an exception, see Singh, Svensson, Wood, and llaghan 2011), research findings of relevance here offer a glimpse of the content of these codes. A 2004 survey of the world's 200 largest companies found that 52.5 percent had a "business code" – a code of ethics or a code of conduct. Of the 105 firms that did have one, most were focused on traditional business concerns such as respecting local legislation and ensuring the quality of their goods or services. However, several issues of more globalized corporate social responsibility were also included in these codes. The five most common ones were: 1) Preventing/preserving/restoring the natural environment (56 percent of the 105 companies with codes; 2) Being a good corporate citizen through charitable donations, educational and cultural contributions, etc. (36 percent); 3) Enhancing quality of life/contributing to sustainable development/improvement (18 percent); 4) Respecting human rights and promoting them wherever practicable (11 percent); 5) Supporting public policies and practices that promote human development and democracy (8 percent) (Kaptein 2004, 19–20). Thus, whereas environmental issues have been adopted by the majority of companies with codes, other ethical issues – particularly those pertaining to human rights and social justice – had not yet made it to the codes or programs of many companies. Chapters 5 and 8 discuss why environmental standards are easier to implement than other forms of standards. Finally, although levels are rising every year, by 2010, just a small fraction of the world's businesses had signed on to the UN Global Compact, the world's largest CSR initiative that is also sanctioned by international governmental organizations.[7]

The significance of the increase in signing up for CSR policies is highly debated, and critics of political consumerism dismiss it as window-dressing. However, the rising use of CSR themes in business codes suggests that there is recognition by a growing number of corporations about the need to deal with consumer and activist pressure on them to act ethically and environmentally and that their reputations are at stake. New research shows that there is a link between the quality of codes of conduct and ethical performance; companies maintaining high-quality codes are significantly more represented among CSR ranking systems for corporate citizenship, sustainability, ethical behavior, and public perception (Erwin 2011, 535). Yet other studies report mixed results on

---

[7] See more at United Nations Global Compact (2010), *Annual Review 2010*, http://www .unglobalcompact.org/docs/news_events/8.1/UN_Global_Compact_Annual_Review_2010.pdf.

the relation between CSR codes of conduct and corporate practices (see Mamic 2005, Kaptein and Schwartz 2008). In sum, corporations are increasingly taking notice of the ethical and environmental demands that are put on them by actors in political settings.

2) *Rise in Corporate Partnerships with NGOs*

Corporate interaction or partnering with NGOs to find common solutions to environmental or human resource problems has risen over time (Dahan, Doh, and Oetzel 2010, Linton 2005). For example, for decades now, McDonald's has cooperated with the NGO Conservation International to raise consciousness about global environmental problems. Over the years, this partnership has focused more on McDonald's global supply chain and how it can be made sustainable in economically achievable ways, including the development of an environmental scorecard in 2004.[8] McDonald's also maintains a partnership with Greenpeace and other business and nonprofit organization leaders in Brazil to establish a moratorium on soybean sourcing to help protect precious areas of the Amazon Rainforest (Goldberg and Yagan 2007, 6). Similarly, Coca-Cola has developed partnerships with WWF, the World Resources Institute, and the Nature Conservancy and has entered roundtable discussions with different national NGOs on water replenishment and stewardship as well as recycling projects some of which are conducted primarily in the United States (Coca-Cola Enterprise 2009, 2009/2010). Furthermore, Unilever, as the manufacturer of Lipton Tea – the world's largest tea company, buying about 12 percent of the world's entire black tea crop – is "working with the Rainforest Alliance to have all of [its] tea certified from sustainable sources by 2015. Such actions are expected to transform the global tea industry," according to president Kevin Havelock (Reuters 2008).[9] Similar developments are evident in other consumer-oriented industries.

In most cases, corporations that seek partnerships with NGOs have been the target of political consumer activism. Marianne Barner, Ikea's director of corporate communications and ombudsman for children's issues, said frankly that Ikea was caught "completely unaware" about the use of child labor in the production commodity chain in the early 1990s: "It was not something we had been paying attention to." Ikea's "buyers met suppliers in their city offices and rarely got out to where production took place.... Our immediate response to the [documentary on Swedish television] was to apologize for our ignorance and acknowledge that we were not in full control of this problem" (Bartlett,

---

[8] This scorecard indicates key product suppliers of potatoes, poultry, pork, beans, and buns to measure water use, energy consumption, solid waste production, air emissions of suppliers, and a sustainable fisheries program.

[9] "Unilever Participates in Industry Forum at the Grocery Manufacturers Association's First Environmental Sustainability" (January 18, 2008), press release on *Reuters*, http://www.reuters.com/article/pressRelease/idUS225168+18-Jan-2008+MW20080118 (accessed August 9, 2012).

Dessain, and Sjöman 2006, 2). As will be discussed in this chapter, Ikea did more than apologize. Activism and media reporting also enter the corporate boardroom more indirectly. Paul Pressler, Gap Inc.'s CEO and president began his letter in the corporation's 2003 social responsibility report by disclosing that "one of the first things my teenage daughter asked was, 'Doesn't Gap use sweatshops?'" (Gap, Inc. 2003; for similar developments on social and family pressure in the Swedish cement industry, see Gillberg 1999). In 2007, Gap worked with the anti-sweatshop charity Global March Against Child Labour to create a certification scheme that would allow it to label its products "sweatshop-free" (*Guardian* 2007b).

These examples and numerous others demonstrate that corporate leaders are aware of political consumer criticism and, in certain cases, actively seek out some political consumer activists to help solve corporate problems. However, critics maintain that many activists are rejected, and that receiving some of them should be interpreted as tactical and clever corporate moves to white-wash their production practices and engage in "activism management." As discussed in Chapter 5, the political consumer organizational settings are also divided on the benefits of collaboration with corporations. Does it help their cause or does it allow big business to co-opt them while corporate practices remain essentially the same (CNN 2008, Fridell 2007)? Regardless of inter-pretation and perspective, these developments show how corporations – for whatever reason – increasingly involve a wider span of stakeholders in their policy discussions and seek partnerships with consumer-oriented NGOs, most of whom are active in the political consumer organizational settings, as a way to help solve globalized problems. Increasingly, therefore, "sandals" and "suits" acknowledge that the complex problems associated with production and pri-vate consumption require the joint efforts of corporations and civil society activists.

3) The Effects of Consumer Boycotts

Boycotting is probably the oldest form of political consumerism. It has been called a weapon and is considered to be a contentious and conflictual way of getting the message across to business and others. The question, however, remains: do boycotts actually *change* corporations' policies and practices?

Occasionally, targeted firms may themselves admit the economic effects of a boycott. Executives of Barclays Bank, targeted by advocates of socially respon-sible investing in the 1980s for their presence in apartheid South Africa, stated in a leaked memo that their market share among students had dropped signif-icantly as a result of the boycott campaign (Smith 1990). Shortly thereafter, Barclays left South Africa. This type of admission is rare, thus rendering the study of boycott effects a much more complex task. Following Smith (1990), it is possible to distinguish between *success* (realization of boycott objectives) and *effectiveness* (achievement of a significant economic impact on the tar-get). High turnout and participation rates for selected boycotts is certainly one type of measurement of success (Friedman 1999); although rarely have studies measured it in specific boycott campaigns. Another problem is that boycotters' objectives are not always stated or clear; a boycott of a particular corporation may involve several different and conflicting complaints; boycotts may have short-term and/or long-term effects; boycotts may be executed according to plan, but still their ultimate goals may have not been met. Boycotts may also be long-term affairs, as illustrated in the decades-long Nestlé boycott, or even recurring McDonald's boycotts. They may also affect the targeted corporations but not necessarily for the reason of the boycott call.

Thus, not only must a number of factors be considered when analyzing boycott success and/or effectiveness, at the same time a boycott may be "successful" without being "effective," or vice-versa. Boycotts may have economic effects in the form of an impact on sales or shareholder values, or symbolic effects by putting a corporation in the negative spotlight by damaging its reputation and goodwill and subjecting it to media scrutiny. And to complicate things further, the simple threat of a boycott may be enough to halt objectionable corporate behavior.

Despite these caveats, there have been attempts to study the direct economic effects of boycott actions. This approach resembles a narrow view on political consumerism's effectiveness, but critics and others often see such effects as hard evidence. From such a perspective, we would expect boycotters to target central values of corporations by, for instance, trying to damage their stocks or shareholder values and reduce the sales of their products during the boycott period. The research around this question is, however, fraught with methodological problems. It is very difficult to ascertain whether boycotts and activism are actually behind the changes of stock and shareholder value or product sales (O'Rourke 2005). Numerous other factors, such as the competition in this particular industrial sector, international stock values, economic developments, and consumer spending, can be behind dynamic changes of a corporation's fortune. Thus, it is no surprise that research on boycotts reveals some contradictory findings. On the one hand, it notices significant negative stock market responses to public disclosures of poor labor and environmental practices (cited in O'Rourke 2005; see also Rock 2001). Studying more directly the effects of boycotts, Pruitt and Friedman (1986) examined twenty-one boycotts that occurred in the United States between 1971 and 1981 and found that consumer boycott announcements were followed by statistically significant decreases in stock prices for the target firms. Another study of sixty-seven U.S. boycotts between 1969 and 1991 reaches similar conclusions, arguing that "one way boycotts work is by damaging stockholder wealth" (Davidson, El-Jelly, and Worrell 1995, 190). On the other hand, Koku, Akhigbe, and Springer (1997), who studied 502 boycotts called in the United States between 1980 and 1993, showed that the value of target firms actually increased (by an average of 0.76 percent) after the announcement of a boycott, and 0.55 percent once it began. Furthermore, no statistically significant difference was found between the market's reaction to an *actual* boycott and the *threat* of a boycott. The authors explain this counterintuitive finding by suggesting that when confronted by a boycott threat, "firms work hard to nullify the impact of actual boycotts or threats of boycott" – not by complying with boycotters' demands directly but by engaging in public relations counteroffensives (Koku, Akhigbe, and Springer. 1997, 20) and in managing activism (Deegan 2001).

However, conventional studies of boycott effectiveness miss an important point: boycotts put activist and consumer criticism on the corporate work agenda, which is why Clouder and Harrison (2005, 92–93) measure what they call a boycott's success as a change in target firms' policies or practices. For example, some corporations, like Ikea (see earlier in this chapter) and H&M, took a new approach to find ways to solve problems with child labor in rug weaving and sweatshop abuses in garment manufacturing (Bartlett, Dessain, and Sjöman 2006). Friedman (1999) adds that the late-1980s tuna boycotts (see Chapter 5), which led Heinz to comply with activists' demands, caused a domino or snowball effect that saw its competitors commit to dolphin-safe practices, after which the boycott was lifted. In other cases, a legacy of boycotting has been an important incentive for opening up to the idea of certifying products through a labeling scheme, as in Unilever's decision to work together with WWF to create MSC (see Chapter 5). These changes in corporate practices and policies may be due to image and branding considerations rather than immediate, direct economic impact of the boycott. Indeed, a boycott's ability to damage corporate reputations through negative media attention has been found to be a greater predictor of boycott effectiveness than financial losses, which signifies the importance of brand reputation as a core resource for corporations (Brayden King 2008; see Chapter 6).

These studies are concerned with boycotts aimed at companies. Studies dealing with boycotts targeting products from specific countries are also difficult to evaluate. While Chavis and Leslie (2007) find that the 2003 U.S. boycott of French wine led to a severe drop in sales for that product; Teoh, Welch, and Wazzan's (1999) analysis of the South African apartheid boycott concludes that there were no significant effects on at least U.S. firms operating in South Africa or on the Johannesburg Stock Exchange.

Some boycott effects are even unintended; thus measuring their influence becomes even more difficult. For example, while boycott organizers have targeted particularly important corporate products, they sometimes find that they cannot force the corporation to make concessions regarding the particular product but rather other products in its line. An example is a 1991 Swedish boycott of the market-leading washing detergent "Via," (also called Omo, Skip, or Persil in other countries), which represented 10 percent of corporate Swedish profits (also called Omo, Skip, or Persil in other countries). Once the green activists failed to convince Swedish Unilever to make its detergent less polluting to waterways, they publicized their boycott call. Although the corporation was ill-prepared for the magnitude of the boycott, it refused to make Via more environmentally friendly. However, it did later introduce the first multinational eco-labeled detergent on the Swedish market. Thus, tracking corporate reactions to particular product boycotts might not register all the effects of political consumer activism on targeted and other corporations (Eiderström 1998).

Boycotters can have diverse objectives, ranging from expressing dissatisfaction with corporate practices to forcing a change in those practices, which makes the assessment of boycott effects difficult. The above brief summary of the literature shows that some boycotts do not have a negative economic effect on their targets, and not all boycotts succeed in changing corporate practices. Moreover, not all are able to successfully communicate their messages to consumers. One problem encountered in this review is that boycott studies, as well as most studies of social movement and interest group impact, often focus only on successful and effective cases. There is, thus, a lack of scholarship to develop a more nuanced analysis of the factors and mechanisms that explain boycott effectiveness and noneffectiveness.

4) *Rise of Ethical Business*

The rise in political consumerism has not only revealed the politics of products to the general public and as corporate leaders. It has also led to an increased use of labeling schemes as well as functioned as an incubator for what is now called "ethical businesses." Reports reveal that the people who decide to establish a company whose business model involves ethical and environmental problem-solving are frequently dedicated to sustainable production and consumption (Watson 2010, Reinhardt, Casadesus-Masanell, and Freier 2004). In some cases, their business point of departure is engagements with political consumerism. Concerned shoppers send signals to the market about a consumer demand for ethical products that are picked up by businesspeople who decide to engage in more sustainable or ethical business. Their market successes lead others to follow suit. Thus, scholars speak of waves of ethical capitalism (see Mirvis 1994, Kennedy 2006). Today, ethical capitalists are found in most areas of political consumerism.

While there is no exact account of the actual rise in ethical businesses, there are important and trend-setting examples. Well-known pioneering ethical businesses include The Body Shop (established in 1976), Patagonia (1972), Ecover (1980), and Whole Foods Market (1980). Their business model is to provide consumers with more environmentally friendly sourced cosmetics, clothing, household detergents and cleansers, and food, respectively. Over the years and after activist criticism about the depth of their commitment to the value-driven business model (cf. Kennedy 2006), many ethical businesses have added concerns about animal testing, garment-workers' rights, and farm animal treatment to their list of business concerns. In the 1990s and 2000s, ethical capitalism mushroomed into a market segment of its own and now has its own distribution and marketing information chains, as exemplified by Ethicalsuperstore.com Ltd. (founded in 2003) and the numerous sustainable lifestyle magazines now on the market in North America and Europe and starting up in the wealthier developing countries.

Among the newer ethical businesses in the garment trade that have received considerable attention is Blackspot shoes. This company started as a political project by the Adbusters Media Foundation in order to provide consumers with the option to buy "earth-friendly, anti-sweatshop, and cruelty-free" shoes. The shoes are available through about 100 retailers worldwide (Adbusters 2011). Some garment companies are committed to ensuring that their products are sourced from manufacturers who comply with the core International Labor Organization conventions. They include American Apparel (founded in 1997), the largest clothing manufacturer in the United States, which has been scrutinized critically by trade unions and women's groups,[10] No Sweat Apparel, founded in 2000, Ethical Threads, a fairtrade company from the early 2000s, and trendy apparel company Nudie Jeans (founded in 2001). All emphasize sustainability and ethics as core business concerns. Nudie Jeans is used by the Swedish government to market domestic manufactured "eco-chicness" (Swedish Institute 2011). The 1990s and 2000s also witnessed a mushrooming of organic, Fairtrade, and slow food restaurants, cafés, and catering services.

In sum, without being able to quantify a rise, several examples of established ethical businesses are visible in the Northern world. Ethical capitalism is also promoted by such newspapers as *Guardian*, which has a directory of ethical fashions and other goods. However, some of these companies also face challenges. For example, while Cafédirect helped mainstream fairtrade coffee in the United Kingdom, the company is currently in the midst of a slowdown. Reasons for this development include challenges from other competitors in the fairtrade market and its adoption of conventional business marketing practices that some observers believe threatens the authenticity of the fairtrade concept (Davies, Doherty, and Know 2010).

5) The Adoption of Ethical Lines by Major Retailers

Not only are ethical businesses on the rise, but mainstream retailers have also started to adopt either third-party certified organic or their own ethical lines. Indeed, transnational corporations are becoming major players in political consumer markets. Certainly, these can be seen as efforts to take green/ethical commerce beyond niche market status and into the mainstream. The development of fair trade (not necessarily FLO-certified) and organic lines in major retailers are good examples of this trend.

---

[10] See for example: Jim Straub (2006), "Who's Your Daddy? Dov Charney serves up paternalism with a creepy smile at American Apparel HQ," *Clamor Magazine*, http://clamormagazine.org/issues/38/aa/straub.php (accessed August 9, 2012).

For example, for several years now, Tesco, the world's fourth-largest retailer with 13 million weekly customers, has marketed more than 1,200 organic and 130 fair trade products (though not necessarily all FLO-certified lines), a good portion of which are part of its own ethical line (Tesco 2008, Nichols and Opal 2005, 183–185). One recent collaboration has been with ethical fashion label Etethica to create a line of recycled clothing in a certified "green" factory in Sri Lanka and sold under the eco-fashion label From Somewhere (*Guardian* 2010).[11] Tesco has also launched a completely new initiative to become a zero-carbon business by 2050, without purchasing offsets, a goal toward which it has made progress: in 2011, it reduced emissions from its baseline portfolio of buildings by 7.7 percent (*Guardian* 2011a, Tesco 2011). Another large British supermarket chain, Sainsbury's, which received the Best Organic Supermarket of the Year award several years in a row from the British Soil Association (see Chapter 5) and the Ethical Award from *Observer Magazine* in 2007, moved all its bananas, Red Label tea, and own-brand sugar in 2008 to fairtrade and committed to switch the remainder of its tea range plus all roast and ground coffee and hot chocolate to fairtrade.[12] Similar developments are found in the United States. Wal-Mart, a highly criticized corporation within the political consumer organizational setting, began expanding its assortment of organic food in 2006 and now even markets its own line of organic and fairtrade goods, including coffee and cotton items. In 2008, it received the Best Green Companies award from Working Mother Media, a private company owned by a media conglomerate. According to a 2010 issue of the U.S. magazine *Private Label*, several companies have joined the "green bandwagon" since 2007 (Berlinski 2010; see also Chapter 5).

In more recent years, the main players in the global coffee industry have also stepped up efforts to enter the market for "sustainable" or "ethical" coffee. As sales of FLO-certified Fairtrade coffee rose in the late 1990s and early 2000s, several large European and American corporations began to offer their own fairtrade-certified coffee as well. The four largest global buyers of coffee, Altria, Nestlé, Procter & Gamble, and Sara Lee (together known as the "Big Four" – they buy about half of the world's coffee beans) all have sustainable coffee lines now (*Fortune* 2002, *Guardian* 2004, Kolk 2005). Nestlé and Procter & Gamble also sell FLO-certified coffee. In this they are joined by Starbucks, which has been one of the top sellers of fairtrade coffee in the United States (Fridell 2007). In January 2011, Sara Lee announced that by 2015, more than 20 percent of its coffee purchases would be certified sustainable using mostly Utz Kapeh and Whole Planet (Sara Lee 2011). Kraft Foods has announced that by 2015, all of its European brands will be sustainably sourced, mostly by the Rainforest

---

[11] See also at Tesco, http://www.tesco.com/greenerliving/greener_tesco/what_tesco_is_doing/tesco_eco_fashion.page (accessed December 11, 2010).

[12] See evidence at Sainsbury's: http://www2.sainsburys.co.UK/food/Fairtrade/100percentFair tradeproducts/more-Fairtrade-products.htm (accessed December 12, 2010).

Alliance (Kraft Foods News Release 2011). Starbucks claims that in 2010, 84 percent of its coffee was ethically sourced using three certification schemes: its own certification label, C.A.F.E practices (launched in 2004), fairtrade or another external audit system (Schmelzer 2010). The number for Starbucks includes TransFair certified coffee sales (around 2 percent of all sales) (Fridell 2009, Jaffee 2010).

This development means that several "sustainable" or "ethical" coffees certified by the Rainforest Alliance or Utz Kapeh are increasingly offered along with fairtrade coffees. All of these labels differ in their standards and certification processes. Indeed, critics point to attempts by large corporations to lower fairtrade certification standards to accommodate their interests more (cf. Davies and Ryals 2010, 328, Wilkinson 2007, cf. Davies, Doherty, and Know 2010, 132, Jaffee 2010, 273). According to political consumer activist networks, these new self-initiated ethical retailer lines share some characteristics in common – their standards are vague, that is, less stringent and transparent than those of FLO, and producers neither benefit from a floor price nor receive a social premium (Fridell 2007, Jaffee 2007, Renard 2005, Jaffe and Howard 2010). For example, Starbucks's C.A.F.E system has been criticized for obscuring the distinction between its own line of certification and that of fairtrade (Macdonald 2007, Raynolds, Murray, and Heller 2007, Cohn and O`Rourke 2011) and Sara Lee's certifier, Utz Kapeh, is said to use unclear statements like "good agricultural practice" (Giovannucci and Ponte 2005, 287). Two additional problems arising from these self-imposed certification labels are the lack of independent monitoring and oversight on the stringency of standards and the inability of producers to exercise influence over these standards (Schmelzer 2010). Thus, retailers' own ethical lines might lead to a dilution of standards and, thus, make consumer choice editing more confusing and even less viable as part of the solution for globalized problems. Competition in forestry certification seems, however, to benefit FSC, (Johansson 2013).

Activists are concerned about other retailers in the food sector as well. Trader Joe's, for example, is widely viewed as a green company but has faced criticism about its organic line because the Cornucopia Institute, a sustainable-agriculture watchdog group, found that an increasing number of organic dairy products come from factory farms with dubious ethical practices (Utne 2010). The problem extends well beyond the food industry. A CBC report, based on an advisory organization that monitors greenwashing (Terra Choice Environmental Marketing 2010)[13] revealed that 95 percent of consumer products

---

[13] The reported study is based on the analysis in Terra Choice Environmental Marketing (2010) Their methodology is based on their "7 sins of greenwashing" (sin of the hidden trade-off, sin of no proof, sin of vagueness, sin of irrelevance, sin of lesser of two evils, sin of fibbing [environmental claims that are simply false], sin of worshipping false labels [fake labels]). They examined "5,296 unique home and family consumer products" and the sample was made up of: "2,583 products found in Canada, 1,960 products found in the US, 753 products found in both countries" (10). They found that "over 85% of 'greener' producers commit one or

making green claims were guilty of some form of greenwashing, either by making claims that were vague, irrelevant, unproven, or just patently false, (*Canadian Broadcasting Corporation* 2011; see also Schwarcz 2007). It was estimated that although the availability of green products has increased over the last three years, false labeling and other types of greenwashing, particularly the lack of proof as well as vagueness, have also increased over time (Terra Choice Environmental Marketing 2010).

Activists fear that greenwashing will delegitimize all types of labels. They argue that consumers unaware of the difference between labels may have a diminished willingness to pay for more expensive fairtrade coffee, which they maintain tackles the problems better. It is also believed that corporations tend to prefer the schemes that place the least demands on them (Renard 2005, Bennett and Lagos 2007; see also Chapter 5 for some examples), and thus their adoption does not really solve the complex problems associated with production and consumption. In addition, observers worry that consumers will be confused by this proliferation of labels, as the differences and relative merits of their claims may not be readily apparent from the label or product itself (Levi and Linton 2003, 426, Renard 2005, 428, Giovannucci 2003, 7). Faced with many choices, consumers seeking to choose between sustainable coffees may simply opt for the least expensive one, effectively treating the labels as equivalents or substitutes. Fairtrade coffee, as a rule, is more expensive than its competitors due to its provision of the price floor and social premium to producers, but "if consumers think that the schemes are all the same, then fairtrade producers will lose out as consumers interested in sustainability might pick the cheapest certified product" (Consumers International and International Institute for Environment and Development 2005, 44).

In sum, many political consumer activists view corporate adoption of ethical lines critically. Fairtrade's more ideological segment, represented by third-world solidarity groups such as Cooperation Sud in France and worldshops, argue that labeling cannot reform free trade and so cannot go far enough in solving complex problems (see Bezençon and Blili 2009, Wilkinson 2007, Jaffee 2010). They fear that the multiplicity of sustainable labels might not only lead to a dilution of standards and thus lessen the potential effectiveness of the market as an arena for politics, but also to confusion on the side of consumers. Yet, its spread shows that business feels the pressure of political consumerism to adapt to it. Whether the ethical lines remain a niche market or develop further cannot yet be determined. The important question is why retailers decide to adopt ethical lines rather than go for full-fledged certification

more of the seven Sins of Greenwashing" (see chart on p. 16 to see which sins were more common). Interestingly, they found that "The use of fake labels . . . is increasing. More than 32% of 'greener' products found in this study carried such a fake label, compared to 26.8% in 2009" (20). See more at http://sinsofgreenwashing.org/findings/greenwashing-report-2010/. This TerraChoice methodology was used in Dahl (2010).

by the political consumer labeling schemes, and which role, if any, political consumer organizational settings have played in this process. To answer some of these questions, we look at the examples of Procter & Gamble and the European hardware chain Clas Ohlson in greater depth (see following sections).

THE CASE OF PROCTER & GAMBLE

In September 2003, Procter & Gamble announced that it would begin selling fairtrade coffee through its premium Millstone line. This decision was the result of a two-year campaign by a wide variety of market-oriented civic groups that used different strategies to pressure the corporation. This was not the first time the corporation was boycotted and bombarded with activist demands; in the mid-1990s, it was the target of animal welfare and rights activism (see Chapter 5). Pressure on Procter & Gamble came both from within, through shareholders, and from the outside, with a coalition of NGOs carrying out a campaign of public education and letter-writing (see Global Exchange 2008, Oxfam 2008). Although some activists were disappointed that the company declined to sell fairtrade coffee through its more popular Folgers brand and refused to commit to buying a minimum of 5 percent of its coffee via fairtrade contracts, the announcement was nonetheless hailed as a victory by at least some important elements of the fairtrade organizational setting (Equal Exchange 2008). Procter & Gamble became the first of the Big Four roasters to offer fairtrade coffee on a large scale. An Oxfam spokesperson called it a "tipping point" (*USA Today* 2003). By the end of 2005, the other members of the Big Four had also begun to offer fairtrade coffee (Jaffee 2007).

This case is instructive for the variety of actors and strategies involved. Development-focused NGOs, a coalition of religious groups (which consists of several Protestant, Catholic, and Jewish organizations), and socially responsible investment firms cooperated in this effort, showing how divergent political consumer activist networks can act as a united force. Moreover, these groups combined traditional strategies such as public education with the more creative tactic of shareholder activism. Although more research is needed to understand the extent to which each strategy influenced the outcome, it seems likely that forcing Procter & Gamble to address a formal shareholder resolution on fairtrade had a significant impact. Experience with being targeted by political consumer activism in the past may also have made the corporation sensitive to the cause-related problems and ready to take a more proactive stance. Such "anticipated reactions" or decisions to modify actions in order to avoid conflicts and problems form an important part of the social science literature on how power is exercised in politics. They show how both individuals and collectivities let prior experience with conflicts (the legacy of conflict) affect their decisions (Stone 1980), in this case, policies and practices to appease the demands of activists.

THE CASE OF CLAS OHLSON

Clas Ohlson is a large retail outlet chain with more than 100 stores in Sweden, Norway, Finland, and the United Kingdom, and is listed on the Swedish stock exchange. Its products for households, technology, and hobbies have been sourced from more than 800 suppliers in at least 30 countries, and more than half of its commodities come from Asia. Today, Clas Ohlson states that "due to demands from customers, employees and other stakeholders, but also to the business opportunities [that social and environmental responsibilities create] sustainable development and CSR (Corporate Social Responsibility) work is fundamental" to its operations.[14] But this was not always the case. In 2005, its sourcing practices were harshly criticized by the Swedish NGO Swedwatch (founded by several important civic associations and funded by the governmental Swedish Development Aid Agency). This criticism led the company to formulate a code of conduct and carry out code monitoring inspections at its Chinese factories. Its positive efforts were rewarded; Banco Fonder AB (now part of Swedbank Robur), an important Swedish SRI actor, classified it as an ethical company. But in 2007, the NGO accused the company of code violations, including the use of environmentally harmful material in product manufacturing, long working hours in the Chinese factories it used, prohibition against unionization, and the lack of factory inspections to monitor code implementation and information to workers on their rights. Certain SRI actors decided to put Clas Ohlson on their negative screening list (a kind of boycott). An interview with the company's chief information officer John Womack conducted for this book,[15] reveals how companies can struggle with corporate social responsibility: "Our industry was a slow starter and some factory owners lack experience with these types of inspection," he said, admitting that his industry has not come as far as the global garment industry. "[Ethical sourcing] is a complex challenge given that we have over 800 suppliers," he stated. "CSR offers us business opportunities and is a way to distinguish us from our competitors." His company's efforts, however, cannot "automatically lead to higher workers' wages. Clas Ohlson is too small of an actor to exercise this kind of influence." Instead, they try to work with their suppliers "on practical issues that we can influence – questions of overtime work, safety clothes, etc."

This case illustrates that larger retailers are pushed by activists to monitor their standards and supplier politics. It makes clear that political consumer pressure can influence the corporate agenda even of companies with a very large number of suppliers. Once ethical goals are formulated and made public,

---

[14] See "Sustainable Development," Clas Ohlson, http://about.clasohlson.com/Company/ Sustainable-development (accessed August 30, 2011).

[15] This interview was conducted in Swedish for this book on October 9, 2008, by Henric Barkman, now a Ph.D. candidate in political science at Stockholm University. All quotations have been translated from Swedish.

the company is further watched and pressured into more encompassing actions and policies. While the interview shows that a single company is not able to solve the industry-wide issues of workers' salaries, it also elucidates how companies that want to engage in ethical responsibility-taking might be able to exert some pressure on their suppliers with regard to important aspects of the everyday well-being of workers.

In this section we have discussed how businesses respond to political consumer demands by deepening or expanding their engagement with corporate social responsibility. Political consumer activism pushes corporations into increased commitment to better business practice and corporations are pulled into them by their need to remain competitive and make profits. Thus, it shows how the logic of capitalism can be used within the political consumer framework (for further discussion, see Micheletti and Stolle 2008). If one corporation in a competitive commodity market is publicly applauded for taking its responsibility seriously, the market instincts of others in the same industry have been found to entice them to follow suit. In particular, well-known brands in sensitive and highly competitive buyer-driven commodity markets – affordable apparel, cosmetics, food, household equipment, DIY goods – have shown themselves to be vulnerable to what might be called a spiral of political consumerism. Corporate commitment comes, however, at a price. Political consumer activists are, by nature, not satisfied unless they reach their goals completely. They thus monitor corporate actions carefully for signs of insufficient commitment or what was earlier discussed as greenwash, sweatwash, and whitewash. In some instances, businesses have begun to experience an overload of responsibility and societal expectations to solve general problems in particular country settings (e.g., the activist claims that are put on Shell Oil in Nigeria, see Holzer 2007). They have also met with growing expectations about the impact that they should make as role leader in their own industry and the need to continually ratchet up their commitments. The impact that they can make as role leader in their own industry, and their need to continually ratchet up their commitments. This experienced sense of responsibility overload leads them at times to promote innovative business commitments and partnerships and even advocate a new role for government.

Nevertheless, political consumer activists remain critical, and many civic groups continue to be suspicious of business. They question whether corporations are doing everything in their power to practice responsibility-taking to the fullest. The question is whether the recent turn toward increased corporate social responsibility will continue and if and how it can solve the global problems identified by the political consumer organizational settings.

PUSHING GOVERNMENT INTO POLITICAL CONSUMERISM

While political consumer activism often emerges from governmental inactivity or inability on certain issues, governments can also directly be targeted to take more political responsibility. In fact, many political consumer groups would like more government involvement and even regulation, for example in the form of engagement in voluntary labeling schemes, regulations regarding animal treatment or human rights abuses in corporations even on foreign soil, or at least government's active support of their goals (see Levi and Linton 2003, Maquila Solidarity Network 2006, Murray 2004; more discussion in Chapter 8). However, for several political consumer issues there has been no easy national or even international legal solution (see Chapter 1). Political consumers individually and collectively try, therefore, to get government engaged through their purchasing practices.[16] Deregulation, privatization, and globalization have turned governments into the single largest consumer in the global economy. On average, between 8 percent and 25 percent of a nation's gross domestic product is spent on public purchasing globally (United Nations Environment Programme 2009a). Among their large purchases are commodities targeted by different political consumer organizational settings: clothing, energy, food, office supplies and equipment, transportation vehicles, construction materials, and surgical instruments. Governmental procurement must accord with the World Trade Organization's rules regarding open, transparent, and nondiscriminatory trade policy. Thus, even if there may be governmental will to practice political consumerism, there are legal restrictions on how much it can use its shopping choices to promote sustainable development. Labeling schemes are an important mechanism here because they help ensure that public procurement is free trade. Governments are allowed within WTO's free trade rules to use information contained in labeling schemes if they meet certain conditions including requirements that the label is based on scientific information, is adopted using a procedure in which all stakeholders (such as government bodies, consumers, manufacturers, distributors, and environmental organizations) can participate, and is accessible to all interested parties.

In terms of commodity focus, green public procurement (GPP) is most advanced. All layers of government include clauses that facilitate green buying in their public procurement policy; some of the governmental differences have been examined in Chapter 4 (see also Erdmenger 2003). Energy use is a central concern. Social considerations – social justice, human rights, and labor conditions and pay – play a more minor role. The UN, World Bank, and OECD promote green and sustainable procurement policies and have commissioned task forces to facilitate better shopping that adheres to the WTO free-trade regulations (UNEP 2009b). Sustainable procurement policies – those involving environmental, social justice, and economic considerations – have been launched in many OECD countries and even rapidly developing countries (including

---

[16] We would like to thank Tomas Mitander, now a Ph.D. student at Karlstad University, for help in collecting some initial materials on public procurement policies.

China). All OECD countries have committed to foster green purchasing on all levels of government and to monitor purchasing processes. Austria, Denmark, Sweden, and Japan have green purchasing governmental institutions or multi-stakeholder institutions (Ochoa, Führ, and Günther 2003). The European Union is the supra-governmental level most engaged in political consumerism, and, as mentioned in Chapter 5, is involved in discussions on labeling schemes. It has developed a public procurement policy and action plans to implement it among its member states. Some of the formulated criteria are based on existing European and national eco-labeling schemes and information collected from stakeholders in industry and civil society. More recently, it has begun to formulate a guide on taking account of social considerations in public procurement policy (European Commission 2010). Green buying is the European Union's main focus. Some of its priority areas are favorable for FSC, MSC, organic food labeling, the EU eco-label and other eco-labels.

Moreover, all layers of government are increasingly considering how they can purchase fairly traded and organically labeled goods through voluntary non-contractual means and to provide alternative consumer choices, for instance by including such goods in vending machines in hospitals and schools. Governments interested in solving climate change and improving public health have focused more of their attention on procuring organic food. Sustainable food initiatives are found in the European Union and the United States and are particularly strong in the United Kingdom. The UK Department for Environment, Food and Rural Affairs (DEFRA) encourages the British National Health Service to set a target of between 30 percent and 60 percent organic ingredients to be used in recipes instead of encouraging caterers to provide an organic option, which it has found to be impracticable (DEFRA 2009). In Sweden, the official goal is to have 25 percent of the food in the public sector organically labeled. Even though governments are only beginning to put green procurement policy into operation and formulate their policies on fairtrade and criteria for sourcing foreign manufactured clothing and equipment, their efforts are showing effects. Scholars find that governmental actions send a signal to the market, for instance in the case of domestically sourced wood and paper purchasing, and have pushed the forest harvesting and processing industry to adopt more sustainable CSR practice, (Simula 2006, 40–42). In the Netherlands, sustainable procurement has even stimulated timber importers to increase their share of certified products.

Of course, problems remain with sustainable public procurement; two specific issues are a limited number of established environmental criteria for products and services and the proclivity of certification schemes to give relative advantage to plantation timber over natural forests, which encourages the promotion of more Southern forest plantations and, according to some political consumer activists, is contrary to the broad goals of political consumerism. Studies demonstrate also that not all governments use the opportunities available through public procurement to shop in a more environmental and ethically responsible way. Sweden is a good case in point (Ahlberg and Bruun 2010). Governments are even sometimes uncertain about the legal possibilities to include environmental criteria in tender documents. So far, the European Union has also noted a lack of political support and coordinated exchange of best practice and information between regions and local authorities (European Commission 2008).

Political consumerism targets government in one other important way. It uses jurisdictions – towns, cities, villages, counties, zones, islands, boroughs – and their local institutions – schools and churches – to create "geographies of responsibilities" (Massey 2004). "Fairtrade settlements and cities" are the best example. Statistics from 2011 show about 1,014 such entities in twenty-two countries across all major continents (Fairtrade Towns 2011). These efforts create communities that undertake consciousness-raising, agenda-setting, public procurement, and market effects (Fairtrade Foundation 2008, Malpass, Cloke, Barnett and Clarke 2007).

As discussed in Chapter 4, most OECD governments operate voluntary eco-labeling certification schemes. Many have also implemented green claim guidelines that inform consumers about choice opportunities, and Nordic countries were among the first to create ethical claim guidelines (see Nordic Consumer Ombudsmen 2005). Many governments are also involved in providing incentives to promote political consumer choice. For example, in 2009, new EU regulations went into effect for the production, control, and labeling of organic products; the European Action Plan for Organic Food and Farming was also implemented that year.[17] Many European countries have been funding farmers' conversion to organic methods for decades; and some scholars suggest countries in the South should do the same (see Calo and Wise 2005). Other governments use nudging instruments such as tax incentives to encourage consumers to purchase more environmentally friendly goods and, in so doing, create consciousness for the environmental and ethical politics of products.[18]

---

[17] This plan sets out twenty-one initiatives to achieve the objectives of developing the market for organic food and improving standards by increasing efficacy, transparency, and consumer confidence. See more information here: http://ec.europa.eu/agriculture/organic/eu-policy/ legislation_en; http://ec.europa.eu/agriculture/organic/eu-policy/action-plan_en.

[18] Governments also take on more indirect roles in the support of political consumerism or individualized responsibility-taking, particularly with regard to environmental products. For example, in the United States, many states and the federal government offer "rebates and incentives through tax breaks, loans, and perks such as allowing hybrid-car drivers to use car pool lanes" as well as "tax incentives for purchases of many hybrid vehicles and energy-saving products" (Milakovich and Gordon 2008). These policies, which result from the Energy Policy Act of 2005 in the United States, can be seen as institutional frameworks that encourage the purchase of certain types of political consumer products through government action (Ward-Jones 2008).

POLITICAL CONSUMERISM – REAL-LIFE PROBLEM SOLVER?

So far, this book's findings have shown how the organizational setting of political consumerism has been able to mobilize consumers over the last decades and how (in part at least as a result of their joint actions) corporations have begun to consider ethical issues in their production. Moreover, although governments are less frequently targeted by political consumer actions, they have been drawn into adopting a more political consumer agenda, which is particularly visible in changing procurement policies and the rise of fairtrade cities. In this section, we examine whether and how political consumerism has been able to solve problems in real life – that is, if it is able to facilitate the changes for workers, farmers, and the environment that form its intentions. Has child labor, for example, been eliminated or reduced because of actions of political consumers and activist groups? How has political consumerism changed farmers' well-being in developing countries? In short, how effective is it in solving real-life problems on the ground?

The empirical evidence for this section is mostly drawn from research on child labor, studies on minimum wages as well as case studies of fairtrade coffee farmers. Wages of factory workers are one of the most essential aspects of the anti-sweatshop movement and perhaps also the most measurable. Child labor was and still is an important substantive target of political consumer activists. It is a high priority for the United Nations, global unions, other civil society associations, and forbidden in many countries. Campaigns against child labor appeal to caring sensitivity of consumers and, as shown in the study of Nike in Chapter 6, can make headline news. Fairtrade labeling is an important choice architecture for the political consumer organizational setting and several political consumers both individual and institutional engage in buying fairtrade products. Importantly, fairtrade is also a critical test of political consumerism as it focuses more on other-regarding values (in addition to self-interested ones) that are explicitly addressed by this labeling scheme. Findings from numerous studies of fairtrade coffee farmers carried out between 2000 and 2011 are synthesized in this section. These studies, which rely primarily on interviews with fairtrade coffee producers or actual comparisons of farmers in both fairtrade and other cooperatives, cover twenty-one cooperatives in six countries, with approximately 20,000 members between them. By comparing the researchers' findings and distilling the commonalities, a clearer picture of the benefits and challenges of fairtrade emerges.

Effects on Wages

The Nike case and the entire apparel industry are probably the most studied examples of anti-sweatshop political consumerism's effectiveness on workers' lives. An unusual comparison examines statistically the impact of anti-sweatshop campaigns in Indonesia on wages and employment in the textile,

footwear, and apparel sectors (including Nike). They compare the wage growth
of workers in foreign-owned and exporting firms before and after the initiation
of anti-sweatshop campaigns as well as in targeted versus non-targeted regions.
They show that these campaigns indeed led to large wage increases for targeted
enterprises, but they also came at a cost. Although they increased wages, the
targeted firms also showed reduced investment and falling profits, and smaller
plants were more likely to close (Harrison and Scorse 2010; for a different
view, see Powell and Zwolinski 2011). In short, whereas many workers certainly directly benefited from the pressures of the movement, in these cases,
corporations were negatively affected.

While research on the direct effects of the political consumer organizational
setting on workers in the South is scarce, there are a few case studies drawing
a slightly less optimistic picture of long-term consequences. One case study
examines four anti-sweatshop campaigns. In most of the campaigns, the workers and activists obtained short-term victories like better wages and working
conditions, but eventually many of the changes were reversed – often because
the targeted factory closed down. Armbruster-Sandoval (2005) concludes that
Northern campaigns are mostly successful in combating sweatshop practices
and fighting for higher salaries when they also include strong local unions.

In a successful 2001 case at the Kukdong plant in Mexico, the workers who
were protesting poor working conditions – extremely low wages, forced over-
time, physical abuse, and gender discrimination – reached out to anti-sweatshop
NGOs, filing an official complaint with WRC (Worker Rights Consortium, see
Chapter 5) in order to achieve tangible changes (Bose 2008; see Rodriguez-
Garavito 2005, 222 for an extensive overview of all actors involved). Here,
the partnership of NGOs constantly pressured Nike, Kukdong managers, and
Mexican state authorities. Despite resistance from the factory, the workers
eventually compelled Nike to overhaul its codes of conduct (Carty 2001). The
workers formed a new union and were able to negotiate substantial wage and
benefit increases (Bose 2008). Another study highlighted that the main impact
of corporate codes of labor under the U.K. ethical trading initiative were found
to be in the areas of minimum wage guarantees and health and safety, but they
had little impact on freedom of association, right to collective bargaining and
reduction of discrimination. Moreover, while the codes "encouraged payment
of the national minimal wage," it was not clear whether this amounted to an
actual "living wage" for workers (Barrientos and Smith 2007, 722). In sum,
while the overall evidence of the positive effects of anti-sweatshop campaigns
on wages is mixed; selected case studies elucidate the conditions that have led
to successful wage increases for workers.

Child Labor

Child labor was an important early substantive target within political consumerism. Although child labor is now regulated in international (including

ILO) guidelines, many national laws, and even through voluntary labeling schemes for organic food and sustainable forests (Forest Stewardship Council; see Chapter 5), several organizational settings are still concerned about its continued presence in manufacturing and agriculture. Child labor has particularly been a concern within anti-sweatshop, organic, and fairtrade political consumerism. Child labor has a strong emotional appeal, and ending it seems – from the Western perspective – to be a feasible policy goal. However, political consumerism does show some limits in its ability to address the problem.

Despite some evidence that economic globalization might reduce child labor when higher household incomes allow parents to remove their children from the workforce (Edmonds and Pavcnik 2002), and despite campaigns by Northern governments, intergovernmental organizations such as the ILO and UNICEF and NGOs (e.g. Oxfam and Save the Children) and marked progress, child labor persists today (see ILO 2009). According to UNICEF, one in six children in the world (or 158 million children between 5 and 14 years of age) are still engaged in child labor (Business and Human Rights Resource Centre 2011). Trade sanctions and import tariffs or political consumerism do not seem able to reduce significantly, let alone eliminate, child labor from all sectors (Maskus 1997, Melchior 1996, see *Globe and Mail* 2011).

The feasibility of the goal to eradicate child labor is at times questioned. For example, the chairman of Nestlé, one of the largest cocoa and coffee buyers, claims that it is nearly impossible to completely eradicate child labor (*Globe and Mail* 2011), and that an alternative policy goal should be to offer schooling for all children in locations with chocolate farms instead (ibid; see also Admassie 2003).

Activists are united on their goal to eradicate child labor and have traditionally deployed different forms of political consumerism in their battle, from boycotts (e.g., of Uzbek cotton in 2009) to buycotts (e.g., buying child-labor-free-labeled goods certified by Rugmark, Care & Fair, and others) to discursive action (e.g. see the case study on the Nike e-mail exchange in Chapter 6) to supporting legal action against companies believed to have contravened OECD guidelines by purchasing goods produced using child labor (e.g. the current lawsuit against Cargill and ICT Cotton for buying Uzbek cotton allegedly cultivated using forced child labor; see Cotton Campaign 2011). But how effective are these actions? While empirical studies are scarce, some research indicates that on its own, market-based activism may be ill-suited for the task.

The first problem is that child labor is more prevalent in developing countries or regions with little or no export industry (UNICEF 1997, Baland and Duprez 2007). Thus, Northern political consumers are restricted in their efforts to affect child labor as a whole. Moreover, there is consensus that boycotts are not an effective method to combat child labor occurring in export sectors in the global South because they may hurt their intended beneficiaries by actually increasing child labor overall by forcing child laborers into other, perhaps even less safe, activities such as prostitution (Basu and Zarghamee 2005, 2009, see also Brown 2006, Edmonds 2007). Finally, simulation analysis indicates that when child labor boycotts result in further political consequences such as trade sanctions, domestic political support for a ban on child labor might diminish as a result (Doepke and Zilibotti 2010).

For this reason, activist groups, including those specifically focusing on children's rights and welfare prefer *buycotts* to fight child labor (e.g. Stop Child Labour 2007). But, depending on underlying economic conditions, they too may be counterproductive. If children are sent by their parents to work because of extreme poverty, again, labeling schemes may simply displace child laborers to a different sector of the economy and often for lower pay (Baland and Duprez 2007, Basu, Chau and Grote 2006, Brown 2006). This is because the labeling scheme, if successful, reduces the supply of child jobs, but unless it is able to tackle the core issue of poverty, the demand for child jobs remains. One empirical study points, however, to ways in which political consumerism can in fact be a positive force. A study of the social labels Rugmark and Care & Fair in the context of the Nepali carpet industry found that households with at least one member working in a certified factory are much less likely to have a child working than other households because these factories offer welfare activities like sponsorship of children's education and day cares. In short, labeling schemes are most effective if the premium paid by Northern consumers helps create or improve services such as education for children (Baland and Duprez 2007, Chakrabarty 2007, Chakrabarty, Grote, and Luchters 2011). The limits in the effectiveness of the fight against child labor demonstrate how difficult it is to reach certain important and fundamental societal goals through political consumerism. Because not all products reach Western markets, they are not available for political consumer influence, so these problems are more likely to persist or at least unlikely to change if only political consumerism is employed as the problem-solving device (see more in Chapter 8). Clearly, local economic conditions, specifically the reasons children are sent to work by their families and the structure of local labor markets, will determine and limit the effect of political consumer actions (Basu and Zarghamee 2005). Policies that tackle poverty directly should be expected to offer a more successful approach to addressing this issue.[19]

Benefits of Fairtrade for the Farmers in Southern Cooperatives

The main benefits of the fairtrade label for producers may be divided into two categories: material and social/cultural, both of which are examined in this section. Our analysis focuses on the coffee market, which is a good test of political consumerism's effectiveness. Not only was Northern concern about the plight

---

[19] The conditional cash transfers programs in Nicaragua, for example, require that parents send their children to school if they want to receive the benefits. They have reduced the probability of a child working underage and the number of hours of child labor significantly (Gee 2010).

of coffee farmers the reason for the establishment of the first fairtrade label, but coffee also continues to be the flagship product for fairtrade mobilizing and marketing (see Chapter 5). Most research shows that fairtrade coffee farmers enjoy a significantly higher income than conventional coffee farmers (Aranda and Morales 2002, Bacon 2005, Bacon et al. 2008, Pérezgrovas and Cervantes 2002, Valkila and Nygren 2010, Boersma VanderHoff 2002).

A case in point is the Majomut co-op in Chiapas, Mexico. In 2002, its fairtrade coffee farmers earned 1,700 USD for their average annual harvest of about 1,500 pounds. Their non-fairtrade counterparts in the region earned 550 USD (Pérezgrovas and Cervantes 2002). However, 2002 was a year when world prices were particularly low; the difference between fairtrade and conventional coffee farmers is not always so dramatic. Fairtrade proponents would argue that higher prices regardless of market price levels are an important goal. Like most commodities, global coffee markets are highly volatile; under fairtrade arrangements, producers earn not only a higher salary but also one that is guaranteed. Fairtrade arrangements also require that coffee buyers extend this pre-financed guarantee to producers at world market rates (Aranda and Morales 2002, González 2002, Lyon 2002). On a global level, the Fairtrade system performs a redistributive function; from 1998 to 2005, 70 million USD were spent by consumers in the United States on purchases from Southern coffee farmers. Based on survey data from Nicaragua, there can be a 10 percent household income difference favoring fairtrade producers (Macdonald 2007). Together, the guaranteed fair price and access to credit ensure a higher standard of living, reduce producers' economic vulnerability, and bring an element of predictability to their business.

However, some scholars remain skeptical. In a comparison of a random sample of coffee-producing households in southern Mexico between fairtrade/organic and conventional growers, the conclusion was drawn that fairtrade cannot alleviate rural poverty, that the price differences between fairtrade and conventional coffee growers were relatively small (about a 300 USD difference in net returns), and that most of the difference in net cash income per hectare comes from differences in yields, not prices (Bradford et al. 2011). Another study (Valkila and Nygren 2010) shows that the superiority of fairtrade coffee prices depends on fluctuating market prices, which have recently been very close to fairtrade coffee prices. In Nicaragua as well it was found that the combination of current coffee sales alone is insufficient to eliminate extreme poverty (Bacon et al. 2008, 264), and the majority of households stated that at some time they have been unable to meet their basic nutritional needs. In sum, while salary differences between conventional and fairtrade farmers exist, the actual life circumstances might not be so different.

In addition to the minimum guarantee, the fairtrade price includes a "social premium" (basically, a higher price for the consumer), which is to be spent at the producers' discretion. FLO encourages co-ops to invest it in local development. Researchers have observed that the social premium has been used to

repay co-op debts, launch economic diversification schemes such as small textile factories and bakeries, invest in infrastructure, including health, education,
and transportation, reinvest in coffee operations in order to improve the quality of coffee or efficiency of production, or simply distribute it evenly among
co-op members. One success story promoted by FLO is that of the Coocafé
consortium in Costa Rica. This organization invests the bulk of its social premium into a social capital fund, which is used primarily to purchase school
supplies and to provide high school and university scholarships; nearly 7,000
scholarships were provided to students in coffee-growing communities between
1997 and 2007 (Ronchi 2002, FLO 2007). While there is agreement that the
infrastructure and organization of farms have improved in fairtrade arrangements, it also seems that the social impact of fairtrade is at times difficult to
evaluate. This is especially the case when farmers in fairtrade cooperatives are
not even aware of the benefits of the social premiums (Valkila and Nygren
2010). Some studies are also unable to separate the effects from the benefits
provided by various rural development projects from those of fairtrade social
premiums (ibid, 331).

Finally, the material benefits of fairtrade production extend beyond producers and their families. A thriving cooperative may provide seasonal employment
that contributes to household incomes and investment in infrastructure such
as roads, and the purchase of hospital and school supplies can be advantageous for the broader community (Aranda and Morales 2002, Pérezgrovas and
Cervantes 2002, Boersma VanderHoff 2002).

Fairtrade has also been found to have other social or cultural advantages.
Successful fairtrade co-operatives allow, for instance, individuals to stay in
their home region instead of migrating in search of work, which producers
argue promotes family and community cohesion (Aranda and Morales 2002,
Pérezgrovas and Cervantes 2002, Murray, Raynolds, and Taylor 2003). Where
the social premium is invested in education, more children have been found to
be enrolled in school and to continue on to the secondary and tertiary levels
(Lyon 2002, Ronchi 2002, CI and IIED 2005). This can be viewed as a long-
term consequence of fairtrade because education is commonly considered an
important activity for combating child labor and for general social development. On a more individual level, producers state that controlling production
gives them a sense of empowerment and pride (Aranda and Morales 2002, Lyon
2002, Méndez 2002, Pérezgrovas and Cervantes 2002). Moreover, producer
organizations with access to more resources can perform functions that the
government is failing to do, such as building health centers and repairing roads
(Macdonald 2007). Other opportunities provided by stronger farmer organizations include direct marketing of coffee and access to training in organic
farming techniques (Murray, Raynolds, and Taylor 2006). Finally, the vast
majority of fairtrade coffee is also organic and shade-grown and in addition to
the environmental benefits – protection of the soil, promotion of biodiversity,
worker safety, and the elimination of synthetic (and often harmful) elements –
it has been noted that in converting to organic methods, producers in Central

America have also revived and adapted traditional indigenous farming techniques. In this way, some producers have found that fairtrade has contributed to a revival and preservation of their culture (Lyon 2002, Boersma VanderHoff 2002).

CHALLENGES OF FAIRTRADE PRODUCTION

Notwithstanding these very real benefits, the FLO fairtrade model has certain drawbacks and faces major challenges. These issues, which can be divided into four categories, demonstrate the complexity of the problems that political consumerism wishes to solve.

Fairtrade Markets in the North Are Stagnant

Because the fairtrade coffee price is often higher than the conventional price – sometimes, sizeably – capacity vastly exceeds demand. Sales of fairtrade coffee are somewhat stagnant in most countries, seemingly unable to attain higher than 3 percent to 4 percent market share. This has ramifications not only for the *number* of producers who have access to the fairtrade market, but also for *which* producers have access to it. Almost all coffee marketed as fairtrade has been high-quality specialty coffee, and under these conditions, importers have been able to choose among a wide variety of producing cooperatives. These expectations of quality tend to eliminate small, poor producers who are unable to meet them due to a lack of expertise and equipment (Frese 2008). Thus, the vast majority of fairtrade producers are mid-sized to large co-ops, leading small growers to lament that Fairtrade production has been captured by "an elite group of producers" (González 2002, quoted in Taylor 2002, 25). In fact, many of the most successful fairtrade coffee co-ops were already well-organized, relatively well-off cooperatives *prior* to receiving fairtrade certification (Taylor 2002). This inability of small producers – arguably those who would benefit most from fairtrade – to enter the fairtrade market is of major concern to a number of producers and researchers (see Calo and Wise 2005, Murray, Raynolds, and Taylor 2003, Renard 2005, Utting-Chamorro 2005).

Due to limited Northern markets, even those cooperatives that have been successful in locating buyers may find Northern demand for fairtrade coffee insufficient. Among the co-ops surveyed in research, the majority were not able to sell their entire crop under fairtrade arrangements. Thus, despite the fact that all of these cooperatives' coffee is produced according to fairtrade guidelines, it is often the case that fairtrade buyers can be found for only a small proportion of the crop. Because these producers were able to sell less than half of their crop on fairtrade markets, researchers find on occasion that fairtrade farmers' quality of life is indistinguishable from that of conventional producers (Bacon 2005). The limits of the fairtrade market are critical qualifications to the above discussion of the benefits of fairtrade coffee (Murray, Raynolds, and Taylor 2003, 16).

Coffee co-ops in this situation are increasingly forging agreements with transnational corporations, selling them coffee directly under private "ethical" or "green" labels that compete with FLO. These schemes are less advantageous for producers than the FLO model in that they usually do not offer a guaranteed minimum price, a social premium, or credit for producers – though they usually offer better returns than conventional coffee markets. While some producers worry that they may be helping these TNCs "fairwash" their corporate image, they seem to have few alternatives (González 2002, Boersma VanderHoff 2002).

Problems with FLO Governance and Monitoring

Generally, political consumerism includes individual acts of participation that are less dependent on hierarchical organization structures. However, it should not be concluded that less hierarchical structures necessarily are more democratic, equal, and transparent. The criticism still stands that certain political consumer institutions and NGOs do not have transparent operating structures. A common complaint among producers is that the FLO model, for all its benefits, is a top-down affair. The development of standards is said to be undemocratic, with Southern producers lacking sufficient voice. Producers have mentioned arbitrariness in the monitoring process, with FLO monitors sometimes having shown limited understanding of local issues or refusing to disclose evaluation results of the inspections carried out as a part of FLO's co-op evaluation process (Lyon 2002, Martinez 2002, Pérezgrovas and Cervantes 2002, Boersma VanderHoff, Jaffe and Howard 2010). Another governance issue that has been raised is that while Fairtrade began as an attempt to create equitable, *direct* relations between consumers and producers, as fairtraded goods are mainstreamed in conventional supermarkets, FLO's approach has become depersonalized, business-like, and marketing-oriented, and is pushed "more by commercial considerations than by solidarity" (Renard 2005, 425; also González 2002, Murray, Raynolds, and Taylor 2003). Indeed, some have made the point that a considerable amount of "the gains from the Fairtrade price are eaten up by the fees that co-operatives must pay to the FLO to qualify as being Fairtrade" (Henderson 2008, 63; see also discussion in Chapter 8).

Some of the case studies from fairtrade communities discussed in this chapter were conducted before 2003, when FLO reorganized itself partly in response to this criticism in order to give producers a greater say in the development of standards and to enable their representation within the organization (Renard 2005). Yet, the extent to which this reorganization has helped solve these problems is unclear. More recently, increases in fairtrade sales, general public awareness, and certain external global developments (e.g., climate change) have prompted the FLO to extend its mission and strategy and revalidate its values to "connect consumers and producers via a label which promotes fairer trading conditions through which producers who are disadvantaged by conventional trade can combat poverty, strengthen their position and take more control over their lives" (FLO-I 2009, 5). Its aims are, therefore, to enlarge fairtrade's scope by broadening its availability to more Southern producers and communities, deepening the commitment of involved participants, and strengthening the FLO infrastructure so that it can more effectively achieve its goals (FLO-I 2009, 9). Extending certification to more kinds of commodities over its sixteen categories (coffee, cocoa, bananas, sugar, rice, honey, tea, wine, flowers, fresh fruit, spices and herbs, sports balls, gold, cotton, juices, and composite products) is also on its agenda (FLO-I 2009, 7). An important new item now labeled nationally is gold (*Guardian* 2011).

The second criticism is more difficult to address and concerns disagreements within the political consumer organizational settings on market shares vs. ideological commitment (see Chapter 5). If Northern fairtrade markets are to be expanded so that a greater number of farmers can gain entrance into fairtrade certification, it is perhaps reasonable to assume that more mainstream marketing and "commercial considerations" (including certification of transnational corporations and plantation production) would be necessary. However, fairtrade's more ideological segment, represented by third-world solidarity groups such as Cooperation Sud in France and worldshops, fear that the mainstream marketing focus is transforming fairtrade into a simple consumer choice that can be performed almost everywhere and a commodity that must compete with conventional goods on the basis of price, taste, and quality. Fairtrade's challenge is, therefore, to work toward a greater market share while, at the same time, giving producers and small farmers a central role in decision making (Jaffe and Howard 2010).

The Fairtrade Model Does Not Address Structural Problems Faced by the South

Some scholars have argued that the fairtrade system reinforces the status quo in that no incentives are offered to help "unsustainable farming communities to develop new sources of income" (Sidwell 2008, 13). Obviously, there are several major factors involved in the chronic poverty of the global South that fairtrade cannot properly or effectively solve. One important matter is that fairtrade is not able to alter Northern protectionism, particularly the trade barriers that work against Southern exports to Northern markets (Gandenberger, Garrelts, and Wehlau 2011). Another is the cash commodity dependence of Southern farmers. While several co-ops have launched projects meant to create new income streams, producers remain heavily dependent on coffee for their income (Aranda and Morales 2002, Fridell 2007, Méndez 2002, Pérezgrovas and Cervantes 2002). Basically, fairtrade and other political consumer labeling schemes continue to export raw materials from the South, which are then refined in Northern industries. Thus, fairtrade does not automatically lead to economic diversification, skills development, and Southern empowerment. This confirms one of the criticisms of political consumerism, that the livelihood of Southern fairtrade coffee producers remains very much dependent on the whims of consumers in the North. Thus, fairtrade is still a limited coping strategy in the absence of structural and policy changes at the macroeconomic level, which would be essential for the overall goal of global poverty eradication. This emphasizes how market-based activism should possibly be understood – as a way to address global problems that governments or international organizations are not willing or able to solve by filling a responsibility gap created by deregulation, protectionism and lack of governmental action. For persistent structural global problems, such as poverty, this form of activism alone has only limited reach (see more in Chapter 8).

ASSESSING EFFECTIVENESS ON BALANCE

The primary goal of political consumerism is to reveal the "hidden politics of products" and to change corporations' sense of responsibility for their commodity chains. It puts the environmental, ethical, and social justice problems associated with production and consumption on the public, governmental, and corporate agenda. It attempts to sensitize consumers about these issues and to force corporations to develop policies and solutions for these problems. Political consumerism has played and continues to play an important role in challenging corporate "race-to-the-bottom" profit-making schemes in several industries. It works on convincing corporations that their bottom line is "triple" and must not only concern profit-making but also workers' rights and the environment globally. Today, many transnational brand corporations are devising strategies to mark themselves as "race-to-the-top" businesses that care about social and environmental responsibility-taking. The investigations in this chapter and others in the book demonstrate that, with few exceptions, government has not generally played a proactive and strong role in pushing business into corporate social responsibility. Instead, these demands have been put forth by political consumer discourse and activism.

This chapter constitutes one of the first studies into the effectiveness of political consumerism and demonstrates clearly that this assessment is not an easy undertaking. The argument here is that evaluating the effectiveness of political consumerism should include a broader analysis that begins with how public awareness is created and also consider that influencing change is a slow and, in some cases, dynamic process with ups and downs and with the main stakeholders playing complex roles.[20] The overall results for political consumer effectiveness are, however, case specific.

This study of the effectiveness process cannot demonstrate a direct causal link between political consumer activists and the outcomes identified in this chapter (see also O'Rourke 2005). In part, this problem is shared with most

[20] For an interesting example of this, see the report on outsourced manufacturing in the Lesotho garment industry (Brea 2007).

studies of power and influence, which have only been able to establish causality by closely tracking particular cases with the help of multi-methods. In the case of political consumerism as illustrated in discussions in this chapter, such a study would require detailed analysis over a considerable period of time. The problem of causality assessment is also compounded because activists have used "hidden" strategies revealed only to corporate targets, according to activists in the Nike case, and do not always publicly display all the tactics they use to push corporations into responsibility-taking. There is, in other words, a diplomatic character of political consumerism that has not yet been explored systematically by social scientists. Some scholars have referred to this phenomenon as "the gun behind the door." Moreover, corporations, as shown in our Nike interview (2004) and elsewhere do not always feel comfortable with admitting that they have been influenced by and made concessions to political activists. Overall, short of showing that organizational settings and movement activists were behind the observed developments over the last decade, this chapter has demonstrated that political consumer activism is paralleled by changing consumer attitudes and behavior to take on responsibility for their shopping decisions, a new focus by corporations on corporate social responsibility, changing governmental approaches to procurement policies, and visible changes in the lives of targeted workers or farmers. However, the chapter also identified some limitations in the effectiveness of political consumerism. These and the general weaknesses and potential of political consumerism as a form of political action and problem-solver are discussed more fully in the last chapter.

8

Political Consumerism's Scope and Challenges

INTRODUCTION

This book presents a unique and comprehensive analysis of the various practices of political consumerism in populations of advanced democracies. It highlights the point that political consumerism is not just about shopping decisions in the supermarket – it goes well beyond considerations of price and material quality of the products to include discursive forms and potentially a commitment to lifestyle changes as well. These action repertoires have a few characteristics in common that do not necessarily fit into the traditional definitions of political participation. Yet, they are symptomatic of the larger transformation and reconfiguration of political participation now occurring across the world. The book shows how these practices might be understood as forms of individualized responsibility-taking. Based on theoretical work on the collapse of responsibility-taking, previous chapters discussed that important sources of political consumerism are in part related to the rising inability of governments to address complex global problems as well as to the development of buyer-driven capitalism. Furthermore, the book has explored the individual and contextual correlates of political consumerism in a cross-national perspective and the organizational settings that have promoted its mobilization.

Most importantly, though, the book offers the first attempt to investigate the effectiveness of political consumerism. This discussion has made clear that there are not many indicators of political effectiveness when it comes to evaluating citizens' political engagements and suggests that effectiveness cannot just be measured through the investigation of policy change. A systematic study of effectiveness must also include measures of attitudinal and behavioral change of the targets of political consumer actions and other involved actors.

The remainder of this chapter presents a critical and reflective outlook on the practice, future, and theoretical understanding of political consumerism.

It consists of four parts. First, it asks about the most important difficulties in the practice of political consumerism by individuals, groups, and even governments and addresses remaining general criticisms of political consumerism as an engine for political and social change. The second section focuses on the latest and newest strategies of the political consumerist organizational settings to overcome or address some of these difficulties. Thirdly, the chapter highlights the theoretical implications of this work for the concepts of political participation and the measurement of political effectiveness. Finally, the most important and exciting research questions in the area of political consumerism that still need answers are identified and discussed.

DIFFICULTIES IN THE PRACTICE OF POLITICAL CONSUMERISM

Chapter 7 discussed the various ways in which political consumerism has become an efficient political tool in solving political problems and also highlighted its limits. Here, the focus is on the difficulties people might encounter in the practice of political consumerism. For example, are there limits to the "reach" of political consumerism? More specifically, are there certain products, sectors, or companies that political consumers are unable to engage or address? Political consumerism as a form of individualized responsibility-taking involves concerned citizens as individuals or collectivities engaging as market actors. As demonstrated often in this book, political consumerism is ideally suited for citizens to challenge producers or retailers of consumer goods for whom brand and image are important. When it comes to companies with little in the way of direct market interactions with individuals, or issues occurring lower down in product chains, it may be difficult for political consumers to engage these actors and put pressure on them through their activism and purchasing decisions. There are some situations in which the use of political consumerism – particularly boycotts and buycotts – is difficult if not impossible when certain products, sectors, firms or even causes are not susceptible to this kind activism. This may be the case if a product or firm in question is not accessible for everyday purchase by individual consumers, if alternatives are not available or too costly, or if the product chain or even the causes for political consumerism are too complex for political consumer tracking. These problems are examined below.

Access/Visibility of the Product or Firm in the Supply Commodity Chain

An important question for the practice of political consumerism is whether the product or firm is visible, identifiable, and accessible to everyday consumers. If not, direct boycotting and buycotting are nearly impossible. This may occur in at least two different scenarios. First, some sectors produce for other firms or for governments, and not primarily for individual consumers. For example, most of the mining sector and the firms that operate in it are generally invisible to many political consumers. Regular citizens are not usually the first consumers of their products (although some do purchase certain metals and minerals such as gold and diamonds). Individuals displeased with the actions of most mining corporations may be better served by going through more traditional political channels such as contacting a politician, signing a petition, or participating in a public demonstration. They may also consider pressuring institutions to change their procurement policies. This may also be the case for products like aircraft, military equipment and weapons, heavy machinery, and natural resources such as oil, natural gas, or coal. For instance, in the late 1990s, activists linked Canadian energy company Talisman with a variety of environmental and human rights offences in the Sudan. Since Talisman is an "upstream" company (that is, low down or distanced from consumers on the supply chain) focusing on extraction, with no gas stations or retail locations to target, political consumers do not usually encounter this company in the context of everyday purchases. Activists opposed to Talisman's Sudanese operations resorted primarily to other, more traditional tactics such as petitions and government lobbying (Kobrin 2003). The case of asbestos provides another example where a lack of access or visibility may hinder the use of political consumerism. There is general scientific consensus that asbestos is a carcinogen and that its industrial use should be avoided (Waldman 2009), and most industrialized countries have banned all uses of asbestos. Canada, particularly Quebec, the world's main producer of this commodity, limits domestic use of asbestos but exports 96 percent of the asbestos it produces – primarily to the South, notably India, Indonesia, and Thailand – where it is used in ways that would be illegal in Canada due to health concerns (Attaran, Boyd, and Stanbrook 2008). Because asbestos is extracted and produced by two firms that do not create consumer goods, there is a limited scope for targeting these actors in consumer society to take responsibility for their practices.

The other aspect of the "access" problem has to do with the fact that political consumerism is principally a Northern phenomenon, and has been, as shown in this book, most practiced in the wealthiest of OECD countries. A political consumer cannot easily target market actors unless the company in question actually sells in the Northern consumer market – and sometimes this is not the case. Thus, some major problems remain unaddressed. For instance, most child labor occurs in the South and, as mentioned in Chapter 7, only a minority occurs in export sectors. The bulk of this child labor takes place in the agricultural sector, for *domestic* consumption (ILO 2006). Therefore, Northern political consumers have no clear or easy targets.

One solution to this problem of access has been the deployment of secondary boycotts or boycotts further down the commodity chain. A secondary boycott is directed at a firm that purchases from or otherwise deals with the "offending" firm. The primary boycott target is the one whose actions are considered offensive, but for strategic reasons, secondary or other targets – usually retailers who buy from the primary target either for resale or for use as inputs in their own products – may be selected and added to the boycott (Friedman 1999). Such strategies have been used in the forestry industry, larger chain restaurants to change their suppliers' animal treatment or labor practices, and in some campaigns by the Humane Society of the United States.[1] Another solution is, of course, to develop further political consumerist mechanisms and platforms, as now being done in the gold trade (www.fairtrade.org.uk/gold/). However, here again, gold is a mined product with considerable identifiable presence and demand in consumer society.

Substitution/Availability of Alternatives

Sometimes, there are no real alternatives to the product or company in question. If the costs of substitution products are high for consumers or if there are no alternatives, political consumerism may not be possible. The pharmaceutical sector, for instance, has been criticized by a wide variety of organizations for its involvement in animal testing (SHAC 2011, PETA 2011) and its lobbying for development and enforcement of strict patent law at the global and national levels, which is perceived to adversely affect access to medicines in developing countries (May 2000, Médecins Sans Frontières 2003, Shiva 2001). But for political consumers interested in taking action, alternative options are limited. Most pharmaceutical drugs are covered by patents and, depending on the availability of generic versions, companies may have a monopoly on their products. Thus, some well-protected sectors and monopolies may simply be off-limits for political consumerism. Other sectors that may offer limited avenues for political

---

[1] For example, activists have successfully targeted a logging company (Daishowa) accused of taking trees on traditional Cree land in northern Alberta. In that case, a company that had no direct interactions with consumers was indirectly targeted via boycotts of its clients – most notably, a clothing retailer and a fast-food chain. This secondary boycott was successful, as Daishowa eventually agreed to suspend its operations on disputed native land. In another example, in 2004, a Florida-based workers group organized a boycott of Taco Bell because it was purchasing tomatoes from suppliers that were considered to be underpaying their workers (*Multinational Monitor* 2005). Rather than make the tomato suppliers the primary target, the Coalition of Immokalee Workers boycotted Taco Bell, a major buyer of Florida tomatoes, until it agreed three years later to pay an extra penny for each pound of tomatoes. Taco Bell, in turn, ensured that its tomato suppliers pass along this surcharge directly to the workers. Another example comes from the Humane Society of the United States, which in 2005 adopted the strategy of boycotting and protesting restaurant chains that had not joined the boycott of Canadian seafood because of issues with the seal hunt. Red Lobster, a major American restaurant chain, was targeted in this way (Prewitt 2005). Along similar lines, animal rights activists opposed to the force-feeding involved in making *foie gras* have frequently organized boycotts of restaurants whose menus include this dish, for example in Toronto in 2005 (Aubin 2005). Although these particular secondary boycotts did not convince either the primary or secondary targets to change their practices, they provide more recent examples of boycotts being deployed against targets that are elusive and hard to reach.

consumerism in this way, depending on the market, include energy, telecommunications, and transportation (air and rail). Boycotting such products may, therefore, involve high risks or require more time and effort in finding alternatives, thus increasing the threshold for activism tremendously and making it more difficult for political consumerist mechanisms to develop.

Complexity of Production

Previous chapters already alluded to the fact that at times the production chain is so complex or long that it is difficult to determine the origins of the product in terms of labor conditions, environmental impact, and so forth. Goods like computers and mobile telephones, automobiles, clothing, home furniture, and other products can have such long and complex chains of production that political consumerist targeting is challenging. Even a simple shirt has multiple links in its chain of production, from cultivation of raw materials to often multi-factory manufacturing and quality control of the end product. The social and environmental impacts at each point in this production chain accumulate to form the politics behind this product and what Iris Young (see Chapter 1) identifies as structural injustices. Some organizational settings for political consumerism have made the conscious decision not to include all problem areas in their assessments. As discussed in Chapter 5, Marine Stewardship Council (MSC) does not include social criteria in its certification scheme. Anti-sweatshop activists made the choice in their early years not to take on the environmental problems associated with cotton growing, cloth dying, and so on for fear of overloading their activist agenda (Interview Andersson 2001).When shopping for a car, for instance, political consumers may select a more fuel-efficient model. They may even be able to find out where the car was assembled. But they will most likely be unable to discern where all automobile parts come from, and under what conditions they are produced, let alone discover the labor and environmental impact of the extraction of the raw materials that go into those auto parts and if the car is designed for both the requirements of women and men. Thus, many such complex goods may be said to suffer from a lack of what can be called "product accountability."

Complexity and Scale of Political Consumer Causes

However, not only are production chains complex and products badly labeled, there are also global problems that are so complex and of such a large scale that they are challenging for political consumerist campaigns and problem-solving. The problem of global climate change mentioned in Chapter 7 is an important example of issue complexity, and because of its large scale, it is riddled with problems coordinating collective action among diverse institutional levels, actors, and spheres. Some problem areas involve contradictory lines of action, while others are highly politicized and, therefore, sensitive, which makes it difficult for necessary stakeholders to join and accept them.

Yet other political consumer causes are not only complex but at times even contain internal contradictions. The inner tensions between the important product dimensions of organic production and fairtrade that involve transport costs and energy, illustrate the value-oriented conflicts that can be present within political consumerist campaigning, institutions, and problem-solving. Consumers concerned about environmental issues, and use of fossil fuels in particular, may scrutinize the produce at their local grocery store to assess the green options and find imported organic apples – perhaps from a developing country – as well as conventionally grown apples from national large agri-business brands and perhaps even some locally grown ones from small organic farmers who fertilize their crops with agri-food industry waste. Although organic agriculture is generally more environmentally friendly, additional considerations about its use of animal waste and fossil fuel consumption and how far these particular organic apples have traveled may complicate the making of fully conscious and consistent choices. Particularly in the absence of a "climate-friendly" or "low carbon" label, the consumer may thus be ill-equipped to make an educated decision about which apple is more sustainable overall. Not only is there often a tension between organics and the concept of a low food-mile diet (see Melchett 2007), but consumers may also find it difficult to access and process information on the net environmental impact of their purchases. This can be even more complicated if the consumer is attempting to support sustainable development in the South and farm animal welfare. In sum, political consumerist labeling may, in its need to simplify messages and devise certification mechanisms, also hide the politics of products from citizens and consumers or be unable to prioritize certain political consumer values over others, thus leaving consumers potentially confused as to which values should determine their shopping choices and also which choices to actually make.

Similar contradictions face political consumers who, concerned about the treatment of animals and the environmental effects of eating meat, decide to go vegetarian. These individuals may increase their intake of soy in order to replace lost protein in their plant-based diet. Yet while this step might solve their ethical concerns about animal welfare, it does not necessarily reduce their environmental footprint. The environmental issues associated with large-scale agriculture are well documented, and soybean production, a common food item for vegetarians, is no exception (Altieri 2009).[2] Thus, it is unclear whether a vegetarian

---

[2] The U.S.-based Organic Consumers Association has noted that Brazilian and Chinese soy is problematic due to clear-cutting (local eradication of forests), monoculture, and other unsustainable practices, and the fact that unlabeled soy from these countries are commonly found in organic tofu and soy milk sold in the United States (Organic Consumer Association 2009).

diet is necessarily more environmentally friendly than one that includes meat from animals raised on smaller, more traditional farms (*New York Times* 2009b). When agricultural practices are comparable, one kilogram of vegetables has a lower environmental impact than one kilogram of meat, as vegetarian diets require less agricultural inputs than non-vegetarian diets, using less water, energy, pesticide, and fertilizer (Marlow et al. 2009, Weber and Matthews 2008). However, when other factors such as transport and fossil fuels are considered, vegetables may lose their environmental advantage. Locally produced meat, for example, has a lower environmental impact than vegetarian food that is flown long distances, especially when the vegetarian food is out of season (Reijnders and Soret 2003, Thibert and Badami 2011). This example reveals the complexity of the decision-making required by political consumers; it is not clear that given the many dimensions of a "good" political consumer choice, they possess the capacity to accurately calculate all the consequences of their choices. As implied in the soy example, it might even be the case that dedicated political consumers will explicitly or inadvertently choose between what they believe to be two good causes – supporting animal-friendly consumption by supplementing their diet with soy and vegetarian options or eating meat in order to oppose deforestation for the sake of growing more soy beans. Quinoa is similarly problematic. Further, given that organic products are characterized by significant price premiums in most markets (see Chapter 4), consumers considering the merits of switching to a vegetarian and/or organic diet face a tangled, complex decision-making calculus involving perceptions of sustainability, ethics, and more traditional factors such as cost and quality. These factors may be in contradiction with one another and, even more problematic, consumers may lack information on the net environmental effects of each alternative.

The discussions of the tensions that may exist between the two values of environmental and animal friendliness deserve further attention. In 2005, activists pressured Whole Foods Market, the top seller of organic food in the United States, to reconsider the use of live lobster tanks (see Corson 2006). Whole Foods created a Lobster Task Force, which after some deliberations decided to stop carrying live lobsters in most of its stores. Rather than obtaining live lobsters directly from fishermen, Whole Foods now sells only frozen raw or cooked lobster from suppliers meeting specific quality standards for humane treatment, handling, and processing (Whole Foods Market 2006), though these standards do not include the safety of the lobster divers, who – in other cases – are known to suffer serious health-related illnesses (Dobbs 1998, Inter Press Service 2011). Some observers charge that this addition of links in the production chain (processing and transportation) makes this lobster *less* environmentally sustainable, and also has the effect of further distancing lobster consumers from the source of their food (Corson 2006). In the process of trying to make the product more ethical, according to these critics, Whole Foods actually made it less environmentally sustainable.

Whole Foods Market has been involved in a number of other debates that demonstrate the different and at times contradictory values pulling political consumers. The textbox on this page explores how this giant of corporate responsibility has become the target of a left-wing activist boycott and also a Republican buycott, in part for a speech given by its CEO John Mackey expressing caution about universal health care. These complexities and contradictions of political consumer values contribute to the difficulties in its practice.

Textbox: The Whole Foods Market Boycott

In a *Wall Street Journal* op-ed on August 12, 2009, Whole Foods Market CEO John Mackey stated his opposition to U.S. president Barack Obama's plans for single-payer health care. Mackey began with a quote from Margaret Thatcher that "The problem with socialism is that eventually you run out of other people's money," and closed by arguing that "A careful reading of both the Declaration of Independence and the Constitution will not reveal any intrinsic right to health care, food or shelter. That's because there isn't any. This 'right' has never existed in America." Reaction was swift. By August 14, major U.S. news outlets were reporting that liberal activists had organized a national Whole Foods boycott in order to voice opposition to Mackey's opinions (*ABC News* 2009). Later that month, it was noted that the boycott was gaining traction (*Undernews* 2009). This boycott bewildered many observers. Some wondered where boycotters would shop, since Whole Foods appears in many ways to be a model of corporate social responsibility, having been placed on *Fortune*'s list of top 100 U.S. employers every year since 1998 and being frequently named the most animal-friendly retailer by PETA. This boycott appeared to be based solely on the CEO's expressed opinions and not about Whole Foods' corporate policies or practices. But a closer look suggests that there were other issues that angered activists. The "Boycott Whole Foods" Facebook group, for instance, stated: "Whole Foods has *built its brand with the dollars of deceived progressives.* Let them know your money will no longer go to support Whole Foods' anti-union, anti-health insurance reform, right-wing activities" (emphasis added) (www.facebook.com/group.php?gid=119099537379). The mention of "anti-union activities" refers to April 2009 reports that CEO Mackey held a secret union-busting meeting with San Francisco employees, and that leaked internal Whole Foods documents reported in a left-oriented magazine listed "remaining 100% union free" as one of its top six corporate goals for the next five years (*Mother Jones* 2009). Mackey's op-ed piece, then, was not the only instigating factor at play in the boycott. Perhaps the most interesting Facebook group claims concern the sense of disillusionment among progressives. The group appears to be saying that Whole Foods, a corporation whose brand is built on consumers' perception of ethics and corporate social responsibility, has revealed its true, nonprogressive face. This episode suggests that activists and political consumers are watching corporations to make sure that their actions match their policies and are, therefore, requiring moral consistency on the part of those companies. Thus, firms with relatively good ethical records, as Whole Foods, may be punished when this is not the case. This example illustrates some of the tough choices facing political consumers. Should corporations who market themselves as socially responsible be held to higher standards? To what extent is it reasonable to expect that such corporations will have "perfect" records? And is it fair to punish such a firm for the opinions of its CEO?

Other complexities concerning political consumerism exist at the psychological level. Research has suggested that some consumers might experience a so-called "moral licensing effect," whereby individuals who engage in altruistic or "good" behavior may subsequently feel licensed or free to engage in self-indulgent or "bad" behavior (Khan and Dhar 2006). The authors posit that "virtuous" acts boost a positive self-concept, which then can be drawn upon to diminish a negative self-concept that might otherwise occur when committing a "hedonic" act. Applied to the study of political consumerism, this suggests that political consumer acts perceived as virtuous give license for consumers to engage in other actions or practices that in some way offset the potential positive effects of their (say) sustainable purchases. Indeed, this is exactly what has recently been suggested by researchers at the University of Toronto (Mazar & Zhong 2010, 494) and elsewhere (cf. Guthman 2009). In their study, participants – all university students – were asked to purchase a basket of goods in an online store composed of mostly either conventional or green products. They were then allocated money and given the option of sharing it with an unidentified person. Finally, they played a computer game that allowed them to accumulate more money. Those who had purchased green products were less likely to share their money relative to those who bought conventional products and were also more likely to lie or steal to make more money in the computer game. The authors propose that for those who buy green products, these purchases can have a licensing effect or moral offset that allows them to engage in "bad" behavior (Zhong, Liljenquist, and Cain 2009, 82).[3] Thus, if individuals consider political consumerism to be a moral act, then it is possible that

---

[3] It is best explained through the metaphor of a moral bank account: "good deeds establish moral credits that can be 'withdrawn' to 'purchase' the right to do bad deeds with impunity" (Merritt, Effron, and Monin 2010, 349). For example, a person who spent an hour at the gym may feel like he or she has earned the right to indulge in dessert, even though doing so may run contrary to his or her weight-loss goals. Moral licensing has also been applied to consumer choices. As Merritt, Effron, and Monin (2010) explain, those who have a chance to establish themselves as ethical spenders might feel licensed to indulge in frivolous purchases. Consistent with this hypothesis, Khan and Dhar (2006) found that those who first imagined doing something altruistic chose a luxury good (designer jeans) over a necessity (a vacuum cleaner) more often than those who

virtuous consumption choices may create licenses to engage in subsequent contradictory ways. The potential challenge is that the subsequent practices could cancel out the original virtuous act, possibly rendering it obsolete.[4] However, newer research indicates that these effects were moderated by existing political consumerism. While moral licensing continued to hold among people who rarely act as political consumers, it was substantially weakened among regular political consumers. This shows that there are important limits to the moral licensing effect. Buying ethically may license compensatory action or practices mostly for those who are not really committed to doing so; however, regular and committed political consumers are much more likely to behave in a way consistent with their values (Hertzman 2011). The potential problems related to moral licensing and their effects on the practice of political consumerism warrant further research (see below).

Difficulties in political consumerism are also expressed in the coordination of efforts in organizational settings. For instance, activists and institutions may want to use political consumerism to solve complex problems but either cannot agree on the degree to which problems actually can be solved or on whether sufficient support among key stakeholders can be mobilized. A good case in point that illustrates both these problems is the attempt in Europe to develop gender labeling schemes, that is standards for assessing whether products and services suit women just as much as men. Gender labels would ensure that products do not depart from and conform to male standards and needs. In the late 1990s the Nordic Council and European Commission responded to requests to investigate the possibility of a gender label by deferring to ongoing Swedish projects. In Sweden, in these years there was considerable public support for creating a labeling scheme as an innovative and voluntary mechanism to promote gender equality and counter what was considered to be state sluggishness on the issue (TCO and LO 2001, 3, Niemann 2004). These feminist scholars and activists convinced the government to appoint a parliamentary commission to investigate the possibility of using voluntary consumer power for a gender equal society (Departementserie 1998, SOU 2001, 9). The Swedish parliament debated the idea, and the large Swedish umbrella unions contributed personnel and monetary resources as well as their prestige to aid the establishment of suitable criteria and standards. They wanted to pattern the gender label after successful eco-labels initiated by the Swedish environmental movement and even one by an umbrella union (see tcodevelopment.com).

had not. By first imagining themselves behaving pro-socially, individuals felt licensed to treat themselves to the frivolous product without guilt.

[4] There were, however, several drawbacks of this experiment. First, Mazar and Zhong (2010) illustrated that green consumerism licensed morally questionable behavior in general; they did not determine whether purchasing green products decreased relevant environment-related behavior. Second, the authors did not control for existing green consumerism. While they identified a moral licensing effect for those forced to buy green products in the laboratory, it is not clear whether these results would hold for actual green consumers.

The gender label, which also involved several academic institutions, civil servants, and officials from different unions, encountered three serious problems: participants could not decide on what to certify; how to formulate the certification criteria, and key stakeholders became increasingly skeptical of the idea. The initial idea of labeling products (such as automobiles, office furniture, and pharmaceutical drugs) and what they called "services" (pension systems, insurance schemes, bank loans, etc.) as women-friendly became more complicated once the unions suggested labeling not only products but also workplaces as women-friendly. This ratcheting-up of problem-solving led to internal disagreements within the project group appointed to develop the idea into practice, and it could not find a sufficient number of companies and workplaces willing to go beyond the mandates of the Swedish Gender Equality Law and allow themselves to be certified. Powerful business leaders declared publicly their dislike of the idea. Thus, gender labeling became too contentious as a problem-solving mechanism even after the unions began to discuss the idea as a management policy and practice learning process. All this led the large unions to reevaluate their commitment to the idea. Among other difficulties, they concluded that establishing a gender label was too resource-intensive and that gender labeling workplaces was too complicated (Interview Amundsdotter 1999, DN Debatt 1999). Thus, even though this multi-stakeholder initiative met with initial public enthusiasm, the need for support from multiple actors meant that new goals were added to the problem-solving agenda which, in turn, made the creation of standards a very taxing and, in this case, unsuccessful process. Modeling all certification after eco-labeling might be, moreover, misleading as not all problems can be solved through this form of assessment and standardization.

All these examples indicate that political consumerism is at times impossible, at other times difficult to practice, and, finally, in almost constant need of campaigns that inform and sensitize people about the impact of their consumer desires and choices and give them advice and nudges about alternative consumer practices and shopping options. In short, activist networks and labeling institutions must be in place to remind consumers that they have a responsibility to take part in this form of problem-solving. Political consumers as well as the actors and institutions wanting to establish labeling schemes need not only adequate financial resources but also a well-rounded and complex understanding of the complex politics of complex products. Otherwise, they may unconsciously run the risk of prioritizing some of their values while undermining others. Moreover, labels must be created so that citizens and consumers are able to understand their content, are able to compare them across products, and trust the provided information. These insights show that the moral goal of individualized responsibility-taking can be difficult to realize in practice. Individualized responsibility-taking through political consumerism is, as discussed in this book, a relatively demanding and challenging task that requires socio-economic, educational, and knowledge resources, and for the activist networks, a series of organizing skills. At the same time, political consumers, activists, and labeling schemes need to be aware of and honest about the scope of their mission. If their goal is to limit climate change, eradicate child labor, or even to demolish glass ceilings in their own countries, solutions must not only be able to identify good products/services to target but may need to go beyond using the market of Northern consumers as their arena for political problem-solving. This may include convincing key stakeholders to take responsibility by engaging in this form of voluntary collective action. It may also involve utilizing tools beyond more conscientious consumerism, including those that represent traditional means of political participation and public policy-making.

THE MATURING OF POLITICAL CONSUMERISM IN THE 2000S

The political consumer organizational setting, its activists and even everyday political consumers are constantly in flux, testing and adopting new more suitable ideas to reach their desired goals. Which current practices can be identified as having the potential to shape and determine the future of political consumer activism and institutions? This book has discussed how the organizational settings are aware of the difficulties in practicing political consumerism. Chapter 5 highlighted their strategies in advancing political consumer causes in a historical and contemporary perspective. In this light, traditional boycotts are now often considered problematic or less effective than the buycott. But even buycotts and labeling schemes are also increasingly forced to deal with the growing complexity and trade-offs among different political consumer values (see last section). This section discusses some recent innovations in political consumerism. Some of them try to address the problematic areas in political consumerism, while others promote more discursive forms or lifestyle changes. Such innovative examples include cradle-to-cradle labeling, innovative forms of buycotts such as carrotmobs, performative and discursive political consumerism, manifestations of lifestyle politics in public institutions, and radical advertisement campaigns for lifestyle politics. Yet, as discussed below, most of these initiatives still struggle with difficulties or limitations.

Labeling Schemes of the 2000s

Labels are an important infrastructure for the practice of political consumerism because they simplify problems in order to provide individual and collective consumers with help to overcome the difficulties and complexities of their shopping choices. Yet, the process to determine label standards is not easy, and labeling bodies must often engage in the complex task of weighing the various consequences for the environment and global equity against one another (Pfaller and Lerch 2005). Other difficulties are that standards or certification criteria can vary somewhat across products and countries, that the labeling schemes must be credible and trustworthy (Crespi and Marette 2005),[5] and that they need to be perceived as most efficient when they are applied simultaneously across various products so consumers can make comparative informed choices (Horne 2009).

In line with the spirit of chain-of-custody labeling employed by the eco-labeling schemes discussed in this book, some companies have started to adopt procedures that claim to take a "cradle-to-cradle" (or C2C) approach in assessing the environmental impact of a product. This evaluation accounts for the entire lifespan of a product by ensuring that all raw materials or parts used in the manufacturing of products both are assembled in an eco-friendly way and do not produce any waste.[6] Another such initiative involves Environmental Product Declarations (EPDs), based on lifecycle assessment, that are to provide transparent, credible environmental footprint data on energy and water consumption, global warming, waste, and air emissions in a standardized manner. The hope is that they will allow consumers with different priorities to fairly compare products (O'Conner and Draper 2011). EPDs have just emerged in North America and have interested several industrial groups (www.environmentalproductdeclarations.com/Guidelines_for_EPD.html).

"Carbon footprint labeling"[7] is a similar development worth mentioning here because it attempts to bundle up different sustainability values and to process a variety of information so that consumers more easily can make better environmental choices, in this case lowering their carbon footprint. Carbon footprint or reduction labels show the amount of carbon dioxide emissions associated with the manufacturing, transportation, and disposal of a product (*Economist* 2007, carbon-label.com/the-label; O'Neil 2009). Again, in future

---

[5] Quite recently, a group of scientists examined the accuracy of MSC (Marine Stewardship Council) sustainability certification labels for Chilean sea bass using genetic analysis, and found that not all of the fish were from the certified sustainable stock on the label (Marko, Nance, and Guynn 2011, 622). They also found that while the suppliers claimed the fish to be from Chile, "they were most likely captured in Antarctic waters, but processed later in Chile." While this is only a single case, it illustrates how the complexities of the supply chain make eco-labeling difficult, and in some cases, it may lead to inaccurate claims and thus lack in credibility.

[6] As the German EPEA (Environmental Protection and Encouragement Agency) web site explains: "The Cradle to Cradle® method of production is in direct contrast to the 'Cradle to Grave' model in which material flows are formed without any conscious consideration of protecting resources. Rather than attempt to reduce the linear material flows and present-day methods of production, the Cradle to Cradle® design concept envisages their redesign into circular nutrient cycles in which value, once created, remains of worth to both man and nature." See (http://epea-hamburg.org/index.php?id=69). An example of this development comes from Desso, a Dutch carpet and textile company that recently began to let its products be evaluated according to a third-party certified C2C label (Confino 2011). For more information on this example see Desso's web site: http://www.desso.com/Desso/home/EN/EN-Cradle_to_Cradle/EN-Cradle_to_Cradle-Cradle_to_Cradleampltsupampgtampltsupampgt.html.

[7] This was originally implemented by the U.K. government in 2006 in cooperation with The Carbon Trust, an environmental organization (*Economist* 2007).

versions, the label might be developed to take the entire lifecycle of the product into account when calculating the carbon footprint.[8]

Buycotts in the 2000s

Buycotts are also developing in new ways in the 2000s and relying on social media platforms and networks to mobilize consumers into episodic events for a political consumer cause. One of the newer forms is a carrotmob, which scholars describe as "a quintessential, new millennium, new media, new social movement organization" (Pezzullo 2011, 137). The carrotmob idea came from a university student in communications in the San Francisco area who wanted to employ social media to help halt climate change. He prepared the event carefully by approaching more than twenty convenience stores in his neighborhood and choosing the one that promised to make the most investment in energy efficiency (*Guardian* 2008b). Then, he mobilized consumers through social media networks to shop at the store on one designated day. Many consumers followed this advice, which turned the idea into a critical mass episodic or short-lived event. Due to its success and media attention, the idea began spreading to other geographic and problem areas. Convenience stores, grocery stores, food markets, and restaurants have been carrotmob targets in different major U.S. cities, the United Kingdom, Argentina, Sweden, Finland, and other countries. Usually, the carrotmob entrepreneurs choose businesses that are willing to commit the highest percentage of their profits in a given day to a particular cause. Unlike most political consumerism, carrotmobs have focused on climate change problem-solving and led to the installation of energy-efficient lighting and solar panels, and other investments that aim at reducing local businesses' CO_2 emissions. The activists combine the logic both of capitalism (the value of profit-seeking) to draw businesses into investing in cause-related problem-solving and

---

[8] However, these labels also have limitations in terms of reach. A main issue is the difficulty of calculating the carbon footprint of products (Röös, Sundberg, and Hansson 2010) because there are many factors contributing to the carbon emissions of products beyond their production or transportation. As *Economist* (2007) explains, carbon footprint labels do not take into account the emissions that arise from the refrigeration/heating of products or from their actual usage. Some scholars maintain that these problems can be overcome if academic researchers become more involved in calculating the correct emission standards. At present, this work has been primarily conducted by NGOs and private business (Weidema et al. 2008). Another concern is that these labels only work when a variety of products use them so that comparisons between products can be made. For example, with frequent display, consumers would gradually learn an "understanding of their carbon number, such as they may understand their daily caloric intake" (McNamara and Grubb 2011, 21). The implication is that if carbon footprint labeling is to operate correctly, it must be adopted generally across different product categories. At the moment, carbon footprint labeling is voluntary (at least in the United Kingdom) (Gray 2010), and corporations may choose which of their products to label and how. Here, again, the suggestion has been that governments should impose these labels on corporations so that they can be used more widely and with unified measurement standards (McNamara and Grubb 2011, 17).

of social media to draw consumers with the desire to engage in individualized responsibility-taking by shopping at the designated retailer. Carrotmobs differ from most contemporary political consumer buycotts because they do not involve a bureaucratic certifying apparatus. However, even these labeling institutions are beginning to use them to promote their cause, for instance when Fairtrade Sweden participated in a carrotmob to encourage consumers to buy fairtrade flowers for Valentine's Day. The initial activity of the university student in San Francisco evolved into a nonprofit organization that offers ideas about how loosely or non-organized consumers can play a role in political consumerism. They are asked to buy products – no matter if they are labeled or not – that reward businesses "who are making the most socially responsible decisions" (carrotmob.org, accessed September 2011). These less confrontational, pro-business, family- and neighborhood-oriented, fun, and quick events are an important innovative approach to the practice and mobilization of political consumer values in the 2000s. They demonstrate how consumers can be mobilized into a critical mass of conscious shoppers that is less reliant on standard political consumer campaigning and that employs the logic of capitalism (cf. Micheletti and Stolle 2007, Micheletti 2007).

Discursive Political Consumerism in the 2000s

Although buycotting now plays a more central role in the politics of the marketplace, innovative discursive political consumerism and mobilization into lifestyle change are growing in importance. The direction of these forms of political consumerism in the 2000s includes increased use of humor, popular culture, and attention-grabbing shocking images for the purpose of mobilization, performative and event-oriented discursive political consumerism, brandjacking, and hacktivism. Some of these developments are discussed in Chapter 5, and others are addressed below.

Over the last ten years, not only has political consumer campaigning increased in general but the campaigns run by the political consumer organizational setting appear to have become more dramatic, shocking, sensational, humorous, and reliant on personal testimony and celebrity backing in order to grab consumer attention (Boström and Klintman 2011, Micheletti and Stolle 2007; see Chapter 5). This is perhaps most visible in the political consumer fight against GMOs and in the animal rights movement, which uses emotional language and imagery to draw attention to the plight of factory farm animals and to promote vegetarian lifestyles (see Chapter 5). Such developments seem to follow a pattern found in other attempts to rally citizens into political action (Valentino, Brader, and Suhay 2008). The organization People for the Ethical Treatment of Animals (PETA) is only one example of many groups that use this style of mobilization, which includes spectacular and humorous images for its fast-food restaurant campaigns targeting Burger King, Kentucky Fried Chicken, and McDonald's. PETA has shifted to employing nude images to get its message across, for example in anti-fur campaigns. PETA continues to frame its cause in this visual way. It has, for instance, attempted to launch a web site that intersperses pornographic pictures with graphic images of animals to "get people talking about veganism, and the changes they can make in their lives to support the rights of animals'" (Hartman 2011). Such steps do not come without controversy and inspire organizations beyond PETA. For instance, the opening of the world's first vegan stripclub, the Casa Diablo Gentleman's Club, provoked considerable discussion because its "vegetarianism pitch is actually part of a broader effort to overhaul vegetarianism's wimpy image and to break, once and for all, the historical ties that bind meat-eating and masculinity" (George 2008, 1). Feminist activists are critical because animal rights issues are addressed at the expense of women's rights (ibid). Such campaigns might alienate women, who account for a disproportionate amount of vegetarians, and even religious supporters of better animal treatment.

Discursive political consumerism is also taking a performative turn that brings people together face-to-face for event-oriented actions. For example, Bank of America and Wells Fargo have become targets of recent protests for their "investments in dirty energy products," as both banks are major lenders to Arch Coal, the second biggest coal company in the United States. Students of Reed College in Oregon have built a human "coal-train," and their performance disrupted business in the main bank lobby area.[9] These actions may seem close to civil disobedience and street theater; they are reminiscent of telephone and fax-bombing campaigns that have engaged protest movements historically and remind us of some political consumer anti-sweatshop actions and culture jamming. They are chosen because other forms of political participation do not easily work; boycotting coal, for example, is not an easy option so protesting or challenging companies in this fashion is an alternative. Targeting a company that is indirectly involved in an undesirable business practice, of course, also occurred within forest stewardship activism but what appears new and innovative here is the performative aspect that is used to both engage citizens in participation and to publicize complaints and demands.

Another example is the "Occupy Wall Street" movement (occupywallst.org), an action initiated by the Vancouver-based culture jamming and consumer-critical group Adbusters, which a few months before the event in 2011 posted a blog calling for people to "flood into lower Manhattan" on September 17 for a "Tahrir moment"[10] in order to take on Wall Street as the "financial Gomorah of America" without until now (2013) specifying more instrumental goals or demands. The protest is directed in part at corporations but also aims

---

[9] For evidence see: "Coal Train Visits Bank of America and Wells Fargo" (May 5, 2011), It's Getting Hot in Here, http://itsgettinghotinhere.org/2011/05/15/coal-train-visits-bank-of-america-and-wells-fargo (accessed October 2011).
[10] For the original blog message, see: http://www.adbusters.org/blogs/adbusters-blog/occupy-wallstreet.html (accessed October 2011).

at general awareness-raising about systematic inequality and the influence of money in politics and the exhibition of sheer wealth. Occupy protests have occurred worldwide and appear also to be associated with discontent over the recent economic and debt crises facing particularly North America and Europe. Whereas the mainstream media largely ignored the protests in the first weeks, new social media reported on it extensively. For example, in August 2011, the "hacktivist" Internet group Anonymous released a video encouraging people to heed to the Adbusters call and join the protest.[11] Mainstream media reported on it once police incidents involving protesters spread. Occupy Wall Street can be seen as a performative protest that involves political consumer mobilizing groups. Whether these kinds of protests will affect corporations and banks is still an open question, but it seems clear that the issue of economic justice will in some ways shape electoral politics in North America and Europe. It will be important to understand how these performative protests with clear discursive political consumer aspects will shape the character of political consumerism in the coming years.

Lifestyle Politics in the 2000s

Lifestyle political consumerism is practiced more widely in the 2000s and has reached public institutions. Again, in many cases, students are taking the lead. For instance, in May 2009, UC Berkeley students successfully protested to stop the opening of a Panda Express fast-food store on their campus because they considered it "unhealthy and unsustainable" (Arias 2009). A number of U.S. universities (Yale, Duke, UCLA, Berkeley, etc.) have also decided to remove trays and disposable packaging from their food facilities in order to reduce unnecessary consumption (Arias 2009, Cummings 2009, College Sustainability Report Card 2011). The slow food movement's spread into the university scene is another good example of this (see Chapter 5 for the origins and goals of the slow food movement). The most important advances seem to have taken place in the United States, where the movement has been reported to double every two-and-a-half years (Parking and Craig 2006). Beyond providing a vehicle to promote a new "way of life," Slow Food USA has been involved in concrete campaigns such as providing direct relief to the victims of Hurricane Katrina (Severson 2008) and the creation and development of Edible Gardens and chapters in more than twenty-two schools (Slow Food USA 2011b) and forty universities (Slow Food USA 2011a), as well as state prisons (Cernansky 2010).

---

[11] See this support post here: Adbusters (August 23, 2011), "Anonymous Joins #OCCUPYWALL-STREET," Adbusters Blog, http://www.adbusters.org/blogs/adbusters-blog/anonymous-joins-occupywallstreet.html (accessed October 2011).

The ideal of slowness emerged in Italy as a reaction to the fastness culture, in particular as represented by fast-food chains like McDonald's, and continues to expand as an alternative lifestyle and politics. The adjective "slow" is becoming a global logo for concern regarding the role of consumption in sustainable development. It is now used to trigger new thinking about how we live our lives and the role of consumption and production in it generally. Slow fish, slow fruit, slow fashion, slow money, slow cities, slow parenting, slow family life, slow travel, slow art, slow media, slow software development, and even slow public policy are some of the areas in which this new thinking is developing (*Guardian* 2009).[12] These efforts want to encourage consumers to evaluate whether they are satisfied with their general well-being, the role of consumption and paid work in it, and how they might want to change their lifestyles. They all share the goal of creating space for living differently, a life that can involve the ideals of face-to-face meetings between producers and consumers and local community solidarity. The slow efforts reflect a general critique of globalized consumer lifestyles and, in some cases, a vision of a different economic system (social economy) that reveal a resistance against the unabated progress of modern society and a negative view of neoliberal governing (Leitner, Peck, and Sheppard 2007, Parking and Craig 2006). Slowness questions the evaluation of time as a cheap economic resource and, as such, offers an alternative assessment of the labor involved in production. Some proponents hope that it will develop into an ideological framework for political consumerism and politics.

Role of Multi-Stakeholders and Government

There is another emerging approach to political consumerism in the 2000s, which emphasizes the inclusion of the multi-stakeholders and within it increasingly also government. While there has been doubt on the side of the political consumer organizational setting and political consumers more generally about governments' ability and willingness to address their issues, scholars and practitioners have arrived at a point when they believe that multiple stakeholders and particularly governments' involvement might give more legitimacy and additional tools to political consumer causes. A "triangle of change" is emerging in political consumerism that involves people, government, and business. In a way, this is a strange twist of the story. While this book started with the idea that political consumerism is a result of government inability, lack of capacity, and willingness to solve complex globalized problems by regulating business, some parts of the organizational setting discussed in Chapter 5 and activists now believe that the general political consumer cause could advance more if government and other stakeholders played a more forceful

---

[12] For more information consult: The World Institute of Slowness, http://www.theworld-instituteofslowness.com/home (accessed October 2011).

role. Activists increasingly believe that corporations, government, civil society worldwide, and consumers globally must cooperate in problem-solving. They generally view multi-stakeholder initiatives as an innovative problem-solving mechanism. However, not every such mechanism meets with activist approval.

Prominent examples of European-based multi-stakeholder initiatives that are generally supported in political consumer activist groups in the garment sector are the Ethical Trading Initiative (a tripartite institution including government, civil society, and business founded in the United Kingdom in 1998) and the Fair Wear Foundation (an international tripartite-run verification initiative founded in 1999 by the Clean Clothes Campaign, among others). Another form of multi-stakeholder effort is the U.K. public sustainable development strategy. It gives government the role of catalyzing sustainable consumption and production practices by providing necessary information and infrastructure, engaging in community-based, deliberative endeavors to change attitudes among people, business, and the media, and implementing incentives for sustainable action. This includes making government a role model by making its procurement policy more sustainable (Sustainable Development Commission 2006, see also Chapter 7). Generally, these new efforts in political consumerism reveal that it cannot stand alone and should be implemented along with more classic government control instruments and government collaboration.

THEORETICAL IMPLICATIONS OF STUDYING POLITICAL CONSUMERISM

This book explores whether and how we can understand political consumerism as a form of political participation, as the taking of political responsibility, and as a solution to complex and globalized political problems. Previous chapters have addressed criticisms from participation scholars about political consumerism as not being measurable, not sufficiently political, self-oriented in character, and unsuitable for classic definitions of political participation. While these issues have been addressed in several chapters, the remainder of this section summarizes the new theoretical insights for political participation research from this book's analysis. First and foremost, previous chapters have shown that political consumerism can be measured in survey research, and its consequences can be researched. Both quantitative analysis of longitudinal survey data as well as qualitative analysis of the organizational setting in previous chapters have shown that political consumerism has established itself in civil society, often is on the rise, and is practiced in multiple ways. Four major forms of political consumerism were identified: boycott, buycott, discursive political consumerism, and lifestyle political consumerism. Within these main forms, major innovations have taken place. Chapter 7 also explored whether political consumerism makes a difference and contributes to solving political problems. In all these ways, this book has compared and measured political consumerism with other forms of political participation and so the question that is still looming is whether political consumerism can or should be regarded as a form of political participation.

This section discusses some of the consequences of classifying political consumerism as political participation and puts in perspective what can be learned from the analysis of its political effectiveness. The first complication inherent in this broadening of political participation is a concern about stretching the concept to include many acts that might seem political, even though their political meaning may actually be debated.

The Discussion about Defining Political Participation

In order to avoid the problem of defining everything as politics, it has been suggested that motivations might be used to distinguish political participation from other forms of societal practices (Micheletti and Stolle 2010, Stolle, Hooghe, and Micheletti 2005, van Deth 2010). In other words, political and societal motivations define an act as political, while nonpolitical motivations render it nonpolitical. In terms of this book, this solution would imply that health-only-oriented vegetarians should not be considered political participants, whereas those motivated by health and animal rights issues would be (Micheletti and Stolle 2010). But this line of thinking runs into problems. It is not clear which types of motivations might qualify as political. Even the classic distinction between public and private and other-regarding versus self-regarding concerns are difficult and easily spillover into each other. Health-concerned vegetarians might, for example, easily make inquiries and demand more health-related labels in their local stores and thus foster a sense of discursive political consumerism in their community that can involve more other-oriented concerns. Moreover, many scholars have argued that the requirement of other-oriented as the only definition of political action is too theoretically demanding (see e.g., Burtt 1993, see also Micheletti 2010, Chapter 1) and just including this aspect as forming the definition of political participation would call into question several conventional acts, including joining a political organization for social or fun reasons or voting for a personal benefit one receives from a candidate. Other boundaries for distinguishing between political action and other societal practices, such as the "public-private divide" have already been questioned in feminist scholarship and are being further challenged through this research agenda. Given changes in social welfare provision that involve privatization and public-private partnerships and the globalization processes discussed in Chapter 1, it seems important not to discount other arenas as targets of political action.

A reconceptualization of political participation also has consequences for how it is measured and analyzed, particularly in survey research. Scholars would not be able to ask any more what people have done to influence politics and society, but mostly would have to focus on why citizens have done it. While

motivations are explicit in current measures of political consumerism in order
to be able to distinguish the phenomenon from other forms of consumption
(most questions ask for shopping choices based on environmental, ethical, or
political considerations), direct motivational questioning is not commonly done
for other types of participation measured in quantitative research (e.g., Why
did you go to vote?).[13]

It seems, therefore, necessary to adapt the definition of political participation
to include all acts that challenge or support *any* powerholders in society that
engage in the allocation of common resources and values. This definition would
create a more realistic picture and richer understanding of political participation in contemporary times. Political acts might be classified on a scale that
identifies them as parliamentary in orientation or outside the parliamentary
sphere; online or offline; government-targeting or multiple-targeting; electoral
or non-electoral; self-oriented or other-oriented, and so on. Moreover, they
can be compared regarding their motivations, activities, performances, and
practices as well as consequences and effectiveness. In short, the overall definition of political participation should be broader and more inclusive, and a
distinction between various types of participation and their differing consequences is a key feature of this step. While this book has begun to draw such
distinctions theoretically and empirically, it has particularly focused on identifying the participational aspects of political consumerism as one example.
This political activity is located in the non-parliamentary, non-electoral, and
multiple-targeted sphere, but it cuts across online and offline as well as other-
and self-regarding in orientations. It might also be the case that with increasing
government backing and involvement in labeling schemes and political consumer initiatives, this activity cuts across the parliamentary/non-parliamentary
divide (see Berlin 2011, 278ff. for a first discussion about this).

Obviously, further research is necessary to show whether these varieties of
political acts across these spheres have similar origins and motivations and
whether they are similarly effective in reaching their goals. Such a theoretical
and empirical research exercise has the potential to enrich our understanding
of the mechanisms of participation and non-participation and possibly even aid
public and other institutions engaged in attempts to draw more citizens into
political engagements. Some scholars hope that it will offer another interpretation of the *decline debate* (see Chapter 2) as more recent research suggests that
there is decline only in conventional and electoral forms of participation while
others are on the rise. Research conducted for this book and elsewhere shows,
however, that conventionally active people use additional tools to express their

---

[13] Of course, the vote choice literature attempts to understand the type of political motivations
behind the vote choice – whether they are candidate-based, issue-based, or policy-based to
name a few. But they are not examined along the lines of self-oriented versus other-oriented
motivations for voting (see one exception in Putnam 1993).

voices but that the emerging forms seem to do little to empower larger groups of people formerly excluded from the political discourse (however, for political consumerism see exceptions in Chapter 3 and below). Thus, the rise of political consumerism does not necessarily compensate for the decline in traditional participation.

The Effectiveness of Political Participation

The debate about political consumerism has also spurred on a discussion about the effectiveness of different forms of participation. While the effectiveness of various political acts has mostly been assumed or at best partially studied in the past, the concept of political consumerism unfolds a new approach that directs researchers to examine political effectiveness more systematically and thoroughly. The fear here has been that political consumerism suggests a simple scenario in which we become "consumers in the great hall of democracy, which we can pluck off the shelves in the shops" (Patel 2007, 312). The idea is that political consumerism might nurture the perception that democratic society can easily be achieved through monetary transactions or perhaps donations to causes (Skocpol 2003). Several chapters in the book have emphasized that effective political consumerism is not simply done in a few minutes over the shopping counter. To be most effective, it needs an active political consumer organizational setting, a conducive infrastructure and resources, and even deliberation on the part of individuals about making consumer choices and the trade-offs involved in more ethical and conventional shopping. Yet before drawing conclusions about the effectiveness of participation, political effectiveness must be defined theoretically so that it can be operationalized for empirical evaluation. In line with the broadening of the concept of political participation we suggest a broader approach to political effectiveness.

Chapter 7 proposed assessing political effectiveness as a multi-level process that goes beyond examining participation effects on public policy and includes how it sets the public agenda, shapes public opinion, public action and the media, and influences all powerholders, including corporations and governments. Effectiveness as a process must even examine whether the targeted problem has been actually solved. Our review shows mixed results. On the one hand, the political consumer organizational setting and political consumers themselves show a heightened awareness of the issues involved in the politics of products and have been able to get their issues on the broad political agenda. On the other hand, the markets for products that address these concerns are still rather small, indicating that behavioral change of political consumers lags behind. Chapter 7 has also shown that governments have tended to address political consumer issues more through their procurement policies (that is, as consumers) than through their law- and policy-makers. Political consumerism has also been indicated in increased corporate social responsibility over the last decades. However, many problems addressed by political consumer activists have not been solved and continued actions or new solutions are called for. It has also become clear that political consumerism cannot heal all wounds – it is not and most likely cannot be designed to fix all problems. In sum, when looked at as a process of affecting change in politics, political consumerism has shown some effectiveness. However, what is lacking in this study is comparative assessment of a variety of political actions repertoires. A similar process evaluation should, therefore, be applied to other forms of political participation as well as other problem-solving mechanisms (e.g., public policy) so that comparisons can be made, ideally for the same type of grievance or problem.

Political consumerism has also been criticized for lacking sufficient legitimacy, mainly for not being fully inclusive. Indeed, one could argue that it shifts the locus of political change to a place where participation opportunities are *ex ante* most unequal. In electoral democracy, one person has one vote, whereas in the market arena some people have more "votes" than others. This inequality-reinforcing mechanism is highly problematic in a world in which inequity is already rampant. Our findings have confirmed that inequality in political consumerism exists along different dimensions – somewhat along income, more-so along educational background and knowledge resources – while bridging or reversing the gap on age and gender (see Chapter 3 for more discussion). The latter point confirms that political consumerism has some mobilizational power through its everyday and informal practice, which potentially mobilizes otherwise inactive people. This is particularly true for women outside the labor force. The book also presents evidence that young people are disproportionately engaged in discursive and lifestyle political consumerism. Thus, political consumerism has the ability to draw in some of the otherwise excluded or passive groups, which also indicates some potential of less conventional forms of political participation to counterbalance the loss in electoral participation (at least numerically). Yet, inequalities in these less conventional and emerging forms also compound and reinforce the existing political inequalities in the traditional forms, as the same active people basically practice more types of participation and have thus multiple opportunities to voice their views. What should be remembered, however, is that the purpose of many political consumer acts is to eradicate worldwide inequalities (e.g. for Southern laborers in general) and to achieve better rights and protection for children, nature, and animals. Thus, although political consumerism like other forms of participation are practiced more by resource-strong citizens, many of them nevertheless aim to achieve more equality for others and, therefore, a more egalitarian world (cf. Verba 2003). It is in this sense that political consumerism fulfills the theoretical demands of the concept of individualized responsibility-taking which state that it is about answerability by those with more affluent resources to solve unaddressed political issues or inequalities that they have contributed to through their consumption patterns and practices (see Chapter 1; Young 2010).

FUTURE RESEARCH IN POLITICAL CONSUMERISM

A wide variety of disciplines are contributing to political consumerism scholarship, and many of them are cited in this book. Historians remind us that political consumerism as a form of political action has long roots (e.g., Glickman 2009, Cohen 2003, Trentmann 2009; see also Chapters 2 and 5), and sociologists, geographers, and anthropologists study closely the relationship between consumption, identity, and community (e.g., Sassatelli 2006, Isenhour 2010, Barnett, Cloke, Clarke, and Malpass 2010, Spaargaren and Oosterveer 2010). More recently, management scholars are focusing on the business case for political consumerism (see references in Chapter 7), political philosophers on its normative merits (e.g., Young 2010, Follesdal 2006), and media researchers on how it increasingly is communicated through social media networks and challenges traditional views of collective action (Dahlgren 2005, Bennett 2006, Bennett and Segerberg 2009; see also Chapter 6). Several social scientists investigate why and how political consumerism becomes institutionalized primarily in labeling schemes (Cashore, Auld, and Newsom 2004ab, 2006, Boström and Klintman 2011, Auld, Gulbrandsen, and McDermott 2008). While this research has contributed greatly to the understanding of the phenomenon, it, admittedly along with this book, has not yet completed the story.

The interdisciplinary research on political consumerism has not yet studied systematically some more exclusive and undemocratic examples. Rather it has focused primarily on publicly visible and generally "politically correct" political consumerism. Second, this research has not explored sufficiently and systematically how political consumerism is unfolding in the Global South; instead it has mostly paid attention to Northern consumer markets and Northern citizens. Third, while several analyses have highlighted the importance of mainstream media and some online tools (such as e-mails and e-mail lists) in mobilizing political consumerism, there has been little research on political consumerism practiced online and the mobilizing effect of social networking sites. Fourth, while political consumerism research has used a wide variety of research methods, including surveys, historical case studies, and comparative events, the laboratory and field experimental research on political consumerism is just starting.

Rarely Studied Cases of Political Consumerism

There are several motivations for and cases of political consumerism that this book and other research have not captured. Future scholarship should study them in detail and use them for theory-building and a more encompassing framework of political consumerism.

One important example that is completely understudied is what is called here *undemocratic political consumerism*. Available evidence offers several cases of how the market has historically been used strategically by groups and political parties and consciously by individuals to intimidate and discriminate members of ethnic, racial, and religious groups. The most well-known undemocratic example is the Nazi-led campaigns and mobilization to boycott Jewish business in the 1930s and 1940s (Encyclopædia Judaica Jerusalem 1971, www. ushmm.org/outreach/en/article.php?ModuleId=10007693). National socialist parties in Sweden, Germany, and elsewhere called on citizens to consciously choose goods (that is, buycott) so that they "don't buy Jewish" (see Micheletti 2010, chapter 2) and, in so doing, engaged in a "cold pogrom" that undermined the livelihood of hundreds of thousands of Jews. This is arguably the clearest example of the ability to use political consumerism and individualized responsibility-taking for an antidemocratic cause. Scholars have also discussed the Ku Klux Klan's (KKK) overall boycott program in the earlier parts of the 1990s as a form of market-based "racial terrorism." KKK-boycotts have targeted African-Americans as well as immigrants. Frequently, KKK activists communicated their boycott and even buycott messages in a much less obvious fashion than those addressed in this book and most research, for instance by alluding to their message in advertisements stating "100 percent" dry cleaners, grocers, and so forth and involving the code "TWK" (Trade with a Klansman), thus implying that this is a boycott choice for KKK products and producers (Blee 1991). Given these historic cases, it would seem apparent that similar less transparent campaigns might still be conducted by a variety of causes today, though they may be less public and visible than those in the past.

Furthermore, some groups might also be seen as engaging in contemporary exclusionary forms of political consumerism. One example is the case of the New Black Panther Party for Self-Defense (NBPP), which promotes black nationalism and empowerment in the United States. However, unlike the earlier Black Panther Party of the civil rights movement, the NBPP is staunchly anti-white and anti-Semitic, and is considered to be a hate organization by the Anti-Defamation League and the U.S. Commission on Civil Rights (Martin 2011, May 2011). Along with engaging in riots, protests, and most notably voter intimidation strategies in Philadelphia during the 2008 election, the group has also used political consumer tactics to advance its cause. In particular, in April 2011, the NBPP announced a "Day of Action and Unity" which called for a boycott of all non-black businesses in addition to street-wide protests and demonstrations (May 2011). This call for boycotts against white businesses is not exclusive to this particular instance (Lyons 2011). Similar activities among African-Americans were used in the 1930s in "don't buy where you can't work" boycott campaigns that were part of the civil rights era and at times included anti-Semitic and anti-white rhetoric; boycotts of Jewish-owned stores were also called (Greenberg 2006). Several scholars might see this form of engagement as an expression of identity politics and a way of empowerment for discriminated groups (Gardberg and Newburry 2010). Similarly charged examples come from India, where a Hindu, anti-Muslim party, called for an economic boycott against Muslims. The argument was that the money from

Muslim businesses is used to destroy Hindus and their religion (Narula 2003); the boycott mobilization led to the looting and burning of Muslim shops and businesses (Engineer 2003).

In whatever way these examples are categorized, this book along with almost all investigations into political consumerism and other forms of political engagement does not address systematically the fact that in some instances, citizen and/or consumer actions do not necessarily and always promote democracy or inclusion (for a short discussion, see Chapter 2). Thus, although political consumerism can empower individuals and has had given political voice to women long before suffrage, it can also be used to support exclusionary causes. Even the notion of reasonable choice that is included in the concept of individualized responsibility-taking that was formulated for this book can be interpreted in very different ways and therefore does not guarantee the underlying motivation or goal for democratic sustainable development.

There are other more recent examples of political consumerism that are understudied, primarily because political consumerism is often understood as a left-wing phenomenon. That is perhaps the case because of the way questions are posed in surveys, which often contain the words "environmental" as priming attributes of political consumerism, indicating a potentially more left-leaning agenda. It might also be that certain political consumer products often mentioned as examples such as organic products or fairtrade products are disproportionately included in the shopping lists of consumers on the political left. In part, this might be one reason why survey scholars often find that political consumers are more left-leaning in orientation (see also discussion in Chapter 3). In sum, whether in quantitative or qualitative studies, right-wing examples of political consumerism are often forgotten in the analysis, although there are several of them available. They include some more loosely organized market campaigns for selected Christian right or traditional family value-oriented causes.[14] Political consumerism seems to be developing as an important action profile here. Pro-life activists advocate "biblical stewardship" as a countervailing market-based force for what they view as left-wing dominated socially responsible investment. The American Family Association fights threats to what it believes are core family values in boycott actions (e.g., against Disney) through its "One Million Moms" and "One Million Dads" units that also employ political consumer discursive actions such as e-mailing the Kellogg Company, Calvin Klein, and other large corporations to stop their TV ads, considered to be offensive to the American family (Religioustolerance.org, American Family Association 2009ab). Thus, several corporations actually end up being criticized from both left and right for the same product but for completely different reasons (e.g., Home Depot and the Walt Disney

---

[14] For more information, see: "Boycott the Home Depot," American Family Association, http://action.afa.net/item.aspx?id=2147496231 (accessed September 26, 2011).

Company) as they are targeted by anti-sweatshop and environmental activists as well as by religious groups.[15]

This discussion points to a general weakness in the scholarship on the phenomenon of political consumerism. It reveals that several motivations for political consumer actions have not been studied and measured sufficiently in historical and contemporary cases. More and different case studies can contribute to our understanding of the variety of causes that motivate political consumerism, and whether all four forms are utilized for these causes. For example, are political consumers of understudied causes advocates of the market as a political arena; do they believe such actions are necessary because individuals must take more responsibility, or because government is not attending to their causes properly?

The question is whether these examples can be studied using the research strategies adopted in this book. First, it seems that additional survey questions are necessary to identify the worries and values that lie behind these other examples of political consumerism, as current questions do not seem to capture them properly. Furthermore, for the study of underground groups that are less eager to reveal their actions publicly for fear of reprisal, other methodological approaches must be employed. Here, more ethnographic approaches, including participant observation, seem appropriate as they find the inklings of activism in very concrete and ordinary gatherings as represented, for instance, by music festivals (cf. Virchow 2007) and perhaps even in everyday shopping encounters that can include discussions about the origin of commodities, owners of shops, and world affairs.

Political Consumerism in Developing Countries

Most scholarship on political consumerism, including this book, has focused primarily on Northern consumers and the Northern organizational setting. When scholars have turned their attention to developing countries they (we) have studied how the Global South is affected by the environmental and human rights problems generated from Northern consumption (see Chapter 1 for a discussion). This book goes, however, a bit further. Chapter 5 highlights the role that developing countries have played as initiators of the organic food movement. Chapter 7 discusses both the effectiveness of Northern-based political consumerism on the lives of Southern producers and critical Southern views about the need to reshape political consumer labeling schemes, which has led to institutional changes. Other scholarship has focused on how Mahatma Gandhi's market-based action repertoire has influenced the strategies

---

[15] For Home Depot, see Chelsea Schilling (June 23, 2010), "'Homo Depot'? Chain Hosts Kiddie Crafts at 'Gay' Festival," *WND*, http://www.wnd.com/index.php?fa=PAGE.view&pageId=170033 (accessed August 9, 2012). Note that some of these examples might be identified as breaching human rights (e.g., gay and abortion rights).

of Northern civil society (e.g., for the U.S. civil rights movement and grape boycott in the 1960s; Ingram 2004, Micheletti 2010, chapter 2). Research has addressed the way Southern countries are dealing with Northern political consumerist demands for fairtrade and organic food (e.g., Raynolds, Murray, and Wilkinson 2007), and even whether Southern citizens are political consumers (see below). More academic attention should, nevertheless, be directed at the phenomenon of political consumerism in both the Global South and Eastern Europe.

These "new consumers" are changing from a traditional lifestyle of lower consumption to one that involves eating more meat, dairy products, fast and processed foods, and less locally grown goods. They are also purchasing and using more cars, major home appliances, and energy, and shopping for a large variety of more globalized consumer goods. Some scholars claim that "consumerism has run rampant in developing countries" and that the new middle-class consumers are "gravediggers of our common and sustainable future" (see for a discussion Lange and Meier 2009, v, 5). Thus, a general fear is that this heightened consumption – combined with the already high Northern levels – will accelerate global climate change and the depletion of common pool resources. Studying social and environmental responsibility among citizens in developing countries and even Eastern Europe is, therefore, a crucial task. Fortunately, some scholars have begun this necessary research. A broad survey of consumers conducted in 2008 indicates that 87 percent of respondents in Latin America and 73 percent in the Asian Pacific region were interested in purchasing ethical products in order to contribute to social or environmental causes – this compared to 59 percent of respondents in Europe and 57 percent of those in North America (Nielsen 2008). Available research also suggests that there is a growing market for organic food in the Middle East, India, Argentina, Brazil, and Vietnam (Lillywhite, Al-Oun, and Simonsen 2010, Dittrich 2009, Rodriguez, Lacaze, and Lupin 2007, Bui 2010, 81, Portilho 2010) and that fairtrade or organic food retailers are present in Argentina, Bangladesh, Brazil, Guatemala, India, Mexico, Nepal, and Pakistan (Witkowski 2005, Dittrich 2009, Portilho 2010) but that the price and availability of labeled goods appear to be a barrier for higher levels of buycott political consumerism (Barbosa, Portilho, Wilkinson, and Dubuex 2011, 10). Brazilian scholarship (ibid.) points to several key areas for future research on how political consumerism is increasingly unfolding in the Global South. They concern the role played by the establishment of a greater number of political consumer-oriented NGOs, more media interest and public education programs on sustainable consumption, an explosion of CSR and corporate citizenship practice on the part of Southern-based corporations, and a proliferation of labeling schemes with some of them more domestic in orientation.

In the study of political consumerism in developing countries and Eastern Europe, the question is whether the phenomenon is becoming institutionalized, and if it is taking a different trajectory than in the North. In terms of its institutionalization, some developing and Eastern European countries have joined the global labeling scheme networks. China and India are well-represented in the IFOAM structure (see Chapter 5), and South Africa, Mexico, Iran, and many other developing countries are IFOAM members. Eco-labeling schemes have been established in Brazil, Hong Kong, Indonesia, and Thailand, among others, and South Africa, Korea, Latvia, and Lithuania are members of fairtrade organizations (FLO-I at www.Fairtrade.net, accessed October 2011). Some scholars believe that the Global South is developing its own version of political consumerism and point to the fact that many Southern countries have been more interested in Alternative Trade Organizations (ATO) and International Fair Trade Association (IFAT) initiatives, which are seen as more open to facilitating Southern empowerment, South-to-South production networks, and the solidarity economy movement than the fairtrade network (Wilkinson and Mascarenhas 2007). Perhaps the different trajectory can be explained as a reaction to state-led and internationally recommended liberalization policies (e.g., see Fernandes 2009, Schild 2007) or to scandals involving transnational corporations (e.g., the disputes concerning Coca-Cola in India and Colombia, Shell Oil in Nigeria, or Nike's garment manufacturing in Indonesia). How Eastern Europe with its different political historical experiences will develop its relationship to consumer society and the politics of products is another interesting development for political consumer scholars to follow. However, before commencing this broad research challenge, it is crucial that scholars from different language and political cultural contexts collate and compare their research results and attempt to find ways to develop the field of comparative political consumerism.

Role of the Internet and Social Media for Political Consumerism

Internet use is ubiquitous in political consumerism. Awareness of corporate practice and information about the politics of products is increasingly visible on web sites and social networking sites where compromising information about corporations, difficult-to-boycott products or critical consumer wit is difficult to hide. Thus, web sites and social networking sites have become important communication tools for political consumer activists. As examined in detail in Chapter 6, for the culture jam on Nike, creator Jonah Peretti used a corporate interface for the order of customized shoes and e-mail forwarding to create and spread corporate critiques and satire. A decade later, such pranks can be found on social networking sites globally. For example, in a recent protest against Dole's and Chiquita's use of fuel based on Canadian tar sands, participants did not just wear tar-covered banana costumes outside of stores selling Dole/Chiquita bananas like in conventional performative protests, but also flooded Dole and Chiquita's Facebook pages with comments. As a response to this prank, both corporations temporarily shut down comments on their Facebook pages. Furthermore, political consumerism can also be practiced online, as consumers increasingly shop for their products on the Internet and use green or ethical shopping guides for their choices. Examples include Good Guide (goodguide.com), Ethical Consumer's Best Buy Label (www.ethicalconsumer.org/ShoppingEthically/BestBuyLabel.aspx), and the shopping sites associated with the labeling schemes discussed in Chapter 5. Apps that help consumers make sustainable choices are now being developed so that this information can be delivered to mobile telephones. With a few exceptions (see Chapter 6) research on online political consumerism and its practice on social networking sites is almost nonexistent or at best ongoing. Clearly, this is an agenda for future research.

New research could shed more light on how social networking sites initiate political consumerism campaigns and mobilize people into them, create awareness and sensitize people in different ways into individualized responsibility-taking, and facilitate the sense of community that may be needed for some forms of political consumerism. It should also attempt to assess whether and how social media promote certain forms of political consumerism over others and, as discussed above on carrotmob buycotts, evaluate whether it has the capacity to innovate the four forms and even include values and groups that prefer more anonymity than those discussed in this book and elsewhere. This research can help answer questions about the importance of performances and emotion for raising awareness of and mobilization into political consumer causes and even probe more fully into the relationships between the Global South and North.

New Methodological Approaches in Political Consumerism

This book has unearthed a number of new insights into political consumerism from its use of a multi-method approach that includes most predominantly survey research but also content and discourse analysis, historical and organizational case studies, fieldwork, interviews, and the synthesis of secondary literatures. While there is a need for survey research to further the study of this phenomenon with regularly asked questions about consumption habits and studies of their roots and consequences, new research methods must be included to reinvigorate this research agenda in order for it to remain sensitive to emerging trends in citizen engagement in politics (Forbig 2005). Our suggestions here include: the development of follow-up questions to classic participation survey items; diaries of daily consumption habits; consumer focus groups; the study of political consumer campaigns in local stores through participant observation, the study of lifestyle communities; field experiments; and lab experiments on consumer choices.

1) Although survey research has reached certain limits in political consumer research, mostly because of social desirability and related overestimation of actual shopping choices (see also Chapter 3), new survey questions

could still shed more light on political consumerism, especially through follow-up questions that ask about the content, target, and goal of political action repertoires. Such information would lead to more insights about the nature of these emerging action repertoires.

2) Another tool could be the study of daily consumption diaries that capture shopping decisions and values and deliberations that shaped them. Such studies, some of which have been conducted in other disciplines, would enhance our understanding of the various motivations of political consumer decisions, in everyday practices further elucidating the maturing of these acts and the detailed motivation behind the purchase of each product.

3) In order to better understand whether and how consumers think about the politics of products, several creative research strategies can be used to determine what consumers think when they see a product of their liking, for instance a nice pair of jeans or a Disney toy. This can even include asking families and children to write letters to Santa and to relate to commercial advertisements in magazines and on television and the Internet. School children can be asked to make drawings that reflect the role of consumption in their lives, for instance by illustrating their own rooms or space. In-depth interviews and focus groups can be utilized to examine people's food, clothing, and other consumer desires and choices. Such discussions would aid the assessment of which values drive shopping decisions. People can also be asked to show their wardrobes and discuss the consumer articles in them; among other aspects such study will help scholars understand levels of consumption (number of similar products) and how people relate to them and which values they relate to different favorite items.

4) The unfolding of political consumer campaigns in local stores can help scholars to better understand how consumers are drawn into political consumerism. By using participant observation and interviews on the spot with shop assistants and consumers, the mobilization of consumers can be examined, and the availability of political consumer goods in stores can be established and consumer strategies identified.

5) Textual analysis of product catalogs, for instance for jeans, shoes, and clothing, close to gift-giving occasions (birthdays, religious holidays, etc.) can help scholars understand more fully the role of marketing in shaping consumer choice and, therefore, how consumers are influenced or feel pressured to shop to celebrate and to purchase goods targeted in commercials and ads. This can include corporate as well as political consumer marketing (see Chapter 5 for examples).

6) Lifestyle communities are only now being studied more intensely. Conventional survey research methods usually do not capture a sufficient number of lifestyle activist practices, which is why the study of such lifestyle communities would be superior. Survey and interview methods

and even participant observation can be used in order to understand how these communities create identities and how deeply or consistently the people living in them practice their values in consumption-related settings. In some cases, research of this character has been and is being conducted in other disciplines. For example, vegetarian and vegan communities or groups can be studied to penetrate how food intake can mobilize into politics.

7) An important new method in the study of political consumerism is the use of field experiments, in which for example, information on common products in stores (in collaboration with stores) can be manipulated. This could be done in toy stores or garment stores, and would generate more insights about the role of caring sensitivity for political consumer action. Such field experiments were in part conducted on eBay, where Hiscox and his co-authors manipulated whether coffee products were fairtrade certified or not in order to understand what effect the certification has on shopping decisions (Hiscox, Broukhim, Litwin, and Woloski 2011).

8) Finally, lab experiments also constitute a valuable addition to research methods. For example, the information people have available to make shopping decisions can be manipulated in multiple ways, and the advantage is that shopping decisions can be linked to previously answered survey questions. Thus, attitudinal and behavioral measures of political consumerism can be linked in a more optimal way. The moral licensing study discussed in this chapter is a good example of this research agenda, which can also include various experiments on how people can be nudged into making new choice decisions and practicing new relations with certain consumer goods.

THE FUTURE OF POLITICAL CONSUMERISM IN A NUTSHELL

Political consumerism as a form of politics and problem-solver of complex globalized problems is summarized and analyzed in this final chapter. Effective political consumerism depends on a series of developments that involve access to environmentally friendly and ethical commodities, the resources to relate to them as a form of participation, and the ability to act on one's values in a variety of settings. Whether it involves boycotts, buycotts, discursive actions, or lifestyle change, political consumerism requires an intricate coordination of stakeholders and a keen sense of the readiness for a variety of forms of action – from more individualized ones to those that demand stakeholders from different walks of life to commit to a collective mechanism for solving problems associated with globalized production and consumption. This book discusses the strengths and weakness of political consumerism as a form of participation and mechanism to solve globalized problems. Among other things, it finds that political consumerism is stronger when it includes a choice architecture, that is, information communication and institutional platforms and mechanisms (labeling schemes) that guide shopping desires and purchase.

Ironically, while political consumerism has developed as a response to responsibility claims for solving complex globalized problems, it also falls short on delivering robust global mechanisms for dealing with the complexities of production and consumption. Four basic difficulties in the practices of political consumerism have been identified in a section above: product access, available alternatives, production chains, scale of causes. Its inability so far to tackle the complex issue of climate change is one of the most telling examples regarding these difficulties here. These weaknesses make consistent practices that follow one's value system a hard task, and raise in some cases the threshold for commitment. Thus, political consumerism, just like responsibility-taking through parliamentary politics, requires a problem-solving approach that brings strange bedfellows together into compromises, bargaining, coalitions, and arrangements whose goal is to benefit all participants as well as the global common good. Political consumerism has over the years engaged different values, interests, and powerholders and is, therefore, in many ways similar to conventional political work.

As political consumerism matures and renews itself in the 2000s, it attempts to deal with a series of problems that perhaps were not envisioned in the 1990s. Keeping to the general value base of political consumerism can be a deep commitment, can require deliberation and perhaps even, as shown by certain lifestyle communities (e.g., the commitment to veganism), a number of choices that can affect how one lives one's life. On the one hand and in some cases, trade-offs between different desired values, so-called moral balancing, might be necessary. This means, for instance, that consumers might need to engage in intricate planning, budgeting, and auditing of their life in order to practice individualized responsibility-taking because they are forced to juggle desires and needs against available resources and the practice of personal values. An illustration is when shopping involves a series of trade-offs between the money in one's wallet, one's concern for the environment, and the dedication to promote social equity through fairtrade. Moral balancing is a process that also might require vetting one's moral framework against the choice architecture institutions of labeling schemes, shopping guidelines, and even Facebook groups and other social media networks that offer encouragements and examples for planning and practicing more dedicated lifestyle change. On the other hand, some political consumer actors might engage in the practice of so-called moral licensing, which means that they act responsibly in one realm but not in others. If moral licensing was widespread, political consumerism would not be able to solve global problems, as responsibility-taking in one area would simply outweigh the lack in another.

Finally, the discussions in this chapter as well as the investigations reported in this book have revealed the emergence of new instruments, mechanisms, and platforms for political consumerism in the 2000s. Importantly, there are three general lessons for future research. First, this book has uncovered serious blind spots in much research on the phenomenon. Less politically correct, undemocratic, and other rarely studied forms of political consumerism should be given their due in the scholarship. Second, a renewal of the methodological repertoire that includes studies constructed to include multi-methods approaches is necessary if scholars are to meet the new challenges to political consumer research identified in this chapter. Third, it is essential that we leave the Northern framework of political consumer studies. Northern scholars must engage more with scholars of and in newer consumer nations so that we can better understand how political consumerism is appraised, practiced, and developed in a comparative global perspective. This research should employ new methodology to study more fully the power relations involved in shopping for a better world. Lastly, it is necessary for political philosophers to study more the fundamental norms and values that lie behind political consumerism. Not only is this form of scholarship necessary for theorizing the phenomenon for further empirical study, it seems acutely important for public and governmental assessments of whether, when, and how political consumerism should be employed as a sanctioning device by governments, corporations, civic groups, and consumers. A current and highly sensitive case-in-point is the ongoing debate on the benefits of boycotts, financial divestments, and product labeling to express opposition to production practices in Israeli-occupied settlements. Clearly, the future of the research on political consumerism and its practice entail interesting and important challenges.

Bibliography

AAAS Science and Technology Policy Yearbook. Washington DC: American Association for the Advancement of Science, pp. 173–181.

ABC News 2009. "Health Care Stirs Up Whole Foods CEO John Mackey, Customers Boycott Organic Grocery Store." Available at http://abcnews.go.com/Business/story?id=8322658&page=1 (accessed October 26, 2011).

Adam Smith Institute. "53: Citizen's Charter: Consumer Rights for Public Service Users," http://adamsmith.org/80ideas/idea/53.htm (accessed February 20, 2011).

Adbusters. 2007. "Blackspot Shoes." Available at http://adbusters.org/metas/corpo/blackspotshoes/info.php (accessed November 1, 2007).

Adbusters. 2011. "Blogs: Blackspot." Available at http://www.adbusters.org/blogs/blackspot (accessed January 4, 2012).

Adbusters. "Submission Guidelines" at the Adbusters web site, http://www.adbusters.org/about/submissions (accessed December 14, 2011).

Admassie, Assefa. 2003. "Child Labour and Schooling in the Context of a Subsistence Rural Economy: Can They Be Compatible?" *International Journal of Educational Development* 23: 167–185.

Ahlber, Kerstin, and Niklas Bruun. 2010. *Public Procurement and Labour in the EU*. Summary of Report No. 3 "Upphandling och arbete i EU." Stockholm: Swedish Institute for European Policy Studies (SEIPS). http://www.sieps.se/sites/default/files/628-2010-3-summary.pdf 2up (accessed December 10, 2012).

Alger, Chadwick F. 2010. "Expanding Governmental Diversity in Global Governance: Parliamentarians of States and Local Governments," *Global Governance* 16: 59–79.

Allego, Aina. 2007. "Unequal Political Participation in Europe," *International Journal of Sociology* 37(4): 10–25.

Almond, Gabriel, and Sidney Verba. 1963. *The Civic Culture*, Princeton, NJ: Princeton University Press.

Altieri, Miguel A. 2009. "The Ecological Impacts of Large-Scale Agrofuel Monoculture Production Systems in the Americas," *Bulletin of Science Technology Society* 29(3): 236–244.

American Family Association. 2009a. "Ask Kellogg Company to Pull Ads from 'The Secret Life of the American Teenager." Available at http://onemillionmoms.com/ IssueDetail.asp?id=329, http://onemilliondads.com/victories.asp (accessed July 16, 2009).

American Family Association. 2009b. "Your Actions Make a Difference! Gap Says 'pro-Christmas' Ad to Air this Weekend." Available at http://action.afa.net/Detail. aspx?id=2147489799 (accessed October 25, 2011).

American Family Association. 2011. "The Home Depot Promotes the Homosexual Agenda." Available at http://action.afa.net/item.aspx?id=2147496231 (accessed September 26, 2011).

Amundsdottter, Eva. 1999. Interviewed by Michele Micheletti for research purposes, Stockholm, Sweden, December 23.

Andersen, Jørgen Goul, and Mette Tobiasen. 2006 (2004). "Who Are These Political Consumers Anyway? Survey Evidence from Denmark," in Michele Micheletti, Andreas Follesdal, and Dietlind Stolle (eds.), *Politics, Products, and Markets: Exploring Political Consumerism Past and Present*, New Brunswick, NJ: Transaction Press, pp. 203–222.

Andersson, Renée. 2001. Interview by Michele Micheletti. April 19. At the time of the interview, Anderson was employed as an officer within Swedish Branch of Amnesty International's section Amnesty Business. Previously she headed Dresscode, a Swedish effort to create a multi-stakeholder framework to regulate working conditions in overseas garment factories used by Swedish apparel corporations.

Animal Aid. No date. Veggie and Vegan. Available at http://www.animalaid.org.uk/h/ n/CAMPAIGNS/vegetarianism/ALL/// (accessed December 13, 2011).

Appiah, Anthony. 1991. "Racism and Moral Pollution," in Larry May and Stacey Hoffman (eds.), *Collective Responsibility: Five Decades of Debate in Theoretical and Applied Ethics*, Lanham: Rowman & Littlefield Publishers, pp. 219–238.

Appleton, A. E. (ed.) 1997. *International Environmental Law Environmental Labelling Programmes*: International Trade Law Implications and Policy Series. Boston, MA: Kluwer Law International.

Aranda, Josefina, and Carmen. Morales. 2002. "Poverty Alleviation through Participation in Fair Trade Coffee Networks: The Case of CEPCO, Oaxaca, Mexico," New York: Fair Trade Research Group (Colorado State University) / Ford Foundation.

Arendt, Hannah. 2006. *Eichmann in Jerusalem: A Report on the Banality of Evil*, London: Penguin Classics.

Argenti, Paul A. 2004. "Collaborating with Activists: How Starbucks Works with NGOs," *California Management Review* 47(1): 91–116.

Arias, Charles. 2009. "Sustainable Dining: Colleges and Corporations Take a Fresh Approach to Food," *Sustainability* 2(4): 215–220.

Armbruster-Sandoval, Ralph. 2005. "Workers of the World Unite? The Contemporary Anti-sweatshop Movement and the Struggle for Social Justice in the Americas," *Work and Occupations* 32(4): 464–485.

Aronczyk, Melissa, and Devon Powers. 2010. "Introduction: Blowing Up the Brand," in Aronczyk and Powers (eds.), *Blowing Up the Brand: Critical Perspectives on Promotional Culture*, New York: Peter Lang, pp. 1–26.

Arts, Bas. 2002. "'Green Alliances' of Business and NGOs: New Styles of Self-Regulation or 'Deal-End Roads'," *Corporate Social Responsibility and Environmental Management* 9: 26–36.

Arvidsson, Adam. 2005. "Brands: A Critical Perspective," *Journal of Consumer Culture* 5(2): 235–258.

Associated Press (AP). 2011. "PETA Lawsuit Seeks to Expand Animal Rights," October 25. Available at http://news.yahoo.com/peta-lawsuit-seeks-expand-animal-rights-222219887.html (accessed December 13, 2011).

Atkinson, Joshua. 2003. "Thumbing Their Noses at 'the Man:' An Analysis of Resistance Narratives About Multinational Corporations," *Popular Communication*, 3: 163–180.

Attaran, Amir, David R. Boyd, and Matthew B. Stanbrook. 2008. "Asbestos Mortality: A Canadian Export," *Canadian Medical Association Journal* 179(9): 871–874.

Aubin, Benoit. 2005. "Duck If You're Still Eating Foie Gras," *Maclean's* 118(48): 86.

Auld, Graeme, Lars H. Gulbrandsen, and Constance L. McDermott. 2008. "Certification Schemes and the Impacts on Forests and Forestry," *Annual Review of Environment and Resources* 33: 187–211.

Avanzi SRI Research. 2003. "Green, Social and Ethical Funds in Europe: 2003 Review," Milan: Avanzi. Available at http://www.avanzi-sri.org/pdf/complete_report_2004_final.pdf (accessed July 14, 2005).

Avanzi SRI Research. 2006. "Green, Social and Ethical Funds in Europe: 2006 Review," Milan: Avanzi. Available at http://www.avanzi-sri.org/pdf/complete_report_2006_final.pdf (accessed December 13, 2006).

Baby Milk Action. 2011. "Every Day 4000 Babies Die from Unsafe Bottle Feeding." Available at http://www.babymilkaction.org/resources/yqsanswered/yqacode.html (accessed December 2011).

Bäck, Henry, Hubert Heinelt, and Annick Magnier. 2006. *The European Mayor*, Wiesbaden, Germany: VS Verlag.

Bacon, Christopher. 2005. "Confronting the Coffee Crisis: Can Fair Trade, Organic, and Specialty Coffees Reduce Small-Scale Farmer Vulnerability in Northern Nicaragua?" *World Development* 33(3): 497–511.

Bacon, Christopher M., V. Ernesto Méndez, María Eugenia Flores Gómez, Douglas Stuart, and Sandro Raúl Díaz Flores. 2008. "Are Sustainable Coffee Certifications Enough to Secure Farmer Livelihoods? The Millennium Development Goals and Nicaragua's Fair Trade Cooperatives," *Globalizations* 5(2): 259–274.

Baek, Young Min. 2010. "To Buy or Not to Buy: Who Are Political Consumers? What Do They Think and How Do They Participate?" *Political Studies* 58(5): 1065–1086.

Baland, Jean-Marie and Cedric Duprez. 2007. "Are Fair Trade Labels Effective Against Child Labor?" Working Paper No. 144: Bureau for Research and Economic Analysis of Development, USA.

Ballinger, Jeffrey. No date. "Chronology of the Nike Sweatshop Labor Campaign 1988–1997," Center for Communication & Civic Engagement. Available at http://depts.washington.edu/ccce/polcommcampaigns/NikeChronology.htm (accessed December 21, 2009).

Balsiger, P. 2010. "Making Political Consumers: The Tactical Action Repertoire of a Campaign for Clean Clothes," *Social Movement Studies* 9(3): 311–329.

Bandy, Joe. 2004. "Paradoxes of Transnational Civil Societies Under Neoliberalism: The Coalition for Justice in the Maquiladoras," *Social Problems* 51(3): 410–431.

Banerjee, Abhijit, and Barry D. Solomon. 2003. "Eco-labeling for Energy Efficiency and Sustainability: A Meta-Evaluation of US Programs," *Energy Policy* 31(2): 109–123.

Bang, Henrik, and Eva Sørensen. 2001. "The Everyday Maker: Building Political Rather than Social Capital," in Paul Dekker and Eric M. Uslaner (eds.), *Social Capital and Participation in Everyday Life*, London: Routledge, pp. 148–161.

Barbaro, Michael, and Felicity Barringer. 2005. "Wal-Mart CEO Sets New Goals to Limit Environmental Impact," *The Tech*, October 25, 2005. Available at http://tech.mit.edu/V125/N49/49long2.html (accessed March 24, 2009).

Barbosa, Livia, Fátima Portilho, John Wilkinson, and Veranise Dubuex. 2011. "Youth, Consumption and Citizenship: The Brazilian Case." Paper presented at the International RC21 Conference, Amsterdam, July 7–9, 2011. Available at http://www.rc21.org/conferences/amsterdam2011/edocs2/Session%2030/RT30-1-Barbosa.pdf (accessed October 21, 2011).

Barham, Bradford L., Mercedez Callenes, Seth Gitter, Jessa Lewis, and Jeremy Weber. 2011. "Fair Trade/Organic Coffee, Rural Livelihoods, and the 'Agrarian Question': Southern Mexican Coffee Families in Transition," *World Development* 39(1): 134–145.

Barkman, Henric. 2008. Interview with John Womack, Clas Ohlson's chief information officer, October 9, 2008. On file with authors.

Barner, Marianne. 2007. "Be a Socially Responsible Corporation," *Harvard Business Review* 85 (7/8): 59–60.

Barnes, Samuel Henry, and Max Kaase. 1979. *Political Action: Mass Participation in Five Western Democracies*, Beverly Hills, CA: Sage.

Barnett, Clive, Paul Cloke, Nick Clarke, and Alice Malpass. 2010. *Globalizing Responsibility: The Political Rationalities of Ethical Consumption*, London: Willey-Blackwell.

Baron, David P. 2003. "Private Politics," *Journal of Economics & Management Strategy* 12(1): 31–66.

Barrett, Susan, and Colin Fudge. 1981. "Examining the Policy-Action Relationship," in Susan Barrett and Colin Fudge (eds.), *Policy and Action, Essays on the Implementation of Public Policy*. London: Methuen, pp. 3–34.

Barrientos, Stephanies. 2008. "Contract Labour: The 'Achilles Heel' of Corporate Codes in Commercial Value Chains," *Development and Change* 39(6): 977–990.

Barrientos, Stephanies, and Sally Smith. 2007. "Do Workers Benefit from Ethical Trade? Assessing codes of Labour Practice in Global Production System," *Third World Quarterly* 28(4): 713–729.

Barry, John. 2005. "Resistance is Fertile: From Environmental to Sustainability Citizenship," in D. Bell and A. Dobson (eds.), *Environmental Citizenship*, Cambridge, MA: MIT Press, pp. 21–48.

Bartlett, Christopher, Vincent Dessain, and Anders Sjöman. 2006. "IKEA's Global Sourcing Challenge: Indian Rugs and Child Labor," Harvard Business School, Case 9-906-414.

Bartley, Tim. 2003. "Certifying Forests and Factories: States, Social Movements, and the Rise of Private Regulation in the Apparel and Forest Products Fields," *Politics & Society* 31(3): 433–464.

Basu, Arnab, Nancy Chau, and Ulrike Grote. 2006. "Guaranteed Manufactured without Child Labor: The Economics of Consumer Boycotts, Social Labeling, and Trade Sanctions," *Review of Development Economics* 10: 466–491.

Basu, Kaushik, and Homa Zarghamee. 2005. "Is Product Boycott a Good Idea for Controlling Child Labor?" CAE Working Chapter #05–14. Ithaca, NY: Cornell University, Center for Analytic Economics.

Basu, Kaushik, and Homa Zarghamee. 2009. "Is Product Boycott a Good Idea for Controlling Child Labor? A Theoretical Investigation," *Journal of Development Economics* 88: 217–220.

Bauman, Zygmunt. 2002. "Foreword by Zygmunt Bauman: Individually, together," in Ulrich Beck and Elisabeth Beck-Gernsheim, *Individualization: Institutionalized Individualism and its Social and Political Consequences*, London: Sage, pp. xiv–xix.

Bauman, Zygmunt. 2007a. "Exit homo Politicus, enter homo Consumens," in Kate Soper and Frank Trentmann (eds.), *Citizenship and Consumption*, London: Palgrave Macmillan, pp. 139–153.

Bauman, Zygmunt. 2007b. *Consuming Life*, London: Polity Press.

Bauman, Zygmunt. 2008. *Does Ethics Have a Chance in a World of Consumers?* Cambridge, MA: Harvard University Press.

Baumgartner, Frank R., and Bryan D. Jones. 1993. *Agendas and Instability in American Politics*, Chicago: University of Chicago Press.

Baura, Gail Dawn. 2006. *Engineering Ethics: An Industrial Perspective*, Burlington, MA: Elsevier Academic Press.

BBC. 1998. "The Pink Pound," *BBC News*, July 31, 1998. Available at http://news.bbc.co.uk/2/hi/business/142998.stm (accessed December 10, 2012).

BBC. 2002. "Gap Hit by 'Sweatshop' Protests," *BBC News*, November, 21, 2002. Available at: http://news.bbc.co.uk/2/hi/business/2497957.stm (accessed December 2011).

BBC. 2009a. "Can Business Stay Green in a Recession?," *BBC News*. Available at http://www.bbc.co.uk/worldservice/business/2009/06/090602_timberland_swartz.shtml? (accessed December 2011).

BBC. 2009b. "'Eat Less Meat' Says Carbon Footprint Burger Chain," *BBC News*, December 8, 2009. Available at http://news.bbc.co.uk/2/hi/in_depth/8395287.stm (accessed December 2011).

BBC. 2010. "Gulf of Mexico oil leak: US sues BP over Oil Disaster," *BBC News*, December 15, 2010. Available at http://www.bbc.co.uk/news/world-us-canada-12005240, (accessed January 12, 2012).

Becchetti, Leonardo, and Marco Castantino. 2010. "Fair Trade in Italy: Too Much 'Movement' in the Shop?" *Journal of Business Ethics* 92: 181–203.

Beck, Ulrich. 1992. *Risk Society: Towards a New Modernity*, London: Sage.

Beck, Ulrich. 1997. *The Reinvention of Politics: Rethinking Modernity in the Global Social Order*, Cambridge, MA: Blackwell.

Beck, Ulrich. 1999. *World Risk Society*, Malden, MA: Polity Press.

Beck, Ulrich, and Elisabeth Beck-Gernsheim. 2002a. "Authors' Preface: Institutionalized Individualism," in Ulrich Beck and Elisabeth Beck-Gernsheim, *Individualization: Institutionalized Individualism and its Social and Political Consequences*, London: Sage, pp. xx–xxv.

Beck, Ulrich, Anthony Giddens, and Scott Lash. 1997. *Reflexive Modernization: Politics, Tradition and Aesthetics in the Modern Social Order*, Cambridge, MA: Polity Press.

Behind the Label. No date. "Conduct Unbecoming: Fighting for Freedom in Sweatshop Uniforms," http://www.behindthelabel.org/infocus.php?infocus_id=95 (accessed December 13, 2011).

Benetton. 2005. "Benetton's Position Regarding the Controversy on Mulesing between the Australian Wool Industry and PETA," September 2005. Available at http://press.benettongroup.com/ben_en/about/facts/fact1 (accessed December 4, 2012).

Benford, Robert D., and Danny L. Valadez. 1998. "From Blood on the Grapes to Poison on the Grapes: Strategic Frame Changes and Resource Mobilization in the Farm Worker Movement," paper for the Annual Meeting of the American Sociological Association, San Francisco, CA, August 21, 1998.

Benjamin, Medea. 2001. "Forward," in Archon Fung, Dara O'Rourke, and Charles Sabel, *Can We Put An End to Sweatshops? A New Democracy Forum on Raising Global Labor Standards*, Boston, MA: Beacon.

Bennett, W. Lance. 1998. "The Un-civic Culture: Communication, Identity, and the Rise of Lifestyle Politics," *PS: Political Science & Politics* 31(4): 740–761.

Bennett, Lance. 2003a. "Communicating Global Activism: Strengths and Vulnerabilities of Networked Politics," *Information, Communication & Society* 6(2): 143–168.

Bennett, Lance. 2003b. "New Media Power: The Internet and Global Activism," in Nich Couldry and James Curran (eds.), *Contesting Media Power*, pp. 17–38. Oxford: Rowman and Littelfield.

Politics," *PS: Political Science & Politics* 31(4): 740–761.

Bennett, W. Lance. 2004a. "Communicating Global Activism," in Win van de Donk, Brian Loader, Paul Nixon, and Dieter Rucht (eds.), *Cyberprotest: New Media, Citizens, and Social Movements*, London: Routledge, pp. 123–146 (reprinted from *Information, Comunication & Society*).

Bennett, W. Lance. 2004b. "Social Movements Beyond Borders: Organization, Communication, and Political Capacity in Two Eras of Transnational Activism," in Donatella della Porta and Sidney Tarrow (eds.), *Transnational Protest and Global Activism*. Boulder, CO: Rowman & Littlefield, pp. 203–227.

Bennett, W. Lance. 2006 (2004). "Branded Political Communication: Lifestyle Politics, Logo Campaigns, and the Rise of Global Citizenship," in Michele Micheletti, Dietlind Stolle and Andreas Follesdal (eds.), *Politics, Products, and Markets: Exploring Political Consumerism Past and Present*, New Brunswick, NJ: Transaction Publishers, pp. 101–127.

Bennett, W. Lance, and Taso Lagos. 2007. "Logo Logic: The Ups and Downs of Branded Political Communication," *The ANNALS of the American Academy of Political and Social Science* 611: 193–206.

Bennett, Lance, Christian Breunig, and Terri Givens. 2008. "Communication and Political Mobilization: Digital Media and the Organization of Anti-Iraq War Demonstrations in the U.S.," *Political Communication* 25(3): 269–289.

Bennett, W. Lance, and Alexandra Segerberg. 2009. "Collective Action Dilemmas with Individual Mobilization through Digital Networks," Seattle: Center for Communication and Civic Engagement, University of Washington, Paper #2.

Berlin, Daniel. 2011. "Sustainable Consumers and the State: Exploring How Citizens' Trust and Distrust in Institutions Spur Political Consumption," *Journal of Environmental Policy & Planning* 13(3): 277–295.

Berlinski, Peter. 2010. "Retailers Sustain Green Initiatives," *Private Label Magazine*, October 2010. Available at http://www.privatelabelmag.com/issues/pl-oct-2010/editorial.cfm (accessed January 4, 2012).

Bernstein, Steven, and Benjamin Cashore. 2007. "Can Non-State Global Governance be Legitimate? An Analytical Framework," *Regulation & Governance* 1(4): 1–25.

Bexell, Magdalena. 2006. "Exploring Responsibility: Public and Private in Human Rights Protection," Ph.D. thesis, Lund University.

Bexell, Magdalena, and Ulrika Mörth. 2010. *Democracy and Public-Private Partnerships in Global Governance*, Basingstoke: Palgrave Macmillan.

Bezençon, Valéry, and Sam Blili. 2009a. "Ethical Products and Consumer Involvement: What's New?" *European Journal of Marketing* 44(9): 1305–1321.

Bezençon, Valéry, and Sam Blili. 2009b. "Fair Trade Managerial Practices: Strategy, Organization and Engagement," *Journal of Business Ethics* 90(1): 95–113.

Bimber, Bruce Allen. 2003. *Information and American Democracy: Technology in the Evolution of Political Power*, Cambridge: Cambridge University Press.

Binay, Ayse. 2005. "Investigating the Anti-Consumerism Movement in North America: The Case of Adbusters," unpublished dissertation, University of Texas, 2005.

Birkland, Thomas A. 1997. *After Disaster: Agenda Setting, Public Policy, and Focusing Events*, Washington, DC: Georgetown University Press.

Birkland, Thomas A., and Regina G. Lawrence. 2002. "The Social and Political Meaning of the Exxon Valdez Oil Spill," *Spill Science & Tehcnology Bulletin* 7(1–2): 17–22.

Blais, André, Elisabeth Gidengil, Neil Nevitte, and Richard Nadeau. 2004. "The Evolving Nature of Non-Voting: Evidence from Canada," *European Journal of Political Research* 43(2): 221–236.

Blee, Kathleen. 1991. "Women in the 1920s Ku Klux Klan Movement," *Feminist Studies* 17: 57–77.

Blee, Kathleen M. 1991. *Women of the Klan: Racism and Gender in the 1920s*, Berkeley: University of California Press.

Blomqvist, Paula. 2004. "The Choice Revolution: Privatization of Swedish Welfare Services in the 1990s," *Social Policy and Administration* 23(2): 139–155.

Blood, Robert. 2000. "Activism and the Internet: From Email To New Political Movement," *Journal of Communication Management* 5(2): 160–169.

Bloomberg. 2010. "Lawsuits Surge as Gulf Oil spill Washes Ashore," May 1, 2010. Available at http://www.bloomberg.com/news/2010-04-30/bp-transocean-face-at-least-23-lawsuits-over-gulf-rig-blast-crude-spill.html, (accessed January 12, 2012).

Boersma, Franz VanderHoff. 2002. "Poverty Alleviation through Participation in Fair Trade Coffee Networks: The Case of UCIRI," Report prepared for Fair Trade Research Group, Colorado State University. Available at http://www.cfat.colostate.edu/research/one-cup-at-a-time/ (accessed April 2007).

Boje, David M. 2001. "Corporate Writing in the Web of Postmodern Culture and Postindustrial Capitalism," *Management Communication Quarterly* 14(3): 507–516.

Booth, Philip, and Linda Whetstone. 2007. "Half a Cheer for Fair Trade," *Economic Affairs* 27(2): 29–36.

Bordwell, Marilyn. 2002. "Jamming Culture: Adbusters' Hip Media Campaign Against Consumerism," in Thomas Princen, Thomas Michael Maniates and Ken Conca (eds.), *Confronting Consumption*, Cambridge, MA: The MIT Press, pp. 237–253.

Borenstein, Seth. 2010. "Oil spill is the 'Bad One' Experts Feared," Associated Press article on MSNBC web site published on April 30. Available at: http://www.msnbc.msn. com/id/36878803/ns/technology_and_science-science/# (accessed January 12, 2012).

Boris, Eileen. 2003. "Consumers of the World Unite!" in Daniel D. Bender and Richard A. Greenwald (eds.), *Sweatshop USA: The American Sweatshop in Historical and Global Perspective*, London: Routledge, pp. 203–224.

Bose, Purnima. 2008. "From Agitation to Institutionalization: The Student Anti-Sweatshop Movement in the New Millennium," *Indiana Journal of Global Legal Studies* 15: 213–240.

Boston Magazine. 2011. "Boiling Point." Available at: http://www.bostonmagazine. com/restaurants/articles/boiling_point/ (accessed October 20, 2011).

Boström, Magnus, Andreas Føllesdal, Mikael Klintman, Michele Micheletti and Mads P. Sørensen (eds.).With editorial assistance from Susanna Lindberg (2004). "Political Consumerism: Its Motivations, Power, and Conditions in the Nordic Countries and Elsewhere," Proceedings from the 2nd International Seminar on Political Consumerism, Oslo, August 26–29, 2004. Available at http://www.norden.org/pub/ velfaerd/konsument/sk/TN2005517.pdf.

Boström, Magnus, and Mikael Klintman. 2011. *Eco-Standards, Product Labeling and Green Consumerism*, London: Palgrave-Macmillan.

Bové, José, and François Dufour. 2001. *The World Is Not for Sale: Farmers Against Junk Food*, London: Verso.

Boycott Israel Goods. 2008. "The BIG Campaign: Information You Need." Available at http://www.norwichpsc.org.uk/Why_Boycott_Israel_The_BIG_campaign_ Information_you_need.pdf (accessed October 25, 2011).

BP. 2010. "BP Establishes $20 Billion Claims Fund for Deepwater Horizon Spill and Outlines Dividend Decisions." Press release, June 16, 2010. Available at http:// www.bp.com/genericarticle.do?categoryId=2012968&contentId=7062966 (accessed January 12, 2012).

Brady, Henry E. 1999. "Political Participation," in John P. Robinson, Phillip R. Shaver, and Lawrence S. Wrightsman (eds.), *Measures of Political Attitudes*, San Diego: Academic Press, pp. 735–800.

Brady, Henry E., Sidney Verba, and Kay Lehman Schlozman. 1995. "Beyond SES: A Resource Model of Political Participation," *American Political Science Review* 89(2): 271–294.

Brañas-Garza, Pablo, and María Paz Espinosa. 2006. "Altruism with Social Roots: An Emerging Literature," *Desarrollo y Sociedad* 58: 245–260.

Brea, Jen. 2007. Unpublished Report for this book: Lesotho Case Study. *Available from the authors*.

Breathing Planet. 2009. "Whirl-Mart Ritual Resistance." Available at http://www. breathingplanet.net/whirl/ (accessed August 4, 2011).

Brécard, Dorothée, Sterenn Lucas, Nathalie Pichot, and Frédéric Salladarré. 2011. "Consumer Preferences for Eco, Health and Fair Trade Labels: An Application to Seafood Product in France." Available at: http://EconPapers.repec.org/RePEc:hal: wpaper:hal-00593744 (accessed December 16, 2011).

Bromberg Bar-Yam, Naomi. 1995. "The Nestlé Boycott: The Story of the WHO/ UNICEF Code for Marketing Breastmilk Substitutes," *Mothering*: 56–63.

Brooks, Ethel C. 2007. *Unraveling the Garment Industry: Transnational Organizing and Women's Work*, Minneapolis: University of Minnesota Press.

Brown, Drusilla. 2006. "Consumer Product Labels, Child Labor, and Educational Attainment." *Contributions to Economic Analysis and Policy* 5: 1.

Buchanan, James M. 1954. "Individual Choice in Voting and the Market," *The Journal of Political Economy* 62(4): 334–343.

Bui, Thi Lan Huong. 2010. "The Vietnamese Consumer Perception on Corporate Social Responsibility," *Journal of International Business Research* 9(1): 75–87.

Bullen, Anna, and Mark Whitehead. 2005. "Negotiating the Networks of Space, Time and Substance: A Geographical Perspective on the Sustainable Citizen," *Citizenship Studies* 9(5): 499–516.

Buller, Henry, and Carol Morris. 2003. "Farm Animal Welfare: A New Repertoire of Nature-Society Relations or Modernism Re-embedded," *Sociologia Ruralis* 43(3): 217–237.

Bullert, B. J. 2000. "Strategic Public Relations, Sweatshops, and the Making of a Global Movement," Working Paper no. 14. Seattle, WA: John Shorenstein Center on the Press, Politics and Public Policy. Available at http://www.hks.harvard.edu/presspol/publications/papers/working_ papers/2000_14_bullert.pdf.

Burchell, J. and Cook, J. 2008. "Stakeholder Dialogue and Organisational Learning: Changing Relationships Between Companies and NGOs," *Business Ethics: A European Review* 17(1): 35–46.

Burma Campaign UK. 2009. "The Dirty List: Companies Supporting the Regime in Burma," Available at http://www.burmacampaign.org.uk/dirty_list/dirty_list_details.html (accessed October 8, 2009).

Burstein, Paul, and April Linton. 2002. "The Impact of Political Parties, Interest Groups, and Social Movement Organizations on Public Policy: Some Recent Evidence and Theoretical Concerns," *Social Forces* 82(2): 381–408.

Burtt, Shelley. 1993. "The Politics of Virtue Today: A Critique and a Proposal," *American Political Science Review* 87: 360–368.

Business and Human Rights Resource Centre. 2011. Available at http://www.business-humanrights.org/Home (accessed December 2011).

Buttel, Frederick H. 2000. "The Recombinant BGH Controversy in the United States: Toward a New Consumption Politics of Food?" *Agriculture and Human Values* 17(1): 5–20.

Buy Nothing Day UK. 2011. "Shop £€$$ Live More." Available at http://www.buynothingday.co.uk/ (accessed December 13, 2011).

Calkins, Laurel Brubaker. 2011. "US Forms Criminal Task Force on Deepwater Horizon Disaster." *Bloomberg*, March 7, 2011. Available at http://www.bloomberg.com/news/2011-03-07/u-s-forms-criminal-task-force-on-deepwater-horizon-disaster.html (accessed January 12, 2012).

Calo, Muriel, and Timothy A. Wise. 2005. *Revaluing Peasant Coffee Production: Organic and Fair Trade Markets in Mexico*, Medford, OR: Tufts University Global Development and Environment Institute. Available at http://ase.tufts.edu/gdae/pubs/rp/revaluingcoffee05.pdf (accessed October 20, 2011).

Cameron, D. R. 1984. "Social Democracy, Corporatism, Labour Quiescence, and the Representation of Economic Interest in Advanced Capitalist Society," in J. Goldthorpe (ed.), *Order and Conflict in Contemporary Capitalism*, Oxford: Oxford University Press, pp. 143–178.

Cammaerts, Bart. 2007. "Jamming the Political: Beyond Counter-Hegemonic Practices," *Continuum: Journal of Media & Cultural Studies* 1(21): 71–90.

Canadian Broadcasting Corporation (CBC). 2011. "Peeling Back Misleading Green Labels: Why Government Needs to Police those 'Green' Claims," March 18, 2011. Available at http://www.cbc.ca/news/business/story/2011/03/18/f-marketplace-erica-johnson-green.html (accessed June 7, 2011).

Canadian Broadcasting Corporation (CBC). 2009. "Naomi Klein." Video clip. Available at http://www.cbc.ca/video/#/Shows/1221254309/ID=1343755750 (accessed October 21, 2011).

Canadian Food Inspection Agency. 2009. "CFIA: Organic Products." Available at http://www.inspection.gc.ca/english/fssa/orgbio/orgbioe.shtml (accessed September 12, 2009).

Canadian Radio-television and Telecommunications Commission (CRTC). 2009. "Communications Monitoring Report 2009." Available at http://www.crtc.gc.ca/eng/publications/reports/policymonitoring/2009/2009MonitoringReportFinalEn.pdf (accessed October 24, 2009).

Carbon Trust. 2011. "Tesco: Case Study," Available at http://www.carbontrust.co.uk/about-carbon-trust/case-studies/carbon-reduction-label/Pages/tesco-carbon-footprinting.aspx (accessed January 12, 2012).

Caring Consumer. No date. Available at http://www.caringconsumer.com/ (accessed May 2, 2007).

Carraro, Carlo. 1999. "The Structure of International Environmental Agreements," in Carlo Carraro (ed.), *International Environmental Agreements on Climate Change*, Dordrecht: Kluwer Academic Publishers, pp. 9–26.

Carty, Victoria. 2001. "The Internet and Grassroots Politics: Nike, the Athletic Apparel Industry and the Anti-sweatshop Campaign," *Tamara: Journal of Critical Organization Science* 1(4): 34–47.

Carty, Victoria. 2002. "Technology and Counter-Hegemonic Movements: The Case of Nike Corporation," *Social Movement Studies* 1(2): 129–146.

Casey, Roseann. 2006. "Meaningful Change: Raising the Bar in Supply Chain Workplace Standards," Corporate Social Responsibility Initiative, Working Paper No. 29. Cambridge, MA: John F. Kennedy School of Government, Harvard University.

Cashore, Benjamin. 2002. "Legitimacy and the Privatization of Environmental Governance: How Non-State Market-Driven (NSMD) Governance Systems Gain Rule-Making Authority," *Governance* 15(4): 503–529.

Cashore, Benjamin, Graeme Auld, and Deanna Newsom. 2004a. *Governing through Markets: Regulating Forestry through Non-State Environmental Governance*, New Haven: Yale University Press.

Cashore, Benjamnin, Graeme Auld, and Deanna Newsom. 2004b. *Governing through Markets. Forest Certification and the Emergence of Non-State Authority*, New Haven and London: Yale University Press.

Cashore, Benjamin, Graeme Auld, and Deanna Newsom. 2006. "Legitimizing Political Consumerism: The Case of Forest Certification in North America and Europe," in Michele Micheletti, Andreas Føllesdal and Dietlind Stolle (eds.), *Politics, Products and Markets: Exploring Political Consumerism Past and Present*, New Brunswick, NJ: Transaction Publishers, p. 181–199.

Castells, Manuel. 1997. *The Rise of the Network Society*, Oxford: Blackwell.

Caul, M. C. 2005. "Rising Political Inequality in Established Democracies: Mobilization, Socio- Economic Status and Voter Turnout, 1960s to 2000," paper presented at the annual meeting of the American Political Science Association, Washington, DC, September 1–4, 2005.

Cave, Michael. 2002. "Just Change It," *Australian Financial Review*, June 14, 2002, p. 12.

Center for Applied Research (CFAR). 1999. Mini-case Study. Nike's "Just do it" Advertisement Campaign. Available at http://www.cfar.com/pdf/nikecmp.pdf, (accessed January 5, 2012).

Cernansky, Rachel. 2010. "Prison Gardens a Growing Trend, Feeding Inmates on the Inside and Food Banks on the Outside," *Planet Green*. Available at http://planetgreen.discovery.com/food-health/prison-gardens growingtrend.html (accessed September 20, 2011).

Chadwick, Andrew 2006. *Internet Politics: States, Citizens, and New Communications Technologies*, Oxford: Oxford University Press.

Chakrabarty, Sayan. 2007. "Do Social Labeling NGOs Have Any Influence on Child Labor?," in Ulrik Grote, Arnab K. Basu, and Nancy H. Chau (eds.), *New Frontiers in Environmental and Social Labeling*, Heidelberg: Physica-Verlag, pp. 59–82.

Chakrabarty, Sayan, Ulrike Grote, and Guido Luchters. 2011. "Does Social Labeling Encourage Child Schooling and Discourage Child Labour in Nepal?" *International Journal of Educational Development* 31: 483–489.

Chandler, A. D., and B. Mazlish (eds.), 2005. *Leviathans: Multinational Corporations and the New Global History*, Cambridge: Cambridge University Press.

Chapman, Roger. 2010. *Culture Wars: an Encyclopedia of Issues, Viewpoints, and Voices*, New York: M. E. Sharpe.

Charles, Daniel. 2001. *Lords of the Harvest: Biotech, Big, Money, and the Future of Food*, Cambridge, MA: Perseus Publishing.

Chavis, Larry, and Phillip Leslie. 2007. "Consumer Boycotts: The Impact of the Iraq War on French Wine Sales in the U.S.," NBER Working Chapter No. W11981. Available at: http://ssrn.com/abstract=879246 (accessed January 4, 2012).

Cherry, Elizabeth. 2006. "Veganism as a Cultural Movement: A Relational Approach," *Social Movement Studies* 5(2): 155–170.

Cherry, Elizabeth. 2010. "Shifting Symbolic Boundaries: Cultural Strategies of the Animal Rights Movement," *Sociological Forum* 25(3): 450–475.

Clark, Duncan, and Richie Unterberger. 2007. *The Rough Guide to Shopping with a Conscience*, New York: Penguin Group.

Clarke, John. 2006. "Consumers, Clients or Citizens? Politics, Policy and Practice in the Reform of Social Care," *European Societies* 8(3): 423–442.

Clarke, John. 2007. "'It's Not Like Shopping': Consumers and the Reform of Public Services," in Mark Bevir and Frank Trentmann (eds.), *Governance, Consumers and Citizens: Agency and Resistance in Contemporary Politics*, Basingstoke: Palgrave Macmillan, pp. 97–118.

Clarke, John, Janet Newman, Nick Smith, Elizabeth Vidler, and Louise Westmarland. 2007. *Creating Citizen Consumers: Changing Publics and Changing Public Services*, London: Sage.

Clary, E. Gil, and Jude Miller. 1986. "Socialization and Situational Influences on Sustained Altruism," *Child Development* 57(6): 1358–1369.

Clean Clothes Campaign (CCC). 1998. Nike Case. November. Available at http://www.cleanclothes.org/companies/nikecase.htm (accessed March 8, 2004).

Clean Clothes Campaign (CCC). 2009. "Demand Change from the World's Giant Retailers," 5 October Available at http://cleanclothes.org/betterbargain (accessed December 10, 2012).

Clean Clothes Campaign (CCC). 2010. "Call for an End to Jeans Sandblasting," Press release, November 18, 2010. Available at http://www.cleanclothes.org/media-inquiries/press-releases/call-for-an-end-to-jeans-sandblasting.

Clifton, Rita, and Esther Maughan. 2000. *The Future of Brands: Twenty-Five Visions*, London: Macmillan Press.

Clouder, Scott, and Rob Harrison. 2005. "The Effectiveness of Ethical Consumer Behaviour," in Rob Harrison, Terry Newholm, and Deirdre Shaw (eds.), *The Ethical Consumer*, London: Sage, pp. 89–104.

CNN Money. 2008. "Corporate Ties Bedevil Green Groups," November 14, 2008. Available at http://money.cnn.com/2008/11/13/news/companies/corporate_green.fortune/index.htm?postversion=2008111409 (accessed August 29, 2009).

Coca Cola Enterprise. 2009. "Clean on our Commitments: Our Journey to 2020," Available at http://www.cokecce.com/assets/uploaded_files/Coca-Cola-CRS-Report_LR.pdf (accessed January 4, 2012).

Coca Cola Enterprise. 2009/10. "Corporate Responsibility: NGOs and Public-Private Partnerships," Available at http://www.cokecce.com/pages/_content.asp?page_id=284 (accessed January 4, 2012).

Cohen, Lizabeth. 2003. *A Consumers' Republic: The Politics of Mass Consumption in Postwar America*, New York: Alfred A. Knopf.

Cohn, Avery, and Dara O'Rourke. 2011. "Agricultural Certification as a Conservation Tool in Latin America," *Journal of Sustainable Energy* 30(1): 158–186.

Colbert, Barry A., and Elizabeth C. Kurucz. 2007. "Three Conceptions of Triple Bottom Line Business Sustainability and the Role for HRM," *Human Resource Planning* 30(1): 21–29.

College Sustainability Report Card. 2011. "Official Website: Food and Recycling," Available at http://www.greenreportcard.org/report-card-2011/categories/food-recycling (accessed July 4, 2012).

Confino, Jo. 2011. "Cradle to Cradle: How Desso Has Adapted to Birth of New Movement," *Guardian*, September 1, 2011. Available at http://www.guardian.co.uk/sustainable-business/cradle-to-cradle-desso-carpet-tiles-innovation (accessed July 5, 2012).

Conford, Philip. 2001. *The Origins of the Organic Movement*. Edinburgh: Floris Books.

Connelly, Brian L., Robert E. Hoskisson, Laszlo Tihanyi, and S. Trevis Certo. 2010. "Ownership as a Form of Corporate Governance," *Journal of Management Studies* 47(8): 1561–1589.

Connor, Tim. 2004. "Time to Scale up Cooperation? Trade unions, NGOs and the International Anti-Sweatshop Movement," *Development in Practice* 14(1&2): 61–70.

Connor, Tim, and Jeff Ballinger. 2005. E-mail conversation between Jeff Ballinger (founder of Press for Change) and Tim Connor (coordinator of the Oxfam Australian Community Aid Program and Nike Boycott). *On file with authors.*

Conover, Pamela Johnston. 1995. "Citizen Identities and Conceptions of the Self," *Journal of Political Philosophy* 3(2): 133–165.

Conroy, Michael E. 2007. *Branded: How the 'Certification Revolution' is Transforming Global Corporations*, Gabriola Island, B.C.: New Society Publishers.

Constance, Douglas H., and Alessandro Bonanno. 2000. "Regulating the Global Fisheries: The World Wildlife Fund, Unilever, and the Marine Stewardship Council," *Agriculture and Human Value* 17: 125–139.

Consumers International. 1999. *Green Claims: Environmental Claims on Products and Packaging in the Shops: An International Study*, London: Consumers International. Available at http://www.consumersinternational.org/media/316960/green%20claims%20environmental%20claims%20on%20products%20and%20packaging%20in%20the%20shops%20an%20international%20study.pdf (accessed October 20, 2011).

Consumers International and International Institute for Environment and Development. 2005. "From Bean to Cup: How Consumer Choice Impacts Upon Coffee Producers and the Environment," London: CI/IIED. Available at http://pubs.iied.org/pdfs/G00265.pdf (accessed October 20, 2011).

Conway, M. Margaret. 2001. "Women and Political Participation," *PS: Political Science and Politics* 34(2): 231–233.

Cook, Gary, David Downes, Brennan Van Dyke, and John B. Weiner. 1997. *Applying Trade Rules to Timber Ecolabeling: A Review of Timber Ecolabeling and the WTO Agreement on Technical Barriers to Trade*. Geneva: Center for International Environmental Law (CIEL).

Cooper, J., and Weaver, K. D. 2003. *Gender and Computers: Understanding the Digital Divide*, Mahwah, NJ: Princeton University.

Cooper, Tim. 2005. "Slower Consumption: Reflections on Product Life Spans and the 'Throwaway Society'," *Journal of Industrial Ecology* 9(1–2): 51–67.

Co-operative Bank 2010. "Ethical Consumerism Report 2010." Available at http://www.goodwithmoney.co.uk/assets/Uploads/Documents/Ethical-Consumerism-Report-2010.pdf?token=22ab1dc5bff9385338c0cbe955c93be219d4cc39|1306941042#PDFP (accessed June 1, 2011).

Corson, Trevor. 2006. "Lobsterpalooza: Boiling Point," *Boston Magazine*, July 2006. Available at http://www.bostonmagazine.com/articles/2006/06/boiling-point/ (accessed July 3, 2012).

Cotton Campaign. 2011. "Switzerland, UK Accept NGO Complaint Against EU Companies Profiting from Uzbek Child Labor." Available at http://www.cottoncampaign.org/2011/03/29/switzerland-uk-accept-ngo-complaint-against-eu-companies-profiting-from-uzbek-child-labor (accessed May 28, 2011).

Courville, S. 2006. "Organic standards and certification," in Kristiansen, P., Taji, A., Reganold, J. (eds.), *Organic Agriculture: a Global Perspective*, Ithaca, NY: Comstock Publishing Associates, pp. 201–219.

Cowan, Emily. 2009. "Belt-Tightening Shoppers Budgeting for Green, Surveys Show," Sustainable Brands official web site. Available at http://www.sustainablebrands.com/news_and_views/articles/belt-tightening-shoppers-budgeting-green-surveys-show (accessed January 5, 2012).

Cowe, Roger, and Simon Williams. 2000. "Who are the Ethical Consumers?" Published by The Cooperative Bank.

Cravey, Altha J. 2004. "Students and the Anti-Sweatshop Movement," *Antipode* 36(2): 203–208.

Crespi, John, and Stéphan Marette. 2005. "Eco-labelling Economics: Is Public Involvement Necessary?" in Signe Krarup and Clifford S. Russell, eds. *Environment, Information and Consumer Behavior*, Cheltenham, UK: Edward Elgar Publishing, pp. 93–107.

Cummings, Glen. 2009. "Turning Higher Education from the Inside Out: A Qualitative Study of Four Colleges and Universities That Made Green Happen," dissertation in Education for the University of Pennsylvania. Available at http://www2 .presidentsclimatecommitment.org/pcc/newsletter/img/22/cummingsdissertation.pdf (accessed September 22, 2011).

Curbday.com. Available at Giveyourstuffaway.com (formally curbday.com).

Curtis, J. E., D. E. Baer, and E. G. Grabb. 2001. "Nations of Joiners: Explaining Voluntary Association Membership in Democratic Societies," *American Sociological Review* 66/6: 783–805.

Dahan, Nicolas M., Jonathan P. Doh, and Jennifer Oetzel. 2010. "Corporate NGO Collaboration: Co-Creating New Business Models for Developing Markets," *Long Range Planning* 43: 326–342.

Dahl, Richard. 2010. "Green Washing: Do You Know What You're Buying?" *Environmental Health Perspectives* 118(6): A246–A252.

Dahlgren, Peter. 2005. "The Internet, Public Spheres, and Political Communication: Dispersion and Deliberation," *Political Communication* 22: 147–162.

Daily Caller. 2011. "New Black Panthers to Protest 'Non-Blacks,'" Available at http:// dailycaller.com/2011/04/19/newblack-panthers-to-protest-non-blacks/ #ixzz1JyLopQjn (accessed October 24, 2011).

Daily Mirror. 2011. "Child Labour Call over Cotton Firms." Available at http://www .mirror.co.uk/news/latest/2010/12/12/child-labour-call-over-cotton-firms-115875– 22779270 (accessed May 28, 2011).

Dalton, Russell. 2008. *The Good Citizen: How a Younger Generation is Reshaping American Politics*, Washington, DC: CQ Press.

Dana, Frank. 2003. "Consumer-Labor Campaigns–Where Are the Workers in Consumer-Worker Alliances? Class Dynamics and the History of Consumer-Labor Campaigns," *Politics & Society* 31: 363–379.

Darby, Kim, Marvin T. Batte, Stan Ernst, and Brian Roe. 2008. "Decomposing Local: a Conjoint Analysis of Locally Produced Foods," *American Journal of Agricultural Economics*, 90(2): 476–486.

Davidson, Debra J., and William R. Freudenburg. 1996. "Gender and Environmental Risk Concerns: A Review and Analysis of Available Research," *Environment and Behavior* 28(3): 302–339.

Davidson, Wallace N. III, Abuzar El-Jelly, and Dan L. Worrell. 1995. "Influencing Managers to Change Unpopular Corporate Behavior through Boycotts and Divestitures: A Stock Market Test," *Business and Society* 34(2): 171–196.

Davies, Iain A. and Lynette J. Ryals. 2010. "The Role of Social Capital in the Success of Fair Trade," *Journal of Business Ethics* 96(2): 317–338.

Davies, Iain A., Bob Doherty, and Simon Know. 2010. "The Rise and Stall of a Fair Trade Pioneer: The Café Direct Story," *Journal of Business Ethics* 92(1): 127–147.

De Sadeleer, Nicolas. 2009. "Environmental Justice and International Trade Law," in Jonas Ebbesson and Phoebe Okowa (eds.), *Environmental Law and Justice in Context*, Cambridge: Cambridge University Press, pp. 447–461.

De Schutter, O. 2008. "Corporate Social Responsibility European Style," *European Law Journal* 14(2): 203–236.

de Tocqueville, Alexis. 2000 [1848]. *Democracy in America.* Edited by J. P. Mayer, translated by George Lawrence. New York: Perennial Classics.

Dearing, James W. and Everett M. Rogers. 1996. *Agenda-setting,* London: Sage.

Deckha, Maneesha. 2008. "Disturbing Images: PETA and the Feminist Ethics of Animal Advocacy," *Ethics and the Environment* 13(2): 35–76.

Dee, Jonathan. 2004. "Reverend Billy's Unholy War," *New York Times Magazine.* Available at http://www.nytimes.com/2004/08/22/magazine/22BILLY.html?page wanted=all (accessed January 2012).

Deegan, Denise. 2001. *Managing Activism,* London: Kogan Page/PRIA.

Deibert, Ronald J. 2000. "International Plug 'n Play? Citizen Activism, the Internet, and Global Public Policy," *International Studies Perspectives* 1: 255–272.

Delanty, Gerard. 2000. *Citizenship in a Global Age: Society, Culture, Politics,* Buckingham: Open University Press.

Delli Carpini, Michael X., and Scott Keeter. 1996. *What Americans Know about Politics and Why It Matters,* New Haven: Yale University Press.

Demeter. Demeter web site: http://www.demeter.net/ (accessed 25 February 2011).

Department for Environment, Food, and Rural Affairs (DEFRA). 2009. "Public Sector Food Procurement Initiative." Available at http://www.defra.gov.uk/farm/policy/ sustain/procurement/health.htm (accessed March 28, 2009).

Department for International Development (DFID). 2008. "Ethical compass." Version archived 23 April 2010. Available at http://collections.europarchive.org/tna/ 20100423085705/dfid.gov.uk/ethicalcompass/

Dery, Mark. 1990. "The Merry Pranksters And the Art of the Hoax," *New York Times.* Available at http://www.nytimes.com/1990/12/23/arts/the-merry-pranksters-and-the-art-of-the-hoax.html?pagewanted=all&src=pm (accessed in January 2012).

Dery, Mark. 1993. "Culture Jamming: Hacking, Slashing, and Sniping in the Empire of Signs," New Jersey: Open Magazine Pamphlet Series, 1993.

DeWinter-Schmitt, Rececca. 2007. "Business as Usual? The Mobilization of the Anti-Sweatshop Movement and the Social Construction of Corporate Identity." Doctoral dissertation. American University (AU), School of International Service (SIS), Washington, D.C. Available at: http://books.google.se/books/about/Business_ as_usual_The_mobilization_of_th.html?id=09xQ1CLDaqUC&redir_esc=y (accessed December 13, 2011).

Dholakia, Ruby R., and Nikhilesh Dholakia. 2001. "Social Marketing and Development," in Paul N. Bloom and Gregory T. Gundlach (eds.), *Handbook of Marketing and Society,* Thousand Oaks, CA: Sage, pp. 486–505.

Digital Journal Reports. 2011. "PETA to Launch Porn Website to Promote Vegan Lifestyle," Available at http://www.digitaljournal.com/article/310658 (accessed October 20, 2011).

Dimbleby, Jonathan. 2001. "Foreword" in Conford, Philip. 2001. *The Origins of the Organic Movement.* Edinburgh: Floris Books 2001, pp. 11–14.

Dimitri, Carolyn, and Catherine Greene 2002. "Recent Growth Patterns in the U.S. Organic Foods Market/AIB-777," Washington, DC: Economic Research Service/USDA.

Dingwerth, Klaus. 2008. "North-South parity in Global Governance: The Affirmative Procedures of the Forest Stewardship Council," *Global Governance* 14(1): 53–71.

Dittrich, Christoph. 2009. "The Changing Food Scenario and the Middle Classes in the Emerging Megacity of Hyderabad, India," in H. Lange and L. Meier (eds.), *The New Middle Classes: Globalizing Lifestyles, Consumerism and Environmental Concern*, London: Springer, pp. 269–280.

DN Debatt. 1999. "Omrimliga krav på jämställdhet." Op-ed colume written by eight CEOs in Swedish business life. *Dagens Nyheter* December 14, p. 2 in Part A of the newspaper.

Dobbs, David J. 1998. "Lobster in the Rain Forest: The Political Ecology of Miskito Wage Labor and Agricultural Deforestation," *Journal of Political Ecology* 5(1998): 83–107.

Dobson, Andrew 2003. *Citizenship and the Environment*, New York: Oxford University Press.

Dobson, Chad, Head of Consumer Choice Council. 2000. Interview by Michele Micheletti, Washington, DC February, 22.

Dodds, David J. 1998. "Lobster in the Rain Forest: The Political Ecology of Miskito Wage Labor and Agricultural Deforestation," *Journal of Political Ecology* 5(1998): 83–107.

Doepke, Matthias, and Fabrizio Zilibotti. 2010. "Do International Labor Standards Contribute to the Persistence of the Child Labor Problem?" *Journal of Economic Growth* 15: 1–31.

Doherty, Dob, and Sophi Tranchell. 2005. "New Thinking in International Trade? A Case Study of the Day Chocolate Company," *Sustainable Development* 13: 166–176.

Dollar, David, and Aart Kraay. 2002. "Growth is Good for the Poor," *Journal of Economic Growth* 7(2): 195–225.

Dollar, David, and Aart Kraay. 2004. "Trade, Growth, and Poverty," *The Economic Journal* 114(493): F22–F49.

Domask, Joseph. 2003. "From Boycotts to Partnership: NGOs, the Private Sector, and the World's Forests," In *Globalization and NGOs: Transforming Business, Government, and Society* (eds.), Jonathan P. Doh and Hildy Teegen. Westport, CT: Praeger Publishers.

Downs, Anthony. 1957. *An Economic Theory of Democracy*, New York: Harper-Collins.

Departementserie. 1998:49. *Jämställdhetsmärkning. Konsumentmakt för ett jämställt samhälle*, Stockholm: Fritzes kundtjänst. Cabinet Government Report.

Duncombe, Stephen. 2002. *Cultural Resistance Reader*, New York: Verso.

Duvall, Benjamin. 2012. "Deepwater Horizon oil spill made a city's worth of air pollution." *EarthSky*, Available at http://earthsky.org/earth/deepwater-horizon-oil-spill-made-a-citys-worth-of-air-pollution (accessed July 10, 2012).

Dworkin, Ronald. 2000. *Sovereign Virtue: The Theory and Practice of Equality*, Cambridge, MA: Harvard University Press.

Easton, David. 1965. *A Systems Analysis of Political Life*, New York: Wiley.

Ebbesson, Jonas and Phoebe Okowa (eds.) 2009. *Environmental Law and Justice in Context*, Cambridge: Cambride University Press.

Economist. 2003. "Non-governmental Organisations and Business: Living with the Enemy," 378(8336): 55–56.

Economist. 2006. "Voting with your Trolley," 381(8507): 81–84.

Economist. "Not the Label: Why Adding 'Carbon Footprint' Labels to Foods and other Products is Tricky," Available at http://www.economist.com/node/9184296 (accessed May 22, 2007).

Edmonds, Eric V. 2007. "The Economics of Consumer Actions against Products with Child Labor Content," in Hugh Hindman (ed.), *Child Labor World Atlas*, New York: ME Sharpe Publishers, pp. 1–10.

Edmonds, Eric V., and Nina Pavcnik. 2002. "Does Globalization Increase Child Labor? Evidence from Vietnam," NBER Working Paper No. 8760. Available at http://www.nber.org/papers/w8760 (accessed January 5, 2012).

Edvardsson, Bo, and Bo Enquist. 2006. "Quality Improvement in Governmental Services: The Role of Change Pressure Exerted by the 'Market'," *TQM Magazine* 18(1): 7–21.

Edvardsson, Bo, Bo Enquist, and Michael Hay. 2006. "Values-Based Service Brands: Narratives from IKEA," *Managing Service Quality* 16(3): 230–246.

Eiderström, Eva. 1998. "Ecolabels in EU Environmental Policy" in Jonathan Golub, (ed.), *New Instruments for Environmental Policy in the EU*, London: Routledge, pp. 190–215.

Eiderström, Eva. 2000. Interview by Michele Micheletti. January 12. Eiderström is Head of the Good Environmental Choice Unit at the Swedish Society for Nature Conservation (Naturskyddsföreningen) and editor of the unit's magazine "Bra Miljöval."

Eiderström, Eva. 2002. Interview via e-mail by Michele Micheletti. December 2.

Eliasoph, Nina. 1998. *Avoiding Politics: How Americans Produce Apathy In Everyday Life*, New York: Cambridge University Press.

Elliot, Kimberly Ann and Richard B. Freeman. 2000. "White Hats or Don Quixotes? Human Rights Vigilantes in the Global Economy," Paper for the National Bureau of Economic Research Conference on Emerging Labor Market Institutions http://www.asiafloorwage.org/documents/Resources-onwages/Background_reading/ONActivism/White%20Hats%20or%20Don%20Quixotes.pdf.

Elliott, Kimberley Ann and Richard Freeman. 2003. *Can Labor Standards Improve Under Globalization?* Washington D.C: Institute for International Economics cited in O'Rourke, Dara 2005. "Market Movements: Nongovernmental Organization Strategy to Influence Global Production and Consumption," *Journal of Industrial Ecology* 9(1–2): 115–128.

Encyclopaedia Britannica. "Individualism" on Encyclopaedia Britannica web site, available at http://www.britannica.com/EBchecked/topic/286303/individualism (accessed February 22, 2011).

Encyclopædia Judaica Jerusalem. 1971. "Boycott, Anti-Jewish," Jerusalem: Keter Publishing House, Band 4, pp. 1278–80.

Engineer, Ashgharali. 2003. *The Gujarat Carnage*, Hyderabad: Orient Blackswan.

Enis, Ben M. 1973. "Deepening the Concept of Marketing," in *Journal of Marketing* 37: 57–62.

Equal Exchange. 2008. "Fair Trade Coffee Leader Unconvinced by Procter & Gamble Announcement," Available at http://www.equalexchange.com/fair-trade-coffee-leader-unconvinced-by-p-g-announcement (accessed April 13, 2008).

Erdmenger, Christoph (ed.) 2003. *Buying Into the Environment: Experiences, Opportunities and Potential for Eco-procurement*, Sheffield, UK: Greenleaf Publishing.

Erwin, Patrick. 2011. *Corporate Codes of Conduct: The Effects of Code Content and Quality on Ethical Performance*, EJournal of Business Ethics 99 (4): 535–548.

Esping-Andersen, Gøsta. 1990. *The Three Worlds of Welfare Capitalism*, Cambridge: Polity Press.

Esty, D.C., M. Levy, T. Srebotnjak, and A. de Sherbinin. 2005. *Environmental Sustainability Index: Benchmarking National Environmental Stewardship*, New Haven: Yale Center for Environmental Law & Policy.

Esty, Daniel C. 2008. "Rethinking Global Environmental Governance to Deal with Climate Change: The Multiple Logics of Global Collective Action," *Faculty Scholarship Series*, Paper 427. Available at http://digitalcommons.law.yale.edu/fss_papers/427 (accessed October 20, 2011).

Ethical Consumer. 2008. "Ethiscore.org Company Information: Procter & Gamble," Available at http://www.ethiscore.org/company.aspx?id=19291 (accessed April 6, 2008).

Ethical Consumer. 2009. "Consumer Boycotts," Available at http://www.ethicalconsumer.org/Boycotts/currentboycotts.aspx (accessed October 8, 2009).

European Commission. 2007. "Green vs. Sustainable Procurement," Available at http://ec.europa.eu/environment/gpp/green_vs_sustainable.htm (accessed November 29, 2007).

European Commission. 2008. "EU organic Logo turns over New Leaf," Available at http://ec.europa.eu/unitedkingdom/press/frontpage/100208_en.htm (accessed January 9, 2012).

European Commission. 2008. "Public Procurement for a Better Environment," Available at http://eur-lex.europa.eu/LexUriServ/LexUriServ.do?uri=COM:2008:0400:FIN:EN:PDF (accessed January 5, 2012).

European Commission. 2009. "Green Public Procurement," Available at http://ec.europa.eu/environment/gpp/index_en.htm. (accessed September 12, 2009).

European Commission. 2010. "Buying Social: A Guide on Taking Account of Social Considerations in Public Procurement," Available at http://ec.europa.eu/social/BlobServlet?docId=6457&langId=en (accessed January 5, 2012).

European Commission. 2011. "Consultation on the proposed EU Green Public Procurement (GPP) criteria for indoors lighting and tissue paper and the related technical background reports," Available at http://ec.europa.eu/environment/consultations/gpp_en.htm (accessed June 14, 2011).

European Commission, DG Health, and Consumers, No date a. "Genetically modified food and feed," http://ec.europa.eu/food/food/biotechnology/index_en.htm (accessed February 20, 2011).

European Commission, DG Health, and Consumers, No date b. "Rules on GMOs in the EU: Labelling," http://ec.europa.eu/food/food/biotechnology/gmo_labelling_en.htm (accessed February 20, 2011).

European Commission. No date. "Organic farming: Logo," http://ec.europa.eu/agriculture/organic/eu-policy/logo_en (accessed 30 March 2011).

European Fair Trade Association. 2007. "Fair Trade 2007: New facts and Figures from an Ongoing Success Story," Available at http://www.european-fair-trade-association.org/efta/Doc/FT-E-2007.pdf (accessed September 12, 2009).

European Greens. 2007. "National election results since 1979," Available at http://www.europeangreens.org/cms/default/dok/167/167260.national_election_results_since_1979@en.htm (accessed October 16, 2007).

European Union, No date. "Treaty establishing the European Economic Community, EEC treaty – original text (non-consolidated version)," http://europa.eu/legislation_summaries/institutional_affairs/treaties/treaties_eec_en.htm (accessed February 20, 2011).

European Values Survey. 2002 ff. Data Set available at http://www.european socialsurvey.org/

EUROSIF. 2010. "European WRI study 2010," Paris: Eurosif. Available at http://www.eurosif.org/images/stories/pdf/Research/Eurosif_2010_SRI_Study.pdf.

Exxon Valdez Oil Spill Trustee Council. Available at http://www.evostc.state.ak.us/ (accessed September 28, 2005).

Fair Trade Center. 2003. "Företagens ansvar: Vad förväntas av det ansvarsfulla företaget?" Stockholm: Fair Trade Center. Available at http://www.fairtradecenter.se/sites/default/files/ansvar_o.pdf (accessed January 8, 2012).

Fairtrade Federation. 2005. "Fair Trade Trends in North America and the Pacific Rim." Available at www.fairtradefederation.org/ht/a/GetDocumentAction/i/278 (accessed June 18, 2009).

Fairtrade Foundation. 2008. "London, the Fairtrade capital of the world." Available at http://www.fairtrade.org.uk/press_office/press_releases_and_statements/october_2008/london_the_fairtrade_capital_of_the_world.aspx (accessed March 28, 2009).

Fairtrade Foundation. 2012. "Fairtrade and Coffee," Commodity Briefing, Available at http://www.fairtrade.org.uk/includes/documents/cm_docs/2012/F/FT_Coffee_Report_May2012.pdf (accessed July 18, 2012).

Fairtrade International. 2011. Official web site. Available at http://www.fairtrade.net/ (accessed October 26, 2011).

Fairtrade Labelling Organizations International (FLO). 2005a. "FLO International: Coffee." Available at http://www.fairtrade.net/sites/products/coffee/markets.html (accessed February 23, 2005).

Fairtrade Labelling Organizations International (FLO). 2005b. "Labelling initiatives," Available at http://www.fairtrade.net/sites/contact/ni.html (accessed July 15, 2005).

Fairtrade Labelling Organizations (FLO) International. 2005c. Personal communication with Cornelia Halm, June 9, 2005.

Fairtrade Labelling Organizations International (FLO). 2007a. "FLO International: Coffee." Available at http://www.fairtrade.net/coffee.html (accessed October 18, 2007).

Fairtrade Labelling Organization (FLO) International. 2007b. "FLO International: Impact Areas." Available at http://www.fairtrade.net/impact_areas.html (accessed November 21, 2007).

Fairtrade Labelling Organization (FLO) International. 2009. "Fairtrade: Leading the Way. FLO Annual Report 2008–09," Available at http://www.fairtrade.net/fileadmin/user_upload/content/2009/resources/FLO_ANNUAL_REPORT_08-09.pdf (accessed July 1, 2009).

Fairtrade Towns. 2011. "Second International Fair Trade Towns Newsletter – August 2011," Available at http://www.fairtradetowns.org/news/second-international-fair-trade-towns-newsletter-august-2011second-international-fair-trade-towns-news letter-august-2011second-international-fair-trade-towns-newsletter-august-2011 second-interna/?lang=fr (accessed January 5, 2012).

Farm Animal Rights Movement (FARM) Underground. "Get Active." Available at http://www.farmunderground.org/getactive/waystogetactive.html (accessed August 2, 2011).

Featherstone, Liza, and United Students Against Sweatshops (USAS). 2002. *Students against Sweatshops: The Making of a Movement*. New York: Verso.

Fernandes, Leela. 2009. "The Political Economy of Lifestyle. Consumption, India's New Middle Class and State-Led Development," in Hellmuth Lange and Lars Meier (eds.), *The New Middle Classes. Globalizing Lifestyles, Consumerism and Environmental Concern*, London: Springer, pp. 219–236.

Ferraro, Paul J., Toshihiro Uchida, and Jon M. Conrad. 2005. "Price Premiums for Eco-Friendly Commodities: Are 'Green' Markets the Best Way to Protect Endangered Ecosystems?" *Environmental & Resource Economics* 32: 419–438.

Ferrer-Fons, Mariona. 2004. "Cross-National Variation on Political Consumerism in Europe: Exploring the Impact of Micro-Level Determinants and Its Political Dimension," paper for the ECPR Joint Sessions, Uppsala, Sweden. Workshop 24, "Emerging repertoires of political action: toward a systematic study of post-conventional forms of participation."

FIBL, IFOAM. 2011. The World of Organic Agriculture. Statistics & Emerging Trends 2011. Available at http://www.organic-world.net/fileadmin/documents/yearbook/2011/world-of-organic-agriculture-2011.pdf (accessed December 10, 2012).

Financial Times. 2010. "US Reveals Criminal Probe over BP spill," *Financial Times*, June 1. Available at http://www.ft.com/cms/s/0/ae859ef2-6d96-11df-b5c9-00144feabdc0.html#axzz2GDlJJVVu,, (accessed January 12, 2012).

Finer, Herman. 1941. "Administrative Responsibility in Democratic Government," *Public Administration Review* 1(4): 335–350.

Finkel, Steven, and Muller, Edward. 1998. "Rational Choice and the Dynamics of Collective Political Action: Evaluating Alternative Models with Panel Data," *American Political Science Review* 92(1): 37–94.

Fix, Michael E., and Karen Tumlin. 1997. "Welfare Reform and the Devolution of Immigrant Policy," Washington DC: The Urban Institute. Available at http://www.urban.org/UploadedPDF/anf15.pdf.

Follesdal, Andreas. 2006 (2004). "Political Consumerism as Chance and Challenge," in M. Michelletti, A. Follesdal and D. Stolle (eds.), *Politics, Products, and Markets: Exploring Political Consumerism Past and Present*, New Brunswick, NJ: Transaction Publishers, pp. 3–20.

Forbig, Joerg (ed.). 2005. *Revisiting Youth Political Participation: Challenges for Research and Democratic Practice in Europe*. Strasbourg: Council of Europe Publishing.

Forest Stewardship Council (FSC). 2005. "What's new." Available at http://www.fsc.org/en/whats_new/news/news/40 (accessed October 20, 2007).

Forest Stewardship Council (FSC). 2007. "FSC National Initiatives." Available at http://www.fsc.org/keepout/en/content_areas/33/1/files/5_1_2_2007_06_29_FSC_National_Initiatives.pdf (accessed June 13, 2007).

Forest Stewardship Council (FSC). 2010. "Synergies: Annual report 2010," Bonn: FSC International Center. Available at http://www.fsc.org/fileadmin/general-assembly/Documents/Announcements_PDF/English/FSC-Annual_Report_2010-ENG.pdf (accessed December 10, 2012).

Forest Stewardship Council (FSC). 2011. "Global FSC certificates: Type and distribution." Bonn: FSC International Center. Available at http://www.fsc.org/fileadmin/
web-data/public/document_center/powerpoints_graphs/facts_figures/2011-06-
15-Global-FSC-Certificates-EN.pdf (accessed December 10, 2012).

Forest Stewardship Council (FSC). No date. "FSC and Fairtrade Dual Certification
Pilot Project." Available at http://www.fsc.org/dualcert.html (accessed August 10,
2011).

Forno, Francesca, and Carina Gunnarson. 2010. "Everyday Shoppers Fight the Mafia
in Italy," in Michele Micheletti and Andrew McFarland (eds.), *Creative Participation: Responsibility-taking in the Political World*, Bolder, CO: Paradigm Publishers,
pp. 101–124.

Forno, Francesca, and Luigi Ceccarini, L. (2006). "From the street to the shops: The
Rise of New Forms of Political Action in Italy," *South European Society & Politics*,
11(2), 197–222.

Forstater, Maya, Jeannette Oelschlaegel, Philip Monaghan, Alan Knight, Meera Shah,
Bjarne Pedersen, Luke Upchurch and Priya Bala-Miller. 2007. "What Assures Consumers on Climate Change?" Available at www.accountability.org (accessed July 31,
2009).

Fortune. 2002. "Crisis in a Coffee Cup." Available at http://money.cnn.com/magazines/
fortune/fortune_archive/2002/12/09/333463 (accessed December 12, 2007).

Fortune. 2003. "Global Five Hundred: The World's Largest Corporations." 148/2:
106–126.

Fraser, Nancy. 2005. "Reframing Justice in a Globalized World," *New Left Review* 36:
69–88.

Frese, Michael. 2008. *Fairer Handel. Eine ökonomische und marketingorientierte Anal-
yse des Fairen Handels*. Saarbrücken: VDM Verlag.

Fridell, Gavin. 2004. "The University and the Moral Imperative of Fair Trade Coffee,"
Journal of Academic Ethics 2(1): 141–159.

Fridell, Gavin. 2007. *Fair-Trade Coffee: The Prospects and Pitfalls of Market-Driven
Social Justice*, Toronto: University of Toronto Press.

Fridell, Gavin. 2009. "The Co-operative and the Corporation: Competing Visions of
the Future of Fair Trade," *Journal of Business Ethics* 86(supplement 1): 81–95.

Fridell, Mara. 2008. "With Friends Like These: the Corporate Response to Fair Trade
Coffee," *Review of Radical Political Economies* 40(1): 8–34.

Friedman, Milton. 1963. *Capitalism and Freedom*. Chicago: University of Chicago
Press.

Friedman, Milton. 1970. "The Social Responsibility of Business is to Increase its Profits." *New York Times Magazine*, September 13. Available at: http://www.colorado
.edu/studentgroups/libertarians/issues/friedman-soc-resp-business.html   (accessed
January 8, 2011).

Friedman, Monroe. 1999. *Consumer Boycotts: Effecting Change Through the Marketplace and the Media*. New York: Routledge.

Friedman, Monroe. 2006 (2004). "Using Consumer Boycotts to Stimulate Corporate Policy Changes: Marketplace, Media, and Moral Considerations," in Michele
Micheletti, Andreas Follesdal and Dietlind Stolle (eds.), *Politics, Products, and Markets: Exploring Political Consumerism Past and Present*, New Brunswick, NJ: Transaction Press, pp. 45–62.

Friström, Anders. 2001. Interview by Michele Micheletti. 16 January. Friström is a staff member of the Swedish Society for Nature Conservation (Naturskyddsföreningen) and one of the people who started the Good Environmental Choice labeling scheme.

FSC-Watch. 2008. "FSC's Greenwash at the Convention for Biodiversity," May 29, 2008. Available at http://www.fsc-watch.org/archives/2008/05/29/FSC_s_greenwash_at_t (accessed December 10, 2012).

Gabszewicz, Jean J., and Tanguy Van Ypersele. 1996. "The Voting Mechanism and Market Allocation: A Note," *European Journal of Political Economy* 12(4): 723–727.

Gale, Fred. 2002. "Caveat Certificatum: The Case of Forest Certification" in Thomas Princen, Michael Maniates and Ken Conca (eds.), *Confronting Consumption*, Cambridge: The MIT Press, pp. 275–299.

Gandenberger, Carsten, Heiko Garrelts, and Diana Wehlau. 2011. "Assessing the Effects of Certification Networks on Sustainable Production and Consumption: The Cases of FLO and FSC," *Journal of Consumer Policy* 34: 107–126.

Gap, Inc. 2003. "Social Responsibility Report 2003." Available at http://www .unglobalcompact.org/system/attachments/7614/original/Gap_Social_Responsibility_ Report_2003.pdf?1282019231 (accessed March 24, 2009).

Gardberg, Naomi, and William Newburry. 2010. "Who Boycotts Whom? Marginalization, Company Knowledge, and Strategic Issues," *Business & Society*. Available at http://bas.sagepub.com/content/early/2010/03/04/0007650309352507.full. pdf+html (accessed October 24, 2011).

Gee, Kevin A. 2010. "Reducing Child Labour through Conditional Cash Transfers: Evidence from Nicaragua's red de Proteccion Social," *Development Policy Review* 28: 711–732.

Gendron, Corinne, Véronique Bisaillon, and Ana Isabel Otero Rance. 2009. "The Institutionalization of Fair Trade: More than Just a Degraded Form of Social Action," *Journal of Business Ethics* 86(supplement 1): 63–79.

George, Lianne. 2008. "'Go Veg! Get Girls!'" *MacLean's*. Available at http://www. macleans.ca/culture/lifestyle/article.jsp?content=20080306_98967_98967 (accessed September 20, 2011).

Gerber, Jurg, Eric L. Jensen with the collaboration of Jiletta L. Kubena. 2007. *Encyclopedia of White-Collar Crime*, Westport, CT: Greenwood Press.

Gereffi, Gary. 2001. "Beyond the Producer-Driven/Buyer-Driven Dichotomy: The Evolution of Global Value Chains in the Internet Era," *IDS Bulletin* 32(3): 30–40.

Gereffi, Gary, Ronie Garcia-Johnson, and Erika Sasser. 2001. "The NGO-Industrial Complex," *Foreign Affairs* 125: 56–65.

Gibson, Clark C., Margaret A. McKean, and Elinor Ostrom. 2000. *People and Forests: Communities, Institutions, and Governance*, Cambridge, MA: MIT Press.

Giddens, Anthony. 1990. *The Consequences of Modernity*, Stanford, CA: Stanford University Press.

Giddens, Anthony. 1996. *Durkheim on Politics and the State*, Cambridge: Polity Press.

Gill, Lesley 2007. "'Right There with You': Coca-Cola, Labor Restructuring and Political Violence in Colombia," *Critique of Anthropology* 27: 235–260.

Gillberg, Minna. 1999. *From Green Image to Green Practice: Normative Action and Self-Regulation*, Lund: Lund Studies in Sociology of Law.

Gilmore, James H. B., and Joseph Pine, II. 2000. *Markets of One*, Boston, MA: Harvard Business Publishing.

Giovanucci, Daniele. 2003a. "Emerging Issues in the Marketing and Trade of Organic Products," in Organization for Economic Co-operation and Development (ed.), *Organic Agriculture: Sustainability, Markets and Policies*, Cambridge, MA: CABI Publishing, pp. 187–199.

Giovannucci, Daniele. 2003b. "Emerging Issues in the Marketing and Trade of Organic Products," published as a monograph on the proceedings of the OECD Workshop on Organic Agriculture, September 2002. Paris: OECD.

Giovannucci, Daniele with Freek Jan Koekoek. 2003c. *The State of Sustainable Coffee: A Study of Twelve Major Markets*, Philadelphia:

Giovannucci, Daniele, and Stefano Ponte. 2005. "Standards as a New Form of Social Contract? Sustainability Initiatives in the Coffee Industry," *Food Policy* 30: 284–301.

Giugni, Marco, and Florence Passy. 1998. "Social Movements and Policy Change: Direct, Mediated, or Joint Effect." Available at http://www.nd.edu/~dmyers/cbsm/vol1/geneva98.pdf (accessed January 5, 2012).

Giugni, Marco, Doug McAdam, and Charles Tilly (eds.) 1999. *How Social Movements Matter*, Minneapolis: University of Minnesota Press.

Glickman, Lawrence B. 2005. "Boycott Mania: As Business Ethics Fall, Consumer Activism Rises," *The Boston Globe*. Available at http://www.boston.com/news/globe/editorial_opinion/oped/articles/2005/07/31/boycott_mania/ (accessed April 2007).

Glickman, Lawrence B. 2009. *Buying Power: A History of Consumer Activism in America*, Chicago, IL: Chicago University Press.

Global Ecolabelling Network. 2005. "Product category list of ecolabelling programs worldwide." Available at http://www.gen.gr.jp/product.html (accessed July 14, 2005).

Global Exchange. 2003. Nike Campaign. Available at www.globalexchange.org/campaigns/sweatshops/nike/faq.html (accessed February 2004).

Global Exchange. 2008. "Advocacy Groups Persuade Procter & Gamble to Offer Fair Trade Certified Coffee." Available at http://www.globalexchange.org/campaigns/fairtrade/coffee/Millstonevictory.html (accessed April 13, 2008).

Global Exchange. No date. "Proctor & Gamble campaign." Available at: http://www.globalexchange.org/fairtrade/coffee/proctorgamble (accessed September 7, 2011).

Global Greens. 2007. "Green Parties Around the World." Available at http://www.globalgreens.org/index.php (accessed October 16, 2007).

Global Market Institute Poll. 2005. "More Than a Third of all Consumers Boycott at Least one Brand." Available at http://www.gmi-mr.com/about-us/news/archive.php?p=20050829 (accessed June 2009).

Globe and Mail. 2011. "Child-Labour Free Cacao Almost Impossible." Available at http://www.theglobeandmail.com/life/the-hot-button/child-labour-free-cocoa-almost-impossible-nestl-head-says/article1953439/?from=sec434 (accessed March 2011).

Globescan 2011. "Shopping Choices Can Make a Positive Difference to Farmers and Workers in Developing Countries: Global Poll," Press Release by Globescan, available at http://www.globescan.com/commentary-and-analysis/press-releases/press-releases-2011/94-press-releases-2011/145-high-trust-and-global-recognition-makes-fairtrade-an-enabler-of-ethical-consumer-choice.html (accessed July 18, 2012).

Goldberg, Cheryl. 1999. "Don't Buy Where You Can't Work," in Lawrence B. Glickman (ed.), *Consumer Society in American History: A Reader*. Ithaca, NY: Cornell University Press, pp. 241–227.

Goldberg, Ray A. and Jessica D. Yagan. 2007. "McDonald's Corporation: Managing a Sustainable Supply Chain," *Harvard Business School*, Case 9-907-414.

González Cabañas, Alma A. 2002. *Evaluation of the Current and Potential Poverty Alleviation Benefits of Participation in the Fair Trade Market: The Case of Unión La Selva, Chiapas, Mexico*. New York: Fair Trade Research Group (Colorado State University) / Ford Foundation.

Goul Andersen, Jørgen, and Mette Tobiasen. 2001. *Politisk forbrug og politiske forbrugere. Globalisering og politik i hverdagslivet*. Aarhus: Magtudredningen, Aarhus Universitet.

Granovetter, Mark. S. 1973. "The Strength of Weak Ties," *American Journal of Sociology* 78: 1360–1380.

Gray, Louise. 2010. "Food Labels to Show 'Carbon Footprint' under Government Plans," *The Telegraph*, January 5, 2010. Available at http://www.telegraph.co.uk/earth/earthnews/6936658/Food-labels-to-show-carbon-footprint-under-Government-plans.html (accessed July 5, 2012).

Greathead, Scott. 2002. "The Multinational and the 'New Stakeholder': Examining the Business Case for Human Rights," *Vanderbilt Journal of Transnational Law* 35(2): 719–727.

Green America. No date. Fair Trade Your Supermarket. Available at http://www.fairtradeyoursupermarket.org (accessed December 13, 2011).

Green Money Journal. 2011. "The 2010 Report on Socially Responsible Investing Trends in the United States," Summer 2011 online issue. Available at http://www.greenmoneyjournal.com/article.mpl?newsletterid=55&articleid=804 (accessed December 10, 2012).

Greenberg, Cheryl. 2006 (2004). "Political Consumer Action: Some Cautionary Notes from African American History," in Michele Michelleti, Andreas Follesdal and Dietlind Stolle (eds.), *Politics, Products, and Markets: Exploring Political Consumerism Past and Present*, New Brunswick, NJ: Transaction Publishers, pp. 63–83.

Greenberg, Josh, and Graham Knight. 2004. "Framing Sweatshops: Nike, Global Production, and the American News," *Media Communication and Critical/Cultural Studies* 1(2): 151–175.

Greenpeace. 2008. "Holding the line with FSC." Amsterdam: Greenpeace International. Available at http://www.greenpeace.org.uk/files/pdfs/forests/HoldingtheLine_LR_ENG.pdf (accessed December 10, 2012).

Greenpeace. 2009. "No need for condoms: GE corn can do the job," January 12, 2009, Greenpeace India web site. Available at http://www.greenpeace.org/india/en/news/no-need-for-condoms-ge-corn (accessed December 10, 20102).

Gruere, G. P., and S. R. Rao. 2007. "A Review of International Labeling Policies of GM Food to Assess India's Proposed Rule," *The Journal of Agrobiotechnology and Management and Economics (ABioForum)* 10(1): 51–64.

Guardian. 2001. "From Diatribe to Dialogue," February 12, 2001. Available at http://www.guardian.co.uk/society/2001/feb/12/voluntarysector.comment1 (accessed January 9, 1212).

Guardian. 2004. "Who is the Fairest of Them All?" November 24, 2004 Available at: http://www.guardian.co.uk/ethicalbusiness/story/0,,1358196,00.html (accessed December 9, 2007).

Guardian. 2007a. "Are Air Miles and Organic Food Compatible?" Greenliving blog, no date Available at: http://www.guardian.co.uk/environment/ethicallivingblog/2007/sep/06/areairmilesandorganicinco (accessed on October 20, 2011).

Guardian. 2007b. "Gap plans 'Sweatshop Free' Labels." November 4, 2007 Available at http://www.guardian.co.uk/business/2007/nov/04/3 (accessed May 27, 2010).

Guardian. 2008a. "Ethical Business: Norway Ejects Mining Giant Rio from Its Pension Portfolio." September 9, 2008 Available at http://www.guardian.co.uk/business/2008/sep/09/riotinto.ethicalbusiness (accessed October 20, 2011).

Guardian. 2008b. "Meet the CarrotMob." September 18, 2008. Available at: http://www.guardian.co.uk/environment/2008/sep/18/activists.carrotmobbing (accessed October 21, 2011).

Guardian. 2009. "Tesco Becomes UK's First Retailer to Display Carbon Footprint on Milk," August 17, 2009. Available at http://www.guardian.co.uk/environment/2009/aug/17/tesco-milk-carbon-footprint.

Guardian. 2010. "Tesco Launches Recycled Clothing Collection," March 2, 2010. http://www.guardian.co.uk/lifeandstyle/green-living-blog/2010/mar/02/tesco-ethical-fashion-range (accessed June 7, 2011).

Guardian. 2011a. "Tesco – Britain's Biggest Retailer Targets Green Growth." May 26, 2011 Available at http://www.guardian.co.uk/sustainable-business/britain-biggest-retailer-green-growth (accessed June 8, 2001).

Guardian. 2011b. "Fairtrade Hallmark Sets the Gold Standard," published on February 14, 2011. Available at http://www.guardian.co.uk/lifeandstyle/2011/feb/14/fairtrade-gold.

Guardian. 2012. "Kalle Lasn: The Man Who Inspired the Occupy Movement." November 5. Availabe at http://www.guardian.co.uk/world/2012/nov/05/kalle-lasn-man-inspired-occupy (accessed December 6, 2012).

Gulbrandsen, Lars H. 2006. "Creating Markets for Eco-Labelling: Are Consumers Insignificant?" *International Journal of Consumer Studies* 30(5): 477–489.

Gudbrandsen, Lars H. 2009. "The Emergence and Effectiveness of the Marine Stewardship Council," *Marine Policy* 33(4): 654–660.

Guthman, Julie. 2009. "Unveiling the Unveiling: Commodity Chains, Commodity Fetishism, and the 'Value' of Voluntary, Ethical Food Labels." In Jennifer Bair (ed.) *Frontiers of Commodity Chain Research*. Stanford University Press, pp. 190–206.

Hall, Peter, and Katheleen Thelen. 2009. "Institutional Change in Varieties of Capitalism," *Socio-Economic Review* 7: 7–34.

Hallam, David. 2003. "The Organic Market in OECD Countries: Past Growth, Current Status and Future Potential," in Organization for Economic Co-operation and Development (ed.), *Organic Agriculture: Sustainability, Markets and Policies*, Cambridge, MA: CABI Publishing, pp. 179–186.

Halpin, Darren. 2004. *The Australian Organic Industry: A Profile*, Canberra: Australian Government Department of Agriculture, Forestry, and Fisheries.

Hamilton, Clive and Elizabeth Mail. 2003. *Downshifting in Australia. A Sea-Change in the Pursuit of Happiness*. Discussion Paper Number 50. The Australia Institute. https://www.tai.org.au/documents/dp_fulltext/DP50.pdf.

Hamm, Ulrich, Friederike Gronefeld, and Darren Halpin. 2002. *Analysis of the European Market for Organic Food*, Aberystwyth, Wales: University of Wales Aberystwyth School of Management and Business.

Hampel, Jürgen, Uwe Pfenning, Matthias Kohring, Alexander Goerke, and Georg Ruhrmann. 2001. "Biotechnology Boom and Market Failure: Two Sides of the German Coin," in G. Gaskell and M. Bauer (eds.), *Biotechnology 1996 to 2000: The Years of Controversy*, London: Science Museum, pp. 191–203.

Handelman, Jay M. 1999. "Culture Jamming: Expanding the Application of the Critical Research Project," *Advances in Consumer Research*, 26: 399–404.

Hansen, Allan Dreyer, and Jon Jay Neufeld. 1999. "Demokrati og studiet af demokratiske identiter," paper for the Conference of the Nordic Political Science Association, Workshop "Nye politisk identitet og institutioner i hverdagen politiske praksis," Uppsala, Sweden, August 19–21.

Harbin, James L., and Patricia Humphrey. 2010. "Whole Foods Market, Inc.," *Journal of Case Research in Business and Economics* 2(May 2010): 1–19.

Hardin, Russell. 2009. *How Do You Know? The Economics of Ordinary Knowledge*, Princeton: Princeton University Press.

Harold, Christine. 2004. "Pranking Rhetoric: 'Culture Jamming' as Media Activism," *Critical Studies in Media Communication* 21(3): 189–211.

Harrison, Ann. 1993. "Openness and Growth: A Time-Series, Cross-Country Analysis," *Journal of Developmental Economics* 93(2): 419–447.

Harrison, Ann, and Jason Scorse. 2010. "Multinationals and Anti-Sweatshop Activism," *American Economic Review* 100(1): 247–273.

Hartman, Kim I. 2011. "PETA to Launch Porn Website to Promote Vegan Lifestyle," Digital Journal Reports, August 23, 2011. Available at http://www.digitaljournal .com/article/310658 (accessed October 20, 2011).

Harvey, David. 2007. *A Brief Introduction to Neoliberalism*, New York: Oxford University Press.

Hassel, Anke. 2008. "The Evolution of a Global Labor Governance Regime," *Governance: An International Journal of Policy, Administration, and Institutions* 21(2): 231–251.

Haste, H., and Amy Hogan. 2006. "Beyond Conventional Civic Participation, Beyond the Moral-Political Divide: Young People and Contemporary Debates about Citizenship," *Journal of Moral Education* 35(4): 473–493.

Hawkins, Brett, Vincent Marando, and George Taylor. 1971. "Efficacy, Mistrust and Political Participation: Findings from Additional Data and Indicators," *The Journal of Politics* 33(4): 1130–1136.

Häyhitö, Tapio, and Rinne, Jarmo. 2008. *Net Working/Networking: Citizen Initiated Internet Politics*, Tampere: University of Tampere.

Hemphill, Thomas A. 2002. "The White House Apparel Industry Partnership Agreement: Will Self-Regulation Be Successful?" *Business and Society Review* 104(2): 121–137.

Henderson, David. 2008. "Fair Trade is Counterproductive- and Unfair," *Economic Affairs*, 28(3), pp. 62–64.

Hertzman, Yale. 2011. "Moral Licensing and Political Consumerism," Honours B.A. thesis. Montreal, QC: McGill University.

Herzog, Harold A., and Lauren L. Golden. 2009. "Moral Emotions and Social Activism: The Case of Animal Rights," *Journal of Social Issues*, 65(3): 485–498.

Hillemans, Carolin. 2003. "UN Norms on the Responsibilities of Transnational Corporations and Other Business Enterprises with Regard to Human Rights," *German Law Journal* 4(10): 1065–1080.

Hilton, Matthew. 2007. "The Banality of Consumption," in Kate Soper and Frank Trentmann (eds.), *Citizenship and Consumption*, London: Palgrave Macmillan, pp. 87–103.

Hirdman, Yvonne. 1983a. "Den socialistiska hemmafrun," in Brita Åkerman, Yvonne Hirdman, and Kajsa Pehrsson (eds.), *Vi kan, vi behövs! Kvinnorna går samman i egna föreningar*, Stockholm: Akademilitteratur AB, pp. 11–59.

Hirdman, Yvonne. 1983b. *Magfrågan: Mat som mål och medel*, Stockholm: Rabén and Sjögren.

Hiscox, Michael. 2007. "Fair Trade as an Approach to Managing Globalization," Memo prepared for the conference on Europe and the Management of Globalization. Princeton, NJ: Princeton University.

Hiscox, Michael, Michael Broukhim, Clare Litwin, and Andreas Woloski. 2011. "Consumer Demand for Fair Labor Standards: Evidence from a Field Experiment on eBay," Available at SSRN:http://papers.ssrn.com/sol3/papers.cfm?abstract_id=1811788 (accessed October 25, 2011).

Hoffman, Martin. 1978. "Psychological and Biological Perspectives on Altruism," *International Journal of Behavioral Development* 1(4): 323–339.

Holbrook, Allyson L., and Jon A. Krosnick. 2010. "Social Desirability Bias in Voter Turnout Reports: Tests Using the Item Count Technique," *Public Opinion Quarterly* 74(1): 37–67.

Holmberg, Hans-E. 1999. *Konsumentundersökning om ekologiska produkter/KRAV*, Stockholm: LUI marknadsinformation AB.

Holt, Douglas B. 2002. "Why Do Brands Cause Trouble? A Dialectical Theory of Consumer Culture and Branding," *Journal of Consumer Research* 29: 70–90.

Holt, Douglas B. 2005. "How Societies Desire Brands: Using Cultural Theory to Explain Brand Symbolism," in S. Ratneshwar and David Glen Mick (eds.), *Inside Consumption, Consumer Motives, Goals, and Desires*, London, UK: Routledge, pp. 273–291.

Holzer, Boris. 2007. "Framing the Corporation: Royal Dutch/Shell and Human Rights Woes in Nigeria," *Journal of Consumer Policy* 30(3): 281–301.

Holzer, Boris, and Mads Sørensen. 2001. *Subpolitics and Subpoliticians*, Arbeitspapier 4 des SBF 536 Reflexive Modernisierung. Munich: University of Munich.

Holzer, Boris, and Mads P. Sorensen. 2003. "Rethinking Subpolitics: Beyond the 'Iron Cage' of Modern Politics," *Theory Culture Society* 20(2): 79–102.

Hooghe, Marc, and Dietlind Stolle. 2003. *Generating Social Capital: Civil Society and Institutions in Comparative Perspective*, New York: Palgrave.

Horne, Ralph E. 2009. "Limits to Labels: The Role of Eco-labels in the Assessment of Product Sustainability and Routes to Sustainable Consumption," *International Journal of Consumer Studies* 33(2): 175–182.

Howard, Marc, James Gibson, and Dietlind Stolle. 2006. "*United States Citizenship, Involvement, Democracy (CID) Survey*," 2006 [Computer file]. ICPSR04607-v1. Washington, DC: Georgetown University, Center for Democracy and Civil Society (CDACS) [producer]; Ann Arbor, MI: Inter-university Consortium for Political and Social Research [distributor].

Hudson, Mark and Ian Hudson. 2009, "Fair-trade Coffee: The Prospects and Pitfalls of Market Driven Social Justice: Brewing Justice: Fair-trade Coffee, Sustainability, and Survival: Fair-trade: The Challenges of Transforming Globalization," *Historical Materialism* 17(2): 237–252.

Human Rights Watch. 2001. "World Report 2001," New York: Human Rights Watch. Available at http://www.hrw.org/wr2k1/.

Human Rights Watch. 2004. "Turning a Blind Eye: Hazardous Child Labor in El Salvador's Sugarcane Cultivation," New York: Human Rights Watch. Available at http://www.hrw.org/en/node/12067/section/13.

Huneke, M. E. 2005. "The Face of the Un-Consumer: An Empirical Examination of the Practice of Voluntary Simplicity in the United States," *Psychology and Marketing* 22: 527–550.

Hunter, Lori M., Alison Hatch, and Aaron Johnson. 2004. "Cross National Gender Variation in Environmental Behaviors," *Social Science Quarterly* 85(3): 677–694.

Huybrechts, Benjamin. 2010. "Fair Trade Organizations in Belgium: Unity in Diversity?" *Journal of Business Ethics* 92(2): 217–240.

Hynes, Maria, Scott Sharpe, and Bob Fagan. 2007. "Laughing with the Yes Men: The Politics of Affirmation," *Continuum: Journal of Media & Cultural Studies* 21(1): 107–121.

IBFAN (International Baby Food Action Network). 2004a. "Nestlé: Breaking the Rules, Stretching the Rules." Available at www.ibfan.org/art/302–17.pdf (accessed March 8, 2005).

IBFAN 2004b. IBFAN Case Studies. Using International Tools to Stop Corporate Malpractice – Does It Work? *IBFAN International Report*. Available at http://www.ibfan.org/art/394-1.pdf (accessed December 4, 2012).

Idemudia, Uwafiokun. 2010. "Re-engaging Corporate Citizenship and Community Development in Africa: The Implications of the Nigerian Experience for CC Theory and Practice," paper presented at the conference "The Dynamics of Citizenship in the Post-Political World," Stockholm University, May 26–28.

Ikea No date. "IKEA US community relations guidelines." Available at http://www.ikea.com/ms/en_US/ikea_near_you/woodbridge/new_wood_app.pdf (accessed December 10, 2012).

Illia, Laura. 2002. "Passage to Cyberactivism: How Dynamics of Activism Change," *Journal of Public Affairs* 3(4): 326–337.

Inglehart, Ronald. 1997. *Modernization and Postmodernization: Cultural, Economic, and Political Change in 43 Societies*, Princeton: Princeton University Press.

Inglehart, Ronald, and Christian Welzel. 2005. *Modernization, Cultural Change, and Democracy: The Human Development Sequence*, Cambridge: Cambridge University Press.

Inglehart, Ronald, and Gabriela Catterberg. 2002. "Trends in Political Action: The Developmental Trend and the Post-Honeymoon Decline," *International Journal of Comparative Sociology* 43(3–5): 300–316.

Ingram, Carolyn. 2004. *In the Footsteps of Gandhi: Conversations with Spiritual Social Activists*, Berkeley: Parallax Press.

Interbrand. 2001. FASB Statements No. 141 & 142. The Impact of Intangible Assets Including Brand. A Special Report by Interbrand, 2001. Available at http://www.pedroguitton.com/phd_knowledge_center/pdf/FASB141-142.pdf (accessed August 29, 2008).

International Coffee Organization. 2005. "Historical Data." Available at http://www.ico.org/asp/display5.asp (accessed June 24, 2005).

International Coffee Organization. 2006. "Overview of the Coffee Market." Available at http://dev.ico.org/documents/icc93–5e.pdf (accessed June 24, 2005 and December 12, 2006).

International Council on Human Rights Policy (ICHRP). 2002. "Beyond Voluntarism: Human Rights and the Developing International Legal Obligations of Companies," Versoix: International Council on Human Rights Policy.

International Federation of Organic Agriculture Movements (IFOAM). 2009. "The Principles of Organic Agriculture." Available at http://www.ifoam.org/about_ifoam/principles/history_of_principles.html (accessed December 10, 2012).

International Federation of Organic Agriculture Movements (IFOAM). 2011. "Organic Agriculture Worldwide Directory of IFOAM Affiliates." Available at http://www.ifoam.org/IFOAM-Membership-Directory-2011_web.pdf.(accessed December 10, 2012).

International Labour Organization (ILO). 2004. "A Fair Globalization: Creating Opportunities for all." Geneva: International Labour Organization. Available at http://www.ilo.org/public/english/wcsdg/docs/report.pdf. (accessed December 10, 2102).

International Labour Organization (ILO). 2006. "The End of Child Labour: Within Reach. Global Report Under the Follow-up to the ILO Declaration on Fundamental Principles and Rights at Work." Geneva: ILO. Available at http://www.ilo.org/public/english/standards/relm/ilc/ilc95/pdf/rep-i-b.pdf (accessed October 20, 2011).

International Labour Organization. 2009. "Accelerating Action against Child Labour: Global Report under the follow-up to the ILO Declaration on Fundamental Principles and Rights at Work 2010." Available at http://www.ilo.org/ipecinfo/product/viewProduct.do?productId=13853 (accessed June 4, 2011).

Internet World Statistics. 2005. *Usage and Population Statistics*. Available at www.internetworldstats.com (accessed August 24, 2005).

Inter-Parliamentary Union 2007. "IPU PARLINE database on national parliaments." Available at http://www.ipu.org/parline-e/parlinesearch.asp (accessed October 24, 2007).

Inter Press Service. 2011. "Lobster Divers in Deep Trouble." Published Jan 3 2011. Available at http://www.ipsnews.net/2011/01/nicaragua-lobster-divers-in-deep-trouble/ (accessed December 10, 2012).

Irving, Sarah, Rob Harrison, and Mary Rayner. 2002. "Ethical Consumerism – Democracy through the Wallet," *Journal of Research for Consumers* 3. Available at: http://www.jrconsumers.com/academic_articles/issue_3 (accessed November 23, 2008).

ISEAL Alliance and AccountAbility. 2011. "Scaling up Strategy: A Strategy for Scaling up the Impacts of Voluntary Standards." Available at http://www.isealalliance.org/sites/default/files/Scaling_Up_Strategy_Final_June2011.pdf (accessed December 10, 2012).

Isenhour, Cindy. 2010. "Building Sustainable Societies: a Swedish Case Study on the Limits of Reflexive Modernization," *American Ethnologist* 37(3): 511–525.

Jabs, Jennifer et al., cited in Andrew Smart 2004. "Adrift in the Mainstream: Challenges Facing the UK Vegetarian Movement," *British Food Journal* 106(2): 79–92.

Jackman, Robert, and Ross Miller. 1995. "Voter Turnout in the Industrial Democracies During the 1980s," *Comparative Political Studies* 27(4): 467–492.

Jacobs, Lawrence R., Fay Lomax Cook, and Michael X. Delli Carpini. 2009. *Talking Together: Public Deliberation and Political Participation in America*, Chicago: University of Chicago Press.

Jaffee, Daniel. 2007. *Brewing Justice: Fair Trade Coffee, Sustainability, and Survival*, Berkeley: University of California Press.

Jaffee, Daniel. 2010. "Fair Trade Standards, Corporate Participation, and the Social Movement Responses in the United States," *Journal of Business Ethics* 92: 267–285.

Jaffee, Daniel and Phillip H. Howard. 2010. "Corporate Cooptation of Organic and Fair Trade Standards," *Agricultural Human Values* 27: 387–399.

James, Deborah. 2002. "Consumer Activism and Corporate Accountability," *Journal of Research for Consumers* 3. Available at http://www.jrconsumers.com/academic_articles/issue_3?f=5790.

Jasper, James M., and Dorothy Nelkin. 1992. *The Animal Rights Crusade: The Growth of a Moral Protest*, New York: The Free Press of Glencoe.

Jacquet, Jennifer, Daniel Pauly, David Ainley, Sidney Holt, Paul Dayton, and Jeremy Jackso. 2010. "Seafood Stewardship in Crisis," *Nature* 467(September): 28–29.

Javeline, D. 2003. "The Role of Blame in Collective Action: Evidence from Russia," *American Political Science Review* 97: 107–121.

Jenkins, J. Craig, and Charles Perrow. 1977. "Insurgency of the Powerless: Farm Worker Movements (1946–1972)," *American Sociological Review* 42: 249–268.

Jennings, M. Kent, and Ellen Ann Andersen. 2003. "The Importance of Social and Political Context: The Case of AIDS Activism," *Political Behavior* 25(2): 177–199.

John, Peter, Sarah Cotterill, Alice Moseley, Liz Richardson, Graham Smith, Gerry Stoker, and Corinne Wales. 2011. *Nudge, Nudge, Think, Think: Experimenting with Ways to Change Civic Behavior*, London: Bloomsbury Academic.

Johns, Rebecca, and Leyla Vural. 2000. "Class, Geography, and the Consumerist Turn: UNITE and the Stop Sweatshops Campaign," *Environment and Planning* A 32(7): 1193–1213.

Johansson, Johanna. 2013. *Constructing and Contesting the Legitimacy of Private Forest Certification in Sweden*. Umea Department of Political Science, Umea University. PhD thesis.

Johnson, Douglas A. 1986. "Confronting Corporate Power: Strategies and Phases of the Nestle Boycott," *Research in Corporate Social Performance and Policy* 8: 323–344.

Johnson, Nicholas, Phil Oliff, and Erica Williams. 2011. "An Update on State Budget Cuts: At Least 46 States Have Imposed Cuts that Hurt Vulnerable Residents and Cause Job Loss," Washington DC: Center on Budget and Policy Priorities. Available at http://www.cbpp.org/files/3-13-08sfp.pdf (accessed February 14, 2012).

Johnston, Josée. 2008. "The Citizen-Consumer Hybrid: Ideological Tensions and the Case of Whole Foods Market," *Theory and Society* 37(3): 229–270.

Jones, Ellis, Ross Haenfler, and Brett Johnson. 2007. *The Better World Handbook*, Gabriola Island, BC: New Society Publishers.

Jordan, Andrew, Rudiger K. W. Wurzel, and Anthony R. Zito. 2003a. "Comparative Conclusions – 'New' Environmental Policy Instruments: An Evolution or a Revolution in Environmental Policy?" *Environmental Politics* 12(1): 201–224.

Jordan, Andrew, Rüdiger K. W. Wurzel, and Anthony R. Zito. 2003b. "'New' Instruments of Environmental Governance: Patters and Pathways of Change" in Andrew

Jordan, Rüdiger K. W. Wurzel, and Anthony R. Zito (eds.), *'New' Instruments of Environmental Governance? National Experiences and Prospects*, Special issue of *Environmental Politics* 12(1): 1–24.

Jordan, Andrew, Rüdiger Wurzel, Anthony Zito, and Lars Brückner. 2006 (2004). "Consumer Responsibility-Taking and Eco-Labeling Schemes in Europe," in M. Micheletti, A. Follesdal, and D. Stolle, *Politics, Products, and Markets: Exploring Political Consumerism Past and Present*, London: Transaction Press, pp. 160–180.

Jowell, Roger and the Central Co-ordinating Team. 2003. *European Social Survey* 2002/2003: Technical Report, London: Centre for Comparative Social Surveys, City University (Data and codebook available at: http://ess.nsd.uib.no (accessed June 3, 2006).

Kaariainen, Juha, and Heikki Lehtonen. 2006. "The Variety of Social Capital in Welfare State Regimes. A Comparative Study of 21 Countries," *European Societies* 8(1): 27–57. Available at http://dx.doi.org/10.1080/14616690500491399.

Kaptein, Muel. 2004. "Business Codes of Multinational Firms: What do They Say?" *Journal of Business Ethics* 50: 13–31.

Kaptein, Muel, and Mark S. Schwartz. 2008. "The Effectiveness of Business Codes: A Critical Examination of Existing Studies and the Development of an Integrated Research Model," *Journal of Business Ethics* 77(2): 111–127.

Katyal, Sonia. A. 2010. "Stealth Marketing and Antibranding: The Love that Dare Not Speak Its Name," *Buffalo Law Review* 58: 795–849.

Katz, Donald. 1994. *Just Do It, The Nike Spirit in the Corporate World*, Holbrook, MA: Adams Publishing.

Keck, Margaret E., and Kathryn Sikkink. 1998. *Activists Beyond Borders: Advocacy Networks in International Politics*, Ithaca, NY: Cornell University Press.

Keck, Margaret E., and Kathryn Sikkink. 1999. "Transnational Advocacy Networks in International and Regional Politics," *International Social Science Journal* 159: 98–99.

Kemikalieinspektionen (Swedish Chemicals Agency). 2008. "Att arbeta med produkt-val i praktiken," Sundbyberg: Kemikalieinspektionen. Available at http://www.kemi.se/upload/Trycksaker/Pdf/Rapporter/Rapport2_08_Produktval_i_praktiken.pdf (accessed December 10, 2012).

Kendall, Brenden E., Rebecda Gill, and George Cleney. 2007. "Consumer Activism and Corporate Social Responsibility: How Strong a Connection?" in *The Debate over Corporate Social Responsibility*, Steve May, George Cheney, Juliet Roper (eds). Oxford: Oxford University Press, pp. 241–266.

Kennedy, Paul. 2006(2004). "Selling Virtue: Political and Economic Contradictions of Green/Ethical Marketing in the United Kingdom," in Michele Micheletti, Andreas Follesdal and Dietlind Stolle (eds.), *Politics, Products and Markets. Exploring Political Consumerism Past and Present*, New Brunswick, NJ: Transaction Publishers, pp. 21–45.

Kennedy, Peter W., Benoit Laplante, and John Maxwell. 1994. "Pollution Policy: The Role for Publicly Provided Information," *Journal of Environmental Economics and Management* 26: 31–43.

Keohane, Robert O. 2003. "Global Governance and Democratic Accountability," in David Held and Mathias Koenig-Archibugi (eds.), *Taming Globalization: Frontiers of Governance*, Cambridge: Polity Press, pp. 130–159.

Keohane, Robert O., and Kal Raustiala. 2008. "Toward a Post-Kyoto Climate Change Architecture: A Political Analysis," UCLA School of Law, Law-Econ Research Paper No. 08–14. Available at http://ssrn.com/abstract=1142996 (accessed October 20, 2010).

Kern, Kristine; Ingrid Kissling-Näf, Ute Landmann, Corine Mauch, and Tina Löffelsend. 2001. *Policy Convergence and Policy Diffusion by Governmental and Non-governmental Institutions: An International Comparison of Eco-labeling Systems.* Working paper. The Open Access Publication Server of the ZBW – Leibniz Information Centre for Economics, Available at https://www.econstor.eu/dspace/bitstream/10419/48973/1/340893192.pdf (accessed December 6, 2012).

Keys, Tracey, and Thomas Malnight No date. "Corporate Clout: The Influence of the World's Largest 100 Economic Entities," *Global Trends*. Available at http://www.globaltrends.com/features/shapers-and-influencers/66-corporate-clout-the-influence-of-the-worlds-largest-100-economic-entities (accessed February 20, 2011).

Khan, Uzma, and Ravi Dhar. 2006. "Licensing Effect in Consumer Choice," *Journal of Marketing Research* 18: 259–266.

King, Brayden G. 2008. "A Political Mediation Model of Corporate Response to Social Movement Activism," *Administrative Science Quarterly* 53: 395–421.

King, Mary. 1999. *Mahatma Gandhi and Martin Luther King Jr.: The Power of Non-violent Action*, Paris: UNESCO.

Kingdon, John W. 1995. *Agendas, Alternatives, and Public Policies*, New York: Harper Collins College Publishers.

Kingsley, Charles. 1850. *Cheap Clothes and Nasty*, London: W. Pickering. Extract available at http://www.historyhome.co.uk/peel/economic/sweat.htm.

Kinney, Eleanor D. 1990. "Rule and Policy Making for the Medicaid Program: A Challenge to Federalism," *Ohio State Law Journal* 51: 855–863.

Kinunda-Rutashobya, Lettice. 2003. "Exploring the Potentialities of Export Processing Free Zones (EPZs) for Economic Development in Africa: Lessons from Mauritius," *Management Decision* 41(3): 226–232.

Kirton, John J., and Michael J. Trebilcock (eds.) 2004. *Hard Choices, Soft Law: Voluntary Standards in Global Trade, Environment, and Social Governance*, Aldershot: Ashgate Publishing Limited.

Kitschelt, Herbert. 1986. "Political Opportunity Structures and Political Protest: anti-Nuclear Movements in Four Democracies," *British Journal of Political Science*, 16: 57–85.

Kittilson, Mikki Caul. 2005. "Changing Patterns of Mobilization, Increasing Bias?: Trends in Participation in Established Democracies, 1960–2003," paper presented at the annual meeting of the American Political Science Association, Washington, DC, September 1–4.

Klein, Naomi. 2000. *No Logo: Taking Aim at the Brand Bullies*, Toronto: Random House.

Klein, Naomi. 2008. *The Shock Doctrine: The Rise of Disaster Capitalism*, Toronto: Random House.

Klint, Jakob. 1997. *Max Havelaar-mærkede produkter – en undersøgelse af forbrugeren og storkunden*, Copenhagen: CASA.

Klotz, Audie. 2002. "Transnational Activism and Global Transformations: The Anti-Apartheid and Abolitionist Experiences," *European Journal of International Relations* 8(1): 49–76.

Knight, Graham, and Jackie Smith. 2008. "The Global Compact and Its Critics: Activism, Power Relations, and Corporate Social Responsibility," in Janie Leatherman (ed.), *Discipline and Punishment in Global Politics: Illusions of Control*, London: Palgrave-Macmillan, pp. 191–214.

Knight, Graham, and Josh Greenberg. 2002. "Promotionalism and Subpolitics: Nike and its Labor Critics," *Management Communication Quarterly* 15(4): 541–570.

Knill, C., and D. Lemkuhl. 2002. "Private Actors and the State: Internationalization and Changing Patterns of Governance," *Governance* 15(1): 41–63.

Knox, Paul L. 2005. "Creating Ordinary Places: Slow Cities in a Fast World," *Journal of Urban Design* 10(1): 1–11.

Kobrin, Stephen J. 2003. "Oil and Politics: Talisman Energy and Sudan," *International Law and Politics* 36: 425–456.

Koenig-Archibugi, Mathias. 2004. "Transnational Corporations and Public Accountability," *Government and Opposition* 39: 234–259.

Koku, Paul, Aigbe Akhigbe, and Thomas Springer. 1997. "The Financial Impact of Boycotts and Threats of Boycott," *Journal of Business Research* 40(1): 15–20.

Kolk, A., and R. van Tulder. 2005. "Setting New Global Rules? TNCs and Codes of Conduct," *Transnational Corporations* 14(3): 1–27.

Kolk, Ans. 2005. "Corporate Social Responsibility in the Coffee Sector: The Dynamics of MNC Responses and Code Development," *European Management Journal* 23(2): 228–236.

Konsumentverket. 2004. "Ekokalkylen." Available at www.ekokalkylen .konsumentverket.se/ (accessed April 2004).

Koopmans, Rund, and Dieter Rucht. 2002. "Protest Event Analysis," in Bert Klandermans and Suzanne Staggenborg (eds.), *Methods of Social Movement Research*, Minneapolis, MN: University of Minnesota Press, pp. 231–259.

Kortbech-Olesen, Rudy. 2004. *The Canadian Market for Organic Food and Beverages*, Geneva: International Trade Centre.

Kraft Foods News Release. 2011. "Kraft Foods expands sustainability goals to build on success." Available at http://www.kraftfoodscompany.com/mediacenter/country-press-releases/us/2011/multi_media_05112011.aspx (accessed June 14 2011).

KRAV. 2010. "KRAV-labelled organic food is worth more." 21 June. Available at http://www.krav.se/System/Spraklankar/In-English/For-Consumers/KRAV-labelled-Organic-Food-is-Worth-More/. (accessed December 10, 2012).

Kriesi, Hans. 1995. 'The Political Opportunity Structure of New Social Movements: its Impact on their Mobilization,' in J. C. Jenkins and B. Klandermans (eds.), *The Politics of Social Protest*, Minneapolis: U. of Minnesota Press; London: UCL Press, pp. 167–198

Kristiansen, Paul. 2006. "Overview of Organic Agriculture," in Kristiansen, Paul, Acram Taji and John Reganold (eds.), *Organic Agriculture: A Global Perspective*, Collingwood, Victoria: Csiro Publishing, pp. 1–23.

Kristiansen, Paul, Acram Taji, and John Reganold. 2006. *Organic Agriculture: a Global Perspective*, Collingwood, Victoria: Csiro Publishing.

Kroll, Gary. 2001. "The 'Silent Springs' of Rachel Carson: Mass Media and the Origins of Modern Environmentalism," *Public Understanding of Science* 10(4): 403–420.

Krueger, Robert, Brian Hicks, and Matt McGue. 2001. "Altruism and Antisocial Behavior: Independent Tendencies, Unique Personality Correlates, Distinct Etiologies," *Psychological Science* 12(5): 397–402.

Kubal, Timothy J. 1998. "The Presentation of Political Self: Cultural Resonance and the Construction of Collective Action Frames," *Sociological Quarterly* 39(4): 539–554.

Kullberg, John F. 2002. "Animal Rights and Human Responsibilities: A Keynote Address," Former Wildlife Land Trust Director, keynote address at the Animal Rights 2002 Conference in McLean, Virginia, July 2, 2002.

Kumar, Nirmalya and Jan-Benedict E. M. Steenkamp. 2007. *Private Label Strategy: How to Meet the Store Brand Challenge*, Boston, MA: Harvard Business School Press.

Kusago, Takayoshi, and Zafiris Tzannatos. 1998. "Export Processing Zones: A Review in Need of Update." Social Protection Discussion Paper No. 9802. Washington DC: The World Bank. Available at http://siteresources.worldbank.org/SOCIALPROTECTION/Resources/SP-Discussion-papers/Labor-Market-DP/9802.pdf (accessed December 10, 2012).

L. A. County Workforce Investment Board. 2011. "Workforce Investment Board Cites Critical Challenges for Employment and Training Programs," News release, February 23. Available at http://www.prnewswire.com/news-releases/budget-cuts-point-to-severe-economic-repercussions-for-la-county-116725159.html.

Lambert-Beatty, Carrie. 2010. "Fill in the Blank: Culture Jamming and the Advertising of Agency," *New Directions for Youth Development* 125(spring): 99–112.

Lane, Jill. 2002. "Reverend Billy: Preaching, Protest, and Postindustrial Flanerie," *The Drama Review* 46(1): 60–84.

Lange, Hellmuth, and Lars Meier (eds.) 2009. *The New Middle Classes: Globalizing Lifestyles, Consumerism and Environmental Concern*, New York: Springer.

Langert, Bob. 2008. "The Best CSR Comment I Have Ever Heard." Available at http://csr.blogs.mcdonalds.com/default.asp?item=309445&DCSext.destination=http://csr.blogs.mcdonalds.com/default.asp?item=309445 (accessed January 5, 2012).

Lash, Scott. 2002. "Foreword by Scott Lash: Individualization in a Non-Linear Mode," in Ulrich Beck and Elisabeth Beck-Gernsheim, *Individualization: Institutionalized Individualism and its Social and Political Consequences*, London: SAGE Publications, pp. vii–xiii.

Lasn, Kalle. 2000. *Culture Jam: How to Reverse America's Suicidal Consumer Binge – And Why We Must*, New York: Quill, Harper Collins Publishers.

Lazzarini, Marilena. 2007. "The Challenge of Being an Ethical Consumer," President of Consumers International. Speech at the International Standards for Business, Government and Society (ISO) Conference, Can Consumers Rely on Fair Trade Claims? May 23. Available at http://www.iso.org/iso/conferences.htm?llNodeId=22212&llVolId=-2000.

Lee, Min-Dong Paul, and Michael Lounsbury. 2011. "Domesticating Radical Rant and Rage: An Exploration of the Consequences of Environmental Shareholder Resolutions on Corporate Environmental Performance," *Business & Society* 50(1): 155–188. Available at http://bas.sagepub.com/content/50/1/155.full.pdf+html.

Leifert, Carlo, and Michael Bourlakis. 2004. "Recent Developments in the Organic Food Market." Available at www.organicagcentre.ca/DOCs/Carlo%20Liefert%20Organic%20Food%20Markets.pdf (accessed May 23, 2005).

Leighley, Jan E. 1995. "Attitudes, Opportunities and Incentives: A Field Essay on Political Participation," *Political Research Quarterly* 48(1): 181–209.

Leitner Helga, Jamie Peck, and Eric Sheppard (eds.) 2007. *Contesting Neoliberalism: Urban Frontiers*, New York: Guilford.

Levi, Margaret, and April Linton. 2003. "Fair Trade: A Cup at a Time?" *Politics & Society* 31(3): 407–432.

Levi, Margaret, and David Olson. 2000. "The Battles in Seattle," *Politics & Society* 28(3): 309–329.

Lewis, Alan, and Craig Mackenzie. 2000. "Support for Investor Activism among U.K. Ethical Investors," *Journal of Business Ethics* 24: 215–222.

Li, Yaojun, and David Marsh. 2008. "New Forms of Political Participation: Searching for Expert Citizens and Everyday Makers," *British Journal of Political Science* 38(2): 247–272.

Lichterman, Paul. 1996. *The Search for Political Community: American Activists Reinventing Commitment*, Cambridge: Cambridge University Press.

Liebhold, Peter, and Harry Rubenstein. 1998. "Between a Rock and a Hard Place," *Labor's Heritage* 9(4): 4–25.

Light, Ryan, Vincent J. Roscigno, and Alexandra Kalev. 2011. "Racial Discrimination, Interpretation and Legitimation at Work," *The ANNALS of the American Academy of Political and Social Science* 634(1): 39–59.

Lijphart, Arend. 1997. "Unequal Participation: Democracy's Unresolved Dilemma," *American Political Science Review* 91(1): 1–14.

Lijphart, Arend, and Marcus L. Crepaz. 1991. "Corporatism and Consensus Democracy in Eighteen Countries: Conceptual and Empirical Linkages," *British Journal of Political Science* 21: 235–246.

Lillywhite, Jay M., Mohammad Al-Oun, and Jennifer E. Simonsen. 2010. "Growth Potential in the Organic Foods Market of a Developing Country," Paper presented at the International Food and Agribusiness Management Association Symposium, Boston, Massachusetts, June 19–22, 2010.

Lindefors, Joel. 2004. Interview by Michele Micheletti. 3 March. At the time of the interview, Lindefors was the coordinator for the Swedish branch of the Clean Clothes Campaign.

Lindefors, Joel. 2005. Interview by Michele Micheletti. 12 May. At the time of the interview, Lindefors was the coordinator for the Swedish branch of the Clean Clothes Campaign.

Lindsey, Brink. 2003. "Grounds for Complaint? Understanding the 'Coffee Crisis'," Cato Institute Trade Briefing Chapter no. 16. Washington, DC: Cato Institute.

Linton, April. 2005. "Partnering for Sustainability: Business-NGO Alliances in the Coffee Industry," *Development in Practice* 15(3&4): 600–614.

Linton, April, Cindy Chiayuan Liou, and Kelly Ann Shaw. 2004. "A Taste of Trade Justice: Marketing Global Social Responsibility via Fair Trade Coffee," *Globalizations* 1(2): 223–246.

Lipschutz, Ronnie D. 2004. "Sweating It Out: NGO Campaigns and Trade Union Empowerment," *Development in Practice* 14(1–2): 197–209.

Lipschutz, Ronnie D. 2006. "Introduction" in Ronnie D. Lipschutz (ed.), *Civil Societies and Social Movements: Domestic, Transnational, Global*, Ashgate: Aldershop, p. 7.

Littler, Jo. 2005. "Beyond the Boycott," *Cultural Studies* 2(19): 227–252.

Livraghi, Renata, and Gabriella Pappadà. 2009. "Tacit Knowledge and Volunteers' Empowerment in the Fair Trade Sector" in S. Destefanis and M. Musella (eds.), *Paid and Unpaid Labour in the Social Economy*, Heidelberg: Physica-Verlag, pp. 221–244.

Locke, Richard M. 2002. "The Promise and Perils of Globalization: The Case of Nike." Working Paper MIT-IPC-02–007. Cambridge, MA: Industrial Performance Center, Massachussets Institute of Technology.

Lockie, Steward, Kristen Lyons, Geoffrey Lawrence, and Kerry Mummery. 2002. "Eating 'Green': Motivations Behind Organic Food Consumption in Australia," *Sociologia Ruralis* 42(1): 23–40.

Lockie, Stewart, Kristen Lyons, Geoffrey Lawrence, and Janet Grice. 2004. "Choosing Organics: a Path Analysis of Factors Underlying the Selection of Organic Food among Australian Consumers," *Appetite* 43(2): 135–146.

Logsdon, Jeanne M., and Harry J. Van Buren III. 2008. "Justice and Large Corporations: What Do Activist Shareholders Want?" *Business & Society* 47, 4: 523–548. Available at http://bas.sagepub.com/content/47/4/523.shortpapers.

Lovan, W. Robert, Michael Murray, and Ron Shaffer. 2004. *Participatory Governance: Planning, Conflict Mediation and Public Decision-Making in Civil Society*, Aldershot: Ashgate Publishing Limited.

Low, William, and Eileen Davenport. 2005. "Postcards from the Edge: Maintaining the 'Alternative' Character of Fair Trade," *Sustainable Development* 13(3): 143–153.

LRF and Ekologiska lantbrukarna. 2001. *Vägen till marknaden. Ekologiska produkter*, Stockholm: LRF.

Lucci, John Paul. 2003. "Enron: The Bankruptcy Heard Around the World and the International Ricochet of Sarbanes-Oxley," *Albany Law Review* 67(1): 211–249.

LUI Marknadsinformation AB. 1999. *Konsumentundersökning om ekologiska produkter/KRAV*, Stockholm: LUI, unpublished report.

Lukes, Steven. 2006. *Individualism*, Colchester: ECPR Press.

Lundqvist, Lennart. 1980. *The Hare and the Tortoise: Clean Air Policies in the United States and Sweden*, Ann Arbor: University of Michigan Press.

Lundsgaard, Jens. 2006. "Choice and Long-Term Care in OECD Countries: Care Outcome, Employment and Fiscal Sustainability," *European Societies* 8(3): 361–383.

Lund-Thomsen, Peter. 2008. "The Global Sourcing and Codes of Conduct Debate: Five Myths and Five Recommendations," *Development and Change* 39(6): 1005–1018.

Lury, Celia. 2004. *Brands: the Logos of the Global Economy*, New York: Routledge.

Lyon, Sarah. 2002. *Evaluation of the Actual and Potential Benefits for the Alleviation of Poverty through the Participation in Fair Trade Coffee Networks: Guatemalan Case Study*, New York: Fair Trade Research Group (Colorado State University) / Ford Foundation.

Lyon, Sarah. 2006. "Evaluating Fair Trade Consumption: Politics, Defetishization and Producer Participation," *International Journal of Consumer Studies* 30(5): 452–464.

Lyon, Sarah. 2007. "Fair Trade Coffee and Human Rights in Guatemala," *Journal of Consumer Policy* 30(3): 241–261.

Lyons, Mike. 2011. "New Black Panther Party Organized March to Scene of Recent Shooting Deaths," *First Coast News*, October 1, 2011. Available at http://www.firstcoastnews.com/news/local/article/221234/3/Day-Of-Action-And-Unity-Calls-For-End-Of-Violence-In-Black-Community (accessed October 24, 2011).

Macdonald, Kate. 2007. "Globalising Justice within Coffee Supply Chains? Fair Trade, Starbucks and the Transformation of Supply Chain," *Third World Quarterly* 28(4): 793–812.

Macedo, Stephen (ed.) 1999. *Deliberative Politics: Essays on Democracy and Disagreement*, Oxford: Oxford University Press.

Macedo, Stephen, Yvette Alex-Assensoh, Jeffrey M. Berry, Michael Brintnall, David E. Campbell, Luis Ricardo Fraga, Archon Fung, William A. Galston, Christopher F. Karpowitz, Margaret Levi, Meira Levinson, Keena Lipsitz, Richard G. Niemi, Robert D. Putnam, Wendy M. Rahn, Rob Reich, Robert R. Rodgers, Todd Swanstrom, Katherine Cramer Walsh. 2005. *Democracy at Risk: How Political Choices Undermine Citizen Participation, and What We Can Do About It*, Washington DC: Brookings Institution Press.

Macken, Deidre. 2001. "The Chain Reaction," *Australian Financial Review*.

Mair, Peter, and Ingrid van Biezen. 2001. "Party Membership in Twenty European Democracies, 1980–2000," *Party Politics* 7(1): 5–21.

Malpass, Alice, Clive Barnett, Nick Clarke, and Paul Cloke. 2007. "Problematizing Choice: Responsible Consumers and Sceptical Citizens" in M. Bevir and F. Trentmann (eds.), *Governance and Consumption*, London: Palgrave, pp. 231–256.

Malpass, Alice, Paul Cloke, Clive Barnett, and Nick Clarke. 2007. "Fairtrade Urbanism? The Politics of Place Beyond Place in the Bristol Fairtrade City Campaign," *International Journal of Urban and Regional Research* 31(3): 633–645.

Mamic, Ivanka. 2004. *Implementing Codes of Conduct: How Businesses Manage Social Performance in Global Supply Chains*, Sheffield: Greenleaf.

Mamic, Ivanka. 2005. "Managing Global Supply Chain: The Sports Footwear, Apparel and Retail Sectors," *Journal of Business Ethics* 59: 81–100.

Mandle, Jay. 2000. "The Student Anti-Sweatshop Movement: Limits and Potential," *The ANNALS of the American Academy of Political and Social Science* 570(1): 92–103.

Maniates, Michael. 2002. "In Search of Consumptive Resistance: the Voluntary Simplicity Movement," in Thomas Princen, Michael F. Maniates and Ken Conca (eds.), *Confronting Consumption*, Cambridge, MA: MIT Press, pp. 199–235.

Maquila Solidarity Network. 2006. "Is Fair Trade a Good Fit for the Garment Industry?" MSN Discussion Paper. Available at http://en.maquilasolidarity.org/sites/maquilasolidarity.org/files/DiscussionPaper1.pdf (accessed October 20, 2011).

Maquila Solidarity Network. No date. Hold a Sweatshop Fashion Show. Available at http://en.maquilasolidarity.org/en/node/654 (accessed December 6, 2012).

Margulies, Philipp. 2003. *The Exxon Valdez Oil Spill*. New York: The Rosen Publishing Group.

Marine Stewardship Council (MSC). 2010. "MSC fishery standard: Principles and criteria for sustainable fishing." Version 1.1, May 1. Available at http://www.msc.org/documents/scheme-documents/msc-standards/MSC_environmental_standard_for_sustainable_fishing.pdf/view.

Marko, Peter B., Holly A. Nance, and Kimberly D. Guynn. 2011. "Genetic Detection of Mislabeled Fish from a Certified Sustainable Fishery," *Current Biology* 21(16): R621–R622.

Marlow, Harold J., William K. Hayes, Samuel Soret, Ronald L. Carter, Ernest R. Schwab, and Joan Sabaté. 2009. "Diet and the Environment: Does What You Eat Matter?" *The American Journal of Clinical Nutrition* 89(5): 1699S–1703S.

Martin, C. Gus (ed.) 2011. *The SAGE Encyclopedia of Terrorism*, Second Edition. New York: Sage Publishing.

Martinez, Maria Elena. 2002. "Poverty Alleviation through Participation in Fair Trade Coffee Networks: the Case of the Tzotzilotic Tzobolotic Coffee Cooperative, Chiapas, Mexico," Report prepared for Fair Trade Research Group, Colorado State University. Available at http://www.cfat.colostate.edu/research/one-cup-at-a-time/ (accessed June 2007).

Maskus, Keith. 1997. Core Labor Standards: Trade Impacts and Implications for International Trade Policy, Washington DC: World Bank International Trade Division.

Massey, Doreen. 2004. "Geographies of Responsibility," *Geografiska Annaler* 86(B): 5–18.

Maucher, Helmut. 1992. *Leadership in Action: Touch-Minded Strategies from the Global Giant*, New York: McGraw-Hill.

Maurer, Donna. 2002. "Movement Progress and the Vegetarian Identity," *Satya* 8(10), Available at http://academic-editor.com/movementprogress.html.

May, Caroline. 2011. "New Black Panthers to Protest 'Non-Blacks,'" *The Daily Caller*, April 19, 2011. Available at http://dailycaller.com/2011/04/19/new-black-panthers-to-protest-non-blacks/#ixzz1JyLopQjn (accessed October 24, 2011).

May, Christopher. 2000. *A Global Political Economy of Intellectual Property Rights: The New Enclosures?* London: Routledge.

May, Larry. 1992. *Sharing Responsibility*, Chicago: Chicago University Press.

May, Larry, and Stacey Hoffman (eds.) 1991. *Collective Responsibility: Five Decades of Debate in Theoretical and Applied Ethics*. New York: Rowan & Littlefield.

Mayors Against Illegal Guns. 2010. "Trace the Guns: The Link between Gun Laws and Interstate Gun Trafficking." Available at http://www.tracetheguns.org/report .pdf.

Mazar, Nina, and Chen-Bo Zhong. 2010. "Do Green Products Make Us Better People?" *Psychological Science* 21(4): 494–498.

McCaughey, Martha, and Michael D. Ayers (eds.) 2003. *Cyberactivism: Online Activism in Theory and Practice*, London: Routledge.

McCourt, W. 2002. "New Public Management in Developing Countries," in Kathleen McLaughlin, Stephen P. Osborne, and Ewan Ferli (eds.), *The New Public Management: Current Trends and Future Prospects*, London: Routledge, pp. 227–242.

McFarland, Andrew. 2010. "Why Creative Participation Today?" in Michele Micheletti and Andrew McFarland (eds.), *Creative Participation: Responsibility-Taking in the Political World*, Bolder, CO: Paradigm Publishers, pp. 15–33.

McNamara, Siobhán, and Michael Grubb. 2011. "The Psychological Underpinnings of the Consumer Role in Energy Demand and Carbon Abatement," *Electricity Policy Research Group Working Paper*, Cambridge: University of Cambridge.

Médecins Sans Frontières. 2003. "Doha Derailed: A Progress Report on TRIPS and Access to Medicines." MSF Briefing for the 5th WTO Ministerial Conference, Cancun, 2003. Available at http://www.accessmed-msf.org (accessed April 4, 2007).

Meeran, Richard. 2011. "Tort litigation against multinationals ("MNCs") for violation of human rights: An overview of the position outside the US." Available at http://www.business-humanrights.org/media/documents/richard-meeran-tort-litigation-against-mncs-7-mar-2011.pdf.

Meidinger, Errol. 2003. "Forest Certification as a Global Civil Society Regulatory Institution" in Errol Meidinger, Chris Elliott and Gerhard Oesten (eds.), *Social and Political Dimensions of Forest Certification*, Remagen-Oberwinter: Forstbuch, pp. 275–292.

Meikle, Graham. 2002. *Future Active: Media Activism and the Internet*, Sydney: Pluto Press.

Melchett, Peter. 2007. "Are Air Miles and Organic Food Compatible?" in "Green Living Blog," *Guardian*, September 6. Available at http://blogs.guardian.co .uk/ethicalliving/2007/09/are_air_miles_and_organic_inco.html (accessed October 20, 2011).

Melchior, Arne. 1996. "Child Labor and Trade Policy," in Bjorne Grimsrud and Arne Melchior, (eds.), *Child Labor and International Trade Policy*, Paris: Organization for Economic Cooperation and Development.

Mellema, Gregory. "Introduction" at Calvin College, Philosophy Department web site. Available at http://www.calvin.edu/academic/philosophy/writings/crintro.htm (accessed July 16, 2007).

Méndez, Ernesto V. 2002. *Fair Trade Networks in Two Coffee Cooperatives of Western El Salvador: An Analysis of Insertion through a Second Level Organization*, New York: Fair Trade Research Group (Colorado State University) / Ford Foundation.

Merk, Jeroen. 2008. "The Structural Crisis of Labour Flexibility: Strategies and Prospects for Transnational Labour Organising in the Garment and Sportswear Industries," Amsterdam: International Secretariat Clean Clothes Campaign. Available at http://www.cleanclothes.org/documents/Structural_Crisis.pdf.

Merritt, Anna C., Daniel A. Effron, and Benoît Monin. 2010. "Moral Self-Licensing: When Being Good Frees Us to Be Bad," *Social and Personality Psychology Compass* 4/5: 344–357.

Meyer, David S. 2006. "Claiming Credit: Stories of Movement Influences as Outcomes," *Mobilization: An International Quarterly* 11(3): 281–298.

Meyer, David S., and Steven A. Boutcher. 2007. "Signals and Spillover: Brown v. Board of Education and Other Social Movements," *Perspectives on Politics* 5: 81–93.

Michael Jantzi Research Associates. 2003. *Social Responsible Investing in Canada: a Market Backgrounder*, Toronto: Michael Jantzi Research Associates, Inc.

Micheletti, Michele. 1990. *The Swedish Farmers' Movement and Government Agricultural Policy*, New York: Praeger.

Micheletti, Michele. 1995. *Civil Society and State Relations in Sweden*. Aldershot: Avebury.

Micheletti, Michele. 2003. "Global (Sub)Political Representation: The Clean Clothes Campaign and No Sweat Movement," paper for the ECPR Joint Sessions Workshop 14.

Micheletti, Michele. 2006 (2004). "Why More Women? Issues of Gender and Political Consumerism," in Michele Micheletti, Andreas Folledal and Dietlind Stolle (eds.), *Politics, Products, and Markets: Exploring Political Consumerism Past and Present*, New Brunswick, NJ: Transaction Press, pp. 245–264.

Micheletti, Michele. 2007. "The Moral Force of Consumption and Capitalism: Anti-Slavery and Anti-Sweatshop," in K. Soper and F. Trentmann (eds.), *Citizenship and Consumption*, London: Palgrave Macmillan, pp. 121–136.

Micheletti, Michele. 2010 (2003). *Political Virtue and Shopping: Individuals, Consumerism, and Collective Action*, Second Edition. New York: Palgrave.

Micheletti, Michele, and Andrew McFarland. 2010. *Creative Participation: Responsibility-Taking in the Political World*. New York: Paradigm Publishing.

Micheletti, Michele, and Cindy Isenhour 2010. "Political Consumerism," in Karin M.
Ekström (ed.), *Consumer behaviour – a Nordic perspective*, Lund: Studentlitteratur,
pp. 133–152.

Micheletti, Michele, and Dietlind Stolle. 2004. "Politiska konsumenter: marknaden
som arena för politiska val," in S. Holmberg and L. Weibull (eds.), *Ju mer vi är
tillsammans*, Gothenburg: SOM-institutet, pp. 103–116.

Micheletti, Michele, and Dietlind Stolle. 2005. "Swedish Political Consumers: Who
They Are and Why They Use the Market as an Arena for Politics" in Magnus Boström,
Andreas Føllesdal, Mikael Klintman, Michele Micheletti, and Mads Sørensen (eds.),
"Political consumerism: Its motivations, power, and conditions in the Nordic
countries and elsewhere," *TemaNord 2005*: 517. Copenhagen: Nordic Council of
Ministers. Available at http://www.norden.org/sv/publikationer/publikationer/2005–
517.

Micheletti, Michele, and Dietlind Stolle. 2006. "Political Consumerism," in Lonnie R.
Sherrod, Constance A. Flanagan, Ron Kassimir (eds.), *Youth Activism: An International Encyclopedia*, New York: Greenwood Publishing Group, pp. 470–476.

Micheletti, Michele, and Dietlind Stolle. 2007. "Mobilizing Consumers to Take Responsibility for Global Social Justice," *The ANNALS of the American Academy of Political
and Social Science* 611(1): 157–175.

Micheletti, Michele, and Dietlind Stolle. 2008. "Fashioning Social Justice through
Political Consumerism, Capitalism, and the Internet," *Cultural Studies* 22(5): 749–
769.

Micheletti, Michele, and Dietlind Stolle. 2009. "Consumers as Political Actors," in
Lynn Walter and Laurel E. Phoenix (eds.), *Critical Food Issues: Problems and State-
of-the-Art Solutions*, Westport, CT: Greenwood Publishing Group, pp. 188–214.

Micheletti, Michele, and Dietlind Stolle. 2010. "Vegetarianism – A Lifestyle Politics?" in Michele Micheletti and Andrew McFarland (eds.), *Creative Participation:
Responsibility-Taking in the Political World*, Bolder, CO: Paradigm Press, pp. 125–
147.

Micheletti, Michele, and Dietlind Stolle. 2012. "Sustainable Citizenship and the New
Politics of Consumption," in Sustainable Citizenship and the New Politics of Consumption. *The ANNALS of the American Academy of Political and Social Science*
644 Issue 1 (November): 88–120.

Micheletti, Michele, Andreas Follesdal, and Dietlind Stolle. 2006 (2003). *Politics, Products, and Markets: Exploring Political Consumerism Past and Present*, Rutgers, NJ:
Transaction Publishers. Second edition.

Micheletti Michele, Dietlind Stolle, and Daniel Berlin. Forthcoming. "Sustainable Citizenship: The Role of Citizens and Consumers in Protecting the Common Good,"
in Andreas Duit (ed.), *Mapping the Politics of Ecology: The Comparative Study of
Environmental Governance*, Cambridge, MA: MIT Press.

Midttun, Atle. 2005. "Realigning Business, Government and Civil Society," *Corporate
Governance* 5(3): 159–174.

Milakovich, Michael, and George Gordon. 2008. *Public Administration in America*,
Wadsworth Publishing.

Miller, Corbett. No date. "Just Sue It," *The Golden Gate [X] Press Magazine*, Publication of the San Francisco State University Journalism Department. Available at
http://express.sfsu.edu/custom/magazine/nike2.html (accessed April 29, 2003).

Minuteman Project. 2009. "About Jim Gilchrist." Available at http://www.minutemanproject.com/about.php (accessed June 28, 2009).

Mirvis, Phillip, and Googins, Bradly P. 2006. "Stages of Corporate Citizenship: a Developmental Framework," *California Management Review* 48(2): 104–26.

Mirvis, Phillip H. 1994. "Environmentalism in Progressive Business," *Journal of Organizational Change Management* 7(4): 82–100.

Mol, Arthur P. J. 2000. "The Environmental Movement in an Era of Ecological Modernisation," *Geoforum* 31: 45–56.

Monaghan, Paul. 2008. "Why the Co-op is Wary of 'Food Miles' Labeling," in "Green Living Blog", *Guardian*, April 24. Available at http://blogs.guardian.co.uk/ethicalliving/2008/04/soil_association_v_coop.html, (accessed June 23, 2010).

Monks, Robert, Anthony Miller, and Jacqueline Cook. 2004. "Shareholder Activism on Environmental Issues: A Study of Proposals at Large US Corporations (2000–2003)," *Natural Resources Forum* 28(4): 317–330.

Moore, Julia A. 2001. "Frankenfood or Doubly Green Revolution: Europe vs. America on the GMO Debate," in Albert H. Teich, Stephen D. Nelson, Celia McEnaney, Stephen J. Lita (eds.), *AAAS Science and Technology Policy Yearbook 2001*. Available at http://www.aaas.org/spp/rd/yrbk01.htm, pp. 173–179.

Morris, Julian. 1997. *Green Goods? Consumers, Product Labels and the Environment*. London: Institute of Economic Affairs.

Mother Jones. 2009. "Whole Foods vs. Unions." Available at http://motherjones.com/mojo/2009/03/whole-foods-vs unions (accessed October 26, 2001).

Multinational Monitor. 2005. "Taco Bell Cracks," *Multinational Monitor* 26(3). Available at http://multinationalmonitor.org/mm2005/032005/lines.htm (accessed November 6, 2009).

Munro, Lyle. 2005. "Strategies, Action Repertoires and DIY Activism in the Animal Rights Movement," *Social Movement Studies* 4(1): 75–94.

Murray, Douglas L., Laura T. Raynolds, and Peter L. Taylor. 2006. "The Future of Fair Trade Coffee: Dilemmas Facing Latin America's Small Scale Producers," *Development Practice* 16(2): 179–192.

Murray, Douglas, L. T. Raynolds and P. L. Taylor. 2003. *One Cup at a Time: Poverty Alleviation and Fair Trade in Latin America*, New York: Fair Trade Research Group (Colorado State University) / Ford Foundation.

Murray, Joy. 2004. "Corporate Social Responsibility Discussion Chapter," *Global Social Policy* 4: 171–195.

Mutz, Diana C. 2002. "The Consequences of Cross-Cutting Networks for Political Participation," *American Journal of Political Science* 46(4): 838–855.

Myers, Norman, and Jennifer Kent. 2003. "New Consumers: The Influence of Affluence on the Environment," *Proceeding of the National Academy of Science* 100(8): 4963–4968.

Nader, Ralph, Eleanor J. Lewis, and Eric Weltman. 1992. "Shopping for Innovation: The Government as Smart Consumer," *The American Prospect* 3(11): 71–92.

Naiman, Alisa, Richard H. Glazier, and Rahim Moineddin. 2010. "Association of Anti-Smoking Legislation with rates of Hospital Admission for Cardiovascular and Respiratory Conditions," *Canadian Medical Association Journal* 182(8): 761–767.

Narula, Smita. 2003. "Hindu Nationalism in India," *Harvard Human Rights Journal* 55: 41–68.

National and International Official Day of Action. 2011. "April 23rd Day of Action and Unity: Mission Statement." Available at http://www.dayofactionmovement.org/mission.html (accessed October 24, 2011).

National Commission on the BP Deepwater Horizon Oil Spill and Offshore Drilling. 2011. "Deep water: The Gulf Oil Disaster and the Future of Offshore Drilling." Available at http://www.oilspillcommission.gov/final-report.

National Museum of American History (NMAH) No date. "Sweatshops in America." Available at http://americanhistory.si.edu/sweatshops/intro/intro.htm.

Natural Resources Canada. 2009. "Chrysotile." Available at http://www.nrcan.gc.ca/smm-mms/busi-indu/cmyamc/content/2006/20.pdf (accessed October 24, 2009).

Neilson, Lisa A. 2010. "Boycott or Buycott? Understanding Political Consumerism," *Journal of Consumer Behaviour* 9: 214–227.

Neilson, Lisa, and Pamela Paxton. 2010. "Social Capital and Political Consumerism: A Multilevel Analysis," *Social Problems* 57(1) 5–24.

Nelson, Joan M. 1979. *Access to Power: Politics and the Urban Poor in Developing Nations*, Princeton, NJ: Princeton University Press.

Nelson, Michelle R., Mark A. Rademacher, and Hye-Jin Paek. 2007. "Downshifting Consumer = Upshifting Citizen? An Examination of a Local Freecycle Community," *The ANNALS of the American Academy of Political and Social Science* 611(1): 141–156.

New York Times. 2005a. "The Naked Supply Chain," A Special Advertising Supplement to the New York Times. Available at http://www.ecestudents.ul.ie/course_pages/btech_es/modules/et4407/Supplementary%20Material/1.%20CSR.pdf (accessed June 2006).

New York Times. 2005b. "Consumers, Long the Targets, Become the Shapers of Campaigns," July 1. Available at http://www.nytimes.com/2005/07/01/business/media/01adco.html (accessed January 9, 2012).

New York Times. 2007a. "Anarchists in the Aisles? Stores Provide a Stage," December 24. http://www.nytimes.com/2007/12/24/us/24shopdrop.html?pagewanted=all (accessed January 9, 2012).

New York Times. 2007b. "Burger King Shifts Policy on Animals," March 28. Available at http://www.uri.edu/artsci/ecn/starkey/201–590_bulletinboard/MurderKing.pdf (accessed January 2012).

New York Times. 2007c. "Fast-growing China says Little of Child Slavery's Role," *New York Times,* June 21.

New York Times. 2009a. "Organic Dairies Watch the Good Times Turn Bad." Available at http://www.nytimes.com/2009/05/29/us/29dairy.html?emc=eta1 (accessed December 4, 2009).

New York Times. 2009b. "The Carnivore's Dilemma." Available at http://www.nytimes.com/2009/10/31/opinion/31niman.html?pagewanted=all (accessed October 20, 2011).

New York Times. 2009c. "Will Big Business Save the Earth?" Available at http://www.nytimes.com/2009/12/06/opinion/06diamond.html?pagewanted=all (accessed October 21, 2011).

New York Times. 2012. "BP Will Plead Guilty and Pay Over $4 Billion" Available at http://www.nytimes.com/2012/11/16/business/global/16iht-bp16.html?nl=todaysheadlines&emc=edit_th_20121116 (accessed December 4, 2012).

Newell, Peter. 2008. "CSR and the Limits of Capital," *Development and Change* 39(6): 1063–1078.

Nichols, Alex, and Charlotte Opal. 2005. *Fair Trade. Market-Driven Ethical Consumption*, London: Sage.

Nie, Norman, Sidney Verba, and John Petrocik. 1979. *The Changing American Voter*, Cambridge, MA: Harvard University Press.

Nielsen. 2008. "Corporate Ethics and Fair Trading: A Nielsen Global Consumer Report," Paper prepared for the Nielsen and the University of Oxford Environmental Change Institute, Oxford, UK. Available at http://se.nielsen.com/site/documents/ CSR_Fairtrade_global_reportOctober08.pdf (accessed October 20, 2011).

Niemann, Cajsa. 2004. "Projekt jämställdhetsmärkning. En undersökning av ett rackligt forsook att utveckla en jämställdhetsmärkning av arbetsplatser," B.A. thesis. Stockholm University: Department of Political Science.

Nijhius, Michelle. 2007. "Beyond the Pale Green: Activists and Small-Scale Farmers are going 'Beyond Organic' to push Local Foods," *Grist*, November 12. Available at http://www.grist.org/article/beyond, (accessed December 7, 2011).

Nike Interview. 2004. Interview with Mary Slayton, director of consumer insights, and Caitlin Morris, senior manager of issues management, November 16, 2004.

Nike. 2010. "Nike & OCF launch $1.5 million Nike employee grant fund for local area non-profits," Press release, May 17. Available at http://www.nikebiz.com/media/pr/ 2010/05/17_GrantFund.html, (accessed December 7, 2011).

Nikebiz. 2007. "NIKE, Inc. Outlines Strategies for Global Growth and Market Leadership across Core Consumer Categories." Available at http://www.nikebiz.com/media/ pr/2007/02/6_growthPlans.html (accessed March 24, 2009).

Nikebiz. 2009. "Workers & Factories: Improving conditions in our contract factories." Available at http://www.nikebiz.com/responsibility/workers_and_factories .html (accessed March 24, 2009).

No Sweat. 2004. "H&M briefing 2004." Available at http://www.nosweat.org.uk/node/ 256 (accessed November 1, 2007).

No Sweat. 2007. "Changing an Industry." Available at http://nosweatapparel.com/ index.html (accessed November 1, 2007).

Nordbrand, Sara and Mats Valentin. 2005. *Människor och miljö i fruktindustrin: Två fallstudier från Chile och Sydafrika*, Stockholm: Swedwatch.

Nordic Consumer Ombudsmen. 2005. "Ethical and Environmental Marketing Claims: a Nordic Guideline." Available at http://www.forbrug.dk/fileadmin/Filer/FO_English/ EthicalEnvironmentalMarketing_2005.pdf (accessed October 21, 2011).

Nordic Council of Ministers. No date. "Om nyckelhålet." Available at http://www .norden.org/sv/nordiska-ministerraadet/ministerraad/nordiska-ministerraadet-foer-fiskeri-och-havsbruk-jordbruk-livsmedel-och-skogsbruk-mr-fjls/livsmedelsmaerkn ingen-nyckelhaalet (accessed March 11, 2010).

Nordic Swan. No date. Frågor och svar om Svanens krav på mjukpapper. Available at http://www.svanen.se/PageFiles/4088/FoS_Svanens_mjukpapperskrav .pdf (accessed April 19, 2011).

Norris, Pippa (ed.) 1999. *Critical Citizens: Global Support for Democratic Government*, Oxford: Oxford University Press.

Norris, Pippa. 2001. *Digital Divide: Civic Engagement, Information Poverty and the Internet Worldwide*, Cambridge: Cambridge University Press.

Norris, Pippa. 2002. *Democratic Phoenix: Reinventing Political Activism*, Cambridge: Cambridge University Press.

Norris, Pippa, Stefaan Walgrave, and Peter Van Aelst. 2005. "Who Demonstrates? Anti-state Rebels, Conventional Participants, or Everyone?" *Comparative Politics* 37(2): 189–205.

Northbourne, Lord. 1940. *Look to the Land*. London: Dent.

Nosi, Costanza, and Lorenzo Zanni. 2004. "Moving from 'Typical Products' to 'Food-Related Services': The Slow Food Case as a New Business Paradigm," *British Food Journal* 106(10–11): 779–792.

O'Connor, Jennifer, and Jack Draper. 2011. "EPDs: The Coming Wave in Eco-Labels" *Building Products Digest*, September 2011. Available at http://blog.russellherder .com/UploadFiles/Uploads/EPDs-The-Coming-Wave-in-Eco-Labels.pdf   (accessed October 24, 2011).

O'Neil, Stacey R. 2009. "Consuming for the Environment: a Proposal for Carbon Labels in the United States," *California Western International Law Journal* 39: 393–440.

O'Rourke, Anastasia. 2003. "A New Politics of Engagement: Shareholder Activism for Corporate Social Responsibility," *Business Strategy and the Environment* 12: 227–239.

O'Rourke, Anastasia. 2005. "How Venture Capital Can Help Build Ecopreneurship," in Michael Shaper (ed.), *Making Ecopreneurs: Developing Sustainable Entrepreneurship*, 2nd Edition. Burlington, VT: Ashgate Publishing, pp. 165–184.

O'Rourke, Dara. 2005. "Market Movements: Nongovernmental Organization Strategies to Influence Global Production and Consumption," *Journal of Industrial Ecology* 9(1–2): 115–128.

O'Toole, Therese, Michael Lister, Dave Mars, Su Jones and Alex McDonagh. 2003. "Tuning Out or Left Out? Participation and Non-Participation among Young People," *Contemporary Politics* 9(1): 45–61.

Obama, Barack. 2010. "Remarks by the President to the nation on the BP oil spill." Speech delivered June 15. Available at http://www.whitehouse.gov/the-press-office/ remarks-president-nation-bp-oil-spill.

Oberholtzer, Lydia, Carolyn Dimitri, and Catherine Greene. 2005. "Price Premiums Hold On as US Organic Produce Market Expands," *U.S. Department of Agriculture, Economic Research Service*, Washington, DC: USDA-ERS.

Ochoa, Amalia, Vivien Führ, and Dirk Günther. 2003. "Green Purchasing in Practice in Six European Cities," in Christoph Erdmenger (ed.), *Buying into the Environment: Experiences, Opportunities and Potential for Eco-procurement*, Sheffield, UK: Greenleaf Publishing, pp. 69–116.

Olson, Mancur. 1969. *The Logic of Collective Action: Public Goods and the Theory of Groups*, Cambridge: Harvard University Press.

Oosterveer, Peter. 2007. *Global Governance of Food Production and Consumption: Issues and Challenges*, Cheltenham: Edward Elgar.

Oreskes, Naomi and Erik M. Conway. 2010. "Denial Rides Again: the Revisionist Attack on Rachel Carson" in Naomi Oreskes and Erik M. Conway, *Merchants of doubt*, New York: Bloomsbury Press, pp. 216–239.

Øresund Food Excellence. 2004. "Organic Foods in Sweden Cheapest of EU Nations." Available at http://www.foodoresund.com/composite-279.htm (accessed January 8, 2012).

Organic Consumers Association. 2009. "Cornucopia Institute: Many Organic Soy Food Brands Importing Beans from China." Available at http://www.organicconsumers .org/articles/article_17999.cfm (accessed November 21, 2009).

Organic Consumers Association. 2011. "Unchain Your Heart." Available at http:// www.organicconsumers.org/valentines/index.cfm (accessed December 5, 2011).

Organic Trade Association. 2004. "The OTA 2004 Manufacturer Survey Overview." Available at http://www.ota.com/pics/documents/2004SurveyOverview.pdf (accessed May 13, 2005).

Organic Trade Association. 2010. "Organic Industry Overview." Available at http:// www.ota.com/pics/documents/2010OrganicIndustrySurveySummary.pdf (accessed June 1, 2011).

Organization for Economic Co-operation and Development (OECD). 2003. "Organic Agriculture: Sustainability, Markets, and Policies," Proceedings from an OECD Workshop, Washington DC, United States, September 2002. Paris: OECD and Wallingford: Cabi.

Organization for Economic Cooperation and Development (OECD). 2008. "OECD Social Expenditure Database (SOCX)." Available at http://stats.oecd.org/ (accessed July 17, 2008).

Orleck, Annelise. 1993. "'We are that Mythical Thing Called the Public': Militant Housewives during the Great Depression," *Feminist Studies* 19: 147–172.

Ostrom, Elinor. 1990. *Governing the Commons*, Cambridge: Cambridge University Press.

Oxfam. 2003. "Patents versus Patients: Five Years after the Doha Declaration," Briefing Paper 95. Available at http://www.oxfam.org.uk (accessed April 13, 2007).

Oxfam. 2008. "Oxfam and Allies Persuade Procter & Gamble to Offer Fair Trade Coffee," Available at http://www.maketradefair.com/en/index.php?file= 12092003132827.htm (accessed December 9, 2007).

Oxfam International. 2004. "Trading Away Our Rights: Women Working in Global Supply Chains," Oxford: Oxfam International. Available at http://www .maketradefair.com/en/assets/english/taor.pdf (accessed December 10, 2012).

Pacelle, Wayne. 2005. "Decisions we Make" in *The Humane Society of the United States (HSUS) Guide to Vegetarian Eating*, Washington, DC: HSUS. Available at http://www.humanesociety.org/assets/pdfs/farm/gve.pdf (accessed December 10, 2012).

Pacheco, Juilianna Sandell, and Eric Plutzer. 2008. "Political Participation and Cumulative Disadvantage: The Impact of Economic and Social Hardship on Young Citizens," *Journal of Social Issues* 64(3): 571–593.

Parking, Wendy, and Geoffrey Craig. 2006. *Slow Living*, New York: Berg Publishers.

Parsons, William. 2005. *Niche Market or an Expanding Industry? Organic Fruit and Vegetable Production in Canada*, Ottawa: Statistics Canada.

Patel, Raj. 2007. *Stuffed and Starved*, London: Portobello.

Pateman, Carole. 1970. *Participation and Democratic Theory*, Cambridge: Cambridge University Press.

Pellizzoni, Luigi. 2004. "Responsibility and Environmental Governance," *Environmental Politics* 13: 541–565.

Pelsmacker, Patrick, Liesbeth Driesen, and Glenn Rayp. 2005. "Do Consumers Care about Ethics? Willingness to Pay for Fair Trade Coffee," *Journal of Consumer Affairs* 39(2): 363–385.

People for the Ethical Treatment of Animals (PETA). 2011. "Shareholder Campaigns." Available at http://www.peta.org/issues/animals-used-for-experimentation/shareholder-campaigns.aspx (accessed October 20, 2011).

People for the Ethical Treatment of Animals (PETA). No date (a). "McCruelty" web site, http://www.mccruelty.com/ (accessed December 13, 2011).

People for the Ethical Treatment of Animals (PETA). No date (b). "Kentucky Fried Cruelty" web site, http://www.kentuckyfriedcruelty.com/ (accessed December 13, 2011).

People for the Ethical Treatment of Animals UK (PETA UK). No date. "Chantelle Houghton asks, 'Eating meat got you down?'" PETA UK web site, http://action.peta.org.uk/ea-campaign/clientcampaign.do?ea.campaign.id=6118&ea.client.id=5 (accessed December 13, 2011).

Peretti, Jonah, and Michele Micheletti. 2006 (2004). "The Nike Sweatshop Email: Political Consumerism, Internet, and Culture Jamming," in Michele Micheletti, Andreas Follesdal, and Dietlind Stolle (eds.), *Politics, Products, and Markets: Exploring Political Consumerism Past and Present*, New Brunswick: Transaction Publishers, pp. 127–142.

Pérezgrovas Garza, Victor, and Edith Cervantes Trejo. 2002. *Poverty Alleviation through Participation in Fair Trade Coffee Networks: The Case of Unión Majomut, Chiapas, Mexico*, New York: Fair Trade Research Group (Colorado State University)/Ford Foundation.

Perrini, Francesco. 2005. "Building a European Portrait of Corporate Social Responsibility Reporting," *European Management Journal* 23(6): 611–627.

Peters, B. Guy, and Jon Pierre (eds.) 2007. *Handbook of Public Administration*, London: Sage Publications.

Peters, B. Guy. 2010. "Meta-Governance and Public Management," in Stephen P. Osborne (ed.), *The New Public Governance: Emerging Perspectives on the Theory and Practice of Public Governance*, London: Routledge, pp. 36–51.

Petersson, Olof, and Sören Holmberg. 2008. *Svenska partibarometrar 2008*, En dokumentation. Stockholm: SNS. Available at http://olofpetersson.se/_arkiv/dr/partibarometrar_2008.pdf.

Petersson, Olof, Anders Westholm, and Goran Blomberg. 1989. *Medborgarnas makt*, Stockholm: Carlssons.

Petersson, Olof, Jörgen Hermansson, Michele Micheletti, Jan Teorell, and Anders Westholm. 1998. *Demokrati och medborgarskap Demokratirådets rapport 1998*. Stockholm: SNS Förlag.

Petrini, Carlo. 2006. *Slow Food: The Case for Taste*, Irvington: Columbia University Press.

Pezzullo, Phaedra. 2011. "Contextualizing Boycotts and Buycotts: The Impure Politics of Consumer-Based Advocacy in an Age of Global Ecological Crises," *Communication and Critical/Cultural Studies* 8(2): 124–145.

Pfaller, Alfred, and Marika Lerch. 2005. *Challenges of Globalization: New Trends in International Politics and Society*. New Brunswick, NJ: Transaction Publishers.

Pfannhauser, Werner, and Markus Reichhart. 2003. "Consumer Attitude and Food Choice," Flair-Flow 4 synthesis report. Paris: Institut National de la Recherche Agronomique.

Pharr, Susan J., and Robert D. Putnam (eds.) 2000. *Disaffected Democracies: What's Troubling the Trilateral Countries?* Princeton, NJ: Princeton University Press.

Phillips, F. 2005. "Vegetarian Nutrition," *Nutrition Bulletin* 30(2): 132–167.

Pickett, Melanie S., Susan E. Schober, Debra J. Brody, Lester R. Curtin, and Gary A. Giovino. 2006. "Smoke-Free Laws and Second-hand Smoke Exposure in US non-Smoking Adults, 1999–2002," *Tobacco Control* 15(4): 302–307.

Pierre, Jon (ed.) 1998. *Partnerships in Urban Governance: European and American Experiences.* Basingstoke: Macmillan.

Pietrykowski, Bruce. 2004. "You are What You Eat: The Social Economy of the Slow Food Movement," *Review of Social Economy* 62(3): 307–321.

Pines, Gina L. S., and David G. Meyer. 2005. "Stopping the Exploitation of Workers: An Analysis of the Effective Application of Consumer or Socio-Political Pressure," *Journal of Business Ethics* 59(2005): 155–162.

Piotrowski, Ralph, and Stefan Kratz. 1999. "Eco-labelling in the Globalised Economy," *Politik und Gesellschaft / International Politics and Society* 1999(4): 430–443. Available at http://www.fes.de/ipg/ipg4_99/ARTPIOTROWSKI-KRATZ.PDF.

Political Action Survey. 1974. Data Set available at the ICPSR web site. http://www.icpsr.umich.edu/icpsrweb/landing.jsp.

Pollan, Michael. 2006. *The Omnivore's Dilemma: A Natural History of Four Meals,* New York: The Penguin Press.

Pollin, Robert, Justin Burns, and James Heintz. 2004. "Global Apparel Production and Sweatshop Labour: Can Raising Retail Prices Finance Living Wages?" *Cambridge Journal of Economics* 28: 153–171.

Porter, Stephen, and Michael E. Whitcomb. 2003. "The Impact of Contact Type on Web Survey Response Rates," *The Public Opinion Quarterly* 67(4): 579–588.

Portilho, Fátima. 2010. "Self-Attribution of Responsibility: Consumers of Organic Foods in a Certified Street Market in Rio de Janerio, Brazil," *Etnográfica* 14(3): 549–565.

Potoski, Matthew, and Neal D. Woods. 2002. "Dimensions of State Environmental Policies: Air Pollution Regulation in the United States," *Policy Studies Journal* 30(2): 208–226.

Powell, Benjamin, and Matt Zwolinski. 2011. "The Ethical and Economic Case Against Sweatshop Labor: A Critical Assessment," SSRN Papers. http://papers.ssrn.com/sol3/papers.cfm?abstract_id=1947569.

Prakash, Aseem, and Matthew Potoski. 2006. *Voluntary Environmentalists: Green Clubs, ISO 14001, and Voluntary Environmental Regulations,* Cambridge: Cambridge University Press.

Prewitt, Milford. 2005. "Red Lobster Faces Protests for not Joining Boycott of Canadian Seafood," *Nation's Restaurant News* 39(22): 1–3.

Princen, Thomas, and Matthias Finger. 1994. *Environmental NGOs in World Politics: Linking the Local and the Global,* London: Routledge.

Pruitt, Stephen, and Monroe Friedman. 1986. "Determining the Effectiveness of Consumer Boycotts: A Stock Price Analysis of Their Impact on Corporate Targets," *Journal of Consumer Policy* 9: 375–387.

Putnam, Robert D. (ed.) 2002. *Democracies in Flux: The Evolution of Social Capital in Contemporary Society,* Oxford: Oxford University Press.

Putnam, Robert D. 1993. "The Prosperous Community: Social Capital and Public Life," *The American Prospect* 13: 35–42.

Putnam, Robert D. 1995. "Bowling Alone: America's Declining Social Capital," *Journal of Democracy* 6(1): 65–78.

Putnam, Robert D. 2000. *Bowling Alone: The Collapse and Revival of American Community*, New York: Simon & Schuster.

Putnam, Robert D., Lewis Feldstein, and Don Cohen. 2003. *Better Together: Restoring the American Community*, New York: Simon and Schuster.

Quintelier, Ellen. 2007. "Differences in Political Participation between Young and Old People," *Contemporary Politics* 13(2): 165–180.

Rainforest Action Network (RAN). 2008. Letter sent to Andre Giacini de Freitas, executive director of FSC International, October 13. Available at http://understory .ran.org/wordpress/wp-content/uploads/2008/10/ran-to-fsc-101308.pdf.

Ramsey, Lisa P. 2010. "Brandjacking on Social Networks: Trademark Infringement by Impersonation of Markholders," *Buffalo Law Review* 58: 851–929.

Rask Jensen, Hans. 2003. "Staging Political Consumption: A Discourse Analysis of the Brent Spar Conflict as Recast by the Danish Mass Media," *Journal of Retailing and Consumer Services* 10(2): 71–80.

Rättvisemärkt. 2004. *Vad kostar rättvisemärkt*, Frågor och Svar om Rättvisemärkt. http://www.rattvisemarkt.se (accessed August 14, 2004).

Raynolds, Laura T. 2000. "Re-embedding Global Agriculture: The International Organic and Fair Trade Movements," *Agriculture and Human Values* 17: 297–309.

Raynolds, Laura T. 2004. "The Globalization of Organic Agro-Food Networks," *World Development* 32(5): 725–743.

Raynolds, Laura T., Douglas Murray, and Andrew Heller. 2007. "Regulating Sustainability in the Coffee Sector: A Comparative Analysis of Third Party Environmental and Social Certification Initiatives," *Agriculture and Human Values* 24(2): 147–163.

Raynolds, Laura T., Douglas Murray, and John Wilkinson. 2007. *Fair Trade. The Challenges of Transforming Globalization*, London: Routledge.

Reed, Darryl. 2009. "What Do Corporations Have to Do with Fair Trade? Positive and Normative Analysis from a Value Chain Perspective," *Journal of Business Ethics* 86(1): 3–26.

Reed, Matthew. 2010. *Rebels for the Soil: The Rise of the Global Organic Food and Farming Movement*. London: Earthscan Ltd.

Reed, Matthew. 2001. "Fight the Future! How the Contemporary Campaigns of the UK Organic Movement Have Arisen from their Composting of the Past," *Sociologia Ruralis* 41(1): 131–145.

Rehbein, K., S. Waddock, and S. B. Graves. 2004. "Understanding Shareholder Activism: Which Corporations are Targeted?" *Business & Society* 43: 239–267.

Reid, Erin M., and Michael W. Toffel. 2009. "Responding to Public and Private Politics: Corporate Disclosure of Climate Change Strategies," *Strategic Management Journal* 30(11): 1157–1178.

Reijnders, Lucas and Sam Soret. 2003. "Quantification of the Environmental Impact of Different Dietary Protein Choices," *The American Journal and Clinical Nutrition* 78(3): 664S–668S.

Reinhardt, Forest, Ramon Casadesus-Masanell, and Debbie Freier. 2004. "Patagonia," Harvard Business School, Case 9-703-035.

Renard, Marie-Christine. 2005. "Quality Certification, Regulation and Power in Fair Trade," *Journal of Rural Studies* 21: 419–431.

Reuters. 2008. "Unilever Participates in Industry Forum at the Grocery Manufacturers Association's First Environmental Sustainability." Available at http://www.reuters .com/article/pressRelease/idUS225168+18-Jan-2008+MW20080118 (accessed January 5, 2012).

Reuters. 2011. "Nestlé Head Emphasizes Profiting from Doing Good." Available at http://www.reuters.com/article/2011/03/22/philanthropy-corporate-idUSN22146666620110322 (accessed May 28, 2011).

Revesz, Richard L. 1997. "The Race to the Bottom and Federal Environmental Regulation: A Response to Critics," *Minnesota Law Review* 82(2): 535–564.

Rice, Robert A. 2001. "Noble Goals and Challenging Terrains: Organic and Fair Trade Coffee Movements in the Global Marketplace," *Journal of Agricultural and Environmental Ethics* 14(1): 39–66.

Risse-Kappen, Thomas (ed.) 1995. *Bringing Transnational Relations Back in: Non-State Actors, Domestic Structures, and International Institutions*, Cambridge: Cambridge University Press.

Ritzer, George. 1983. "The McDonaldization of Society," *Journal of American Culture* 6(1): 100–107.

Ritzer, George. 2004. *The McDonaldization of Society*. Thousand Oaks, CA: Pine Forge Press.

Robertson, David. 2006. *International Economics and Confusing Politics*, Cheltenham: Edward Elgar Publishing.

Robin, Marie-Monique. 2010. *The World According to Monsanto: Pollution, Corruption, and the Control of the World's Food Supply*, New York: New Press.

Robinson, B. A. 2006. "Boycott of Walt Disney: Further Developments." Available at http://www.religioustolerance.org/disney3.htm (accessed July 16, 2009).

Rochon, Thomas R., and Daniel A. Mazmanian. 1992. "Social Movements and the Policy Process," *The ANNALS of the American Academy of Political and Social Science* 528(July): 75–87.

Rock, Michael. 2001. "Public Disclosure of the Sweatshop Practices of American Multinational Garment/Shoe-Makers/Retailers: Impacts on their Stock Prices," Technical paper 252. Washington, DC: Economic Policy Institute.

Rodriguez, Elsa, Victoria Lacaze, and Beatriz Lupin. 2007. "Willingness to Pay for Organic Food in Argentina: Evidence from a Consumer Survey." Paper presented at the 105th EAAE Seminar, Bologna: March 8–10, 2007. Available at http://www.bean-quorum.net/EAAE/pdf/EAAE105_Paper067.pdf (accessed October 20, 2011).

Rodriguez-Garavito, César. 2005. "Global Governance and Labor Rights: Codes of Conduct and Anti-Sweatshop Struggles in Global Apparel Factories in Mexico and Guatemala," *Politics & Society* 33: 203–233.

Rodrik, Dan. 1999. *The New Global Economy and the Developing Countries: Making Openness Work*. Washington, DC: Development Council.

Roff, Robin Jane. 2007. "Shopping for Change? Neo-liberalizing Activism and the Limits to Eating non-GMO," *Agriculture and Human Values* 24(4): 511–522.

Ronald McDonald House Charities. "Our History". http://rmhc.org/who-we-are/our-history/ (accessed February 20, 2011).

Ronchi, Loraine. 2002. "The Impact of Fair Trade on Producers and Their Organisations: A Case Study with Coocafé in Costa Rica." PRUS (Poverty Research Unit at

Sussex) Working Chapter No. 11. Available at http://www.sussex.ac.uk/Units/PRU/wps/wp11.pdf (accessed January 5, 2012).

Röös, Elin, Cecilia Sundberg, and Per-Anders Hansson. 2010. "Uncertainties in the Carbon Footprint of Food Products: a Case Study on Table Potatoes," *The International Journal of Life Cycle Assessment* 15(5): 478–488.

Rootes, C. 1997. "Shaping Collective Action: Structure, Contingency and Knowledge," in R. Edmondson (ed.), *The Political Context of Collective Action*. London & NY: Routledge, pp. 81–104.

Rose, Nikolas S. 1999. *Powers of Freedom: Reframing Political Thought*, Cambridge: Cambridge University Press.

Rosenkrands, Jacob. 2004. "Politicizing Homo Economicus: An Analysis of Anti-Corporate Websites," in Wim Van De Donk, Brian D. Loader, Paul G. Nixon, and Dieter Rucht (eds.), *Cyberprotest: New Media, Citizens and Social Movements*, New York: Routledge, pp. 57–76.

Rosenstone, Steven J., and John Mark Hansen. 1993. *Mobilization, Participation, and Democracy in America*. New York: MacMillan.

Ross, Andrew (ed.) 1997. *No Sweat: Fashion, Free Trade, and the Rights of Garment Workers*. London: Verso.

Ross, Andrew. 1997. "After the Year of the Sweatshop: Postscript," in *No Sweat: Fashion, Flee Trade, and the Rights of Garment Workers*. New York: Verso, pp. 291–296.

Rostgaard, Tine. 2006. "Constructing the Care Consumer: Free Choice of Home Care for the Elderly in Denmark," *European Societies* 8(3): 443–463.

Rothstein, Bo. 1987. Corporatism and Reformism: The Social Democratic Institutionalization of Class Conflict. *Acta Sociologica* 30: 295–311.

Rubenson, Daniel, André Blais, Patrick Fournier, Elisabeth Gidengil, and Neil Nevitte. 2004. "Accounting for the Age Gap in Turnout," *Acta Politica* 39(4): 407–421.

Rubik, Frieder. 2005. *The Future of Eco-labelling. Making Environmental Product Information Systems Effective*, Sheffield: Greenleaf Publishing.

Ruggie, John G. 2003. "Taking Embedded Liberalism Global: the Corporate Connection" in David Held and Matthias Koenig Archibugi (eds.), *Taming Globalization: Frontiers of Governance*. Cambridge, MA: Polity Press, pp. 93–129.

Ruggie, John G. 2006. "Remarks by John G. Ruggie." Speech delivered at a forum on corporate social responsibility co-sponsored by the Fair Labor Association and the German Network of Business Ethics, Bamberg, Germany, June 14. Available at http://www.reports-and-materials.org/Ruggie-remarks-to-Fair-Labor-Association-and-German-Network-of-Business-Ethics-14-June-2006.pdf.

Ruggie, John G. 2009. "3rd Annual Responsible Investment Forum: Keynote address." Speech delivered at 3rd Annual Responsible Investment Forum, New York, January 12. Available at http://www.reports-and-materials.org/Ruggie-address-to-Responsible-Invest-Forum-12-Jan-2009.pdf.

Rumbo, Joseph D. 2002. "Consumer Resistance in a World of Advertising Clutter: The Case of Adbusters," *Psychology & Marketing* 19(2): 127–148.

Sabatier, Paul A. 1991. "Toward Better Theories of the Policy Process," *PS: Political Science and Politics* 24(2): 147–156.

Sabel, C., A. Fung and D. O'Rourke. 2000. "Ratcheting Labour Standards: How Open Competition can save Ethical Sourcing," in Raj Thamotheram (ed.), *Visions of Ethical Sourcing*, London: Financial Times-Prentice Hall. Chapter available at http://www2 .law.columbia.edu/sabel/papers/fintimes.pdf.

Sandlin, Jennifer A. 2007. "Popular Culture, Cultural Resistance, and Anti-Consumption Activism: An Exploration of Culture Jamming as Critical Adult Education," *New Directions for Adult and Continuing Education* 115: 73–183.

Sara Lee. 2011. "Press release: Sara Lee launches ambitious five-year sustainable coffee plan." Available at http://www.saralee.com/en/NewsAndMedia/News/2011/SaraLeelaunchesambitiousfive-yearsustainablecoffeeplan.aspx (accessed June 7, 2011).

Sassatelli, Roberta, and Federica Davolio. 2010. "Consumption, Pleasure and Politics: Slow Food in the Politicio-Aesthetic Probeimization of Food," *Journal of Consumer Culture* 10: 202–231.

Sassatelli, Roberta. 2006. "Virtue, Responsibility and Consumer Choice: Framing Critical Consumerism," in John Brewer and Frank Trentmann (eds.), *Consuming Cultures, Global Perspectives. Historical Trajectories, Transnational Exchanges*, Oxford: Berg Publishing, pp. 219–250.

Sasser, Erika N., Benjamin Cashore, Aseem Prakash, and Graeme Auld. 2006. "Direct Targeting as an NGO Political Strategy: Examining Private Authority Regimes in the Forestry Sector," *Business and Politics* 8(3): 1–32.

Scan. 2009. "Scan saluför två ekologiska certifieringar." Press release, November 17. Available at http://www.scan.se/sitebase/default.aspx?idnr=vEso1DBBonYKTiz8okSgcmdNAuJQ8oVTLNK8HXlvGbEttTKjGKaj8K2mNIZe.

Schild, Verónica. 2007. "Empowering 'Consumer-Citizens" or Governing Pool Female Subjects?: The Institutionalization of Self-Development in the Chilean Social Policy Field." *Journal of Consumer Culture* 7(2): 179–203.

Schlozman, Kay Lehman. 2010. "Creative Participation: Concluding Thought from the Land of the Boston Tea Party," in Michele Micheletti and Andrew McFarland (eds.), *Creative Participation: Responsibility-Taking in the Political World*, Bolder, CO: Paradigm Publishers, pp. 171–185.

Schmelzer, Matthias. 2010. "Marketing Morals, Moralizing Markets: Assessing the Effectiveness of Fair Trade as a Form of Boycott," *Management & Organizational History* 5(2): 221–250.

Schumpeter, Joseph. 1942. *Capitalism, Socialism and Democracy*, New York: Harper & Brothers.

Schurman, Rachel. 2004. "Fighting Frankenfoods: Industry Structures and the Efficacy of the Anti-Biotech Movement in Western Europe," *Social Problems* 51(2): 243–268.

Schurman, Rachel, and William Munro. 2006. "Ideas, Thinkers and Social Networks: The Process of Grievance Construction in the Anti-Genetic Engineering Movement," *Theory and Society* 35(1): 1–38.

Schurman, Rachel, and William Munro. 2009. "Targeting capital: A Cultural Economy Approach to Understanding the Efficacy of Two Anti-Genetic Engineering Movements," *American Journal of Sociology* 115(1): 155–202.

Schwarcz, Joe. 2007. *An Apple a Day: The Myths, Misconceptions, and Truths about the Foods We Eat*, Toronto: Harper Collins.

Schwartz, Priscilla. 2009. "Corporate Activities and Environmental Justice: Perspectives on Sierra Leone's Mining," in Ebbesson and Okowa (eds.), *Environmental Law and Justice in Context*. Cambridge: Cambridge University Press, pp. 429–446.

Seidman, Gay. 2008. "Transnational Labour Campaigns: Can the Logic of the Market Be Turned Against Itself?" *Development & Change* 39(6): 991–1003.

Seidman, Gay W. 2003. "Monitoring Multinationals: Lessons from the Anti-Apartheid Era," *Politics & Society* 31(3): 381–406.

Seijts, Gerald, and Michael Sider. 2006. "PETA's 'Kentucky Fried Chicken, Inc' Campaign," in Gerald H Seijts, *Cases in Organizational Behavior*, Thousand Oaks, CA: Sage Publications.

Sennett, Richard. 2006. *The Culture of the New Capitalism*, New Haven: Yale University Press.

Severson, Kim. 2008. "Slow Food Savors Its Big Moment," *The New York Times*, July 23, 2008. Available at http://www.nytimes.com/2008/07/23/dining/23slow.html?pagewanted=1 (accessed October 24, 2011).

Shapiro, Ian, and Casiano Hacker-Cordon (eds.) 1999. *Democracy's Value*, Cambridge: Cambridge University Press.

Shaw, Deirdre, Gillan Hogg, Elaine Wilson, Edward Shui, and Louise Hassan. 2006. "Fashion Victim: The Impact of Fair Trade Concerns on Clothing Choice," *Journal of Strategic Marketing* 14: 427–440.

Shaw, Randy. 1999. *Reclaiming America: Nike, Clean Air, and the New National Activism*, Berkeley: University of California Press.

Sherrod, Lonnie R. 2006. *Youth Activism: an International Encyclopedia, Volume 2*. Greenwood Publishing Group. http://books.google.ca/books?id=pnvJC_8-KGQC&dq=internet+political+consumerism&source=gbs_navlinks_s.

Sherry, John F. Jr. 1998. "The Soul of the Company Store. Nike Town Chicago and the Emplaced Brandscape," in *ServicsScapes: The Concept of Place in Contemporary Markets*, NTC Business Books. American Marketing Association, pp. 109–146.

Shirky, Clay. 2008. *Here Comes Everybody: How Change Happens When People Come Together*, London: Penguin Books.

Shiva, Vandan. 2001. *Protect or Plunder? Understanding Intellectual Property Rights*, London: Zed Books.

Short, Katherine. 2003. "Is Eco-Labelling Working: For Marine Ecosystems, WWF and the MSC?" in Bruce Phillips, Trevor Ward and Chet Chaffee (eds.), *Eco-labelling in fisheries: What is it all about?* Oxford: Blackwell Science, pp. 181–185.

Siaroff, Alan. 1999. "Corporatism in 24 Industrial Democracies: Meaning and Measurement." *European Journal of Political Research* 36: 175–205.

Sidwell, Marc. 2008. "Unfair Trade" Adam Smith Institute Paper accessed at http://es.scribd.com/doc/25689582/Marc-Sidwell-Unfair-Trade.

Sierra Club. 2006. "Inhumane Treatment of Farm Animals." http://www.columbia.org/pdf_files/husbandry.pdf.

SIFO. 2001. *Vad händer med Sverige?* Stockholm: SIFO, unpublished report.

Sikkink, Kathryn. 1986. "Codes of Conduct for Transnational Corporations: The Case of the WHO/UNICEF Code," *International Organization* 40: 815–840.

Silvey, Rachel. 2004. "A Wrench in the Global Works: Anti-Sweatshop Activism on Campus," *Antipode* 36(2): 191–197.

Simonson, Peter. 2001. "Social Noise and Segmented Rhythms: News, Entertainment, and Celebrity in the Crusade for Animal Rights," *The Communication Review* 4(3): 399–420.

Simula, Markku. 2006. "Public Procurement Policies for Forest Products and Their Impacts, Draft Discussion Paper," Food and Agricultural Association of the United Nations, http://www.fao.org/forestry/11153–ocd5c4f14302b06791405f3bb09328f12.pdf, (accessed August 9, 2012).

Singh, Jang B. 2006. "A Comparison of the Contents of the Codes of Ethics of Canada's Largest Corporations in 1992 and 2003," *Journal of Business Ethics* 64: 17–29.

Singh, Jang, Göran Svensson, Greg Wood, Michael Callaghan. 2011. "A Longitudinal and Cross-Cultural Study of the Contents of Codes of Ethics of Australian, Canadian and Swedish Corporations," *Business Ethics: A European Review* 20(1): 103–119.

Sjöström, Emma. 2008. "Shareholder Activism for Corporate Social Responsibility: What Do We Know?" *Sustainable Development* 16: 141–154.

Ski, David E. 1985. *The Simple Life: Plain Living and High Thinking in American Culture*, New York: Oxford University Press.

Sklar, Kathryn Kish. 1998. "The Consumers' White Label Campaign of the National Consumers' League 1898–1919," in Susan Strasser, Charles McGovern, Matthias Judt, Daniel S. Mattern, Christof Mauch, and David Lazar (eds.), *Getting and Spending: European and American Consumer Societies in the 20th Century*, Cambridge: Cambridge University Press, pp. 17–36.

Skocpol, Theda. 2003. *Diminished Democracy: From Membership to Management in American Civic Life*, Norman, OK: University of Oklahoma Press.

Sligh, Michael, and Carolyn Christman. 2003. *Who Owns Organic? The Global Status, Prospects, and Challenges of a Changing Organic Market*, Pittsboro, NC: Rural Advancement Foundational International.

Slow Food USA. 2011a. "Slow Food on Campus," Available at http://www.slowfoodusa.org/index.php/programs/details/slow_food_on_campus/ (accessed July 4, 2012).

Slow Food USA. 2011b. "Slow Food in Schools Projects," Available at http://www.slowfoodusa.org/index.php/programs/in_schools_detail/national_education_projects/ (accessed July 4, 2012).

Sluiter, Liesbeth. 2009. *Clean Clothes: A Global Movement to End Sweatshops*, New York: Pluto Press.

Smart, Andrew. 2004. "Adrift in the Mainstream: Challenges Facing the UK Vegetarian Movement," *British Food Journal* 106(2): 79–92.

Smith, Jeffrey. 2010. "Monsanto: The World's Poster Child for Corporate Manipulation and Deceit: Part 1," *The Huffington Post*, 18 January. Available at http://www.huffingtonpost.com/jeffrey-smith/monsanto-the-worlds-poste_b_427035.html.

Smith, Michael B. 2001. "'Silence, Miss Carson!' Science, Gender, and the Reception of 'Silent Spring,'" *Feminist Studies* 27(3): 733–752.

Smith, N. Craig. 1990. *Morality and the Market: Consumer Pressure for Corporate Accountability*, London: Routledge.

Smith, N. Craig, C. B. Bhattacherya, David Vogel, and David I. Levine (eds.), 2010. *Global Challenges in Responsible Business*, Cambridge: Cambridge University Press.

Smith, Paul. 1997. "Tommy Hilfiger in the Age of Mass Customization," in Andrew
    Ross (ed.), *No Sweat: fashion, free trade, and the rights of garment workers*, London:
    Verso, pp. 249–262.
Smith, Paul M., Donald B. Verrilli, Julie Carpenter, and Deanne E. Maynard. 2003. "The
    First Amendment and the 2002 Term (at least until September)," *Communications
    Lawyer* 21(2): 26–28.
Smith, Thomas, and Gregory Stevens. 2002. "Hyperstructures and the Biology of Inter-
    personal Dependence: Rethinking Reciprocity and Altruism," *Sociological Theory*
    20(1): 106–130.
Socialist International. 2008. "Member parties of the Socialist International."
    Available at http://www.socialistinternational.org/viewArticle.cfm?ArticlePageID=
    931 (accessed July 9, 2008).
Soil Association. 2001. *Organic Food and Farming Report 2000*.
Soil Association. 2010. "Organic Market Report." Available at http://www
    .soilassociation.org/LinkClick.aspx?fileticket=bTXno01MTtM=&tabid=116   (ac-
    cessed June 1, 2011).
Solum, Lawrence B. "Legal Theory Lexicon 022: Intention" Available at http://
    lsolum.typepad.com/legal_theory_lexicon/2004/02/legal_theory_le_3.html (accessed
    February 20, 2011).
Sønderskov, Kim Mannemar. 2009. "Different Goods, Different Effects: Exploring the
    Effects of Generalized Social Trust in Large-N Collective Action," *Public Choice*
    140(1–2): 145–160.
Sønderskov, Kim Mannemar, and Carsten Daugbjerg. 2011. "The State and Consumer
    Confidence in Eco-Labelling: Organic Labelling in Denmark, Sweden, the United
    Kingdom and the United States," *Agriculture and Human Values* 28: 507–517.
Soper, Kate. 2007. "Re-thinking the 'Good Life': the Citizenship Dimension of Con-
    sumer Dissatisfaction with Consumerism," *Journal of Consumer Culture* 7(2): 205–
    229.
Soper, Kate and Frank Trentmann. 2008. *Citizenship and Consumption*, New York:
    Palgrave MacMillan.
Sørensen, Eva. 1997. "Brugeren og demokratiet," *Grus* 53: 81–96
SOU. 2001:9. Reglerna kring och inställningen till frivillig jämställdhetsmärkning av
    produkter och tjänster. Stockholm: Fritzes kundtjänst. *Governmental Report*.
Spaargaren, Gert, and Arthur P. J. Mol. 2008. "Greening Global Consumption: Redefin-
    ing Politics and Authority," *Global Environmental Change* 42(1): 273–287.
Spaargaren, Gert, and Peter Oosterveer. 2010. "Citizen-Consumers as Agents of Change
    in Globalizing Modernity: The Case of Sustainable Consumption," *Sustainability*
    2(7): 1887–1908.
Spar, Debora L., and Lane T. La Mure. 2003. "The Power of Activism: Assessing the
    Power of NGOs on Global Business," *California Management Review* 45(3): 78–
    101.
Stahler, Charles. 2010. "How Many Youth in the U.S. Are Vegetarian?" *The Vegetarian
    Research Group*. Available online: http://www.vrg.org/journal/vj2010issue3/2010_
    issue3_youth_poll.php (accessed February 2011).
Stahler, Charles. 2011. "How Often Do Americans Eat Vegetarian Meals? And How
    Many Adults in the U.S. Are Vegan?" *The Vegetarian Research Group*. Available
    online: http://www.vrg.org/journal/vj2011issue4/vj2011issue4poll.php.

Steffens, Melanie C. 2005. "Implicit and Explicit Attitudes towards Lesbians and Gay Men," *Journal of Homosexuality* 49(2): 39–66.

Steger, Marie Anne, and Witt, Stephanie L. 1989. "Gender Differences in Environmental Orientations: A Comparison of Publics and Activists in Canada and the US," *Western Political Quarterly* 42: 627–649.

Steinberg, Marc. 1998. "Tilting the Frame: Considerations on Collective Action Framing from a Discursive Turn," *Theory and Society* 27: 845–872.

Stiglitz, J. E., and A. Charlton. 2005. *Fair Trade For All: How Trade Can Promote Development*, Oxford: Oxford University Press.

Stolle, Dietlind, and Elisabeth Gidengil. 2010. "What do Women Really Know? A Gendered Analysis of Varieties of Political Knowledge," *Perspectives on Politics* 8(1): 93–109.

Stolle, Dietlind, and Laura Nishikawa. 2011. "Trusting Others – How Parents Shape the Generalized Trust of Their Children," *Comparative Sociology* 10(2) 281–314.

Stolle, Dietlind, and Marc Hooghe. 2006 (2004). "Consumers as Political Participants: Shifts in Political Action Repertoires in Western Societies," in Michele Micheletti, Andreas Follesdal and Dietlind Stolle (eds.), *Politics, Products, and Markets: Exploring Political Consumerism Past and Present*, New Brunswick, NJ: Transaction Press, pp. 101–125.

Stolle, Dietlind, and Marc Hooghe. 2004. "Emerging Action Repertoires – An Empirical Investigation of New Forms of Participation," paper delivered at the ECPR Joint Sessions Workshop "Emerging Repertoires of Political Action" in Uppsala April 13–18.

Stolle, Dietlind, and Marc Hooghe. 2005. "Inaccurate, Exceptional, One-Sided or Irrelevant? The Debate About the Alleged Decline of Social Capital and Civic Engagement in Western Societies," *British Journal of Political Science* 35(1): 149–167.

Stolle, Dietlind, and Marc Hooghe. 2011. "Shifting Inequalities: Patterns of Exclusion and Inclusion in Emerging Forms of Political Participation," *European Societies* 13(1): 119–142.

Stolle, Dietlind, and Michele Micheletti. 2005. "The Gender Gap Reversed," in Brenda O'Neill and Elisabeth Gidengil (eds.), *Gender and Social Capital*, London: Routledge.

Stolle, Dietlind, March Hooghe, and Michele Micheletti. 2005. "Politics in the Supermarket: Political Consumerism as a Form of Political Participation," *International Political Science Review* 26(3): 245–269.

Stolle, Dietlind, Michele Micheletti, and Daniel Berlin. 2010. "Politik, konsumtion och delaktighet," in *Fokus 10: En analys av ungas inflytande*, Stockholm: Ungdomsstyrelsen, pp. 316–341.

Stone, Clarence. 1980. "Systemic Power in Community Decision Making: A Restatement of Stratification Theory," *American Political Science Review* 74(4): 978–990.

Stop Child Labour. 2007. "The Consumer and Child Labour." Available at http://www.stopchildlabour.net/reportsanddownloads/Child_labour_Sec5.pdf (accessed August 15, 2009).

Stop Huntingdon Animal Cruelty (SHAC). 2011. "History of SHAC." Available at http://www.shac.net/SHAC/history.html (accessed October 25, 2011).

Story, Louise. "Advertising; Consumers, Long the Targets, Become the Shapers of Campaigns," July 1, 2005. *New York Times*. http://www.nytimes.com/2005/07/01/business/media/01adco.html (accessed December 10, 2012).

Strømnes, Kristin. 2005. "Political Consumption in Norway. Who, Why – and Does it Have Any Effect?" in Magnus Boström, Andreas Føllesdal, Mikael Klintman, Michele Micheletti and Mads P. Sørensen (eds.), *Political Consumerism: Its Motivations, Power, and Conditions in the Nordic Countries and Elsewhere*, pp. 113–144. Proceedings from the 2nd International Seminar on Political Consumerism, Oslo, Norway, August 26–29.

Strømnes, Kristin. 2003. *Folkets makt: Medborgerskap, demokrati, deltakelse*. Oslo: Gyldendal Akademisk.

Sun, William H. 1997. "Performative Politics and International Media," *The Drama Review* 41(4): 510.

Sustainable Development Commission (SDC). 2006. "Sustainable Development in Government: Fifth Annual Report." Available at http://www.sd-commission.org.uk/publications/downloads/sdig_report_2006.pdf (accessed October 25, 2011).

Sustainable Development Commission (SDC) and the National Consumer Council (NCC) 2006. "I will if you will: Towards sustainable consumption." Available at www.sd-commission.org.uk/publications/downloads/I_Will_If_You_Will.pdf.

Sveriges Radio (Swedish Public Radio) 2009. "Grisar skållades levande på slakteri." Reports on pig welfare on Swedish farms. March 17. Available at http://sverigesradio.se/sida/artikel.aspx?programid=3437&artikel=2821922.

Sveriges Radio (Swedish Public Radio) 2010. "Ekot granskar grisfabriken i Sverige." Public radio series investigating pig factories in Sweden. Available at http://sverigesradio.se/sida/gruppsida.aspx?programid=3437&grupp=7709.

Sweatfree Communities. No date (a). Sweatfree Communities. http://www.fairworkplace.org/articles/take-action/get-involved.html (accessed December 14, 2011). See also http://www.sweatfree.org/resources.

Sweatfree Communities. No date (b). "Sweatfree communities campaigns in the US," Available at http://www.sweatfree.org/campaign_contacts (accessed December 5, 2011).

Swedish Institute. 2011. "Eco Chic: Towards Sustainable Swedish Fashion." Available at http://www.si.se/English/Navigation/Current-projects2/Facing-the-future/Facing-the-Future–Sustainability-the-Swedish-Way/Eco-Chic – Towards-Sustainable-Swedish-Fashion (accessed January 5, 2012).

Swedish Society for Nature Conservation (SSNC) (Svenska naturskyddsföreningen). 2010. "SSNC resigns from forest certification in Sweden," June 16, http://www.naturskyddsforeningen.se/in-english/About-us/latest-news/?news=15246.

Talen, Bill. 2003. *What Should I do if Reverend Billy is in My Store?* New York: The New Press.

Tallontire, Anne, Erdenechimeg Rentsendorj, and Mike Blowfield. 2001. "Ethical Consumers and Ethical Trade: A Review of Current Literature," *Policy Series* 12. Chatham, UK: Natural Resources Institute.

Tamm Hallström, Kristina, and Magnus Boström. 2010. *Transnational Multi-Stakeholder Standardization: Organizing Fragile Non-State Authority*, Cheltenham: Edward Elgar.

Tarrow, Sidney. 2000. "Mad Cows and Social Activists: Contentious Mechanisms in the Trilateral Democracies," In Susan Pharr and Robert Putnam, (eds.), *Disaffected Democracies: What's Troubling the Trilateral Countries*, Princeton: Princeton University Press, pp. 270–290.

Tarrow, Sidney. 2005. *The New Transnational Activism*. Cambridge: Cambridge University Press.

Taylor, Peter L. 2002. *Poverty Alleviation through Participation in Fair Trade Coffee Networks: Synthesis of Case Study Research Question Findings*, New York: Fair Trade Research Group (Colorado State University) / Ford Foundation.

TCO and LO. 2001. *Projekt jämställdhetsmärkning. Slutrapport*. Stockholm: TCO and LO. Umbrella Union Co-operative Report.

Teixeira, Ruy. 1992. *The Disappearing American Voter*, Washington DC: Brookings Institution.

Telegraph. 2010. "Food labels to show 'carbon footprint' under Government plans." Available at http://www.telegraph.co.uk/earth/earthnews/6936658/Food-labels-to-show-carbon-footprint-underGovernment-plans.html (accessed October 20, 2011).

Teoh, Siew H., Ivo Welch, and C. Paul Wazzan. 1999. "The Effect of Socially Activist Investment Policies on the Financial Markets: Evidence from the South African Boycott," *Journal of Business* 72: 35–89.

Teorell, Jan, Mariano Torcal, and José Ramon Montéro. 2007. "Political Participation: Mapping the Terrain," in Jan W. van Deth, José Ramon Montéro and Anders Westholm (eds.), *Citizenship and Involvement in European Democracies: A Comparative Analysis*, London: Routledge, pp. 334–357.

Terra Choice Environmental Marketing. 2010. "The Sins of Greenwashing," Home & Family Edition at http://sinsofgreenwashing.org/ (accessed October 2011).

Tesco. 2008. "Tesco Diets." Available at http://www.tesco.com/health/food/healthy_eating/tesco_food/organic.page (accessed January 5, 2012).

Tesco. 2011. "CSR Report." Available at http://www.tescoplc.com/media/60113/tesco_cr_report_2011_final.pdf (accessed January 5, 2012).

Thaler, Richard, and Cass Sunstein. 2008. *Nudge: Improving Decisions about Health, Wealth and Happiness*, London: Penguin Books.

The Walt Disney Company. 2008. "The Walt Disney Company 2008 corporate responsibility report." Available at http://disney.go.com/crreport/home.html.

Thibert, Joel, and Madhav D. Badami. 2011. "Estimating and Communicating Food System Impacts: A Case Study in Montreal, Quebec," *Ecological Economics* 70(10): 1814–1821.

Thompson, Craig J., and Gokcen Coskuner-Balli. 2007. "Enchanting Ethical Consumerism: The Case Of Community Supported Agriculture," *Journal of Consumer Culture* 7(3): 275–303.

Thompson, Craig J., and Zeynep Arsel. 2004. "The Starbucks Brandscape and Consumers' (Anticorporate) Experiences of Globalization," *Journal of Consumer Research* 31: 631–642.

Thoreau, Henry David. 1854. *Walden; or Life in the Woods*. Boston: Ticknor and Fields.

Tobiasen, Mette. 2004. "Political Consumers in Denmark," paper for the ECPR Joint Sessions, Uppsala, Sweden. Workshop 24 "Emerging repertoires of political action: toward a systematic study of post-conventional forms of participation."

Tobiasen, Mette. 2005. "Political Consumerism in Denmark," in Magnus Boström, Andreas Føllesdal, Mikael Klintman, Michele Micheletti, and Mads P. Sørensen (eds.), *Political Consumerism: Its Motivations, Power, and Conditions in the Nordic Countries and Elsewhere*, Copenhagen: Nordic Council, pp. 113–144.

Torjusen, Hanne, Lotte Sangstad, Katherine O'Doherty Jensen, and Unni Kjærnes. 2004. "European Consumers' Conceptions of Organic Food: A Review of Available Research," Oslo: National Institute for Consumer Research. Available at http://www.organichaccp.org/haccp_rapport.pdf.

Toronto Star. 1998. "Daishowa Boycott Did Its Job," Available at http://tao.ca/~fol/pa/forestp/daifolp/ts980618.htm (accessed October 20, 2011).

Trentmann, Frank. 2004. "Beyond Consumerism: New Historical Perspectives on Consumption," *Journal of Contemporary History* 39(3): 373–401.

Trentmann, Frank. 2007. "Citizenship and Consumption," *Journal of Consumer Culture* 7(2): 147–158.

Trentmann, Frank. 2008. *Free Trade Nation.* Oxford: Oxford University Press.

Trentmann, Frank. 2009. "Crossing Divides: Consumption and Globalization in History," *Journal of Consumer Culture* 9(2): 187–220.

Tsai, Shu-pei. 2006. "Investigating Archetype-Icon Transformation in Brand Marketing," *Marketing Intelligence & Planning.* 24(6): 648–663.

Tuck, Richard. 2008. *Free Riding.* Cambridge, MA: Harvard University Press.

Tucker, Arnold. 2010. "Sustainable Consumption by Certification: The Case of Coffee," in Louis Lebel, Sylvia Lorek and Daniel Rajesh, (eds.), *Sustainable Production Consumption System,* New York: Springer, pp. 179–199.

Tucker, Richard. 2002. "Environmentally Damaging Consumption: The Impact of American Markets on Tropical Ecosystems in the Twentieth Century," in Thomas Princen, Michael F. Maniates, and Ken Conca (eds.), *Confronting Consumption,* Cambridge, MA: MIT Press, pp. 177–195.

UK Parliament. "The Impacts of Spending cuts on Science and Scientific Research." http://www.parliament.uk/business/committees/committees-a-z/commons-select/science-and-technology-committee/inquiries/former-inquiries/spending-cuts/ (accessed June 9, 2011).

UK Press Office. 2009. "Thousands to Cycle Naked Against the Environmental Credit Crunch." Available at http://www.pressdispensary.co.uk/releases/c992275/Thousands-to-Cycle-Naked-Against-the-Environmental-Credit-Crunch-.php (accessed June 28, 2009).

Ulrich, Jens. 1999. "Den demokratiske deltagelses potentialer i det senmoderne samfund – en teoretisk ramme for studiet af politisk identitet," paper for the Conference of the Nordic Political Science Association, Workshop "Nye politisk identitet og institutioner i hverdagen politiske praksis," Uppsala, Sweden, August 19–21.

UN Conference on Trade and Development (UNCTAD). 2009. "World investment report 2009: Transnational corporations, agricultural production, and development." Geneva: UNCTAD. Available at http://www.unctad.org/Templates/WebFlyer.asp?intItemID=5037&lang=1.

UN Development Programme, UN Environment Programme, World Bank, and World Resources Institute. 2000. "World resources 2001–2002: People and Ecosystems: The Fraying Web of Life." Washington, DC: World Resources Institute. Available at http://www.wri.org/publication/world-resources-2000-2001-people-and-ecosystems-fraying-web-life.

UN Development Programme, UN Environment Programme, World Bank and World Resources Institute. 2003. "World resources 2002–2004". Washington, DC: World Resources Institute. Available at http://www.wri.org/wr2002.

UN General Assembly. 2007. "Report of the Special Representative of the Secretary-General on the Issue of Human Rights and Transnational Corporations and other Business Enterprises, John Ruggie: Business and Human Rights: Mapping International Standards of Responsibility and Accountability for Corporate Acts." UN document A/HRC/4/35, available at http://documents.un.org/.

UN General Assembly. 2008. "Protect, Respect and Remedy: A Framework for Business and Human Rights: Report of the Special Representative of the Secretary-General on the issue of human rights and transnational corporations and other business enterprises, John Ruggie." UN document A/HRC/8/5. Available at http://documents.un.org/.

UN General Assembly. 2011. "Report of the Special Representative of the Secretary-General on the issue of human rights and transnational corporations and other business enterprises, John Ruggie: Guiding principles on business and human rights: Implementing the United Nations 'Protect, Respect and Remedy' Framework." UN document A/HRC/17/31. Available at http://documents.un.org/.

Undernews. 2009. "Whole Foods Boycott Idea Hitting the Internet." Available at http://prorev.com/2009/08/whole-foodsboycott-idea-hitting.html (accessed October 26).

UNICEF. 1997. "The State of the World's Children 1997: Four Myths about Child Labour." Available at http://www.unicef.org/sowc97/report/myths.htm (accessed August 15, 2009).

United Nations Conference on Trade and Development (UNCTAD). 2006. World Investment Report 2006. FDI from Developing and Transition Economies: Implications for Development. Available at http://www.unctad.org/en/docs/wir2006_en.pdf (accessed September 11, 2007).

United Nations Conference on Trade and Development (UNCTAD). 2004. World Investment Report 2004: The Shift Towards Services. Available at http://www.unctad.org/en/docs/wir2004_en.pdf (accessed January 6, 2005).

United Nations Environment Programme (Division of Technology, Industry, and Economics; Sustainable Consumption & Production Branch). 2009a. "Activities: What UNEP offers to governments." Available at http://www.unep.fr/scp/procurement/activities.htm (accessed March 24, 2009).

United Nations Environment Programme (Division of Technology, Industry, and Economics; Sustainable Consumption & Production Branch). 2009b. "Marrakech Task Forces: Sustainable Public Procurement." Available at http://www.unep.fr/scp/marrakech/taskforces/procurement.htm (accessed March 24, 2009).

United Nations Environment Programme (UNEP). 2010. "ABC of SCP: Clarifying Concepts on Sustainable Consumption and Production." Nairobi: UNEP. Available at http://www.uneptie.org/scp/marrakech/pdf/ABC%20of%20SCP%20-%20Clarifying%20Concepts%20on%20SCP.pdf.

United States Department of Agriculture – Foreign Agriculture Service. 2002. "Canada Organic Products: Organic Food Industry Report 2002." Available at http://www.fas.usda.gov/gainfiles/200201/135683121.pdf (accessed May 13, 2005).

United States Holocaust Memorial Museum. 2011. "The Boycott of Jewish Businesses," Available at http://www.ushmm.org/outreach/en/article.php?ModuleId=10007693 (accessed September 26, 2011).

United States Senate Committee on Environment and Public Works. 1990. "Oil pollution act of 1990." Available at http://epw.senate.gov/opa90.pdf.

Urwin, Derek W. 1995. *The Community of Europe: A History of European Integration since 1945*. Second edition. London: Longman.

USA Today. 2003. "P & G to Give Boost to Small Farmer." Available at http://www .usatoday.com/money/industries/food/2003-09-15-fairtrade_x.htm (accessed April 6, 2008).

Utne. 2010. "The Eco-Myth of Trader Joe's," Utne Reader. Available at http://www. utne.com/Environment/The-EcoMyth-of-Trader-Joes.aspx (accessed June 7, 2011).

Utting, Peter. 2008. "The Struggle for Corporate Accountability," *Development and Change* 39(6): 959–975.

Utting-Chamorro, Karla. 2005. "Does Fair Trade Make a Difference? The Case of Small Coffee Producers in Nicaragua," *Development in Practice* 15(3&4): 584–599.

Vabø, Mia. 2006. "Caring for People or Caring for Proxy Consumers?" *European Societies* 8(3): 403–422.

Valentino, Nicholas A., Ted Brader, and Elizabeth Suhay. 2008. "Is It Immigration or the Immigrants? The Emotional Influence of Groups on Public Opinion and Political Action," *American Journal of Political Science* 52(4): 959–978.

Valkila, Joni, and Anja Nygren. 2010. "Impacts of Fair Trade Certification on Coffee Farmers, Cooperatives and Laborers in Nicaragua," *Agriculture and Human Values* 27: 321–333.

Van Aelst, Peter, and Stefaan Walgrave. 2001. "Who Is That (Wo)man in the Street? From the Normalisation of Protest to the Normalisation of the Protester," *European Journal of Political Research* 39: 461–486.

van De Donk, Wim, Brian D. Loader, Paul G. Nixon, and Dieter Rucht (eds.) 2004. *Cyberprotest: New Media, Citizens, and Social Movements*, New York, NY: Routledge.

van Deth, Jan W. 2001. "Toward a Theory of Everything?" paper presented at the ECPR Joint Sessions, Grenoble, France, April 6–11.

van Deth, Jan W. 2010a. "Is Creative Participation Good for Democracy?" in Michele Micheletti and Andrew S. McFarland (eds.), *Creative Participation: Responsibility Taking in the Political World*, Boulder, CO: Paradigm Publishers, pp. 146–170.

van Deth, Jan W. 2010b. "Political Sociology: Old Concerns and New Directions" in Subrata K. Mitra, Malte Pehl, Clemens Spiess (eds.), *Political Sociology – The State of the Art*, Opladen: Barbara Budrich Publishers, pp. 105–126.

van Deth, Jan W., and Martin Elf. 2000. "Political Involvement and Apathy in Europe 1973–1998," Working Papers Mannheimer Zentrum für Europäische Sozialforschung.

van Deth, Jan W., José Ramón Montero, and Anders Westholm (eds.) 2007. *Citizenship and Involvement in European Democracies: A Comparative Analysis*, New York: Routledge.

Van Riel, Cees B. M., and Anouschka Van den Ban with Evert-Jan Heijmans. 2001. "The Added Value of Corporate Logos: An Empirical Study," *European Journal of Marketing* 35(3–4): 428–440.

Van Schuur, Wijbrandt H., and Gerrit Voerman. 2010. "Democracy in Retreat? Decline in Political Party Membership: The Case of the Netherlands," in Barbara Wejnert (ed.), *Democratic Paths and Trends: Research in Political Sociology*, Bingley, UK: Emerald Group Publishing Limited, Volume 18, pp. 25–51.

Vegetarian Journal. 2005. Yearly edition, http://www.vrg.org/journal, accessed April 2010.

Vegetarian Journal. 2009. Yearly edition, http://www.vrg.org/journal, accessed April 2010.

Vegetarian Resource Group. 2011. "The Market for Vegetarian Foods." Available at http://www.vrg.org/nutshell/market.htm (accessed December 13, 2012).

Verba, Sidney. 2003. "Would the Dream of Political Equality turn out to be a Nightmare?," *Perspectives on Politics* 1(4): 663–679.

Verba, Sidney and Norman H. Nie. 1972. *Participation in America: Political Democracy and Social Equality*, New York: Harper and Row.

Verba, Sidney, Norman H. Nie, and Jae-on Kim. 1978. *Participation and Political Equality.* Chicago: The University of Chicago Press.

Verba, Sidney, Kay Lehman Schlozman, and Henry E. Brady. 1995. *Voice and Equality: Civic Voluntarism in American Politics*, Cambridge, MA: Harvard University Press.

Verhoog, Henk, and Jan de Wit. 2006. "Organic Values and Animal Production," in Matthias Kaiser and Marianne Lien (eds.), *Ethics and the Politics of Food*, Wageningen: Wageningen Academic Publishers, pp. 92–93.

Vigeo. 2011. Vigeo Rating: Green, Social and Ethical Funds in Europe 2011 Review, Available at http://www.famigliacristiana.it/allegati/2012/4/green-social-and-ethical-funds-in-europe-2011_final_2799689.pdf.

Vinken, Henk, and Isabelle Diepstraten. 2010. "Buy Nothing Day in Japan: Individualizing Life Courses and Forms of Engagement," *Young* 18(1): 55–75.

Virchow, Fabian. 2007. "Performance, Emotion, and Ideology: On the Creation of 'Collectives of Emotion' and Worldview in the Contemporary German Far Right," *Journal of Contemporary Ethnography* 36(2): 147–164.

Vissers, Sara Marc Hooghe, Dietlind Stolle, and Valérie-Anne Mahéo. 2011. "The Impact of Mobilization Media on Off-Line and Online Participation: Are Mobilization Effects Medium-Specific?" *Social Science Computer Review* 1–18.

Vissers, Sarah, and Dietlind Stolle. 2012. "Spill-over Effects Between Facebook and on/offline Political Participation? Evidence from a Two-Wave Panel Study," Paper prepared for the panel "New Media Use Among Citizens and Parties," held during the Canadian Political Science Association Annual Meeting, June 15–17, 2012, in Edmonton, AB. Available at http://www.cpsa-acsp.ca/papers-2012/Vissers-Stolle.pdf (accessed July 4, 2012).

Vitak, Jessica, Paul Zube, Andrew Smock, Caleb T. Carr, Nicole Ellison, and Cliff Lampe. 2011. "It's Complicated: Facebook Users' Political Participation in the 2008 Election," *Cyberpsychology, Behavior & Social Networking* 14(3): 107–114.

Vogel, David. 2005. *The Market for Virtue: The Potential and Limits of Corporate Social Responsibility*, Washington, DC: Brookings Institution Press.

Vogel, David. 2006 (2004). "Tracing the American Roots of the Political Consumerism Movement," in Michele Micheletti, Andreas Follesdal, and Dietlind Stolle (eds.), *Politics, Products and Markets: Exploring Political Consumerism Past and Present*, New Brunswick, NJ: Transaction Press, pp. 83–101.

Wacziarg, Romain, and Karen Horn Welch. 2008. "Trade Liberalization and Growth: New Evidence," *The World Bank Economic Review* 22(2): 187–231.

Waldman, Linda. 2009. 'Show Me the Evidence': Mobilisation, Citizenship and Risk in Indian Asbestos Issues. IDS Working Paper 329. Brighton, UK: Institute of Development Studies.

Walsh, W. H. 1970. "Pride, Shame and Responsibility," *The Philosophical Quarterly* 20(78): 1–13.

Ward-Jones Richard S. 2008. "Environmentally Friendly Cars: Promoting and Increasing their USE in the UK," *Earth & Environment* 3: 282–317.

Warneken, Felix, and Michael Tomasello. 2009. "The Roots of Human Altruism," *British Journal of Psychology* 100(3): 455–471.

Warner, Jamie. 2007. "Political Culture Jamming: The Dissident Humor of The Daily Show With Jon Stewart," *Popular Communication* 5(1): 17–36.

Washington Post 2007. "States' Immigrant Policies Diverge: In Differences, Some See Obstacles for a National Law," *Washington Post*, October 15.

Wasserman, Debora, and Charles Stahler. 1998. "Reader Survey Results," *Vegetarian Journal* 17(1): available online at www.vrg.org/journal/vj98jan/981coord.html (accessed April 2009).

Watkins, Kenny, and Penny Fowler. 2002. *Rigged Rules and Double Standards: Trade, Globalisation, and the Fight against Poverty*, Oxford: Oxfam International.

Watson, John. 2010. "Capitalist Housing Developers as Green Activists," in Michele Micheletti and Andrew McFarland (eds.), *Creative Participation as Responsibility-Taking in the Political World*, Bolder, CO: Paradigm Publishers, pp. 80–100.

Weaver, R. Kent, and Bert A. Rockman (eds.) 1993. *Do Institutions Matter? Government Capabilities in the United States and Abroad*, Washington, DC: Brookings Institution.

Weber, Christopher L., and H. Scott Matthews. 2008. "Food-Miles and the Relative Climate Impacts of Food Choices in the United States," *Environmental Science and Technology* 42(10): 3508–3513.

Weidema, Bo, Mikkel Thrane, Per Christensen, Jannick Schmidt, and Soren Lokke. 2008. "Carbon Footprint: A Catalyst for Life Cycle Assessment?" *Journal of Industrial Ecology* 12(1): 3–6.

Welzel, Christian, and Ronald Inglehart. 2005. "Demokratisierung und Freiheitsstreben: Die Perspektive der Humanentwicklung," *Politische Vierteljahresschrift* 46(1): 62–85.

Wessells, Cathy, Holger Donath, and Robert J. Johnston. 1999. *U.S. Consumer Preferences for Ecolabeled Seafood: Results of a Consumer Survey*, Rhode Island: Department of Environmental and Natural Resource Economics, University of Rhode Island, unpublished report.

West, Gale E., and Bruno Larue. 2005. "Determinants of anti-GM Food Activism," *Journal of Public Affairs* 5(3–4): 236–250.

Whole Foods Market. 2006. "Whole Foods Market Stops Selling Live Lobsters," Available at http://www.wholefoodsmarket.com/values/live-lobster.php (accessed July 4, 2012).

Wickstrom, Maurya. 2006. *Performing Consumers. Global Capitalism and its Theatrical Seduction*, New York: Routledge.

Wiegandt, Ellen. 2001. "Climate Change, Equity, and International Negotiations," in Urs Luterbacher and Detlef F. Sprinz (eds.), *International Relations and Global Climate Change*, Cambridge, MA: MIT Press, pp. 127–150.

Wier, M., L. G. Hansen, L. M. Andersen, and K. Millock 2003. "The Role of Government Standards and Market Facilitation," in Organization for Economic Co-operation and Development (ed.), *Organic Agriculture: Sustainability, Markets and Policies*. Cambridge, MA: CABI Publishing.

Wikström, D. 2003. *Willingness to Pay for Sustainable Coffee: A Choice Experiment*, Master's Thesis. Luleå, Sweden: Luleå University of Technology.

Wilkinson, John. 2007. "Fair Trade: Dynamic and Dilemmas of a Market-Oriented Global Social Movement," *Journal of Consumer Policy* 30(3): 219–239.

Wilkinson, John, and Gilberto Mascarenhas 2007. "Southern Social Movements and Fair Trade" in Laura T. Raynolds, Douglas Murray, and John Wilkinson (eds.), *Fair Trade: the Challenges of Transforming Globalization*, New York: Routledge, pp. 125–137.

Wilks, Rick. 2008. Seminar discussion at the Glasshouse Forum meeting on "A Consuming Society", London, January 24.

Willer, Helga, and Lukas Kilcher. 2011. *The World of Organic Agriculture 2011: Statistics and Emerging Trends*, Bonn: IFOAM and FiBL.

Willer, Helga, and Minou Yussefi. 2000. *The World of Organic Agriculture 2000: Statistics and Emerging Trends*, Bonn: IFOAM.

Willer, Helga, and Minou Yussefi. 2001. *The World of Organic Agriculture 2001: Statistics and Emerging Trends*, Bonn: IFOAM.

Willer, Helga, and Minou Yussefi. 2003. *The World of Organic Agriculture 2003: Statistics and Future Prospects*, Tholey-Theley, Germany: IFOAM.

Willer, Helga, and Minou Yussefi. 2004. *The World of Organic Agriculture 2004: Statistics and Emerging Trends*, Bonn: IFOAM.

Willer, Helga, and Minou Yussefi. 2005. *The World of Organic Agriculture 2005: Statistics and Emerging Trends*, Bonn: IFOAM.

Willer, Helga, and Minou Yussefi. 2006. *The World of Organic Agriculture 2006: Statistics and Emerging Trends*, 8th Revised Edition. Bonn: IFOAM.

Willer, Helga, and Minou Yussefi. 2007. *The World of Organic Agriculture 2007: Statistics and Emerging Trends*, Bonn: IFOAM.

Willer, Helga, and Minou Yussefi. 2008. *The World of Organic Agriculture 2008: Statistics and Emerging Trends*, 10th Revised Edition. Bonn: IFOAM.

Willer, Helga, and Kilcher, Lukas (eds.) 2009. *The World of Organic Agriculture – Statistics and Emerging Trends 2009.* IFOAM, Bonn; FiBL, Frick; ITC, Genf.

Willer, Helga, and Kilcher, Lukas (eds.) 2010. *The World of Organic Agriculture – Statistics and Emerging Trends 2010.* IFOAM, Bonn and FiBL, Frick.

Willer, Helga, and Kilcher, Lukas (eds.) 2011. *The World of Organic Agriculture – Statistics and Emerging Trends 2011.* IFOAM, Bonn and FiBL, Frick.

Willigan, Geraldine E. 1992. "High-Performance Marketing: An Interview with Nike's Phil Knight," *Harvard Business Review* 91–101.

Wilson, David C., and Darren W. Davis. 2011. "Re-examining Racial Resentment: Conceptualization and Content," *The ANNALS of the American Academy of Political Science* 634(1): 117–133.

Winter, Gerd (ed.) 2006. *Multilevel Governance of Global Environmental Change: Perspectives from Science, Sociology and the Law*, Cambridge: Cambridge University Press.

Winters, Alan L. 2004. "Trade Liberalisation and Economic Performance: an Overview," *The Economic Journal* 114(493): F4–F21.

Winthrop, Delba. 1975. "Aristotle and Political Responsibility," *Political Theory* 3(4): 406–422.

Witkowski, Terrence. 2005. "Fair Trade Marketing: An Alternative System for Globalization and Development," *Journal of Marketing Theory and Practice* 13(4): 22–33.

Wolfinger, R. and S. J. Rosenstone. 1980. *Who Votes*, New Haven: Yale University Press.

Wollebæk, Dag, and Per Selle. 2003. "The Importance of Passive Membership," in Marc Hooghe and Dietlind Stolle (eds.), *Generating Social Capital: Civil Society and Institutions in Comparative Perspective*, New York, NY: Palgrave MacMillan, pp. 67–88.

Woodside, Sven. 2001. "Every Joke is a Tiny Revolution – Culture Jamming and the Role of Humour," http://www.nassio.com/sven/ Master's Thesis, University of Amsterdam, the Netherlands.

World Bank. 2005. "World Development Indicators," Available at http://devdata.worldbank.org/dataonline/ (accessed June 23, 2005).

World Bank. 2006. "World Development Indicators," Available at http://devdata.worldbank.org/dataonline/ (accessed March 7, 2006).

World Bank. 2007. "World Development Indicators," Available at http://devdata.worldbank.org/dataonline/ (accessed October 13, 2007).

World Values Survey. 1981ff. Data Set available at the ICPSR web site, available at http://www.icpsr.umich.edu/icpsrweb/landing.jsp.

Worm, Boris, Edward Barbier, Nicola Beaumont, J. Emmett Duffy, Carl Folke, Benjamin Halpern, Jeremy Jackson, Heike Lotze, Fiorenza Micheli, Stephen Palumbi, Enric Sala, Kimberley A. Selkoe, John Stachowicz, and Reg Watson. 2006. "Impacts of Biodiversity Loss on Ocean Ecosystem Services," *Science* 314(5800): 787–790.

Worrell, Richard, and Michael C. Appleby. 2000. "Stewardship of Natural Resources: Definition, Ethical and Practical Aspects," *Journal of Agricultural and Environmental Ethics* 12(2): 263–277.

Wuthnow, Robert. 1998. *Loose Connections: Joining Together in America's Fragmented Communities*, Cambridge, MA: Harvard University Press.

Wuthnow, Robert. 1999. "Mobilizing Civic Engagement: The Changing Impact of Religious Involvement," in T. Skocpol & M. P. Fiorina (eds.), *Civic Engagement in American Democracy*, Washington, DC: Brookings Institution Press, pp. 331–363.

Young, Iris Marion. 1994. "Gender as Seriality: Thinking about Women as a Social Collective," *Signs: Journal of Women in Culture and Society* 19(3): 713–738.

Young, Iris Marion. 2002. *Inclusion and Democracy*, Oxford: Oxford University Press.

Young, Iris Marion. 2004. "Responsibility and Global Labor Justice," *The Journal of Political Philosophy* 12(4): 365–88.

Young, Iris Marion. 2006. "Responsibility and Global Justice: A Social Connection Model," *Social Philosophy and Policy* 23(1): 102–130.

Young, Iris Marion. 2010. *Responsibility for Justice*, Oxford: Oxford University Press.

Young, Rick. 2002. Interview by Michele Micheletti December 13. At the time the interview was conducted, Young had initiated a citizen's initiative on sustainable coffee procurement in the city of Berkeley.

Zadek, Simon. 2004. "The Path to Corporate Responsibility," *Harvard Business Review* 82(12): 1–9.

Zadek, Simon. 2007. "Reinventing Global Trade: the MFA Forum," Open Democracy. Available at http://www.opendemocracy.net/globalization-institutions_government/global_mfa_4528.jsp (accessed January 5, 2012).

Zaitchik, Alexander. 2003. "Colombia's other Deadly Coke," New York Press July 16–22. Available at http://killercoke.org/downloads/nypressv16i29.pdf.

Zhong Chen-Bo, Katie A. Liljenquist, and Daylian M. Cain. 2009. "Moral Self-Regulation: Licensing & Compensation" in David de Cremer (ed.), *Psychological Perspectives on Ethical Behavior and Decision-Making*, Charlotte, NC: Information Age, pp. 75–86.

Zukin, Cliff, Scott Keeter, Molly Andolina, Krista Jenkings, and Micheal X. Delli Carpini. 2006. *A New Engagement? Political Participation, Civic Life, and the Changing American Citizen*, Oxford: Oxford University Press.

Zweifel, Stefan, Juri Steiner, and Heinz Stahlhut. 2007. *In Girum Imus Nocte Et Consumimur Igni – the Situationalist International (1957–1972)*, Basel, Switzerland: Museum Tinguely.

Zwick, Detlev, Janice Denegri-Knott, and Jonathan E. Schroeder. 2007. "The Social Pedagogy of Wall Street: Stock Trading as Political Activism? *Journal of Consumer Policy* 30(3): 177–199.

Index

For EU product safety concerns, contact us at Calle de José Abascal, 56–1°,
28003 Madrid, Spain or eugpsr@cambridge.org.

www.ingramcontent.com/pod-product-compliance
Ingram Content Group UK Ltd.
Pitfield, Milton Keynes, MK11 3LW, UK
UKHW011326060825
461487UK00005B/378